Collective Behavior

David A. Locher
Missouri Southern State College

Prentice
Hall

Upper Saddle River, New Jersey 07458

Library of Congress Cataloging-in-Publication Data

Locher, David A.,
  Collective behavior / David A. Locher
      p. cm.
  Includes bibliographical references and indexes.
  ISBN 0-13-088668-8
    1. Collective behavior. 2. Social movements. I. Title.
  HM866. .L63 2002
  303.48′4—dc21

                                          2001035848

VP, Editorial Director: Laura Pearson
Senior Acquisitions Editor: Chris DeJohn
Editorial Assistant: Christina Scalia
Executive Managing Editor: Ann Marie McCarthy
Production Liaison: Fran Russello
Editorial/Production Supervision: Marianne Hutchinson (Pine Tree Composition, Inc.)
Prepress and Manufacturing Buyer: Mary Ann Gloriande
Art Director/Cover Designer: Jayne Conte
Cover Art: Timepix
Director, Image Resource Center: Melinda Lee Reo
Manager, Rights & Permissions: Key Dellosa
Image Specialist: Beth Boyd
Photo Researcher: Karen Pugliano
Marketing Manager: Chris Barker

For permission to use copyrighted material, grateful acknowledgment is made to the copyright
holders on pages 315–316, which are hereby made part of this copyright page.

This book was set in 10/12 New Century Schoolbook by Pine Tree Composition, Inc.,
and was printed and bound by Hamilton Companies.
The cover was printed by Phoenix Color Corp.

©2002 by Pearson Education, Inc.
Upper Saddle River, New Jersey 07458

Printed in the United States of America
10 9 8 7 6 5 4 3 2

ISBN 0-13-088668-8

Pearson Education Ltd., *London*
Pearson Education Australia PTY. Limited, *Sydney*
Pearson Education Singapore, Pte. Ltd.
Pearson Education North Asia Ltd., *Hong Kong*
Pearson Education Canada, Ltd., *Toronto*
Pearson Educación de Mexico, S.A. de C.V.
Pearson Education—Japan, *Tokyo*
Pearson Education Malaysia, Pte. Ltd
Pearson Education, Upper Saddle River, *New Jersey*

Contents

6   Individualist Approaches to Collective Behavior   71

7   General Categories of Collective Behavior   87

11   Fads and Crazes: The Furby Frenzy   174

12   Millennialism: Y2K and the End of the World As We Know It   191

16   The Pro-Life And Pro-Choice Movements   289

Preface

This book is for all those who are curious about collective behavior. It explores the major sociological ideas that have been applied to the understanding of unusual group behavior, and the many and varied forms that such behavior can take. The study of collective behavior is the attempt to understand why things do not always happen according to the norms of society, and why people sometimes do terrible or silly things without being able to adequately explain their motives to outsiders.

I have been teaching collective behavior to undergraduate students for several years. Each time I taught the course in the past, I tried a different combination of books, articles, and various other materials. My students were often less than thrilled with juggling so many different sources of information and I found the multitude of materials difficult to manage. I could not find one text that was sufficiently comprehensive and also filled with up-to-date examples. This book is intended to fill that void. My goal was to create one textbook that provides students and instructors with all of the basic materials needed for a semester of learning about collective behavior.

I wrote this book with the undergraduate student in mind. All too often my students find their textbooks difficult to understand *even when they find the subject interesting*. They become confused or frustrated and, as a result, they don't do the reading at all or they read the words without fully understanding the information. I have endeavored to create a textbook that reduces this obstacle to learning. I firmly believe there is no such thing as a textbook that is too easy to read. Although some theoretical discussions are necessarily dense, a novice can read this book without undue confusion. Whenever possible, difficult concepts are explained using clear, concise terms. I also tried to avoid unnecessarily complex sentence structure. No one learns if they can't understand what they are reading.

There are certain qualities that I look for in a textbook. It must examine all of the major theories of collective behavior and classic social movement theories. A strong textbook must define the various categories of collective behavior and provide interesting examples of each one. It needs examples of events that have occurred within the students' lifetime—things that they actually remember. Equally important, though, it must also discuss the classic examples which sociologists are familiar and comfortable with. Finally, it ought to clearly demonstrate how each of the most useful theories can be used to understand exactly what happens during those episodes, and why. This allows the students to fully understand the theories and their application to events in the real world. This book is designed to fulfill all of those criteria.

While the student was foremost in my mind, I also took the instructor's needs into account while creating this text. The entire book is structured in much the same way my course is structured: discussion of the major theories, followed by definition and examples of specific categories of collective behavior, finally ending with application of the theories to specific, recent examples. I suspect that many other instructors follow a similar pattern in their teaching. Classes always go smoother when the structure of the textbook matches the pedagogical style of the instructor. My goal was to give instructors a book that provides most of what the students will need for the entire semester. The examples are recent, eliminating the need for numerous photocopied handouts. The theory chapters are in-depth, eliminating the need to place classic books on reserve at the library. The analyses are detailed enough to help students understand how to do their own research into collective events and episodes.

I also structured the book in such a way as to allow the instructor to pick and choose which theories and events to focus on. Most instructors will likely find this flexibility and versatility useful. Chapters and sections are self-contained and specific. Vital information that crosses over boundaries is briefly summarized in multiple chapters. This periodic, intentional redundancy allows instructors to require only those chapters that fit their course outline without leaving out any important material that students need to get from their reading. Each chapter contains enough information to allow a reader to understand it without having read all prior chapters. In the end, this repetition not only allows flexibility but will also help novice readers remember the most important concepts and ideas.

Chapter 1 provides the reader with a general sense of what collective behavior is, as well as a brief outline of the theoretical perspectives that have been developed over the last century. Chapters 2 through 6 examine each of those theories in great depth. Chapter 7 gives descriptions and examples of many different forms of collective behavior. Chapters 8 to 12 each examine a recent episode of collective behavior. They include riots, fads, rumors, and hysterias. Each of these chapters also includes a section applying one or more of the theories to the specific event. Chapter 12 briefly applies all of the theories to one specific event, discussing the similarities and differences between the various perspectives. This shows the reader how the theories are used as well as illuminating some of the advantages and shortcomings of each.

Part II of this book focuses on social movements. Chapter 13 discusses why social movements have been traditionally considered a form of collective behavior, and why many social movement researchers do not accept the collective behavior approach. Chapter 14 discusses four of the classic social movement theories. Chapter 15 looks at specific examples of successful and unsuccessful social movements. Chapter 16 examines the Pro-Life and Pro-Choice movements in the United States. It includes analyses of both movements using all four of the classical theories.

I hope that you find this book as fascinating to read as I found it to write. I could not have completed the book without the help of my wife Melissa, who read at least two drafts of each chapter with minimum complaint. I'd also like to thank everyone at Prentice Hall, including Nancy Roberts, Allison Westlake, Christopher DeJohn, Christina Scalia, and Shawna Kelly. I would particularly like to thank all of the people like Shawna who, when I complained that I could not find a textbook that I liked, said "Why don't you write one?" Thanks, too, to all of the students I have taught over the years, particularly Dan. Finally, thanks to every teacher I ever had. I've learned something from every one of you.

Earlier drafts of these chapters were reviewed by Hank Johnston Ph.D., San Diego State University; Thomas J. Sullivan, Northern Michigan University; Randy Stoecker, University of Toledo; Eric L. Hirsch, Providence College; Chad E. Litton, Southeastern Oklahoma State University; Ralph R. Smith, Southwestern Missouri State University; Oleg I. Gubin, University of Utah; and Michael J. Webber, University of San Francisco. Their comments and suggestions helped make this a better textbook.

David A. Locher
Missouri Southern State College

Chapter 1

Introduction to Collective Behavior

Collective behavior can be fascinating, terrifying, and amusing. It can be violent and deadly, or silly and harmless. Episodes of collective behavior have been reported as long as there has been a written record of human activity. Throughout history, crowds of people have engaged in behavior that struck observers, and sometimes the participants themselves, as unusual, bizarre, deviant, unexpected, or just plain odd. This book will introduce readers to a broad range of collective behavior and some of the theories that have been created to help understand and explain such behavior.

What Is Collective Behavior?

What is collective behavior? Are screaming fans at a football game taking part in collective behavior? What about participants in a riot? What exactly determines whether or not an event is considered an episode of collective behavior?

In the most general sense, *collective behavior* is any event during which a group of people engages in unusual behavior. ("Unusual" in the sense that it is not expected, not what people normally do in that setting, and not what those people normally do.) Collective behavior falls outside of normative

1

expectations for the situation and/or participants. It goes against the standards of conduct or social expectations of a given group or society. It is a group form of deviant behavior. Attempts to formulate more specific definitions all ultimately fail because they exclude some forms of collective behavior.

There have been many different definitions of collective behavior over the years. Originally called "mob behavior" or "mass hysteria," collective behavior was once believed to occur when people lost their ability to reason and became temporarily insane (see "History of the Study of Collective Behavior," below). Researchers have since realized that many different types of unusual events do not at first glance seem to possess the frightening, irrational qualities of a riot, a lynching, or other forms of "mass hysteria." These include fads and crazes, rumors, miracles and religious sightings, UFO sightings, millennial movements, and social movements.

All of these forms of collective behavior involve groups of people doing things that they would not normally do. They all occur much more often than the examples of mob violence and brutality that originally drew researchers to the study of collective behavior. Most cause little or no harm to participants. They occur in similar ways and for similar reasons. All of them can be examined using the same theoretical frameworks.

Collective behavior can take many forms. Some are obvious, and some are not. For example, football fans who cheer when their team scores a touchdown are not engaging in collective behavior because their behavior is expected within the setting (a sporting event) and for the participants (sports spectators). Cheering is routine behavior. However, if a large number of fans suddenly ran out onto the field and disrupted the game, then this unusual and unexpected behavior would qualify as collective behavior. The participants have deviated from the norms of the situation and engaged in behavior that is neither accepted nor expected under the circumstances.

Understanding collective behavior can be even more complicated, though. If this new behavior becomes ritualized, and every time a winning touchdown is scored the fans rush the field, then it becomes routine and expected. Once it becomes a ritual, it ceases to be collective behavior. Others may find the behavior annoying and disruptive, but it is not collective behavior because it is expected within the setting.

Collective behavior is always relative to the social rules and expectations. Those rules and expectations change over time. Therefore, no list can ever capture all potential forms of collective behavior, and any collective behavior can be transformed into ritual or routine behavior over time. It is the unusual, unexpected nature of collective behavior that makes it so interesting and also so difficult to study. This book will explore, examine, and analyze several different types of collective behavior in later chapters. By the time a reader reaches the end of this book, he or she will have a firm sense of what makes collective behavior different from other forms of group behavior.

Is Collective Behavior Really "Odd"?

Some researchers argue that referring to an episode of collective behavior as "bad" is value-laden. They believe that judging the episode in any way precludes objective, empirical understanding. However, there is an important difference between calling an *episode* "violent and terrible" and calling the *participants* "violent and terrible." Most collective behavior theories start with the assumption that participants are normal people, and all of them recognize that the behavior would not have occurred under different circumstances. Riots *are* terrible: They almost always result in the destruction of property and the injury or death of participants and bystanders. There is no reason to pretend otherwise. However, only someone who does not understand the sociological perspective would then confer that same judgment upon the participants themselves. The same is true for episodes that are unusual but not harmful: Fainting for no reason is not normal social behavior. Participants who pass out because they believe they are victims of a nonexistent toxic gas are not behaving as they normally would. The event stands out because it isn't typical behavior.

All collective behavior deviates from the norm to some extent. The more extreme the episode, the more obvious the gap between participants' behavior during the episode versus their behavior at other times. It is as unusual to participants as it is to observers. They are not "barbarians," "deviants," "suckers," or "idiots," even if the behavior itself seems barbaric, deviant, credulous, or inconceivably foolish in hindsight. Collective behavior can be bizarre. It can be ugly. It can be amusing. It is not wrong to say so and does not compromise one's status as a scientist. One can objectively study a particular event and conclude that the behavior was horrific. To pretend that distinctly unusual behavior is normal and commonplace does not aid the pursuit of knowledge. However, to make foolish statements like "I would never act that way" is another thing entirely. Learning to separate evaluations of the behavior from feelings about participants is an important step for any researcher. Some never learn the difference between the two. As a result, they condemn collective behavior participants with impunity or they pretend that killing strangers is perfectly normal social behavior. Neither position helps our understanding of collective behavior.

Why Study Collective Behavior?

Most of the time, people do what they are supposed to do. Most crowds do not turn violent. Restaurant diners don't usually run for the exits. People don't typically attach themselves to a rubber band and throw themselves off of a bridge. When these things do happen, they attract our attention because they are unexpected. Why, then, should we bother to study something that usually doesn't happen? There are several reasons.

1. It is important for individuals to understand why such terrible (or silly) things happen. The more we understand about such events, the less likely we are to get caught up in collective behavior. Understanding the dynamics that make a rumor spread and gain acceptance makes one less likely to accept them. Knowing the pattern that riots tend to follow can allow one to leave a situation before it becomes dangerous. Even more importantly, one individual can often steer a crowd away from potentially destructive behavior. Knowledge leads to better decisions.

2. It is important for researchers to understand why such terrible (or silly) things happen. Deviant behavior is a huge specialty within sociology. Researchers dedicate their entire careers to understanding why some people violate certain social norms, how those norms are created, why they change, and so on. Collective behavior is a type of deviant group behavior. We want to know why a mob turns violent for the same reason that deviant behavior researchers want to know why some individuals kill—so that we can keep it from happening in the future. Few would disagree that the world would be a better place without lynchings, riots, and other forms of mob violence. The more scientists understand why collective behavior occurs, the more likely we as a society will be able to avoid it in the future.

3. It happens more often than one might think. Although collective behavior doesn't occur every day, it does happen with alarming frequency. There are riots, rumors, fads, etc., year after year after year. These episodes are unusual when compared to normative social behavior but not uncommon. While nowhere near as common as normative behavior, collective behavior happens too often to ignore. It would be foolish to dismiss collective behavior as being too rare to bother understanding.

4. It is interesting. We all know that people normally stand and wait for a bus, or wait in line for their turn at a store checkout line. It is difficult to understand why people might suddenly start tearing down a bus stop and throwing rocks at cars, or why they might begin running, kicking, and screaming, trying to force their way to the front of a line. These things attract our attention because they don't happen every day. There is nothing wrong with wanting to learn more about something just because it seems interesting.

5. It may reveal information about common social behavior. Understanding why people sometimes do "odd" things may also help us understand why they typically do "normal" things. Thousands of researchers study typical, everyday behavior. A few scientists specializing in the "odd" stuff isn't going to hurt. Learning about human behavior under unusual circumstances can expand our understanding of society in general. Studying the breakdown of social order is an excellent way to increase understanding of social order.

There are undoubtedly other reasons to study collective behavior. Early pioneers within the field seem to have simply wanted to understand how seemingly normal, rational people could engage in such seemingly abnormal, irrational behavior. In exactly the same way that meteorologists started out trying to understand hurricanes and tornadoes, the early collective behavior scholars tended to focus on the most extreme forms of collective behavior. They paid particular attention to the destructive and deadly forms, such as riots and lynch mobs, because they wanted to understand behavior that frightened them.

The History of the Study of Collective Behavior

Collective behavior has been with us as long as there have been groups of people. However, scientists have only focused their attention on collective behavior for about the last century or so. In that time, several different perspectives and specific theories have been developed.

The Beginnings of the Study of "Mass Hysteria"

Charles Mackay's *Extraordinary Popular Delusions & The Madness of Crowds,* originally published in 1841, is arguably the first modern work focusing on collective behavior. *The Madness of Crowds* gave many people their first glimpse into the odd and often silly world of collective behavior. This book is still considered something of a classic today. However, Mackay was not a social scientist. He approached the topic much as a historian or journalist would. His book provides what seem to be accurate and well-researched accounts of collective behavior, but he does not make any serious attempt to explain *why* the episodes occurred.

In 1895, Gustave LeBon published *The Crowd: A Study of the Popular Mind.* Unlike Mackay, LeBon did not simply describe collective episodes for the amusement of readers. His book was a serious attempt to provide a theoretical explanation for the terrible mob violence that took place in France during and after the French Revolution. LeBon, a psychologist, tried to explain how ordinary citizens could engage in such bloodthirsty behavior and then return to their normal lives. He created what has come to be known as Contagion Theory.

The basic premise of Contagion Theory is that episodes of mob violence, riots, lynchings, and so forth, are driven by animal instincts within us. LeBon believed that these animalistic urges spread throughout a "maddening crowd" like an infection. The members of a mob or crowd are all reduced to the level of the most violent and animalistic member of the group through this contagion.

The Crowd was heavily weighed down with LeBon's own social and political opinions. However, the study of collective behavior rapidly grew once sociologists and psychologists in the United States were exposed to LeBon's ideas. As a result, several different branches of contagion theory have developed over the decades.

Theories of Collective Behavior

Robert Park, an American studying in Germany, wrote his dissertation on crowd behavior in 1904. Park's work, later published in various collections (see Park 1967a, 1967b, 1972), stripped away most of LeBon's political views while retaining most of LeBon's insights into mob behavior. This led to a well-defined theory of collective behavior. Park, along with Ernest Burgess, further refined Contagion Theory in *Introduction to the Science of Sociology* (1921). Here the term "collective behavior" was first used. Park and Burgess referred to social unrest, crowds, publics, sects, social contagion, mass movements, the crowd mind, propaganda, and fashion as forms of collective behavior.

Herbert Blumer, a sociologist who studied under Park, combined LeBon's and Park's ideas into his own version of Contagion Theory in 1939. The key to Blumer's version is the "acting crowd," an excited group that moves toward a goal. Blumer identified five steps that turn a collection of individuals into an active crowd: social unrest, exciting event, milling, common object of attention, and common impulses. All three versions of Contagion Theory are examined in depth in Chapter 2.

The Death of "Mass Hysteria"

Contagion Theory assumes that the individuals lose their ability to reason or to think rationally during a collective episode. When applied to mob violence, as the early studies often were, this provides us with the comforting idea that participants were "hysterical," "temporarily insane," or "hypnotized." This perspective allows episodes to be viewed as temporary aberrations, and one can find comfort by looking for the conditions that allowed this irrational behavior to occur. However, sociologists began to realize that not all forms of collective behavior involve irrational, hysterical, or violent behaviors.

For example, fads began to gain attention in the United States during the 1940s and '50s. Were the people who bought Hula-Hoops™ or crammed themselves into telephone booths under the grips of mass hysteria? Had they somehow "caught" insanity? Contagion Theory just didn't work well when attempting to explain these relatively mild and harmless events. Parents did not go to a store for a gallon of milk, fall prey to a milling crowd, and suddenly act out an irrational urge to buy their child a Hula-Hoop.™ Children asked (or begged and pleaded with) their parents, who went to the store and bought one. These types of harmless, silly collective behavior were not new, but sociologists had never focused their attention on them before. Clearly, a new theoretical perspective was needed. Several have been created.

The Emergent Norm Perspective   Ralph Turner and Lewis Killian introduced what they called the "Emergent Norm Perspective" in *Collective Behavior* (1957). The basic premises of the emergent norm perspective are fairly simple: Most people follow the norms of any situation most of the time. However, when a group of individuals find themselves in a situation where they do not know what to do, they must create new norms for the situation. Once everyone believes they know what behaviors are appropriate, they engage in those behaviors. This process is rational and logical. The behavior only seems hysterical or insane in hindsight.

Further, not all behaviors within a collective behavior episode are the same. Turner and Killian created a classification schema that places participants into different categories based on their reasons for taking part in an episode. Participants may be ego-involved, concerned, insecure, curious spectators, or exploiters. Each of these individuals have their own reasons for taking part in an episode, and none of them are irrational or insane.

No matter which of these categories a participant belongs to, his/her behavior will be rational and consistent as long as the individual remains in that situation. The participants are doing what they always do: obeying the norms that dictate behavior. The Emergent Norm Perspective is the focus of Chapter 3.

The Value-added Theory   In 1962, Neil Smelser published *Theory of Collective Behavior*. Like Turner and Killian, Smelser did not characterize collective behavior as mass hysteria or irrational mob behavior. He argues that collective behavior is a reaction to social conditions and circumstances that lead to unusual behavior. The behavior seems rational to the participants at the time. People don't stop thinking; they adjust their thinking to the situation they find themselves in.

Value-added Theory provides researchers with a set of circumstances required to "assemble" an episode of collective behavior. Like the manufacture of material goods, if one of the steps is missing, the final product cannot be produced. Each step is necessary, but none is sufficient to produce collective behavior. These steps are: structural conduciveness, structural strain, generalized belief, precipitating factors, mobilization of participants, and the actions or reactions of social control agents.

Smelser views collective behavior as episodes of group behavior that relieve some social strain. Participants are rational and sane. They may be fully aware of what they are doing and may be doing so for reasons that seem perfectly logical according to the generalized belief accepted by those within the situation. The behavior only looks irrational to outsiders who do not accept the generalized belief. Chapter 4 takes an extensive look at the Value-added Theory.

The SBI/Sociocybernetic Perspective   Since the early 1970s, Clark McPhail has been accumulating a body of work that centers on the "SBI" (symbolic interactionist/behaviorist) or "Sociocybernetic" perspective. It is behaviorist in the sense that it focuses on the organization of convergent behavior within gatherings. It is interactionist in the sense that this convergent behavior is viewed as the result of meaningful interpretations or instructions for response supplied by participants and others. This perspective focuses on the ways in which people regulate their own behavior. It also looks at how people directly influence the behavior of others.

For McPhail, collective behavior is just another form of group behavior. The perspective follows an extremely broad definition of collective behavior, one that includes routine and ritual behavior. For this reason, most SBI studies focus on events that other sociologists would not consider collective behavior. Further, much more emphasis is placed on analyzing exactly how a crowd comes together, behaves, and disperses. Unlike the earlier theoretical perspectives, little emphasis is placed on understanding why the episodes occur in the first place. The theory is useful for description and analysis, rather than understanding and prediction. The evolution of McPhail's theory is examined in Chapter 5.

The Individualist Theories   A completely separate strain of collective behavior theories developed not too long after Contagion Theory appeared. Called "Convergence Theory," "Learning Theory," and "Social Identity Theory," the individualist theories all assume that collective behavior comes from within the individuals. Collective behavior reveals innate tendencies, learned patterns of behavior, or identity-based yearnings that the participants more or less possessed before they entered the collective event. Collective behavior is viewed not as normal people doing abnormal things, but as potentially abnormal people expressing their inner tendencies or desires.

Floyd Allport began this tradition in 1924 with *Social Psychology*. In that book, he spelled out a Convergence Theory that essentially argues that certain kinds of people tend to gather (converge) in certain kinds of places. If people with violent tendencies converge, the situation is ripe with potential group violence. If gullible people converge, the situation may develop into mass delusion or odd flights of fancy. The behavior of the crowd tells us all that we need to know about the participants.

Neil Miller and John Dollard expanded on this basic idea in *Social Learning and Imitation* (1941). Their Learning Theory also assumed that people arrived at the scene of collective behavior with certain tendencies already in place. Unlike Allport, they argued that these tendencies were learned, rather than innate. Prior responses to various situations had taught people to behave in certain ways under similar circumstances. Once people with similar interests began to pay attention to the same cues, they were likely to engage in similar behaviors in response.

The most recent addition to the individualist approach to collective behavior comes from Michael Hogg and Dominic Abrams. They published *Social Identifications: A Social Psychology of Intergroup Relations and Group Processes* in 1988. Many of the assumptions of their Social Identity Theory seem quite similar to Learning Theory. People with similar self- and group-identities are likely to focus on similar issues and events. Under some circumstances, large groups of these people may decide, out of a sense of group identification, to engage in unusual behavior. Collective behavior, then, is driven by the individual participants' personal characteristics. The individualist theories of collective behavior are examined in Chapter 6.

All of the individualist theories focus on the participants as the key to understanding why collective behavior occurs. The situational and structural theories all focus on the circumstances surrounding the episode. One assumes that participants' behavior reveals something about those people, the other assumes that it reveals something about the circumstances those people found themselves in. This fundamental difference in the perspectives has yet to be fully bridged.

Social Movements

Although considered a form of collective behavior by many researchers, social movements are also considered important enough in their own right to merit a great deal of study and analysis by specialists. This book examines social movements in Part II. Social movements entail groups of individuals engaging in behavior that is outside of the norms for the situation. For this reason, they are considered a form of collective behavior by many. All of the collective behavior theories mentioned above can be applied to social movements. However, compared to other forms of collective behavior social movements are organized, generally endure over a relatively long period of time, and sometimes produce dramatic change within a society. Because of these differences, there are theories intended solely for the explanation and analysis of social movements.

Mass Society Theory   In *The Politics of Mass Society* (1959), William Kornhauser argued that social movements attract socially isolated people who feel personally insignificant. Social movements are more personal than political, because they give a sense of meaning and purpose to people who otherwise feel useless. Kornhauser's Mass Society Theory argues that people with the weakest social ties are the easiest to mobilize in a social movement. Social movements are led by individuals pursuing their own psychological interests and followed by those with few social ties.

Relative Deprivation Theory   Relative Deprivation Theory argues that social movements form when any group of people feels deprived of what they think they should have. "Relative deprivation," a sociological concept dating back to 1949 (Stouffer), refers to the subjective feeling that one has less than one deserves. In 1971, Denton Morrison applied this concept to social movements in "Some Notes Toward Theory on Relative Deprivation, Social Movements, and Social Change." He argued that whenever people feel dissatisfied, believe that they have a right to their goals, and believe that they will not be able to achieve those goals via conventional means, they will form a social movement organization in order to achieve those goals. People are motivated by their sense of unjust deprivation and their belief that they can change it.

Resource Mobilization Theory   Resource Mobilization Theory focuses on the ability of any social movement organization to successfully acquire and manage resources. These may include money, votes, media coverage, volunteer labor, or anything else that could potentially help or hinder the success of the social movement. In 1966, Meyer Zald and Roberta Ash published "Social Movement Organizations." They focused on the success or failure of a social movement organization and how the groups' ability to gain and manage resources effected the organizations. Since then, Zald and John McCarthy have expanded the resource mobilization approach into a full-fledged theory. While the Mass Society and Relative Deprivation theories attempt to explain why a social movement develops, Resource Mobilization Theory seeks to analyze and potentially predict the success of a movement once it has formed. Groups that successfully mobilize available resources are likely to succeed. Those that lack such resources, or waste them, are likely to fail. Assistance and support from powerful people in society is particularly important.

Political Process Theory   The Political Process Theory of social movements was first fully formulated by Douglas McAdam in his 1982 book *Political Process and the Development of Black Insurgency 1930–1970*. Political Process Theory considers both internal and external factors equally important. Ideology and beliefs are just as important as material resources, as are political connections and the overall social structure. The theory is an attempt to combine the best of Mass Society, Relative Deprivation, and Resource Mobilization theories together into a more historical and political perspective. The idea is to look at the social and political conditions that make individual and group action possible, likely or unlikely, and successful or unsuccessful. A movement is likely to form when people believe that something in society needs to change, that it isn't going to change without a push from organized citizen activism, and that they can accomplish the desired changes. The movement is likely to succeed when social, political, and historical conditions are in the group's favor and when the group takes advantage of all available means of reaching its goals. This includes assistance from those with power, but does not place as much importance upon it as Resource Mobilization Theory. Each of these social movement theories is examined in Chapter 14.

It is important to remember that all of these theories should be judged by how useful they are, not by whether or not they "make sense" or seem logical. One should always ask, "How will this theory help me as a researcher understand collective behavior?" Does it explain important aspects of the episode? Is it useful? Does it help us understand how such events could be prevented in the future? If the answer to any of these questions is "no," then the theory fails. No matter how intrinsically appealing a theory may seem, if it does not provide scientists with a way of predicting and ultimately controlling destructive behavior, it is useless. These are the questions that one should keep in mind while reading Chapters 2 through 6 and Chapter 14.

Chapter 2

Social Contagion Theory

Contagion Theory looks at the social events and conditions that make crowd behavior possible. The theory is most closely associated with three writers: Gustave LeBon, Robert Park, and Herbert Blumer. LeBon focused on the situational factors at work in a crowd setting. He established the roots for what became the first sociological theory of collective behavior. However, LeBon was a historian and philosopher, not a scientist. His work is loaded with his own social and political opinions. Park, a trained sociologist, restated LeBon's ideas in more social-psychological terms and explained how contagion occurs socially, within the dynamics of a group. A few years later, Blumer expanded on Park's writings and applied the concept of contagion to a broad range of group behavior. These three forms of Contagion Theory all share the basic premise that people can be made temporarily insane, irrational, or illogical within a crowd, and that they will return to normal as soon as they leave the situation.

The word "contagion" refers to a rapidly spreading infection, such as a plague or flu. It was first used in 1546 by Giralamo Fracastor, who was writing about infectious diseases. A somewhat old-fashioned term, it is now used as a metaphor for anything that spreads quickly from person to person. The first modern theory of collective behavior used contagion to describe the transmission of thoughts, ideas, or behavior from one individual to an entire group of people. Contagion theorists refined the concept, using the slightly more specific term "social contagion" to refer to this process.

The Contagion Theory of collective behavior is based upon the idea that moods and thoughts become contagious within certain types of crowds. Once infected with these thoughts, behavior becomes irrational or illogical and people do things that they normally would not do. Any individual in the crowd who already has the idea becomes the carrier. Under the right circumstances, other members of the crowd become infected. This process of contagion is not instantaneous and it can only occur under certain circumstances. First, a crowd of people must focus attention on the same event, person, or object. Crowd members begin to influence each other as soon as this common focus occurs. As excitement grows, individuals lose their self-consciousness, enter into something like a frenzy state, and cease to think before they act. Once crowd members have reached this condition, any idea or behavior offered by any member of the group is almost certain to receive support from all other members of the group. In this way, the entire crowd is reduced to the level of what LeBon called "its lowest members."

Gustave LeBon

Gustave LeBon published *The Crowd: A Study of the Popular Mind* in France in 1895. The book is a timely account of how the entire social structure in France had irreversibly changed in almost every way over the prior one hundred years. The book became an important first step in the development of a working theory of collective behavior for several reasons. First, LeBon looked at crowd behavior in a general sense. He attempted to explain why all crowd events occur, rather than focusing on the unique, specific details of any one particular episode. Further, he included social and social-psychological factors in his writing. He did not assume that crowd members were psychologically disturbed or abnormal before they took part in the event. Instead, he focused on the factors that occur within any crowd that make it possible for normal people to engage in abnormal or even barbaric behavior. Finally, although LeBon discusses politics at great length, for the most part he does not consider it an important part of his analysis. Most writers prior to LeBon focused entirely on the details of particular episodes, blaming the event on either unique political conditions prior to the episode, or on the psychological makeup of the crowd itself. LeBon kept his analysis general and theoretical. This makes it possible to apply his ideas to any collective episode in virtually any culture.

The history of France prior to 1895 was extremely violent and tumultuous. LeBon was writing at a time when the basic structure of French society had been repeatedly destroyed and rebuilt (Harvey 1968). The French Revolution, far bloodier and more violent than the American Revolution, began in 1789, and it was not until the late 1800s that order began to be restored. During that time, France saw the rise and disintegration of numerous political leaders and governments. The final blow was the defeat of Napoleon

III by Prussia in 1870. Yet another French government was created. This new government was the beginning of true popular democratic rule in France, a time LeBon called "a period of transition and anarchy." For the first time in French history, ordinary citizens held some political rights and power. The violent history of France and the new role of common citizens in the operation of French society led LeBon to consider the force of what he called *the mass* as an important factor in world history.

A wide variety of horribly violent episodes occurred before, during, and after the first French Revolution, including countless episodes of mob violence against individuals with little or no political power. LeBon gives detailed accounts of some of these events, including a three-week episode known as "the September Massacres" in which ordinary French citizens took it upon themselves to execute, one by one, over one thousand prisoners (mostly clergy and nobles) in Paris. He reprints eyewitness accounts of ordinary individuals hacking helpless men to death day after day, all of whom returned to their normal daily routines after the prisons had been emptied.

LeBon was trying to figure out how seemingly ordinary people could take part in such tremendous violence and then apparently revert to their normal selves within hours or even minutes. He concluded that it must be caused by the transmission of mental infection, a "contagion," similar to the deadly plagues which had swept through Europe in 1347, 1350, 1665, and 1721 (Karlen 1995). Such epidemics were still common in LeBon's time, so readers in 1895 would have been familiar with the concept and clearly understood the idea that LeBon meant to convey by using the term "contagion."

LeBon's Contagion Theory

To put it simply, LeBon believed that any time a crowd of people formed, all members of the crowd would be reduced to the level of the least intelligent, roughest, and the most violent member of the group:

> The whole of the common characteristics with which heredity endows the individuals of a race constitute the genius of that race. When, however, a certain number of these individuals are gathered together in a crowd for purposes of action, observation proves that, from the mere fact of their being assembled, there result certain new psychological characteristics, which are added to the racial characteristics and differ from them at times to a very considerable degree. (1982 [1895]:v).

In other words, people act differently when they are in crowds. LeBon called this the "unconscious activity of crowds," believing it to be beyond individual control. He argued that we rarely understand exactly what we are doing, or why, and in some situations this leads to what he called "the extreme mental inferiority of crowds." Crowds are quick to act, do not take time to reason, and can be quite powerful. For LeBon, it is important to study crowds in order to understand how little they are affected by laws and how greatly they are affected by any opinion loudly expressed by a member. He argued that crowds are led by emotion, not reason or ideas of fairness. A collective mind is formed, and the "psychological crowd" becomes a single entity capable of sudden and dramatic behavior.

LeBon states that a psychological crowd can be formed by people who are not in the same place at the same time. However, he never really explains how this can happen and does not give any specific examples. The only hints are some vague references to speculative crazes such as the Dutch Tulip Bulb mania of 1634 to 1636, which has since become heavily overanalyzed (see Mackay 1980 [1841] for information, see Blumer 1969 [1939], Smelser 1962, Turner and Killian 1957 for examples of analysis, see Miller 1985 for discussion of the overanalysis and misinterpretation of the mania).

The rest of LeBon's discussion of crowds focuses entirely on groups of people collected together in the same place at the same time. The process of becoming part of a psychological crowd has three components:

1. The individuals feel invincible and anonymous.
2. Contagion occurs.
3. Members of the group enter a state of suggestibility.

First, the individuals feel *invincible and anonymous*. This allows people to engage in behavior that they would normally repress out of fear and self-consciousness. Anonymity also allows behavior without worrying about the personal consequences. Those who are normally timid become brave, feeling the power of numbers on their side. Those who are normally law-abiding might openly flaunt the law, believing that they will not be caught or punished.

Second, *contagion* occurs. In this "hypnotic phenomenon," sentiments and actions become contagious to the extent that individuals are willing to sacrifice personal interest in the name of collective interest. For example, they might be willing to charge into a line of armed police officers or soldiers. This type of behavior does not occur because crowd members aren't thinking, but because the welfare of the crowd as a whole becomes more important to them than their own personal comfort or safety.

LeBon does not explain how this contagion takes place. He seems to believe that it is something like mass hypnosis, although at times he describes it more as a simple reduction of all members to their "lowest common factors." At least once, he indicates that the infection is literal, mentioning that madness is transmitted like any other infectious illness. This inability to account for how contagion occurs is the weakest aspect of LeBon's work.

Finally, the group enters into *suggestibility*. At this point, people are not conscious of their own behavior. Their attention becomes focused on the same object or event. Those members who disagree with the impulses of the crowd are unable to resist because they feel outnumbered. Even if they try, they are ignored by the crowd unless they can provide an attractive or satisfying alternative. Crowd members are now acting without thinking and may engage in behavior that they would find appalling in more thoughtful moments. They may also engage in heroic behavior that they would normally be afraid to try, but LeBon argues that crowds are almost always destructive.

Crowds can believe almost anything because they rely on their imagination and impulses, rather than logic. Their behavior becomes a simple reaction to emotional images that they find terrifying or attractive. They may even collectively hallucinate. For example, thousands routinely gather in places around the world and collectively "see" miracles that dispassionate observers cannot detect. LeBon cites a case where an entire ship's crew clearly saw a large number of men floating on wreckage and waving for help. When they got closer to the "wreckage," it turned out to be some tangled tree branches and leaves. As LeBon puts it, a "fact simultaneously verified by thousands of witnesses" is always wrong. People are most likely to perceive things incorrectly when in the presence of many others and when all members of a crowd agree on something, because their individual intellect is suppressed. Crowd members interpret things according to their expectations, not reality. Crowds cannot be led through logic or reasoning. Those who guide the crowd do so through startling images which strike the imagination of the crowd. The leaders of the various French revolts did not carefully argue their points. They declared their intentions with short, emotionally charged phrases like "death to them all!" that led to such useless but emotionally significant events as the charging of the Bastille. As LeBon points out, the Bastille held no prisoners at the time of its "liberation." Revolutionaries stormed it because it was an emotional symbol of tyranny to many people.

Situational variables such as time of day, temperature, terrain, etc., which LeBon called *immediate factors*, only have an effect in relationship to *remote factors* such as the attitudes, beliefs, and predisposition of the crowd members. People in a crowd setting will happily ignore clear evidence which contradicts their beliefs, preferring to pretend that they are right rather than face uncertainty or admit that they might be wrong. Perhaps most important of all, the apparent approval of other crowd members can make absolutely any action seem honorable. Even when engaged in criminal behavior, participants do not think of themselves as criminals. Participants in the September Massacres boasted of having taken part, and several later demanded medals of honor for their act of "patriotism." Under crowd circumstances, participants believe that their actions are not only justified, but glorious.

Summary

LeBon is much more of a philosopher and historian than a scientist. *The Crowd* relies on thought and conjecture rather than empirical study. Some of his concepts are quite outdated. For example, LeBon frequently uses the term "race" in a way that is much closer to our current use of such terms as culture, temperament, or ethnicity. He also refers to "women, children, and savages" as being illogical, irrational, and fickle. Such views seem horribly sexist and racist to a modern reader. Further, portions of the book focus much more on politics and revolution than on collective behavior. In spite of all this, LeBon managed to create a theory that was still in use until at least the 1950s, and which is the basis for a perspective that is still used in collective behavior research today. The next step in the development of Contagion Theory did not take long to emerge.

Robert Park

Less than ten years after the publication of *The Crowd,* Robert Park, an American studying in Germany, published his dissertation, *The Crowd and the Public (Masse und Publikum* 1904). Park's ideas were later refined in "Collective Behavior," a chapter in *Introduction to the Science of Sociology* that Park co-authored with Ernest Burgess in 1921. With a writing style much more concise than LeBon's, Park restated LeBon's key points while also making them more empirical and much more social-psychological. The most obvious example of this is the concept of contagion. LeBon believed that people literally catch mental illness from each other, and claimed that "numerous" physicians had contracted madness from working with deranged patients. Park ignores this aspect of LeBon's writing and instead developed a sociological explanation for how ideas spread rapidly through crowds. People imitate and reinforce each other's behavior, and this *circular reaction* produces the effect of social contagion.

Park's Contagion Theory

Park bases his theory on *emergent interaction*. He argues that people engage in "intense interaction" during periods of stress or disorder. Through this emergent interaction, individuals are more actively attuned to each other than they normally would be. Their behavior is social because their thoughts and behavior are influenced by the actions of every other member of the crowd. It is collective because each person acts under the influence of the group's mood. They behave in accordance with norms that all members unconsciously accept and reinforce in each other. This interactive effect on each member by all other members leads individuals to think and act alike. If one person acts decisively, others will imitate him or her. This reinforces the behavior, making the first person believe that their action was correct and simultaneously convincing others as well. Soon, every member of the crowd has adopted the behavior. This *circular reaction* produces contagion. People reinforce each other's behavior by mimicking it, until everyone is acting the same. They all believe that it is the correct or desirable behavior under the circumstances, because that it is what everyone else is doing.

Robert Park was the first person to name collective behavior as a distinct specialty within sociology. Unfortunately, his definition of collective behavior in *Introduction to the Science of Sociology* is vague: "the behavior of individuals under the influence of an impulse that is common and collective, an impulse, in other words, that is the result of social interaction" (1921: 865). This makes it sound as if almost all social behavior is collective behavior. If, for example, a large number of people decide to go to the beach because the weather is hot, few sociologists would argue that this is collective behavior even though it seems to be behavior based on a common impulse. Later in the same book Park redefined collective behavior as "the processes by which societies are disintegrated into their constituent elements and the processes by which these elements are brought together again into new relations to form new organizations and new societies" (1921: 924–25).

These obtuse definitions fail to make Park's position clear. It is apparent when reading his work that Park's conception of collective behavior is simple: Crowd members behave the same because they lose their ability to think clearly and rationally. Once that happens, they mindlessly imitate other crowd members. In this way, every member of the crowd becomes as violent as the most violent member, as impulsive as the most impulsive member, as irrational as the most irrational member, and so on. Park points out that at any time any member of the crowd can act as a leader or instigator simply by acting decisively. The role may pass throughout the crowd continuously, with no one person holding the position for long.

The crowd suppresses differences among members. Members all focus their attention on some event or object. They stop critically weighing alternatives before acting. They become emotional and highly suggestible. Park clearly considers crowd members irrational. Like LeBon, Park believes that crowd formation is dictated by social factors within the group. It is when members start to influence each other that they begin to form a psychological crowd. Park points out that this influence can occur even when the individuals are not in the same place at the same time. As long as individuals are somehow aware of each other's behavior, and this directly influences their own state of mind and subsequent behavior, a crowd mentality exists. This *collective mind* comes about through the disappearance of individual self-consciousness, when feelings and thoughts of members all move in the same direction. Once this collective mind forms, a crowd exists.

As mentioned earlier, this process occurs through social interaction. Whatever other crowd members do is defined as right, and everything else is defined as wrong. Person A imitates B who imitates C who imitates A. A feedback loop is created, with all members of the group forming a sort of circle in which the behavior of each individual becomes the model for all others. This continues until the behavior is unanimous. If everyone else is throwing rocks, then throwing rocks seems like the only acceptable behavior.

Park specifically states that crowds form much more readily during times of social instability. People engage in "something akin to the milling process in the herd" of animals (1924: 226). Park meant *milling* to refer to aimless behavior. People are agitated or excited but have no direction or purpose. It is during this stage that contagion occurs and sets the stage for suggestibility. Members of the crowd engage in mindless behavior (milling) instead of quietly thinking about what is going on. Soon, their behavior becomes impulsive.

The only concept that Park introduces that cannot be traced directly to LeBon or other writers is that of "ecstatic" or "expressive crowds." These are crowds that do not engage in any purposeful behavior. They do not form a goal. Instead, they may engage in such behaviors as dancing, shaking, shouting, and so on, in an attempt to express their ecstatic feelings. They engage in any behavior that makes them feel united. Some types of religious revivals are good examples of ecstatic crowds. Participants may holler, dance, jump, roll around on the ground, or speak in tongues. All engage in behavior that does not occur when they are alone. Within the ecstatic crowd setting, the behavior is its own goal. A more extreme form of expressive crowds are celebratory riots. Large crowds of sports fans might destroy a stadium out of sheer joy over winning an important game. Tearing down goal posts and ripping up bleachers is not intended to produce any social or political change; people engage in the mass destruction as a way of expressing their joy.

Summary

Although trained as a philosopher, Robert Park went on to become an important force in social psychology. His writing, while circular and at times seemingly confused, clearly brought LeBon's concept of the psychological crowd one step closer to being a solid theory of collective behavior. It is Park's emphasis on the social nature of crowd formation and the role of interaction in contagion that sets *The Crowd and the Public* a step ahead. Perhaps more than any other theory within sociology, Contagion Theory has progressed the way that scientific theories are supposed to occur: in small steps, each scientist cutting out more and more excess while fine-tuning those concepts that turn out to be useful. The final stage of fine-tuning can be found in the writings of Herbert Blumer.

Herbert Blumer

Like Park, Blumer is an American sociologist primarily interested in small-group interaction. His conception of collective behavior is much more specific than Park's, and includes "crowds, mobs, panics, manias, dancing crazes, stampedes, mass behavior, public opinion, propaganda, fashion, fads, social movements, revolutions, and reforms" (1969: 67). Although still a bit unfocused, Blumer's list allows us to finally reach an idea of what all forms of collective behavior have in common from the contagion perspective: groups of people doing things that they would not normally do because they are not thinking clearly. This makes it fundamentally different from normal group activity.

Unfortunately, Blumer's writings can easily confuse most readers. For example, he uses the term "collective behavior" to refer to normal group behavior *and* collective behavior. In "The Field of Collective Behavior" (1969), normal group activity is called "collective behavior" and crowd behavior is referred to as "*collective behavior*" (italics in original), "spontaneous collective behavior," and finally "elementary collective behavior." He then uses the term "collective behavior" to refer to the study of these types of behavior! Once the reader gets past this confusion and learns to make sense of Blumer's writing, the theory itself turns out to be a straightforward elaboration of Park's theory.

Blumer's Contagion Theory

Blumer's is the most advanced version of Contagion Theory. From Blumer's perspective, all that matters are the mechanisms that allow people to collectively break through established rules and routines of group life. Under normal circumstances, people engage in what he calls *interpretive interaction*. They interpret the words and/or actions of others and base their behavior on those interpretations. However, in a crowd situation people engage in *circular reaction,* where they react without thinking or interpreting (see Figure 2.1). Like LeBon and Park, Blumer assumes that individuals reach a point where they cease to think rationally about their behavior. The mechanisms that allow this to occur are milling, collective excitement, and social contagion.

Blumer's conception of *milling* is much more developed than Park's use of the term. Blumer believed that any collective episode begins with people behaving in an aimless and random manner. Their attention has been drawn

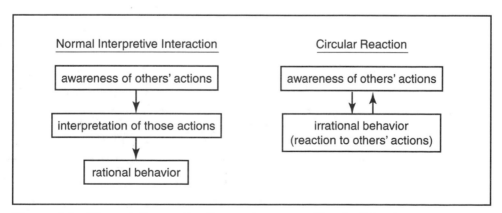

Figure 2.1   Blumer's Intepretive Interaction versus Circular Reaction

by some sort of excitement, which causes tension among the crowd. During milling, people become extremely sensitive and responsive to each other, increasingly preoccupied with each other, and decreasingly responsive to ordinary external stimuli. In other words, they pay so much attention to each other that they start to ignore the rest of the world. They respond to each other quickly and unwittingly, but do not respond to outsiders at all. This milling process prepares people to act collectively.

The next stage, *collective excitement,* is a more intense form of milling. The excited behavior of others makes it difficult to think about anything else and sets the stage for contagious behavior. People have become emotionally aroused, unstable, unresponsive to logic, and irresponsible.

At this point, *social contagion* becomes dominant. Blumer defined contagion as the rapid, unwitting, irrational dissemination of a mood, impulse, or behavior. People become so worked up, emotional, and distracted that they are unable to think clearly. Instead, they imitate the behavior of those around them. They lose their social resistance because they lose self-consciousness. They also lose the ability to interpret the actions of others. Instead of interpreting, thinking, and then acting, they quickly and blindly react to whatever goes on around them. They are more likely to follow impulses. Behavior spreads like wildfire throughout the crowd. A common focus of attention occurs, and a common set of beliefs form. This makes it possible for the crowd to act with unity and purpose (see Figure 2.2).

Blumer also introduces the concept of *the mass* as a unique type of collective social group. This is quite different from LeBon's use of the term, which refers to the general citizenry of a territory. For Blumer, a mass is different than a crowd because it is composed of anonymous individuals who do not directly interact with each other. This means that they cannot engage in milling. Instead, they are faced with exactly the opposite situation: no behavioral cues to help them decide what to do. Therefore, unlike a crowd, members of a mass tend to be extremely self-conscious. They act based in response to an object that has gained their attention and on the basis of impulses

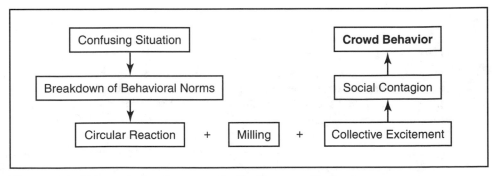

Figure 2.2   Blumer's development of collective crowd behavior

aroused by it. Examples of masses would include all the people who closely follow a murder trial on television or the individuals who decide to build bomb shelters in their back yards after watching a television documentary about communism. Masses are most often composed of detached and alienated individuals who focus on things that are interesting but puzzling. They are confused and uncertain in their actions. Although they act separately, the fact that they act in the same manner means that members of a mass can have a tremendous impact on society or social institutions. For example, if only 1 percent of the population of the United States were to decide that they needed fat-free cookies tomorrow, 2.8 million boxes of cookies would be sold in one day. This slight shift in mass taste could cause a shift in the entire food retailing industry. Each member of the mass acts to fill his or her own needs in response to vague impulses in relation to some focus of attention. It is the common focus of attention that makes the group a mass.

Summary

Although lacking focus and discipline in his writings, Blumer did manage to assemble a more complete version of Contagion Theory. In essence, he argues that crowds and masses engage in what can be called collective behavior. In crowds, milling and contagion effectively eliminate independent thought among members. This can result in behavior that is bizarre and difficult for outsiders to understand. People engage in behaviors that they would never dream of doing by themselves. In masses, independent behavior converges through collective attention. This produces uniform behavior among individuals who interpret some object of attention in the same way and decide to engage in the same course of action. In their most extreme and enduring forms, crowds and masses can eventually lead to the development of new social institutions. Blumer considered this possibility for social change and integration the most important and intriguing aspect of collective behavior.

Discussion

Contagion Theory focuses on the factors that allow individuals to engage in behavior in groups that they would never perform when alone. Starting with LeBon, the contagion theorists were primarily concerned with explaining why terrible and violent group behavior occurred. LeBon, Park, and Blumer all believed that these events are created by the breakdown of normal critical thinking and can occur any time people gather. LeBon literally believed that this breakdown is contagious, but recognized that social factors also play a role. Park expanded on the social and psychological mechanisms that make contagion possible and introduced the concept of circular reaction. Blumer argued that circular reaction is far more important than any pre-existing attitudes among crowd members. He focused almost entirely on the psychological changes that occur when individuals find themselves in crowd situations. Blumer also expanded the concept of collective behavior to include the mass. He argued that members of a mass operate under a different set of stresses than members of a crowd, and therefore engage in collective behavior for different reasons.

Core Assumptions

All contagion theorists assume that collective behavior occurs because of the mental state of participants. This social-psychological focus carries over into the next theory that we are going to examine in Chapter 3, "The Emergent Norm Perspective."

The contagion theorists also share the assumption that members of collective behavior crowds are irrational, experience a loss of self-control, and act without thinking. Members are literally infected with the bad ideas of others. LeBon, Park, and Blumer all believe that the entire crowd can be reduced to the level of the least intelligent, most violent member of the group. This social contagion allows otherwise good people to do radical or terrible things.

Evaluation

The contagion theory is no longer used in modern collective behavior research for a few reasons. The theory itself is sometimes vague and contradictory. Neither Park nor Blumer ever seem to be able to develop a concise, complete definition of what collective behavior is, and both spend more time discussing exceptions than analyzing it. When using Blumer's version, for example, researchers would be forced to choose between more than one way to classify the type of collective behavior, more than one set of specifications they should use to analyze it, and so on. This makes it difficult to use the theory at all. For example, imagine a biologist trying to study a particular insect. The first thing she would want to do is place the new species into a specific category based on particular characteristics. Now, imagine that there are several different classification schemas, and the unknown insect can be placed into different categories, depending on which schema is used. Before the insect (or collective episode) can be analyzed, it has to be placed into an understood category. This allows other researchers to understand what makes that example similar to other, known examples as well as what makes it different or unique.

In the end, sociologists relying on Contagion Theory are forced to conclude that the participants lost their ability to reason. Research has failed to support this assertion. First-hand observation by Turner and Killian (Chapter 3), McPhail (Chapter 5), and others revealed that individual behavior within a crowd is neither as universal nor as irrational as the Contagion theorists believed.

More than any other factor, however, it is the development of the Emergent Norm perspective that sealed Contagion Theory's fate. Turner and Killian (to be discussed in the next chapter) succeeded in borrowing and modifying the most useful aspects of Contagion Theory while eliminating the assumption that participants behave irrationally. As researchers have studied more and more episodes of collective behavior over the decades, exceptions to social contagion have become increasingly obvious. In order to continue, someone had to find a way past the assumption that bad thoughts are contagious like a germ or a virus.

Chapter 3

The Emergent Norm Perspective

In 1957, Ralph Turner and Lewis Killian published what they called an incomplete theory of collective behavior. Following closely in the tradition of Robert Park and particularly Herbert Blumer, *Collective Behavior* aimed "more at assembling existing ideas than at innovation" (1957: v). Turner and Killian were perhaps too modest. Their book, which has been revised twice since the original edition, is an attempt to explain virtually all facets of collective behavior from a social-psychological perspective. They managed to retain almost all of the theoretical elements of Contagion Theory while letting go of the assumption that crowd members become irrational, illogical, or temporarily insane. Their "Emergent Norm Perspective" is based on the premise that collective behavior participants remain rational. This seemingly small change dramatically increases the usefulness of the theory.

The Emergent Norm Theory can be briefly summarized as follows:

1. Collective behavior can occur whenever people find themselves in a situation where they are confused or don't know what to do.
2. When people don't know what to do, they look around to see what other people are doing.
3. As soon as any member of the group engages in any behavior, all other members of the group wait to see what will happen. If there are no negative reactions to the behavior, then they all assume the behavior is ac-

ceptable within the group and become likely to engage in that behavior themselves. Through this process of circular reinforcement, new group norms emerge.

4. Because most people conform to the norms of their social surroundings most of the time, they will follow the group's new, emergent norms. They engage in unusual behavior not because of any mental deficiency, but because it seems like the right thing to do under the circumstances.

Turner and Killian begin by defining "collective behavior" as instances in which "change [rather than stability], uncertainty [rather than predictability], and disorganization [rather than stable structure]" are characteristic (1957: 3, brackets in original). By 1987, they elaborated on this, defining collective behavior as "those forms of social behavior in which usual conventions cease to guide social action and people collectively transcend, bypass, or subvert established institutional patterns and structures" (1987: 3). According to Turner and Killian, social life usually operates smoothly but conditions sometimes arise where the standard norms do not apply. New norms emerge in these situations. People follow these *emergent norms* just as they usually follow social norms throughout their day. This statement sums up the basis of the Emergent Norm Perspective: People generally conform to the norms of any given situation and when the situation calls for the creation of new norms, they simply follow the new guidelines. Turner and Killian shift their focus onto the process that allows new rules for behavior to quickly develop.

The idea that the group exhibits normative constraint over the individual throughout collective behavior episodes clearly distinguishes the Emergent Norm perspective from Contagion Theory. Turner and Killian argue that group norms drive individual behavior during collective events just as they do in most other situations. It is the norms themselves that are different. Contagion theorists would argue that a man engages in violent crowd behavior because he has lost his sense of who he is and throws rocks without thinking because he has been infected with the idea and cannot resist. Turner and Killian would argue that the same man is throwing rocks because it is what everyone else in the situation is doing and therefore it seems to him like the right thing to do in that situation. Collective behavior is caused by conformity.

Emergent Norm theory is firmly grounded in Symbolic Interactionism, a social-psychological perspective that focuses on the importance of meaning and interpretation as driving forces behind human behavior. According to Symbolic Interactionists, we all interpret our surroundings and base our behavior on whatever meaning we attribute to those surroundings. When we are around other people, we all work together to socially define what is going on. This *definition of the situation* is important to us, and dictates our behavior.

Turner and Killian apply this perspective directly to collective behavior. Rather than starting with the assumption that there is something wrong with participants, they began by assuming that the social circumstances themselves must have allowed individuals to engage in odd or unusual behavior without feeling as if they were doing anything wrong. Individuals will not engage in every behavior that is suggested. Instead, they can be guided only in directions that match their attitudes or already-chosen course of action. Crowd behavior is partially influenced by participants' motives but is most strongly guided by norms that emerge as an event takes place.

The component of Turner and Killian's theory most often used by researchers today is their five-part classification of participants. They argue that there are five different reasons for taking part in a collective episode, and therefore up to five different types of participants present at any event. This schema can be applied with the Emergent Norm perspective and with other theories as well.

The Emergent Norm Process

As mentioned earlier, Turner and Killian define collective behavior as specific instances in which traditional norms and/or patterns of behavior seem inadequate or inappropriate to those individuals within the situation (see Figure 3.1). Key to this conception of collective behavior is what Turner and Killian call *crowds:* short-lived, loosely knit, and disorderly collectivities. Crowds are required for collective behavior to occur. A collectivity has formed once new norms that contradict or reinterpret the norms and/or organization of society begin to emerge. Therefore, to Turner and Killian the study of collective behavior is the study of collectivities. This is important because they simply treat collectivities as a special category of small social group and

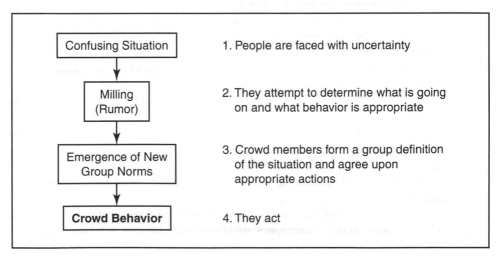

Figure 3.1 Development of Collective Behavior from the Emergent Norm Perspective

apply small group theory and research to a wide spectrum of collective behavior events. In fact, they trace their own roots to Emile Durkheim and his work on the effects of groups on individual thought, as well as Gabriel Tarde, who studied people's imitation of other humans. They combined this with Park and Blumer's interest in the influence of the group on the individual to form the basis of the Emergent Norm Perspective.

Our behavior in any group setting is heavily influenced by what seems to be appropriate in that particular situation. We tend to be quieter at funerals than at concerts, for example. We often judge our own behavior by comparing it to those around us. We use other people as *reference groups* to determine correct behavior. However, crowd members develop new norms that may be totally at odds with the norms of the dominant culture. The other people in the situation act as a temporary reference group, and their behavior seems to indicate that standard cultural norms do not apply.

It is important to remember that the people in the situation perceive the new norms as appropriate under the circumstances. They do not engage in behavior that would normally seem bizarre just because they want to; they do it because it seems like the right thing to do at that time and in that setting. If you were walking in a park and saw someone in a pond calling for help, you would probably assume that the person could not swim and try to help. However, what if there were ten other people pointing at the individual and laughing? Would you still dive into the water, or would you guess that the person was simply joking to amuse his or her friends? The behavior of others always gives us important clues that help us define what behaviors are correct. How do you think you might behave if you were in a movie theater and everyone else suddenly ran to a fire exit? Other people aren't just sharing space with us, they are constantly shaping our social environment.

Individuals normally have little or no influence over group norms. One person cannot redefine appropriate theater behavior simply by running toward the exit. However, under emergent norm circumstances the entire group may define the situation based on the behavior of one individual. If the theater is filling with smoke, running toward an exit may signal to all others present that they are in danger. Although it takes a careful reading of Turner and Killian's work to pick up on this, it is the participants' definition of the situation that most heavily influences their chosen course of action. If they believe they are in immediate danger, they may behave in a way that seems shocking to those who later read about individuals injured in a mad rush for the exits. The definition of the situation is heavily influenced by any individual behavior that seems to confirm what crowd members already suspect or believe to be true.

Turner and Killian stress that throughout this process of perception, definition, and action, members of the group do not act "as one," as earlier scholars of collective behavior had asserted. Instead, the members of the group act as individuals, but choose similar behaviors for similar reasons. The group does not have a mind, a conscience, self-control, or a sense of self-esteem. However, each individual member of the collectivity does possess these things, and these influence their behavior. More importantly, different roles may be assigned as the group forms. Observation, photographs, film and video evidence all show that members of a group almost never act exactly the same as every other member, but most of them do behave similarly to each other. In a riot, for example, it is rare for all individuals to throw rocks at the police. Some throw rocks, some yell or gesture, some loot and steal, and others merely watch the events unfold. Behavior in a group setting is not just caused by attitudes toward an object (such as a police car). They are also guided by attitudes toward one's self, the group, and so on.

The idea that social groups sometimes develop new norms quickly in times of confusion or doubt points to another key difference between the Emergent Norm Perspective and Contagion Theory. Turner and Killian maintain Park and Blumer's idea of circular reaction or circular reinforcement, but consider contagion an unimportant factor. Circular reinforcement, as discussed in the previous chapter, refers to the tendency of all people in a situation to simultaneously imitate and reinforce each other's behavior. Any behavior that does not elicit social disapproval becomes defined as acceptable within that situation. Others become likely to engage in the same behavior. Turner and Killian argue that the circular reinforcement which occurs in crowds is the process that makes the emergence of new group norms possible, and also explains why it can happen so quickly. They do not believe contagion is an important part of this process. The reinforcement and reaction may occur quicker in an emergent situation than in normal everyday life, but that is only because the circumstances call for quick decisions.

This is a complicated way to state a simple idea: You cannot understand collective behavior without understanding the effects of the group on individual attitudes and behavior *and* the effects of the individual on group attitudes and behavior. Prior to the publication of the first edition of *Collective Behavior* in 1957, most theorists focused entirely on one or the other.

Turner and Killian also make it clear that collective behavior is not particularly irrational. For example, they note that lynchings (which are often used to illustrate the purely "irrational" nature of violent group behavior by earlier theorists) can serve as an effective tool to maintain social stratification. If the goal of the individuals involved is to maintain fear and compliance on the part of a specific social group, then the participants may decide to take part for reasons that are quite rational. The fact that we do not like or understand the behavior, no matter how horrifying, does not qualify it as irrational.

Regardless of the type of collective behavior examined, communication is a key factor. If communication breaks down, the normal coordination of social roles begins to collapse. People are not certain that they can count on others to do what they are supposed to do. Different group members may develop different understandings as to what is expected of them and lose confidence in their expectations of others' behavior. The result of this confusion can be a new set of normative expectations for what had previously been a typical situation. It is when members of a collectivity communicate at least partially with each other but not with those outside the group that new norms may emerge.

Ambiguity leads to the spread of rumors because individuals are all trying to define the situation at hand. Information, definitions, and directives for action cannot be validated through normal channels of communication. Decisions about what to do must be made quickly. There may be confusion over what to do even when the situation seems clear. When the situation is unclear, this confusion becomes greatly magnified.

Although Turner and Killian do not state their theoretical ideas in clearly delineated terms, they do spell out the six conditions necessary for the development of a crowd and therefore for the occurrence of collective behavior:

1. Uncertainty of potential participants as to appropriate behavior within the situation.
2. Urgency; a feeling that *something* must be done, soon.
3. Communication of mood and imagery within crowd.
4. Constraint; the sense that one should conform to the norms of the crowd.
5. Selective individual suggestibility; individual acceptance of mood and imagery consistent with the crowd.
6. Permissiveness; attitudes and behaviors that are normally inhibited in society may be expressed within the crowd.

Uncertainty

Turner and Killian argue that people hate confusion and would rather believe something negative or dangerous rather than face doubt. In times of uncertainty, many want to be told what to do because it gives them guidelines to follow and alleviates the confusion, doubt, and anxiety created by the circumstances. To support this point, Turner and Killian discuss famous conformity studies (Sherif 1936) demonstrating that people, faced with a question to which the answer is impossible to know, adjust their answers to match those around them. People all assume that the group answer is better than their own. This experiment illustrates a point that Turner and Killian consider crucial to understanding collective behavior: More uncertainty leads to more suggestibility from others. In a situation where correct responses are unclear, most rely on the judgement of others. In situations where people are confused by those around them, they seek certainty. Acting confident (even if totally wrong) places one quickly into a position of leadership.

Although Turner and Killian never refer to the term themselves, social psychologists have developed the concept of informational influence (Sherif 1936) to explain what happens when people find themselves in new or confusing situations. We base our own behavior on the behavior of those around us. Our basic human tendency is to look around to see what other people are doing. We use other people as a source of information, and their words and behavior guide our own thoughts and actions. In the drowning example referred to above, we use the actions of other witnesses to help us decide if the person is really in trouble or is simply playing a joke. We don't conform to their behavior because we feel pressure to do so, but also because we honestly think it is the right thing to do under the circumstances. If everyone else seems upset, then we define the situation as an emergency and behave appropriately. In this way, our own behavior becomes similar to that of others in the situation. This effect has been thoroughly documented over the years, and perhaps the most striking factor is that people walk away from the situation believing that they have engaged in the correct behavior. If many people are confused at the same time, they may all base their definition of the situation on the actions of one person who seems to know more than they do. This is how one decisive individual can end up dictating the behavior of an entire crowd, even if that person has no real idea what is going on. The fact that they *seem* to know more encourages others to follow their lead.

A part of this process frequently involves accepting rumors that make the behavior seem acceptable or even necessary. All members of the crowd believe that they understand what is going on, and they follow any behavior that seems to fit that understanding.

Urgency

This process of rumor construction is possible because groups do not cease to act when confusion sets in. Instead, they try to figure out what to do next. Having no idea what to do next produces a sense of urgency: The longer they do nothing, the more overwhelmed they become by the sense that they need to take action soon. The agreement and solidarity of collectivities does not suddenly appear, it is developed socially within the group. This often takes place during milling, the process whereby individuals behave in a restless manner.

The assumption that milling must take place for new norms to emerge makes it seem as if the theory can only be applied to collective episodes preceded by a gathering of people in a confusing situation. This is not the case. It is not the physical act of milling that is important, but rather the psychological state of confusion, agitation, and yearning for direction. Whenever peoples' behavior is influenced by the behavior of others, milling can take place. People can be separated by hundreds of miles, but if they all experience the same uncertainty about a common focus of attention, they can be said to "mill." Milling is an attempt to act in the face of uncertainty. It can be quiet, as in a church service when individuals silently look around to determine how other people are reacting to a loud noise. Milling can also be long-distance. Through telephones and the Internet, people can now communicate with others from thousands of miles away in an attempt to acquire more information. No matter what form it takes, this urgent desire for information explains the rapid spread of rumors. Likewise, the urgent desire for direction explains the sometimes rapid spread of behavioral norms.

Communication of Mood and Imagery

Communication within the crowd indicates to each member what is happening, what is likely to happen next, and what actions and attitudes are appropriate. Through rumor and milling, the crowd participants are able to reach consensus. This communication makes it possible for each individual to form a similar definition of the situation. It also indicates what attitudes and behaviors are likely to be accepted within the crowd and which ones will be rejected or punished. Without this communication between members, individuals remain isolated from and independent of each other and a crowd cannot form. Crowd members perceive every other member of the group as a potential source of information. This increased awareness and attention toward others is one more reason why crowd members are so quick to imitate the behavior of others within the group.

Constraint

Participants' ideas about what is acceptable or unacceptable to other members of the group may be totally mistaken. Nevertheless, they are far less likely to engage in any behavior that they believe will be rejected. This leaves them with nothing to do except engage in those behaviors that they believe will be accepted by other members of the crowd. Group pressure to conform is a powerful force, and this is particularly true in the heightened state of group-awareness that crowd members find themselves in.

It is important to remember that only some behavioral patterns are acceptable to crowd members. One member of the crowd can dampen the mood of the entire group by going too far and therefore spoiling the event for others. In other words, only certain paths of behavior are acceptable to any crowd. A crowd that is rapidly becoming violent is not going to accept suggestions to sit down, join hands, and sing. Similarly, a crowd that is sitting down and singing is not going to tolerate one member who suddenly starts throwing rocks. It is not acceptable to scream or fight at the sight of a religious vision. It is not acceptable to hug and kiss strangers in a riot. Once a crowd has begun to define the situation, only behaviors that fit that definition will be tolerated.

Turner and Killian turn here to famous experiments by Asch (1951), which demonstrated that people faced with answers that are clear but go against the rest of a unanimous social group will often give the same wrong answer as everyone else. Participants in those experiments gave the wrong answer, knowing that it was incorrect, because everyone else gave that an-

swer. They felt as if they should. They felt constrained by other members of
the group, even though there was no attempt by other group members to persuade them.

As mentioned earlier, the idea of group constraint truly separates the
Emergent Norm Perspective from earlier theories of collective behavior. Participants may appear to be engaged in completely anti-social behavior to a
dispassionate outside observer, but within the group that behavior is socially accepted, sanctioned, and encouraged. People may even be afraid to do
otherwise.

Selective Individual Suggestibility

Selective individual suggestibility refers to the tendency of individuals to become more and more polarized to the apparent attitudes held by other members of the crowd. They become more and more likely to accept any
information, belief, or behavioral cue that fits the mood of the crowd. They
are also increasingly likely to reject any new piece that does not fit into this
mindset. Members therefore become ever more attuned to increasingly specific suggestions and behavioral cues. If the crowd seems to be angry, individuals become likely to accept suggestions for violent or destructive behavior. If
individuals are being told by other members of a craze that their collectible
dolls are gaining value faster than they can buy them, they become likely to
purchase even more. Eventually, members of the crowd convince themselves
that only one course of action is appropriate. They often believe this so firmly
that doing nothing at all would seem like a failure of some sort.

Permissiveness

Permissiveness may seem to contradict constraint at first glance. After all,
how can the group be constrictive and permissive at the same time? It is constrictive in the sense that it inhibits expression of any feelings out of sync
with those of the group. For example, imagine being the only person cheering
for the away team on the home side of the bleachers at a home football game.
However, the group is also permissive in the sense that it allows the expression of attitudes and behaviors that are not accepted in any *other* setting. A
similar type of permissiveness is often present at social parties: It may be
perfectly acceptable to shout, yell, and get drunk to the point of passing out
at a party, behavior that would be condemned in almost any other setting.
This permissiveness allows some people to engage in behavior that they
would do much more often if social circumstances frequently allowed it. And,
just as those who like to shout and drink heavily are more likely to attend
certain parties, those individuals who are predisposed to behave in certain
ways are likely to seek out situations that allow the desired behavior.

Not all forms of collective behavior involve the release of pent-up feelings. It is doubtful, for instance, that participants in the goldfish swallowing

fad of the 1920s had long yearned to swallow live fish in front of an audience. On the other hand, many types of collective behavior do allow for this sort of release. No matter how much an individual hates another social group, he or she is unlikely to scream insults in public unless surrounded by a large group of like-minded individuals. Riots allow for the expression of destructive, violent, and anti-social or anti-establishment feelings. Spontaneous celebrations allow behaving in a manner that is totally out of line with one's public image. Religious revival events allow for exuberant behavior that would seem unbecoming in everyday life. Many forms of collective behavior allow participants to engage in behavior that they desire, but that is unacceptable in most social circumstances.

Classification of Participants

Turner and Killian are most well known and most often cited for their simple classification schema for collective behavior participants. Turner and Killian divide collective behavior participants into five categories. These categories are based on two factors: the motivation of the individual for joining the event and the behavior of the individual throughout the event. Oddly, the labels most frequently given to some of these categories do not come from Turner and Killian's most recent edition of their textbook. Turner and Killian do not give specific labels to these categories in the first edition of *Collective Behavior,* and by the third edition they dropped the fifth category altogether. The labels "Ego-involved" and "Ego-detached" are commonly used in the literature, although Turner and Killian have dropped those labels since their second edition. The labels used in this chapter are a blend of those used by Turner and Killian between 1957 and 1987. The five categories are:

1. The Ego-involved/Committed
2. The Concerned
3. Insecure
4. Spectators
5. The Ego-detached/Exploiter

The Ego-involved/Committed

The committed participant is deeply and personally involved with the event. He or she is motivated by a sense that some action is demanded. These individuals may be incensed, frightened, or elated. Any intense emotion related to the event will make the individual feel deeply involved at a personal level. They define the situation as demanding immediate action. Pre-existing orientations guide them toward specific action. They are emotionally involved in the event and will take a strong position of leadership, if required, in order to accomplish their goal. For example, those who are most angry or outraged at a perceived social injustice may also be most likely to begin hurling insults or rocks at police officers.

The Concerned

Concerned participants are not as personally involved as the committed participants. They also have less clearly defined attitudes. They believe that something should be done, but they are not personally involved enough to believe that it falls to them to decide what, when, and how action should be carried out. They are concerned about the issues surrounding the event, but not as much as the ego-involved participants. A person whose house is burning down is involved; his or her neighbors are concerned. Because they have less personal stake in the event, concerned participants are more likely to follow than to lead. Using the riot as a continuing example, concerned participants may yell or throw things, but are likely to do so only after others (ego-committed participants) have defined it as the appropriate course of action. They take part out of concern for those on the side of the conflict with whom they identify. Group loyalty is a major factor for the concerned participant. Statements like "we had to do something, they were hitting our people" exemplify this attitude.

The Insecure

The insecure participant derives direct satisfaction from participation in a crowd, regardless of the circumstances. It is the sense of power, belonging, or identity that this participant is interested in. They may not know what the issues are, and don't particularly care. Those who are of what Turner and Killian call "generally insecure status" are included in this category. There are two factors that draw insecure participants into a crowd. First, there is the sense of power and unanimity that comes with joining a large group. The crowd makes insecure members feel physically powerful, socially important, and (perhaps most importantly), a part of something. Second, the "righteousness" of the crowd itself is appealing to insecure individuals. We tend to base our personal standards of right and wrong on the norms of groups that we identify with. In an emergent norm situation, no one in the group contradicts the new norm and no one outside of the group matters at that moment. The certainty that one is doing the right thing and that everyone universally agrees is artificially created within the crowd. This provides a tremendous sense of security to socially insecure individuals.

Spectators

Curiosity is an important human trait. Spectators are often drawn to certain types of collective episodes out of curiosity about the crowd itself, not about the event that drew the crowd in the first place. They may gather to watch a small group of individuals engage in fad behavior. They might not even know what is going on, and are usually relatively inactive. For example, at political protests curious spectators may dramatically outnumber actual participants.

Spectators are an important part of many types of collective behavior for three reasons. First, they are important because official counts often lump them in with active participants. News broadcasts may announce that over one thousand people took part in a particular protest when, in fact, several hundred of those individuals were there to watch the protest, not take part in it. Some may have been hoping to see an exciting clash between protesters and authorities. People are often drawn to a site by the presence of a large crowd of people. It is not unusual for large numbers of people to walk up to (and effectively join) a crowd and only then ask what is going on.

Second, spectators provide crowd members with an audience for any behavior. Most people do not behave the same when they are aware of being watched. Their behavior often swings to extremes: They may become much more subdued, or much more active. This applies to crowd members as well. The awareness that people are watching can magnify whatever behavioral tendencies already exist within the crowd. It also creates the illusion that they support the actions of the crowd.

The third reason that spectators are important is because they are sometimes drawn into the event and become active participants. They might find the crowd's action personally meaningful and decide to join in. They might decide that the crowd is doing something fun or exciting. They may feel outrage at the way participants are being treated, and leap to their defense. Spectators are often treated as participants by authorities in riotous situations. Those spectators who are teargassed, physically hit or pushed, or aggressively shouted at (all common police tactics for dispersing crowds) may become angry and retaliate. Within seconds they can be converted from curious spectators into ego-involved or concerned participants.

The Ego-detached/Exploiters

The ego-detached participant, also referred to as an exploiter, has only his or her own personal interests in mind. They join an event if it suits their own goals, and manipulate the event as much as possible in order to achieve them. Turner and Killian refer to these participants as "the person whose inhibitions are already down before crowd action develops," including "drunks, psychopaths, and petty criminals" (1957: 110). In other words, there are people walking around in society who generally want to engage in various forms of socially unacceptable behavior. Collective behavior episodes provide them with the excuse for doing these things.

Crowd behavior always represents some sort of deviation from ordinary social norms. Exploiters are people who jump at the chance to engage in such deviance. This may even include deliberate instigators who, with a preconceived plan, push the crowd in the desired direction. For instance, they may begin shouting, or actively encourage others to engage in a particular course of action. Unlike the ego-involved participant who often leads the crowd in a desired direction, the exploiter manipulates the crowd in order to achieve some personal goal not related to the group. Turner and Killian recount an instance when older men at a riot could be seen actively encouraging younger men to fight. They literally pushed the younger men toward the fights but were careful to stay out of the scuffles themselves. The involved participant leads primarily by example; the detached instigator often leads through words alone.

Those who speak first, loudest, or most vigorously may create the impression that they express the feelings of the entire crowd. These instigators usually do not take part in the action that they so loudly encourage. Often cautious and deliberate, their actions clearly demonstrate self-control.

Instigators are not the only ego-detached participants in a collective event. Exploiters are those individuals who do not take part in the primary crowd activity at all, but rather engage in their own selfish actions within the context of the group event. Two examples that easily come to mind are looters and merchants. Looters use the cover of a riot or other disturbance to steal as much merchandise as possible. The issues that unite active participants do not motivate exploiters, and their behavior only seems similar at first glance. There is an obvious and significant difference between destroying property out of rage or frustration versus stealing property for one's own personal gain or future use. Merchants or vendors are another type of exploiter that appear at a wide variety of collective events. Those who sell souvenirs such as mugs or T-shirts are clearly not involved in an event in the same way that other participants are. They do not define the situation the same way that the ego-involved and ego-concerned participants do. To exploiters, the event is simply another opportunity to make a profit.

Discussion

Turner and Killian argue that collective behavior participants behave the way they do because of the situation they find themselves in. They are following the norms of the crowd, just as almost all of us generally follow the norms of whatever situation we find ourselves in. The circular reinforcement that Park and Blumer first described is, according to Turner and Killian, nothing more than the process of individuals collectively defining appropriate behaviors within a specific situation. The emerging norms of the situation are the source of collective behavior and the most important aspect of the entire process.

Core Assumptions

Turner and Killian assert that individuals engaged in collective behavior are simply doing what they always do: following the norms of their social surroundings. They focus most of their attention on the group dynamics that occur during several different types of collective behavior. In each, they argue that the influence of the group on the individual accounts for otherwise incomprehensible behavior.

Turner and Killian also assume that collective behavior can occur absolutely anytime any group of people are faced with uncertainty. Preexisting social or personal stress may make an event more likely, but are not necessary. Instead, it is the peculiar stress of social uncertainty itself that creates a sense of urgency within crowd members and drives them to collective behavior. Participants might be relaxed and happy right up until they enter the situation that causes confusion and leads to crowd formation.

Finally, the Emergent Norm perspective is based on the assumption that not all participants take part in collective events for the same reasons and therefore do not engage in identical behaviors. There may be up to five different categories of participants at any one event, and each is there for different reasons. Each engages in different patterns of behavior. Each hopes to achieve something different by taking part. This typology has proven to be highly useful and, as Turner and Killian intended, can be used with theories other than the Emergent Norm perspective.

Evaluation

The typology of participants is useful for sociologists working from a variety of perspectives. For this reason, it is almost always mentioned in any book about collective behavior, including introductory sociology textbooks. However, the Emergent Norm Theory itself has been somewhat neglected by researchers compared to the theory discussed in Chapter 4 (see, however, Aguirre et al. 1998, Turner 1996). This is probably because of the problems with Turner and Killian's writing (poor organization, dense writing style, etc.) and the theoretical roots of the theory itself.

As stated earlier, the Emergent Norm perspective is based on Symbolic Interactionism. Symbolic Interactionism concerns itself almost entirely with individual perception and small-group dynamics. As such, it is a natural for the analysis of collective behavior. However, many of the researchers drawn to the study of collective behavior come from other theoretical paradigms. They tend to focus on different issues. As sociologists look for social-level variables that create collective behavior, they may overlook this theory because it focuses on situational and personal-level variables. A more structure-oriented researcher, for example, might chose to focus on the social and political conditions that led up to a particular episode. They concern themselves with the historical precedents that "created" the event. The Emergent Norm Perspective, by contrast, focuses almost entirely on conditions within the crowd at the time of formation. This approach may lead many sociologists to disregard Emergent Norm Theory as "too psychological." Turner and Killian's theory considers the conditions of the moment at least as important as (if not more important than) the general social conditions leading up to that moment.

As we will see later in this book, the theory is useful in examining the dynamics of various types of collective behavior. However, it might be the case that Emergent Norm Theory does not answer the social and historical questions that some researchers ask.

Chapter 4

The Value-Added Theory

In 1962, Neil J. Smelser published what he called a new and controversial theory of collective behavior. In a dramatic departure from earlier theorists, Smelser focused on the structural social conditions that lead up to what his book's introduction called "collective seizures." Smelser argued that the factors leading to collective behavior are social, not psychological. He claimed to be able to explain why collective episodes occur where they do, when they do, and in the ways they do. Rather than looking inside the minds of the participants, he focused on the social structure itself.

Smelser's Value-Added Theory has its roots in Functionalism. To oversimplify a bit, functionalists assume anything that exists for a long time in society, or that occurs over and over, must serve some sort of benefit or function for society. Using this perspective, Smelser assumed that collective behavior must serve some sort of function. He decided that collective behavior occurs as a sort of relief valve for pent-up tension or strain in society. Whenever tension exists, the potential for collective behavior also exists. The greater the strain, the greater the likelihood of an episode.

The most basic assertions of Smelser's theory can be briefly summarized as follows:

1. Collective behavior is not caused by mysterious forces. Clearly identifiable determinants drive a collective episode.

2. Collective behavior is not caused by the psychology of the participants, but rather by the conditions within the social structure, organization, or specific setting.

3. Collective behavior is driven by strain experienced by participants within a social setting. The unusual behavior acts as a release for participants, lessening their strain. It is not normative, institutionalized, or ceremonial behavior.

4. There are determinants that must be present in order for any form of collective behavior to occur. The determinants are: structural conduciveness, structural strain, generalized belief, precipitating factors, mobilization of participants, and social control. If any determinant is lacking, there will be no outburst. If all of the determinants are present, then collective behavior is immanent.

At no point does Smelser refer to pathology, contagion, temporary insanity, or any other mental or psychological condition of participants. He specifi-

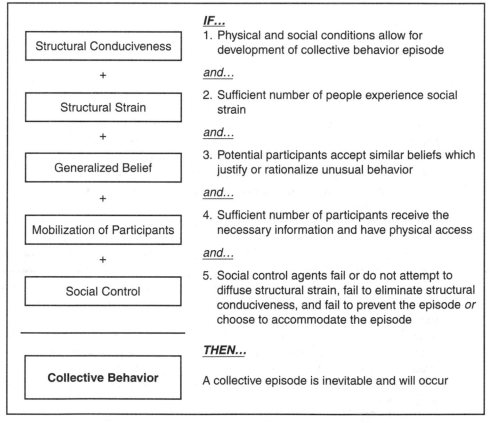

Figure 4.1   The development of Collective Behavior from the Value-Added Perspective

cally argues that psychological factors are created and driven by social factors. Like Turner and Killian (Chapter 3), Smelser assumes that collective behavior participants maintain the ability to reason. Circumstances and social factors create a situation where illogical or irrational behavior seems logical and rational to those within the situation. These circumstances must come about in a particular order for an episode of collective behavior to occur (see Figure 4.1).

Components of Social Action

According to Smelser, all social behavior is driven by one of four components of social action. These components are: values, norms, organized individual motivation in roles and collectivities, and situational facilities. Different forms of collective behavior relate to each of these four components.

Values

Values provide a general source of legitimacy for social behavior. In any society, behavior is judged at the most general level according to societal values. If behavior goes against social values, it is condemned. If behavior seems to mesh with social values, then it is generally accepted.

Norms

Norms give specific guidelines as to how these values are to be enacted. They are the formal and informal rules and laws that we are expected to follow.

Individual Mobilization of Motivation

Smelser uses the phrase "the individual mobilization of motivation for organized acts within roles and collectivities" to refer to the third component of social behavior. He meant for the reader to understand that social behavior occurs within the context of a social structure. Society creates certain social organizations to fulfill certain functions. Social organization and social structure influence and sometimes even dictate individual behavior. We are often judged by how well we fulfill the demands of a particular role, such as student.

Situational Facilities

Situational facilities, the fourth component of social behavior, are the means and obstacles that facilitate or hinder the attainment of goals. These include tools, skills, and knowledge.

Values guide what we as a society desire, norms guide how we go about getting what we desire, individual motivation guides the structure or organization that we create in order to achieve that which we desire, and situational facilities guide how successful we are in achieving it. For example, "financial independence" is an American value. Getting a higher education is one normative way to go about getting it. In order to gain higher education in the United States, a person must attend a college, university, or other institution of higher learning. These institutions represent the social organizations that our society has created to provide the transfer of knowledge. Economic resources, availability of loans and scholarships, and proximity to such institutions all contribute to a person's ability to attend. They represent the situational facilities required to attend college.

For any action that sociologists analyze, Smelser wants us to ask: What values legitimize this action? What norms keep it coordinated and relatively conflict-free? In what ways is the action structured into roles and organizations?, and What kind of situational facilities are available? These four components of behavior are important to the extent that they form the basis of Smelser's conceptualization of collective behavior. He argues that collective behavior can be classified and analyzed under the same conceptual framework as any social behavior. The primary difference is that collective behavior falls outside of normative expectations. Collective behavior occurs when strain is exerted on one or more of the four components of action and established ways of relieving the strain are not available. Any time there is strain on societal values, norms, social organizations, or resources, collective behavior is likely to occur.

The Value-Added Process

The term "value-added" is borrowed from the field of economics. In economics, value-added refers to the idea that each step toward a finished product adds value to the resources used. For instance, before an automobile can be assembled iron ore must be mined. The first step of production (mining) has added value to the iron ore. The ore must then be made into steel, which is worth more than the ore. The steel is then stamped or formed into parts, which must be assembled into an automobile. Each step (mining, milling, stamping, assembling, etc.) moves the materials closer to becoming a final product. Painting, shipping, and selling are the final stages. What were once raw materials are now valuable consumer products.

The term "value-added" is somewhat misleading when applied to collective behavior. Collective behavior does not have inherent monetary value. In fact, some forms end up costing millions of dollars in damages. Smelser was actually referring to the stages of assembly as a metaphor for the steps that must occur before a collective episode is possible. If a step is skipped in assembling a car, nothing is created. One cannot assemble a car out of raw iron ore, without the smelting, stamping, and forming. The steps must also occur in the proper order. It isn't possible to stamp raw iron ore into car parts. In exactly the same way, certain things must occur in a certain order before any episode of collective behavior becomes possible. Smelser calls these factors "determinants." It is a step-by-step process. Once the first several determinants are present, then the collective episode becomes increasingly likely.

In Smelser's original formulation, there were six determinants of collective behavior. The determinants are labeled structural conduciveness, structural strain, growth and spread of a generalized belief, precipitating factors, mobilization of participants for action, and the operation of social control. The Value-Added Theory has been gradually modified over the years as it is used in research. It can be said that Neil Smelser owes a particular debt of gratitude to sociologist Jerry M. Lewis, who has modified and applied the Value-Added Theory to numerous collective episodes over the last few decades (see, for example, Lewis 1972, 1982a, 1982b, 1989 and Lewis and Kelsey 1994). This gradual evolution of the theory has created some changes that will be noted throughout our look at Smelser's theory.

Structural Conduciveness

The first determinant of collective behavior is structural conduciveness. This refers to any factors in the social and/or physical environment that make collective behavior possible. This determinant creates the conditions that make the collective behavior possible, but cannot cause an episode to occur by itself.

Each form of collective behavior has its own factors of structural conduciveness. The factors that make a panic possible are not the same as the factors that make a consumer craze possible. Riots, for example, require a number of people to be in the same place at the same time. An empty cornfield lacks the most basic component of structural conduciveness that would make a riot possible. If, for some reason, hundreds of people gather in the field to hear a speaker, then one of the basic components of conduciveness (a gathering of people) has been met. Any social or physical factor that makes any form of collective behavior possible is a part of the structural conduciveness. This determinant is present in many places virtually all of the time. The more factors of structural conduciveness are present, the more likely the event is to occur. However, no collective episode will occur until the other determinants are present.

Smelser refers almost exclusively to societal factors in his original discussion of conduciveness. He does not mention physical surroundings. However, researchers (including Smelser) have since realized that physical factors within a situation may permit or inhibit social action as much as social factors. The right weather, time of day, week, and year, and the actual physical layout of a space all contribute to the likelihood of collective behavior. Dry, hot weather makes forest fires more likely by creating circumstances under which trees will readily burn. Many forms of human behavior are similarly dictated by mundane variables like the weather. The easier it is for a collective episode to occur, the more structural conduciveness is present.

In the United States, riots almost always occur during warm, dry weather, often over the weekend. This is not because people experience more rage when the weather is sunny. It is because they are more likely to be out and about during nice weather. In fact, it used to be that the hotter the weather got, the more likely a riot became. Many of the riots that occurred before the 1980s started in the middle of heat waves. July and August were the months most likely to erupt in violence. This was because more and more people would gather outside as it got hotter, trying to catch a cooling breeze. The proliferation of air conditioning throughout the United States has modified our behavior. In many parts of the country, once the temperature rises above a certain point people begin to avoid going outdoors because it is cooler inside. The more homes and businesses have air conditioning, the less people gather outside during hot weather. Fewer people gathering outside means less structural conduciveness for mob behavior. Riots are now more likely to occur in the spring/early summer and the late summer/fall than in July or August.

The social characteristics of those present in a situation can also contribute to the structural conduciveness. Young men are more likely to engage in violent, aggressive behavior than older, gender-mixed crowds. Therefore, a heavy-metal concert has more structural conduciveness for a riot than an opera. Both events may draw thousands of people to a particular location to watch a performance. However, one crowd is more likely to erupt in violence if the performance is interrupted. On the other hand, both crowds may be equally likely to panic and crush each other if a fire breaks out in the theater. Both situations contain structural conduciveness for some forms of collective behavior.

Some structural conduciveness is present any time people gather or communicate. The particular form of collective behavior that is possible varies dramatically from situation to situation. Some forms of collective behavior require people to be in the same place at the same time (lynchings, riots, and panics), while others (fads, social movements, and crazes) do not. Some are more likely to occur in urban settings, some in rural surroundings. Collective behavior is possible much more often than it actually occurs. It does not occur more often because the other necessary determinants are not always present to produce the action.

Structural Strain

Collective behavior is interesting to us because it is not normal behavior. People do things that they would not normally do, in situations where the behavior is not expected. Smelser argues that this unusual behavior is driven by social factors leading up to the event. Structural strain, the second determinant of collective behavior, drives participants to engage in such unusual behavior. Anything that causes stress, tension, or anxiety to participants makes them likely to do things that they would not normally do. Collective behavior becomes much more likely if the strain is caused by ambiguities, deprivations, conflicts, or discrepancies that somehow coincide with any factors of conduciveness. Strain alone cannot cause the event, but if the strain is compatible with the structural conduciveness, the raw materials of the event have been assembled. The episode becomes much more likely to occur.

In his original formulation of the Value-Added Theory, Smelser discussed strain in purely social terms. He argued that strain is primarily caused by any event that does not meet cultural standards or personal expectations, strain is a result of insufficient reward or too much responsibility in performing a task, not enough power, conflict of societal values, etc. Unemployment, poverty, fear of unemployment, fear of poverty, discrimination, worry about the coming of a new century, natural disasters, or war could all be sources of social strain. Researchers have since pointed out that physical factors such as the architecture of a sports stadium, extreme heat, electrical blackouts, or traffic jams can also be sources of structural strain. Some forms of collective behavior are caused by long-standing strain that originates from within the root of a culture. Others are caused by temporary strain that is short-lived and unique to the situation. For example, the dissonance between societal values about equality and treatment of minorities is a source of general stain within society. Being trapped in an elevator for hours is a source of specific strain for those inside the elevator. These different levels and types of strain will potentially lead to different forms of collective behavior. They may even overlap. The people trapped in the elevator may also be worried about social changes.

It doesn't matter how grand or small, how long-lasting or temporary the strain is. When people feel strain, they want to get rid of it. It makes them uncomfortable, uncertain, and anxious. If you are thirsty, you drink. If you are hungry, you eat. However, what if your discomfort is caused by worry about the state of the economy? How do you fix the problem? The more strain people are under, the more likely they are to engage in unusual behavior. The more vague or general the strain is, the more likely they are to feel anxious or helpless. Anything that seems to release their tension is welcomed as a good thing.

Structural strain makes the other determinants important. If there is enough structural strain present, people become more and more likely to engage in bizarre behavior. It makes people believe things they would not normally believe, think things they would not normally think, and do things they would not normally do. Structural strain can make an ordinary event turn into the catalyst for an explosive release. If a white man hits a black man in a community with little racial tension, there is a chance that someone will call 911 and report the assault. In a community that has a great deal of racial tension the same event could become the trigger for an explosive riot, a lynching, or a revolutionary social movement.

Anxiety is the particular form of structural strain most likely to lead to collective behavior. Although Smelser states that anything that places people under stress can lead to collective behavior, he argues that anxiety leads to the widest variety of behaviors. Anxiety revolves around the unknown. People feel anxious, but cannot pin down the source of their unease. The strain that they feel is vague, and the behavior that they choose as an outlet for those feelings can take virtually any form. It all hinges on how they choose to define their anxiety, and how they decide to go about alleviating it.

The connection between the anxiety and the behavior might not be obvious or even logical. Anxiety caused by an economic depression can become the trigger for fads, crazes, panics, riots, religious revivals, social movements, or any other form of collective behavior. As long as the behavior gives participants something to focus their energy and attention on, it is likely to occur. Which behavior participants take part in is dictated by the generalized belief that they attach to their strain.

Generalized Belief

Once participants are in a situation that makes a particular form of collective behavior possible and they experience strain that makes that form of behavior more likely, the crucial next step involves the formation of a generalized belief. Potential actors must come to share a definition of the situation that makes a particular course of action seem logical, rational, desirable, or unavoidable. The generalized belief supplies meaning within the situation. This belief identifies a source of strain, attributes certain characteristics to the source, and specifies certain responses as possible or appropriate. The generalized belief makes the behavior seem appropriate to the participants. In other words, it gives people something to do that they believe will eliminate or reduce the strain and anxiety they are feeling.

It is important to note that the generalized belief does not have to be based on truth. If participants believe a wild rumor, they will act as if the rumor is true. It does not matter how odd or illogical this belief seems to observers, or how the participants feel about it later. At that moment, it takes away the uncertainty and anxiety that they have been experiencing and replaces them with certainty and conviction. Many riots have begun because of rapidly spreading beliefs that later turned out to be unfounded. At the time of the episode the participants believed the rumor and it made their next actions seem logical. For example, in the Detroit race riots of 1943, whites believed that a white baby had been thrown from a bridge by blacks, that a white woman had been attacked on the bridge by black men, and that blacks were trying to force whites out of the Belle Isle area. Blacks believed that a black baby had been thrown from the bridge by white sailors, that white men had attacked a black woman, and that whites were trying to force blacks out of Belle Isle. None of these rumors were true, but participants behaved as if they were. These specific rumors fit what they already believed about members of the other race, gave them a specific reason to attack, and justified their violent actions.

The growth and spread of a generalized belief is crucial for a collective episode. It is the belief that determines what participants will do next. Even though structural conduciveness and strain are often present in society, there will be no collective outburst until a generalized belief forms. Furthermore, the particular details of the generalized belief will dictate what form of collective behavior does occur. For example, an angry mob can choose to attack law enforcement officers, attack each other, march to town hall for a quiet protest, or simply disperse and go home. The generalized belief determines which of these potential behavioral patterns occurs. Smelser lists five specific types of generalized belief. Each type of belief leads to a different form of collective behavior, and justifies or rationalizes the behavior in the minds of participants.

Hysterical Beliefs

Hysterical beliefs transform an ambiguous situation into a specific threat. Premonitions of disaster and fear are two forms of hysterical beliefs. Participants become convinced that something terrible is about to happen. Hysterical beliefs may seem to explain a past event or situation, report a present one, or predict a future one. "The recent floods were a warning that the world is going to end on Thursday," "There is more crime than ever before because society as we know it is ending," and "The market is crashing and the value of my stocks is going to evaporate by five o'clock" are all examples of hysterical beliefs. There doesn't have to be any particular reason why the catastrophe is supposed to occur, it just is. Hysterical beliefs generally lead to some sort of panic. The panic may take the form of stampeding for fire exits, selling off stocks at brutally low prices, or heading for the wilderness with a gun and survival supplies. It doesn't matter if the participants fear death in a fire, financial ruin, or attack by Martians. The driving force behind the behavior, a hysterical generalized belief, is the same.

Wish-fulfillment Beliefs

Wish-fulfillment beliefs reduce ambiguity by producing what is believed to be an effective solution to the problem, or by predicting some sort of positive event. Anxiety is replaced with hope and confidence. Participants believe that something wonderful is going to happen, or that they can prevent something terrible from happening if they perform the right behavior. "The economy is about to enter a period of unprecedented growth" would be an example of the former, "The world is going to end on Thursday *unless we pray!*" an example of the latter. Wish-fulfillment beliefs often include a magical faith in individuals, objects, or values; anything that provides the necessary hope. They lead to behaviors that we can generally categorize as crazes. Examples would include speculation booms, certain fads, some types of religious or political revivalism, faith healing, etc. In all of these different crazes, participants believe that they are getting in on something good, or that their behavior is going to make something good happen instead of something bad. Wish-fulfillment beliefs provide a bright hope that the source of strain is about to disappear, or that the participants themselves can eliminate it.

Hostile Beliefs

Hostile beliefs are similar to wish-fulfillment beliefs, except the action required to fix the problem involves removing an agent or object perceived as a threat or obstacle. In other words, the specific fear is focused onto a scapegoat: "The world is going to end on Thursday unless we burn the witches!" The strain and anxiety become focused into anger and hatred that requires action against some individual, group of individuals, or institution. Hostile beliefs are the driving force behind violent episodes such as scapegoating, mob lynchings, and many riots. Participants come to believe that all of their strain is caused by one specific target. This target can be as specific as a particular individual or as general as "the government," "foreigners," or "the New World Order." Participants genuinely believe that if they can only eliminate or destroy the target of their hatred, that everything will be good again and the strain will disappear.

Norm-oriented Beliefs

Norm-oriented beliefs envision either replacing or renewing and reinforcing a threatened normative structure. Participants want to reorganize the basic organization of a social institution. They want to either restore, protect, modify, or create social norms. This often takes the form of either trying to pass new laws, or abolish existing ones. Many social movements are driven by norm-oriented beliefs, particularly reform movements and counter movements. The war on drugs is a good example. Almost every ill in American society is blamed on illegal drugs. Participants in the movement believe that if illegal drugs were eliminated in the United States, the entire society would benefit in a variety of ways. Spousal abuse, absenteeism, poverty, and violent crime would all be eliminated by the creation of one simple norm. Alcohol was outlawed in the United States during Prohibition for exactly the same reasons. Movements aiming to establish (or repeal) laws, desegregate (or keep segregated) schools, acquire (or prevent) government subsidies, restrict (or ease) immigration, increase (or decrease) taxes are all driven by norm-oriented beliefs. They all attempt to control the inadequate, ineffective, or irresponsible behavior of other individuals.

Of course, the members of the movement always have their own beliefs about exactly who is being irresponsible and what would improve the situation. It is common to find a movement aimed at creating a particular change, and another aimed at preventing it, both with the justification that they are trying to save society. Norm-oriented generalized beliefs make a connection, no matter how illogical, between a general source of strain and a specific course of action. They believe that their actions are for the good of all society.

Value-oriented Beliefs

Value-oriented beliefs envision replacing a threatened value system. Although the complaints are often much more vague and general than norm-oriented beliefs, the "solution" is usually simple and straightforward. Cult formation, secession from a parent political or religious body, group withdrawal into isolation, and social or political revolution are all examples of collective behavior driven by value-oriented beliefs. Participants seek to construct a more satisfying culture. They have a preoccupation with the highest moral bases of social life, and a vision of future harmony and stability. The source of strain is identified as inherent within the culture itself, so participants seek to withdraw from it or reshape it in their own image. Value-oriented beliefs attribute the structural strain to a problem inherent in a particular societal value. The only way to eliminate the strain is to change the value.

Precipitating Factors

In Smelser's original formulation of the theory, precipitating factors or events comprise the next determinant in the process. Some sort of occurrence sparks the beginning of the episode. This occurrence ties in with the particular conduciveness, strain, and generalized belief within the situation. Smelser argued that this gives the generalized belief concrete, immediate substance. Using riots as an example, many cities have the necessary conduciveness and strain for a riot to occur at virtually any time. Individuals may believe that there is racial inequality and police brutality, and deeply resent it. However, it takes a specific incident, such as the death or injury of an arrestee, to spark the actual riot.

Many researchers today simply place precipitating factors within the determinant of generalized belief. Precipitating factors sometimes seem to create the generalized belief, while other times they seem to be meaningful only as defined by already existing beliefs. Some collective episodes do not seem to have specific precipitating factors at all. Precipitating factors and generalized belief are so intertwined as to sometimes be indistinguishable. In a sense, precipitating factors have been demoted from the level of determinant to the level of a component within the determinant of generalized belief. Precipitating factors are not necessary for the construction of all types of collective episodes. They are no longer considered a determinant of collective behavior by many researchers and will not be treated as one throughout the rest of this book.

Mobilization of Participants

The final stage in the value-added process of collective behavior is the actual mobilization and organization of action. In a situation where structural conduciveness, strain, and a generalized belief exist, the only thing left is the actual mobilization of participants for action. The behavior of leaders is important at this stage. The collective episode itself has begun. Those who act first or who attract the attention of potential participants may be able to dictate what behaviors are appropriate or acceptable. This shapes the behavior of the rest of the participants.

Mobilization of participants involves both the action of the individual participants and the ability of people to get to the event itself. People cannot become participants in an event if they do not have the ability to get to where the action is. Riots can only occur if individuals are already present or can quickly congregate. In order to take part in a consumer craze, an individual must have access to information about the product and must have the means to purchase the product. Social movements only occur if enough people can be mobilized and motivated to give their time and/or money to the cause.

Leadership is important for this determinant. If potential participants are actively encouraged to take part in the collective episode by leaders they know and trust, the event is likely to be much larger than if they had been discouraged. The right person at the right time may capture the attention of a crowd and send them into a frenzy, or pull them out of one. Leaders within the event may preach for calmness or immediate action, peacefulness or violence, thoughtfulness or malice. Once the event has begun, the effectiveness of leaders may be reduced or eliminated. Timing is the key issue. Calling for calm and peaceful assembly has a much greater effect on a crowd that is merely considering violent action than it does on a crowd actively engaged in rioting.

Social Control

The operation of social control is more of a counter-determinant. At any stage, the actions of formal and informal social control agents can end the process before the collective episode begins. Smelser discussed two broad types of social control: those that minimize conduciveness and/or strain, and those that are mobilized after an event begins. Any action that effectively reduces or eliminates structural conduciveness or strain will prevent the episode from occurring. Successful efforts at minimizing the first few determinants disrupt the value-added process and make it impossible for the latter determinants to come into play.

Social control agents may include police, courts, media, religious authorities, community leaders, etc. Any individual or group with legitimate authority within a particular setting represents social control in that setting. For example, a schoolteacher is a social control agent in his or her classroom, but not on the beach. A lifeguard is a social control agent on the beach, but not on a street corner. If the appropriate social control agents fail to recognize the presence of conduciveness and strain or fail to diffuse them before a generalized belief can form and mobilization occurs, then prevention becomes impossible. Although social control agents sometimes attempt to prevent an episode that has already begun, it is impossible to do so. Instead, the social control agents must choose to deter, redirect, or accommodate the event.

Deterrence

It is sometimes possible to deter participants from continuing their behavior once it has begun. For example, changes were made to the New York Stock Exchange as a result of the crash of October 24, 1929. These controls were instituted specifically to stop the panic selling that occurred when trading outpaced tickertape information. Changes continue to be made. Some stock markets now shut down automatically if prices fall too fast, because online trading once again made it possible for the volume of trade to outpace tracking systems in the early 1990s. In this case, social control agents have devised a crude but effective way of eliminating a key factor of structural conduciveness: If there is no trading, there can be no selling. Those in charge hope that once people have had a chance to think things through, the market can reopen and restrained trading will resume. President Franklin Roosevelt employed a similar tactic during the Great Depression when he declared a "bank holiday," allowing all U.S. banks to close down long enough for him to give a speech on the radio, assuring citizens that their money was safe. Both of these are examples where the conduciveness is temporarily eliminated. In the first example, making it impossible to buy or sell securities for a few hours makes it impossible for a panic to continue. In the second, making it impossible to withdraw money from banks also made it impossible for panicked customers to take out all of their money and collapse banks. Each of these tactics is intended to allow structural strain to dissipate after the episode has already begun. Social control agents could also potentially eliminate the strain itself. This is much more difficult, and sometimes impossible. There was tremendous social strain throughout the United States in the decades of the 1950s and '60s over the civil rights of African-Americans. Changing segregation laws put many prejudiced whites under strain, but not changing the laws kept blacks and less prejudiced whites under strain. No one official action could eliminate strain for both sides. There was no way for social control agents to eliminate the social strain for everyone.

It is also sometimes possible for social control agents to deter collective behavior by simply overwhelming participants in the early stages of mobilization. If police dramatically outnumber participants in the initial stages of a riot or violent protest, they often successfully quell the behavior before it becomes too widespread to handle. Unfortunately, the other possible outcome is that their behavior may enrage onlookers and become the factor that sparks off massive, widespread violence.

Accommodation

Except in situations where authorities can immediately eliminate the conduciveness or strain or where they can simply overwhelm participants through force, social control agents often have little choice but to accommodate the episode. Authorities routinely accommodate some forms of collective behavior, such as fads, fashions, and nonviolent group behavior. Police often direct traffic and act as security guards at nonviolent protests and certain types of religious events. Merchants and the media often provide information to participants in consumer fads, fashions, and crazes. It is not uncommon for local news broadcasters to report on the availability of products that have suddenly become scarce. Law enforcement officials sometimes "look the other way" during collective behavior episodes. These are all examples of accommodation.

Redirection

Redirection is more difficult and less common than prevention, deterrence, or accommodation. In this situation, authorities do not eliminate the conduciveness or strain, but somehow manage to shape the generalized belief and/or mobilization for action. They redirect the attention of participants. A hypothetical example of redirection would be if a city official could somehow turn the attention of hot, angry residents away from starting a riot by offering them free ice cream if they hurry to the municipal swimming pool down the street. If participants' desire for ice cream and cool water outweighs their immediate anger, then they might redirect their attention. Another example would be getting members of a wartime anti-immigration movement to redirect their energy into helping out in a government-sponsored war effort. The group still gets to focus their anxiety on a scapegoat, but a different one. Instead of scapegoating immigrants within their own society, they are putting that energy into selling war bonds or filling sand bags in order to "do something" about members of another society.

Discussion

Smelser's Value-Added Theory focuses on the social causes of collective behavior, not psychological factors. The Value-Added Theory argues that participants are reacting to structural strain according to generalized beliefs that they accept at the time of the episode. They are not reduced to temporary insanity, nor are they behaving irrationally. Their behavior is rational according to their definition of the situation. They have not lost the ability to reason, they are simply basing their reasoning on generalized beliefs that may or may not be true. It is only when the behavior falls outside of societal norms that we consider it irrational.

Core Assumptions

Smelser assumes that abnormal group behavior is caused by stress and anxiety experienced by the group. The collective action is taken in order to ease the strain. Any time people are under strain, there is a potential for collective behavior. If the other determinants fall into place, then an episode will occur. It is only a question of what form the outburst will take.

More importantly, he assumes and argues that collective behavior is only different from any other group behavior because it falls outside of normative expectations for the situation. If a group of people believe that a blizzard is heading their way, they might stock up on canned food and batteries. This fits our expectations for the situation, and we think nothing of it. If another group of people believe that the world is going to end at midnight, they might gather their friends and pray. This behavior is perfectly logical within the context of the belief, but we define the behavior as abnormal because we define the belief as irrational. When people collectively engage in behavior that we expect them to engage in, it is simply social behavior. When they engage in behavior that we do not expect, it becomes collective behavior.

Collective behavior is defined as a social phenomenon. It does not rely on the psychological state of participants, except to the extent that social forces alter them. People engage in collective behavior because it alleviates strain caused by external factors.

Evaluation

Unlike the Contagion and Emergent-Norm perspectives, the Value-Added perspective makes it possible to analyze any form of collective behavior ranging from the apparently inhuman (lynchings, mob violence, riots) to the apparently rational (organized social movements) to the silly (fads, crazes). Furthermore, it is hypothetically possible to predict when and where episodes of collective behavior might break out in the future. Using weather as a metaphor, the Value-Added Theory describes what makes clouds, why they gather, and what conditions are necessary for them to make rain. Meteorologists cannot predict rain months ahead of time. However, they do know that when a moist warm front is overrun by a cold front in a low-pressure condition, rain is almost inevitable. They know this because they understand why the rain happens. Likewise, using the Value-Added perspective, we understand why collective behavior happens and therefore what conditions make it likely.

Smelser's Value-Added Theory classifies forms of collective behavior not according to the behavior of participants, but by the motives and beliefs that drive their behavior. The focus is on clearly defining and understanding the forces driving behaviors that may outwardly appear to be baffling and incomprehensible behavior, but actually follow identifiable patterns. If Smelser's core assumptions are correct, it is possible to trace the beginning of any form of collective behavior. It is also possible to understand, at every stage of development, why the event may either dissipate or amplify. Crowd behavior, once thought mysterious, becomes predictable once the generalized belief forms and solidifies. A researcher can observe the process, understanding and predicting each following phase of activity.

For many researchers, the Value-Added Theory's biggest drawback is its functionalist roots. When applying the Value-Added Theory to episodes of collective behavior, it is tempting to assume that conduciveness, strain, and a generalized belief exist because the theory says so. Some sociologists argue that this makes Value-Added Theory difficult (if not impossible) to use as an effective tool of explanation. However, this same trap can occur when attempting to explain collective behavior with any theory. Each of the theories discussed in this book assumes that certain factors must be present in order for the episode to take place. It is the researcher's job to do enough research to determine if those factors do, in fact, exist. It is not enough to argue that they must be present just because the theory says they should be.

Chapter 5

The Assembly Perspective and Sociocybernetic Theory

Since the late 1960s, Clark McPhail has been actively engaged in the first-hand study and documentation of public gatherings. Working with colleagues and students, McPhail has carefully observed hundreds, perhaps thousands of events such as public rallies, protests, and sporting events (see, for example, McPhail 1994). Based on these observations, he has developed an approach to collective behavior that in some ways is fundamentally different from any other theorist. McPhail views collective behavior as any organization or coordination of individual activity. In daily life, people frequently come together and form temporary groups. Within these gatherings they somehow manage to coordinate their behavior to allow everyone to meet their goals. McPhail is interested in how the processes of assembling gatherings and coordination of behavior are accomplished. Unlike almost all other theorists of collective behavior, he is not trying to explain atypical behavior like fads, crazes, riots, or lynchings. Instead, he attempts to construct a theory that can explain *all* group behavior, including those rare instances when behavior does not follow expectations. He therefore focuses almost all of his attention on group behavior that is typical, routine, and/or ritualized.

There are several different labels for McPhail's perspective. It is often called the Social Interactionist/Behaviorist (SBI) perspective because the theory's roots are clearly tied to Symbolic Interactionism (like the Emergent Norm Perspective) and also to Psychological Behaviorism. Behaviorism looks at human behavior from a mechanical perspective, breaking down our thoughts, feelings, and behavior into a series of small decisions and actions. Both of these outlooks are evident in McPhail's writings. Others simply refer to McPhail's approach as the Assembly Perspective because of the intense focus on the patterns by which humans *assemble* into gatherings. McPhail himself now refers to his theory as the Sociocybernetic Theory of Collective Action. This label will be explained in-depth later in this chapter.

McPhail argues that:

1. Individuals are not driven mad by crowds, and do not lose cognitive control during group events.
2. Individuals are not compelled to participate in collective behavior by some "madness-in-common." No psychological condition, cognitive style, or predisposition distinguishes participants from nonparticipants.
3. The majority of behaviors in crowds are neither universal within the group nor "mad." The vast majority of the time that people come together in large gatherings they engage in perfectly normal, expected behavior.

These conclusions are based on years of carefully documented, firsthand research. As conclusion number #3 indicates, McPhail does not restrict himself to the study of unusual or unexpected group behavior. This focus on typical, routine group behavior is the heart of the Assembly Perspective. He argues that all gatherings, whether peaceful and organized or violent and chaotic, operate the same way. An organized event that goes exactly as planned is just as interesting to him as a spontaneous riot. McPhail studies planned, routine events because they occur much more often than atypical episodes. From his perspective atypical episodes are rare and unusual and not worthy of special study. He is interested in assembling processes, assembled gatherings, and dispersal processes.

Assembling Processes

The first stage of any gathering is the assembly process. In order to take part in any gathering, participants must receive assembling instructions, have access to the event location, and not be deflected or distracted from the goal of taking part (see Figure 5.1).

Assembling Instructions

Assembling instructions can be verbal ("Hey, let's go see the parade tomorrow at noon") or written ("Main Street will be closed from 11:00 A.M. until 2:00 P.M. Saturday for the Harvest Days parade"). They can be received in person, over the telephone, or through media sources such as the radio, television, and newspapers. McPhail states that we are most likely to receive as-

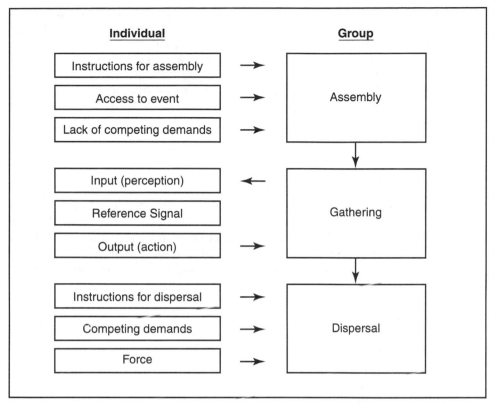

Figure 5.1   The stages of Collective Action according to the Assembly Perspective

sembling instructions informally through friends and acquaintances. In fact, most people go to gatherings with people they know. The more "nudges" from friends, media, and so on, an individual receives, the more likely he or she is to make an effort to attend the event.

Access

Access is a simple variable. People either have a way of getting to an event, or they do not. The more difficult it is for a particular individual to get to the location of an event, the less likely they are to attend. An individual cannot become part of a gathering if he or she has no way of getting to the event.

Distractions

Competing desires or demands for time and attention reduce the likelihood that an individual will attend a particular event. For example, if you have an important exam on Friday, you may be less likely to go to a party or concert on Thursday. Also, many individuals who intend to go to a particular event end up doing something else instead. A group of friends on their way to a political rally may encounter someone they know who invites them to a party. A student on her way to the library may bump into friends on their way to a campus demonstration. In either of these scenarios, the person must choose between the event they originally wanted to attend and the newly offered social opportunity. Anything that distracts people from attending or demands their time and attention makes their attendance less likely.

Assembled Gatherings

It is important to understand that McPhail claims that crowd behavior is not at all like many earlier social theorists believed it to be. He argues that crowd behavior is almost never coordinated or unanimous. The overwhelming majority of gatherings involve many small groups of people who know each other and who gather in the same place at the same time in order to take part in expected behavior as part of a large group. Rarely do all members of the gathering behave exactly alike, and their attention is usually on each other as much as it is on the focus of the event itself. This applies to such routine and uneventful activities as going to a sporting event, taking part in a social protest, or attending a large college class.

Dispersal Processes

As McPhail points out, most gatherings disperse (break up) routinely in response to instructions from others, because of competing demands, or by force. It is extremely rare for violence or panic to break out. For instance, when a concert or football game is over, fans usually leave in an orderly manner.

Instructions for Dispersal

A common way for gatherings to disperse is at the instruction of a crowd member or organizer. "Go home people, it's over," "We're closing in ten minutes," and "Come on, let's go home" are all examples of this type of instruction. These instructions can be general or specific ("Please exit through the south door in an orderly manner"). Some members of the gathering may go home, while others may choose to reassemble somewhere else. It is common for a small percentage of sports spectators to gather at a bar or restaurant near the stadium after the game. Groups of friends and relatives may have scheduled a party or cookout at one of their homes after a parade or other public event. Some concert venues schedule after-show parties at other locations. Each of these is an example of large gatherings receiving instructions for dispersal and simultaneously receiving assembling instructions for smaller gatherings.

Competing Demands

Sometimes members of the gathering leave simply because something else is going to start somewhere else. Spectators at a house fire might want to get home to eat dinner. Students listening to a campus speaker may have to leave at a certain time to take a midterm exam. Although McPhail does not mention this in his writings, many riots end when rioters and looters go home to sleep or go to work. Competing demands make an individual more likely to leave any type of gathering. Those members who have nothing else to do and nowhere else to go are much more likely to stay until forced to leave.

Force

Although most police forces do not have much experience handling large gatherings, it is often left to them to disperse a crowd that is deemed unruly, too large, or in violation of some law or ordinance. Even in these conditions of enforced dispersal, most gatherings quietly and orderly move to a different location or break up. Alternative instructions ("We aren't hurting anyone. We're staying right here!") are most likely to be given by two categories of individuals. Those who have traveled the farthest to attend the gathering have the most effort invested and may therefore want to keep the gathering together. Those with the most free time on their hands have no competing demands. Both categories of participants may have nowhere else to go, and both may be motivated to keep the gathering together.

This Assembly Perspective has been modified over the years by McPhail himself. He has created a more specifically formulated theory, which he calls the Sociocybernetic Theory of Collective Action.

The Sociocybernetic Process

McPhail's approach is truly an attempt to alter the study of collective behavior. He argues that other theorists have tried to come too far, too fast. They have tried to explain something that has not been carefully described, defined, and catalogued. In what he sees as an attempt to make up for this failure on the part of other sociologists, McPhail has spent a great deal of time and attention actually observing public gatherings all over the United States, particularly campus crowds and demonstrations. His focus has been on the components that make collective action possible. Traditional collective behavior such as riots, panics, and crazes are far too rare and unusual to warrant special attention. McPhail argues that all public gatherings should be examined using the same criteria.

Much of what McPhail writes may seem confusing at first. This is because certain terms are used in ways that might seem odd to a student of collective behavior. The theory is built on terms and definitions that are potentially confusing to the reader because McPhail's approach to collective behavior is so different from all of the other theories that we have analyzed. Some of the terms are commonly used by other collective behavior researchers, but not with the same meaning that McPhail intends.

Gatherings

McPhail (1991, 1997) disregards the term "crowd," preferring the term *gatherings*. A gathering is any number of people in the same place at the same time. A gathering forms any time people are around each other. The use of this term in place of more precise labels is revealing: McPhail only seeks to explain behavior that occurs in a face-to-face setting. This means that fads, crazes, and various other forms of collective behavior that occur over a period of time throughout a wide area are of no interest to McPhail. He does not attempt to define, classify, or explain them. Most other theorists attempt to explain these activities. McPhail considers them beyond the scope of his theory.

Collective Behavior/Collective Action

In spite of his statements that "nothing is intrinsically collective behavior" and "definitions are arbitrary" (1991: 154), McPhail develops what he calls "a working definition of collective behavior":

- two or more persons
- engaged in one or more behaviors (e.g., locomotion, orientation, vocalization, verbalization, gesticulation, and/or manipulation)
- judged common or concerted
- on one or more dimensions (e.g., direction, velocity, tempo, or substantive content) (1991: 159)

Since that time, he has completely abandoned the term collective behavior in favor of the term "collective action" (McPhail 1997).

Any time two or more people are in the same place at the same time, they form a gathering. As soon as two or more of them engage in any behavior that is the same (common) or requires cooperation (concerted), it is collective behavior. All that is required is that the behavior appears to be in synch in direction, speed, or the nature of the behavior itself. For example, two people walking on a sidewalk may be heading in the same direction at the same velocity. Members of a concert audience may chant "Encore!" at the same rate. Other pedestrians or chanting fans match each of these behaviors (walking and chanting) in substantive content.

Although at first glance this may seem like a specific definition, careful analysis reveals several problems. There is the issue of judging behavior of others to be "common or concerted." Judged by whom? By what criteria? McPhail criticizes other theorists for relying on their own judgment when evaluating the actions of others, but in this definition he has made a similar mistake himself. Much more importantly, this definition effectively classifies as "collective behavior" or "collective action" *any* behavior engaged in by *any* two or more people at the same time. Using this definition, three people walking in the same direction on a sidewalk are engaged in collective behavior because their behavior is common in direction and velocity. A person buying a movie ticket from a ticket agent is an example of collective behavior, since the behavior of the buyer and seller is cooperative (concerted). Two drivers stopped for a red light constitute collective behavior. Two people fighting, making love, or sitting on a park bench are now engaged in collective behavior. All of these are examples of two or more people engaged in common or concerted behavior that is the same in nature, direction, or speed. Any time two or more people engage in the same behavior, even if they are unaware of each other and are therefore not influenced by each other, it's collective behavior. Any time two or more people cooperate in any way, they are engaged in collective behavior.

By creating such a broad definition of collective behavior and "collective action," McPhail has made it virtually impossible to distinguish between routine, ritualized, organized behavior, and what is more commonly referred to as collective behavior by most sociologists. McPhail justifies this by his repeated observation that most group behavior is peaceful and orderly. He does not seem to consider that peaceful and orderly group behavior is already intensely examined within a variety of general sociological theories. Social psychologists have intensely studied such normative group behavior for decades (see, for example, Allport 1969). McPhail attempts to classify and define *all* group behaviors as collective behavior. Only one small portion of such behavior is unusual, unexpected, or outside of social norms and he considers them to be a minor variance. He has gone so far as to argue that the concept of collective behavior itself should be abandoned (McPhail 1997). However, McPhail's current definition of "collective action" is the same as the definition of collective behavior discussed above.

Cybernetic Systems

"Cybernetic" means self-governing (see Figure 5.2). For example, a furnace thermostat is self-governing. When the temperature drops below a chosen level, the thermostat automatically turns on the furnace. When the temperature reaches a chosen level, it shuts the furnace off. The thermostat and furnace are part of a self-governing system. The thermostat compares the current room temperature (input) to the temperature setting (reference point) and decides whether or not the furnace needs to run. It can continue to

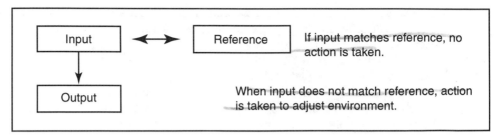

Figure 5.2 A Cybernetic (self-regulating) System

maintain the room temperature for a long period of time without any direct assistance from outsiders.

When applying this concept to human behavior, McPhail states that:

> The basic idea is that human beings are purposive actors and that, unless physically constrained (a phenomenon that sometimes occurs in very dense crowds), they control their own behavior by means of self-instructions regarding the achievement of their goals and objectives (1991: xxv).

This is an obtuse way of stating something simple: People have expectations and preferences. For McPhail, these expectations are a reference point against which we constantly measure our condition. Human behavior is viewed as a constant process of making adjustments in behavior (output) in order to match our perceptions (input) to our desired state (reference signals) (see Figure 5.3). Whenever possible, we engage in behavior that we believe will allow us to match our preferences. If a person is thirsty, his or her goal is to stop being thirsty. If at home, he or she is likely to get a drink from the refrigerator. If they are at a restaurant, they might ask a waiter or waitress to bring them something to drink. The individual will engage in whatever behavior seems necessary to produce the desired result, quenching of thirst.

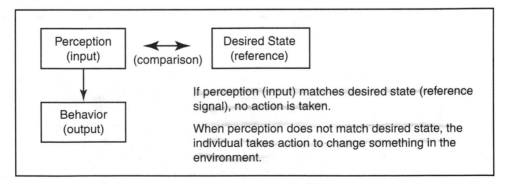

Figure 5.3 The Cybernetic model of human behavior

This can apply to major or minor goals. The process can be as simple as "I want to sit up, so I will engage in the muscle contractions necessary to move my body into an upright position."

Reference Signals

Whenever McPhail uses the terms "reference signals" he is alluding to the individual's standards for judgment. Going back to the thermostat analogy, if you set your home thermostat at 72 degrees Fahrenheit, 72° becomes the reference signal. It is the temperature that the thermostat refers to when deciding if the furnace should be switched on. McPhail argues that humans engage in the same process. When deciding to sit or stand, desired level of comfort is the reference signal. When deciding whether or not to get a drink of water, desired level of thirst is the reference signal. This is a complex way of saying that we make decisions about behavior based on what we expect or desire. If we desire a drink, we get it. McPhail assumes that we do so because we have evaluated our perception or *input* (thirst) against our desired state or *reference signal* (not thirsty), and decided that an action or *output* had to be made. This is a conscious effort to adjust our perception ("I'm thirsty") to our expectation ("I shouldn't be thirsty").

McPhail never uses the terms "goal," "expectations," or "definition of the situation," but all of these are implied within his conception of reference signals. When he uses the term *reference signals,* he means the standard by which people judge a situation. People act to achieve a goal, or meet an expectation, based on their definition of the situation. Keeping this in mind makes the theory easier to understand and simplifies the awkward "input/reference/output" terminology that McPhail uses.

Self-Instructions

McPhail bases much of his writing on the idea that human beings follow internal commands to engage in action. We mentally decide to do something, then tell ourselves to physically do it. McPhail bases his model of human behavior on mechanical and computer models. Such models are used to create machines or computer software that can engage in self-regulating behavior. As such, the decision-making process implied in self-instruction is an assumed step, not one that has been empirically demonstrated.

This mechanistic approach to human behavior is an important component of the Sociocybernetic Theory. McPhail consistently observes that groups of individuals often behave differently from each other. Self-instructions are McPhail's attempt to explain why individuals might behave so differently from each other at one moment when so clearly influenced by others at another moment. For example, an individual may instruct herself to obey the commands of a group leader one second, but if police appear she may instruct herself to retreat to safety. When self-instructions originate from unique individual reference signals, behavior is individualistic. When self-instructions relate to common or shared reference signals, group behavior occurs. The idea of self-instructions largely ignores the emotional component of human behavior, as well as the non-rational ways in which we quickly react to anything that startles, alarms, or frightens us.

For McPhail, all group behavior is a form of collective action. It is important to remember that he consistently bases his theory on the fact that he defines all group or social behavior as collective behavior. As he puts it, "purposive action requires that two or more persons set similar reference signals with respect to which they adjust their individual actions to make their respective perceptions correspond to those similar reference signals" (1991: 207). In other words, people must want the same thing or agree on a goal in order to act together. According to the Sociocybernetic Theory of Collective Action, this can happen in one of three ways:

1. Two or more people can independently create similar reference signals and behave accordingly. This only applies to simple or elementary forms of collective action. For example, if two people separately decide they are thirsty and move toward a drinking fountain at the same time, they are engaged in collective action. They do not need to communicate directly with each other in order to do this.

2. Two or more people can interdependently create similar reference signals and behave accordingly. This can apply to more complex forms of collective action. It also requires that the individuals communicate directly with each other. They negotiate a common reference signal. For example, two friends standing in a long line might decide to give up waiting, leave the line, and go get something to eat or drink instead.

3. Two or more people can adopt a reference signal developed by a third party and behave accordingly. This can lead to the creation of complex collective action. Although participants do not have to communicate directly with each other, the third party must be able to communicate directly with each participant. People who find themselves in a confusing situation may follow the suggestions or commands of a self-appointed leader. For example, witnesses to an accident may suddenly engage in complicated and orchestrated activities in order to help rescue the victims if told to do so by a paramedic or police officer. Workers at a factory may suddenly shut down their machines and engage in a sit-down strike at the urging of a fellow worker. Students might leave a class in order to take part in a campus protest organized by a political activist. All of these are examples of actions engaged in by individuals who have collectively adopted a common reference signal from a third party.

McPhail argues that members of large gatherings almost never simultaneously engage in the same behavior at the same time. People actively choose from moment to moment whether or not to engage in the same behavior as those around them. Most of them do not act the same most of the time. The theory essentially argues that what most other researchers call mass hysteria, crowd behavior, or collective behavior never really happens. Events at the "Woodstock '99" concert held in Rome, New York, in July of 1999 illustrate his point. At the end of the last performance audience members set the stage and adjoining trailers on fire, and pulled down and destroyed large sound and light equipment. To most theorists, this is a clear example of a riot. McPhail, however, would be quick to point out only a few hundred out of 225,000 audience members actually took part in the destruction. Because he would consider all 225,000 concertgoers members of the same gathering, he can argue that less than 1 percent of the gathering members engaged in violent or destructive behavior. The "riot" becomes characterized as nothing more than a minor problem within the gathering, possibly by a relatively small number of people who did not want to obey instructions for dispersal.

Of course, most other theorists would argue that the few hundred rioters make up a distinct crowd within the larger mass of people. Therein lies the greatest difference between the Sociocybernetic Theory and all of the other perspectives that this book examines: McPhail focuses on the large number of people in that place and time who did not take part in riotous behavior. The other theories of collective behavior would all focus on the people who did riot, and try to determine why they did. Where most theorists see a group of individuals who simultaneously engaged in unexpected, atypical behavior, McPhail sees a small anomaly within a much, much larger gathering of individuals who did what they were expected to do. The concert went almost entirely as planned and expected, and almost all audience members did what they were supposed to do the entire time. Even those individuals who instructed themselves to take part in destructive, atypical behavior only did so for an hour at the end of a seventy-two hour event. In short, McPhail would argue that there was no mass riot. Instead, he would define the destruction as a brief outburst of destruction by a few isolated individuals.

Similarities to the Emergent Norm Perspective

Although McPhail is consistently critical of the Turner and Killian, there are several similarities between the Emergent Norm perspective and Sociocybernetic Theory. These are due to the fact that both perspectives are based in part on Symbolic Interactionism. This common theoretical root leads to similar concepts and ideas in both perspectives. The reader may have noticed that McPhail's "developing similar reference signals" seems remarkably similar to Turner and Killian's conception of creating a collective definition of the situation. Likewise, "adopting reference signals developed by a third party" closely resembles Turner and Killian's concept of individuals conforming to an emergent group norm (see Chapter 3). McPhail borrows ideas that appear within the Emergent Norm perspective, but hides them behind terms and labels quite different from Turner and Killian's. The Assembly Perspective's basic premise is the same as the Emergent Norm Perspective: when people behave the same it is because they all define a situation the same and/or because the situation seems to call for a particular course of action. McPhail simply places more emphasis on the individual's attempt to maintain some equilibrium between perceptions (input) and expectations (reference signals).

He argues that people within a gathering attempt to acquire information, and to develop a "collective or convergent orientation." This process, in which people come to focus on the same object or issue and develop similar attitudes and beliefs toward it, seems to be identical to Turner and Killian's "common focus of attention."

McPhail most resembles Emergent Norm theorists when he states that "the sights and sounds" of other crowd members expressing feelings ("evaluations" of the situation) similar to one's own "may affect the individual's adjustments in the intensity, volume, or duration of his or her applause, cheers, boos, throwing, and the like" (1991: 211). In other words, the sight of other people expressing feelings that match our own encourages more obvious expressions of those feelings, and seeing others express feelings opposite of our own discourages such bold displays. The behavior of individuals is directly influenced by others within the situation. If others display behavior that seems to coincide with our own feelings, then we feel those feelings reinforced and express them with even more intensity. This is precisely the point that Contagion theorists and Emergent Norm theorists make when they discuss "circular reaction" or "circular reinforcement." As Turner and Killian put it, in a group "certain attitudes are elicited and reinforced, so that individuals act in accordance with attitudes which would not necessarily have become *dominant* had they been acting purely as individuals" (1957: 15, emphasis in original). McPhail defines this effect as the interdependent development of a common reference signal. Turner and Killian would simply call it creating a collective definition of the situation.

Further, McPhail goes on to state in the accompanying endnote that those in an audience who do not know when to applaud will wait for others to applaud first. They will allow others to define the situation, letting them know when a specific behavior is appropriate. Once the behavior of others seems to indicate that a behavior is called for, they themselves engage in that behavior. For McPhail, these individuals are adopting the reference signals of others. Turner and Killian would view it as following the group's behavioral norms.

McPhail states that the interdependent creation of shared desires or goals can happen whenever individuals are faced with a mutual problem, defined as "unfamiliar phenomenon," "accident or emergency," or "disruption or blockage of activity." Surely the reader can see the parallels between this statement and those of Turner and Killian (Chapter 3).

These conceptual similarities between the Emergent Norm perspective and the Sociocybernetic Theory of Collective Action are important precisely because McPhail heavily criticizes Turner and Killian throughout his writings. The focus is different, but the underlying assumptions about what drives individuals to behave the way that they do when part of a larger group are the same. It can even be argued that McPhail's theory is just a variation of or elaboration upon the Emergent Norm perspective.

Discussion

McPhail argues throughout his writings that collective behavior theorists are wasting their time by focusing their attention too narrowly. He specifically states that "Theories of the crowd and crowd behavior should not be theories of rare events" (1991:225). By this, he means that the vast majority of social behavior is cooperative, normative, and routine. Therefore, he considers those instances where order collapses and groups collectively engage in unexpected behavior to be too few to bother studying. However, McPhail fails to consider the fact that those "rare" events happen fairly often in every society. He also fails to consider that the two types of behavior are in fact fundamentally different.

For example, the study of deviant behavior has long been a specialty within the field of sociology. Deviant behavior is the study of those instances in which individuals engage in behavior that we as a society do not condone or accept. Most members of society obey the law most of the time. However, the relatively small number of people who engage in relatively few acts of deviance within society cause a tremendous loss of life, property, and security year after year. Millions of individuals and billions of dollars are dedicated each year to enforcing the law and punishing those lawbreakers who get caught. The fact that deviance is rare or unusual compared to social conformity does not mean that researchers should not attempt to isolate the causes for such behavior.

The same can be said for sociologists studying collective behavior. The fact that events like riots, crazes, panics, and hysterias are rare compared to typical social behavior does not mean that they are not worthy of special attention and study. It does not seem relevant to McPhail that collective behavior theorists and students might be interested in the "rare" episodes *because* they are unusual and atypical. General sociological theorists have been attempting to explain social behavior for quite some time. Most of their theories include the sort of typical public behavior that McPhail includes under the headings of "collective behavior" or "collective action." Almost all other theories of collective behavior, on the other hand, seek to explain the atypical, abnormal, unusual group behaviors that are not addressed anywhere else in sociological study. The Assembly Perspective is not intended to explain these peculiar episodes. Instead, McPhail aims to describe all public group behavior.

Core Assumptions

McPhail starts by assuming that collective behavior is essentially the same as all other group behavior. For example, he does not believe that it is worth trying to explain why a peaceful demonstration can suddenly turn into a violent riot, simply because most peaceful demonstrations do not. This goes directly against what all other collective behavior theorists mentioned in this book believe to be true. They all believe that those episodes of unusual group behavior, where individuals engage in patterns of behavior that are not expected under the circumstances, are distinctly different from normal public behavior and therefore deserve to be examined and explained in their own right. McPhail's disagreement with this basic premise of collective behavior allows him to make sweeping and damning statements about all other collective behavior theorists. He repeatedly states that they are all wasting their time; that focusing on unusual events cannot yield any important information. Some readers will agree with this assumption, and some will not. Those who agree with McPhail's conception of collective behavior will find the Assembly Perspective useful for categorizing and cataloging a wide variety of public gatherings. Those who do not agree will find it a useless typology.

Evaluation

Apparently, no researchers other than McPhail have used the Sociocybernetic Theory to analyze any episodes of collective behavior or collective action. Although the general conception of human behavior as sociocybernetic seems to be a source of discussion, particularly in Europe, there do not appear to be any collective behavior researchers actually using the approach to analyze public gatherings.

McPhail's conception of collective action and his Sociocybernetic Theory are only useful to those individuals who believe that a riot is fundamentally no different from a peaceful demonstration, or that people waiting for a bus together are engaged in exactly the same social and psychological processes as a group of people swallowing goldfish, looting a burning store, or taking part in a lynching. For those who wish to understand the abnormal, deviant behavior, this theory is weak at best. McPhail's insistence on treating a riot or a lynch mob as if it were identical to an orderly procession leaves us with no tools for prevention of those horrible events. The theory may be coherent, but is it useful?

As he writes, "Theories of the crowd and crowd behavior should not be theories of rare events" (1991: 225). Of course, this begs the question "Why not?" Most collective behavior researchers are interested in determining exactly what makes it possible for a group of people to engage in socially deviant behavior that they would not normally perform and that is not expected under the circumstances. McPhail considers this a useless pursuit. He argues that routine, ritualized, and organized group behavior is no different than episodes of collective or crowd behavior (as defined by other sociologists).

In one sense, McPhail may be right: People might always follow similar decision-making processes whenever they engage in public behavior. However, Turner and Killian already made this point back in 1957. They argued that humans typically follow behavioral norms for any situation, and when the situation is unusual or confusing new norms can emerge to guide them. For example, "[in a crowd] . . . certain attitudes are elicited and reinforced, so that individuals act in accordance with attitudes which would not necessarily have become dominant had they been acting as individuals" (1957:15). People express feelings matching the behavior of those around them and suppress those that differ from the crowd behavior. McPhail makes a remarkably similar argument when he states that "the sights and sounds [of other crowd members] . . . may effect the individual's adjustments in the intensity, volume, or duration of his or her applause, cheers, boos, throwing, and the like" (1991: 211). The similarity is striking, especially considering McPhail's heavy criticism of the Emergent Norm perspective.

The Sociocybernetic Theory is probably most useful for two things. First, its language and terminology might attract more behaviorist-oriented researchers into the field. The theory seems designed to appeal to individuals with a precise, abstract approach to human behavior. The old "Social Interactionist/Behaviorist" label clearly revealed the behaviorist roots of the theory. This rigid mathematical model of human thought and behavior would surely appeal to those researchers who find the more general, philosophical style of Turner and Killian too vague and imprecise. In other words, it can be viewed as a sort of variation of Emergent Norm Theory intended for use by those researchers who prefer specific models of human behavior based on mechanical and mathematical reasoning.

The second useful component of the Sociocybernetic Theory of Collective Action may be the idea that collective behavior is not so different from normal group behavior as we sometimes think. Although this conception of collective behavior has been criticized above, it would not hurt researchers to remember that collective behavior is not as bizarre as it may sometimes seem. Early attempts to explain collective behavior were marred by incorrect assumptions about the "brutal" and "animalistic" behavior of participants. The Assembly Perspective is a deliberate attempt to correct and counter these errors. However, McPhail's efforts to define collective episodes as exactly the same as normative behavior certainly goes too far to be useful to many researchers.

The Emergent Norm Theory and Value-Added Theory both allow us to examine unusual group behavior while still assuming rational thought amongst participants. McPhail's insistence that participants retain rational thought is therefore not as revolutionary as he seems to think. It fits in quite well with other modern conceptions of collective behavior.

However, McPhail's argument that all group behavior is the same phenomenon, whether orderly and normative or violent and unexpected, runs counter to all other current theories of collective behavior. If a researcher hopes to understand why a group of people engages in a particular episode of unusual behavior, then he or she needs a theory that seeks to explain the unusual. The Sociocybernetic Theory of Collective Action is not that theory. On the other hand, if a researcher seeks to understand the effects of groups on individual behavior within orderly gatherings, the Sociocybernetic Theory can be quite useful. A researcher who is interested in how public gatherings form, how they influence behavior, and how they disperse will find much of interest in the Assembly Perspective. Those interested in the dynamics that turn some public gatherings into unexpected, frightening, or silly events will have to look elsewhere.

Chapter 6

Individualist Approaches to Collective Behavior

A different conception of collective behavior appeared not too long after the development of Contagion Theory (Chapter 2). Contagion theorists like LeBon and Blumer focused heavily on the process whereby an individual loses his or her ability to reason clearly and think rationally. Other theorists, to be discussed in this chapter, share a totally different sense of what goes on in a crowd. They believe that people only engage in behavior that they (as individuals) already possess some inner drive or tendency toward. Crowds do not drive people mad and crowd members do not lose their ability to think. On the contrary, crowds simply allow people to engage in behavior that they desire but normal circumstances do not permit. These theories are generically referred to as "Convergence Theories."

Convergence Theory focuses heavily on the characteristics and drives that individuals bring to a crowd. Convergence Theory argues that people in crowds only engage in those behaviors that they have an individual predisposition for (see Figure 6.1). Convergence theorists argue that individuals within a crowd are still individuals and if they act mad it is only because the presence of others allows them to do so. Collective behavior allows people to follow the true inner feelings that they normally repress in polite society. This explanation is *individualist* in the sense that it places the drive for collective behavior within the individuals. Situations do not create collective behavior, individuals do. When violent individuals gather, violent group

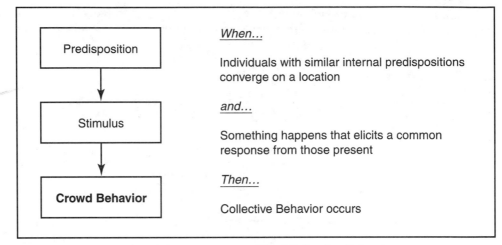

Figure 6.1   The general Convergence model of Collective Behavior

behavior becomes likely. Collective behavior is dictated by individual tendencies rather than by crowd circumstances. Convergence theorists focus most heavily on acts of mob violence such as riots and lynchings.

The Convergence perspective does recognize that people may be encouraged to act violent in some situations. However, they claim that those individuals who do not have an inner tendency toward violence will not engage in violent behavior no matter how strongly circumstances encourage it. According to Convergence Theory, a person's behavior in a crowd is ultimately dictated by his or her own inner drives.

Particular types of people *converge* in particular settings. Similar people are drawn together because they are attracted to the same events. The individuals who are in an art museum on a Monday afternoon probably have certain things in common with each other, just as those individuals who choose to go to a radical political rally are similar to each other in some ways. Members of each group share certain social characteristics and behavioral tendencies. This is why, convergence theorists argue, a riot is more likely to occur at a rock concert or certain types of political events than at an art gallery opening or during a church service. Individuals who are more likely to be attracted to a loud, exciting, and potentially violent event are psychologically different from those individuals who are attracted to quiet, reserved events. Since the individuals comprising the groups have different characteristics, each group has different characteristics. A crowd comprised of intoxicated young male concert fans is fundamentally different than a crowd of funeral attendees.

Convergence Theory began with Floyd Allport (1924). Miller and Dollard (1941) also popularized it in a different form. They emphasized social factors and appealed to then-popular ideas about human nature. In the United States, we seem to prefer to believe that individuals are responsible for their own behavior at all times. For example, we believe that successful people possess inner characteristics that make them successful, and unsuccessful people lack these qualities. This outlook has made individualistic explanations for collective behavior quite popular with the general public since Convergence Theory first appeared in the early 1920s.

The basic premises of the convergence perspective can be summarized as:

1. People are not driven insane or transformed by a crowd. Individuals retain their core personality traits.
2. Even in a crowd situation people behave in ways that match their individual predisposition. For example, people with violent tendencies are likely to engage in violent behavior, peaceful individuals are not.
3. People with certain predispositions will tend to converge at particular events or at particular times and places. This means that members of crowds will tend to have various things in common with each other. Whenever people with a predisposition toward a particular behavior gather, that behavior could potentially occur within the crowd.
4. Collective behavior is nothing more than the mass release of those internal, individual tendencies or predispositions. These tendencies may be brought out or encouraged by circumstances, but no individuals will engage in a behavior that he or she does not possess a tendency toward. Individuals are not transformed by crowds, although they may be provoked or encouraged. This encouragement is enough to bring out the behavior in an individual who has a predisposition toward it. Those who do not will refuse to engage in the behavior no matter how strongly others encourage it.

The last point explains why some individuals seem to leap at the chance to engage in looting, while others do not. Some types of crowds seem willing to start a riot at the drop of a hat, while others will remain quiet and cooperative under extreme duress. No matter how much strain a situation puts on them, some people just do not engage in outlandish behavior. These behavioral differences are inside of us, and external circumstances can draw out the good, the bad, or the ugly within us.

This chapter is going to examine two forms of Convergence Theory. It concludes with an analysis of Social Identity Theory, a much more recent addition to the individualistic approach to collective behavior. Social Identity Theory is a hybrid theory that combines elements of the original Convergence perspective with elements of the Emergent Norm perspective (Chapter 3).

Floyd Allport

In the early 1900s, Floyd Allport began to formulate an explanation of collective behavior that was almost the opposite of the Contagion theorists. Allport began with the argument that "there is no psychology of groups which is not essentially and entirely a psychology of individuals" (1924: 4). In other words, a group of people only possesses the qualities of the people who make up that group. If a number of impulsive, violent people gather together, they form an impulsive and potentially violent group. A group composed entirely of intelligent, thoughtful, and gentle individuals will be a group that acts intelligently, thoughtfully, and without violence. According to Allport there is no such thing as the "group mind" that LeBon and Park described (see Chapter 2). Allport argues that group phenomena such as collective behavior can only be explained through underlying psychological processes. Although individual action may be facilitated or even intensified by crowd dynamics, group behavior always originates within the individual drives of the crowd members.

Allport approached collective behavior from a much more psychological perspective than other collective behavior theorists of the time. He believed that individuals are always responsible for their own behavior, even in crowd settings. Like LeBon, Allport was horrified by the behavior that mobs and crowds sometimes engage in. Unlike LeBon, Allport believed that normal people would never perform such behavior regardless of the circumstances. He argues that crowd members are not mentally impaired by those around them. Rather, they sometimes allow their own worst impulses to rise to the surface. Allport sought to explain crowd behavior without letting individuals off the hook for their behavior. The result was Convergence Theory.

Allport's Convergence Theory

According to Allport, although the excitement or confusion of a crowd may encourage individuals to engage in particular behaviors, people only engage in behavior that they are inclined toward in the first place. No amount of pressure, confusion, or reinforcement from others could lead a person into behavior that he or she did not already have the capacity to engage in alone. If someone engages in violent behavior in a crowd, it is because that person has violent tendencies. People only engage in behaviors for which they have a *predisposition*. These individual predispositions, added together, determine the behavior of a group.

If people always gathered randomly, we would expect behavioral predispositions to be irregular, and collective behavior would never occur. A few people within a crowd might engage in a behavior, but the rest would not join in. The result would always be wide variations of behavior within any group. However, not all crowds are haphazardly formed. Key to Allport's theory is the idea that many groups do not form randomly or by accident. People are often in particular places at particular times for a reason. Those who *converge* at particular events are likely to share certain predispositions. This convergence explains why certain groups act with unity: they are made up of individual people who share certain behavioral tendencies in common.

Allport states that there are two basic types of innate human responses, "avoidance" and "approach." He views *all* human behavior as a learned modification of these two responses. We *avoid* anything that is unpleasant and *approach* anything that is interesting or desirable. Allport sees everything we do as a learned version of this. Everyday behavior is dictated by our drives to avoid anything negative and seek out anything positive. We will attempt to overcome anything that interferes with these drives.

Convergence occurs when people are brought together by a common interest in overcoming interference with some response they have learned in order to satisfy their drives. In other words, people are interested in the same thing so they go to the same place. In this way, a group of like-minded individuals is formed. Those individuals who are least inhibited are likely to act first. Their behavior acts as a model for other members of the group, encouraging them to drop their own inhibitions. This process of modeling behavior is called "social facilitation." If the majority of group members share a predisposition for that particular behavior, it will appear to observers as if the entire group spontaneously decided to do the same thing. If the majority do not possess that particular tendency, the behavior will not catch on within the group.

From Allport's perspective, both of these situations are examples where individuals behave according to their own internal disposition. Although they are influenced by external facilitation, ultimately it is their own internal drives that determine whether or not they join in. A crowd can only engage in violent behavior if the majority of crowd members possess violent tendencies. Therefore, if a crowd does turn violent, it is because the individuals within the crowd were violent people before joining the crowd. People will only engage in behavior for which they have a predisposition. External cues such as social facilitation merely reinforce the internal impulse.

However, Allport does believe that crowd formation makes individuals much more likely to follow impulses that they would normally keep hidden or even remain unaware of. He believes that humans are conditioned to submit to the will of the majority. This goes all the way back to the "primitive ascendance of direct physical power": We instinctively follow the majority because we fear what they may do to us if we do not comply.

Further, people believe that it is okay to engage in behavior that they might normally suppress because they manage to rationalize their own participation. In *Social Psychology,* Allport states that people go through a three-step process in convincing themselves that it is desirable to engage in behavior within the group that is normally socially condemned:

1. "Even if I get caught, they can't punish me without punishing *everybody,* which is impossible" (1924: 312, emphasis in original).

The individual falsely convinces him- or herself that the sheer number of fellow group members protects him or her from punishment. This is not the same as anonymity. The person is not worried about being identified, because they believe that any punishment of specific individuals would be unjust. They feel untouchable.

2. "Such large numbers of people can't be wrong" (312).

This goes back to Allport's claim of our inherent conditioning to follow the will of the majority. Looking around, we simply convince ourselves that such the behavior must be acceptable if so many other people are doing it.

3. "Since so many will benefit by this act, it is a public duty and a righteous deed" (313).

"So many people" refers to the other members of the group. Allport believed (like LeBon) that crowd members not only engage in socially condemned behavior, they somehow convince themselves that it is a great or honorable thing to do. In Allport's theory, this is achieved by thinking of other group members as comrades of a sort. If the behavior is desired by all of them, and they seem to think that it's a good idea, then taking part in the behavior is to all their benefit and therefore an act of public duty.

None of these rationalizations force people to do anything that they do not possess the drive to do. They are encouraged to choose one potential behavior over another, but the behavior must exist within them as a predisposition in the first place.

Summary

Allport saw collective behavior as the group release of innate individual behavioral tendencies. People with similar predispositions tend to converge and form groups due to their similar interests and similar learned techniques for satisfying innate drives.

From the Convergence Theory perspective, the crowd does not drive sane people to madness. A "mad" crowd is driven by people sharing similar anti-social tendencies.

Neil Miller and John Dollard

In *Social Learning and Imitation* (1941) Neil Miller, a psychologist, and John Dollard, a social anthropologist, took Allport's theory one step further. Applying even more specific psychological principles to human behavior, they created what they called "Learning Theory." Their goal was to create an integrated science of human behavior. Although Learning Theory does not focus exclusively on collective behavior, Miller and Dollard did dedicate more than one chapter of their book to analyzing of crowd behavior, including a well-documented lynching.

Learning Theory is different from Allport's Convergence Theory only in its emphasis on the learned patterns behind individual behavior. It is the same in its reliance on the gathering or convergence of similar people into groups, and on the theoretical assertion that individuals only engage in behavior that they possess a personal tendency toward.

Social attitudes changed between the 1920s and the 1940s. In Allport's time, individual behavioral tendencies were believed to be innate. Differences between different races, ethnicities, or social classes were often believed to be genetically inherited. Miller and Dollard, however, argued that these tendencies were simply learned responses to various drives. In other words, they believed that all humans had certain drives. As we grow up in society, we learn particular ways of satisfying these drives. Whereas Allport could be interpreted as arguing that members of certain social categories are inherently predisposed to behave in certain ways, Miller and Dollard argue that people have *learned* to behave in those ways.

Miller and Dollard's Learning Theory

According to Miller and Dollard, in order to learn a person must want something ("drive"), notice something ("cue" or "stimuli"), do something ("response"), and get something ("reward"). They argue that crowd behavior is nothing more than common responses to stimuli. In other words, when the members of a crowd act the same, it is because they have the same responses to their circumstances. Individuals have learned various responses to various stimuli as they have grown up in society. When faced with a cue, those individuals automatically respond in whatever way they have learned.

Like most other collective behavior theorists before the 1960s, Miller and Dollard focused heavily on violent crowds. In fact, they characterize "crowds and crowd-mindedness" as "a continual danger to an orderly social life" (1941: 218). They argue that aggressive or violent behavior is specifically driven by frustration. Frustration is caused whenever an individual is blocked from satisfying a drive. Miller and Dollard called this the "Frustration-Aggression Hypothesis," though it is now sometimes referred to as the "Deprivation-Frustration-Aggression Hypothesis." Individual deprivation causes aggression in the form of violent behavior.

Miller and Dollard began their analysis of crowd behavior with the statement, "People in a crowd behave about as they would otherwise, only more so" (1941: 218). Although they stated that the "more so" is at times extremely important, it is clear that they placed more emphasis on the idea that people behave according to their own individual tendencies, whether alone or in a crowd. When faced with a set of circumstances, people act in whatever way their learned patterns guide them.

What Miller and Dollard call "drive stimuli" and "crowd stimuli" determines the strength of individual responses to any cues. *Drive stimuli* are the excitation that a person experiences inside, regardless of whether others are present. They are the initial individual responses to any situation. *Crowd stimuli* have to do with the excitation created by other crowd members. The behavior of others provokes, encourages, or modifies the strength of response from drive stimuli. In other words, when an individual notices something he or she has an immediate, internal reaction. This reaction is modified, magnified, or reduced by the behavior of others. Although circumstances might alter our behavior somewhat, we still behave according to our own individual tendencies. "Strength of response" is the measure of individual action taken under both of these stimuli. A person notices something, responds to it in whatever way he or she has learned to, and then sometimes modifies this response based on the action of others. The result is a majority of crowd members behaving in similar ways.

Miller and Dollard view collective behavior as any instance where a group of people engages in behavior that is in some way unusual or unexpected. They believe that all examples of collective behavior begin when a common stimulus (focus of attention) is noticed and responded to by a large part of the crowd. Once a common response occurs, the individuals begin to think of themselves as a group and other members of the crowd heavily influence their behavior. In other words, people first respond to something in whatever way their own personal, internal tendencies drive them. These drives are then modified by other members of the crowd (see Figure 6.2).

They argue that crowd stimulus is stronger under certain conditions. In fact, if the drive stimulus is sufficiently dangerous, frustrating, or aggression-provoking, crowd stimulus does not matter at all. For example, Miller and Dollard argue that if something explodes and bursts into flames, people run

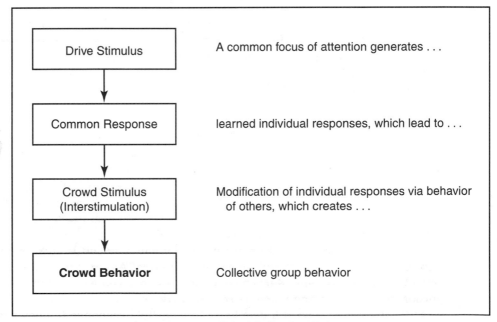

Figure 6.2   Miller and Dollard's model of Collective Behavior

from it, regardless of what others are doing. However, most of the time the drive stimulus is much more neutral, and this is when individual behavior is most influenced by group dynamics. Crowd stimulus is stronger and more important when crowd members experience *interstimulation, proximity, numbers, anonymity,* and leaders with a *prestige factor.*

Interstimulation

Interstimulation is the process that generates crowd stimulus. It refers to the actual excitement created by others. Miller and Dollard illustrate interstimulation by giving an example where it cannot occur: if a number of people who are blindfolded and wearing earplugs are placed in a room, interstimulation cannot occur. The ability to communicate, to see and hear each other, makes interstimulation possible.

Proximity

The closer people are to each other, the more they influence each other's behavior. Intense proximity tends to lead to intense interstimulation and, hence, intense crowd stimulus.

Numbers

The larger a crowd is, the more each member of the crowd feels protected. This reduces each member's self-editing of responses. More importantly, a large crowd makes each member feel as if others share his or her feelings and desires. Being surrounded by hundreds of like-minded individuals is enough to convince some people that the vast majority of society agrees with them about something. Miller and Dollard also argue that as we grow up we have learned to obey the will of large numbers of people for the sake of our own personal safety. We have learned that it is safer to go along with a large crowd than it is to go against it.

Anonymity

Miller and Dollard argue that large crowds make people feel anonymous. People have learned that they are less likely to be punished for their actions if their identity is unknown.

Prestige Factor

Finally, crowd stimulation is more intense when a crowd leader holds some sort of prestige as recognized by crowd members. Again, Miller and Dollard argue that this has been learned over time. As children we are taught to obey authorities. Parents and teachers consistently urge us to do as we are told. As a result, we grow up with a deeply rooted, learned response to obey the commands of anyone who seems like an authority figure.

Any or all of these factors can combine to increase crowd stimulus. However, it is important to remember that no matter how strong the crowd stimulus may be, it cannot create behavior that the individual does not possess a predisposition toward:

> "Responses evoked by crowd excitation are ready-made. Apparently, no considerable amount of learning new responses takes place under crowd conditions" (1941: 228).

Miller and Dollard clearly believe that collective behavior is only possible when a crowd contains a majority of members who possess a predisposition to engage in that particular behavior.

Summary

Although Miller and Dollard place much more emphasis on the learned, rather than innate or inborn, nature of individual response, they still clearly accept the convergence model of collective behavior. Learning Theory views collective behavior as driven by the individual behavioral predispositions within the crowd. Those individual predispositions or tendencies have been learned over time. If violent people converge at a certain time and place and a drive stimulus occurs, they are likely to respond with violence. Crowd interstimulation will increase this tendency. On the other hand, a crowd of people who do not possess violent tendencies will not engage in violence, no matter what. It is simply not within their personal characters to do so. Each crowd's initial response to the drive stimulus will be different, and consequent crowd stimuli will reinforce and encourage that response.

Each of us has a certain repertoire of potential behaviors. We carefully choose among those potential behaviors when faced with mild or unexciting circumstances or stimuli. We have learned to engage in those behaviors that are most socially acceptable. However, when faced with unusually exciting stimuli we may initially react in a way that is socially unacceptable. If we are in a crowd of people, and if many of them also react in the same way, then crowd conditions encourage us to continue and perhaps even increase the behavior. Social conditions allow us to engage in behavior that we would normally repress. In this way, the crowd allows our inner tendencies to come out. No matter how we act on a regular basis, collective behavior allows us to follow our true inner feelings. Irrational people create irrational crowds, and quiet, calm people create quiet, calm crowds.

Michael Hogg and Dominic Abrams

In the 1980s, there was an effort by Michael Hogg and Dominic Abrams to modify and in some ways resurrect the individualist approach to collective behavior. Social Identity Theory argues that much of what we do is driven by our self-images. These self-images exist in relationship to the social roles that we occupy. For example, if you are playing football, you act in ways that you believe a player should behave while playing football. When you are on a date, you act the way that you believe a date should behave. In every situation, whatever identity is called attention to will determine how we behave. Hogg and Abrams apply their own brand of Social Identity Theory to collective behavior.

Although they argue that convergence theorists are reductionist because they seek to explain the behavior of a group by looking at individuals, Hogg and Abrams' own version of Social Identity Theory is really a modification of the same individualist approach. In *Social Identifications: A Social Psychology of Intergroup Relations and Group Processes* (1988) they argue that collective behavior is the result of the formation of a group identity within a crowd. Individuals orient their behavior according to this new identity.

Although Social Identity Theory seems at first glance completely different from the contagion theories, there is a clear link between Learning Theory and Social Identity Theory when applied to collective behavior. Argyle (1957) made an argument similar to Learning Theory when he stated that "suggestion" is best classified with "imitation," and both can be explained as behavior learned through the satisfaction of various needs. However, Argyle went on to state that "An individual (or group) is said to be exposed to 'threat' or 'ego-involvement' if he believes that he stands to gain or lose by his performance" (1957: 148). Argyle conceptualized people as performing roles in an attempt to impress others. He shared Miller and Dollard's focus on the satisfaction of needs, but creates a stepping stone to Hogg and Abrams by arguing that the need most commonly sought to be fulfilled is the need to be accepted or approved of by those making behavioral suggestions. In other words, people modify and monitor their behavior within a group in the hopes of achieving or maintaining acceptance from other group members.

Hogg and Abrams begin with the idea that we are influenced by others, and that our own behavior is often driven by social forces. However, like Miller and Dollard and Argyle, they also argue that the driving force behind collective behavior occurs mostly within the individuals involved.

Hogg and Abrams' Social Identity Theory

Hogg and Abrams seek to explain how a group of individuals can act collectively. They start with certain assumptions about the nature of society and the nature of people, and the interrelationship between people and society.

Hogg and Abrams characterize society as "a web of social categories." Each of these social categories has a level of power and status relative to all others. Social categories can include things like nationality, race, class, occupation, sex, religion, and so on. These categories only exist in relation to each other. For example, "male" is meaningless unless their are other gender categories to compare males to, and "upper class" means nothing if there are no classes below it. Categories can also come and go over time within any culture. "Computer programmer" is a social category that simply did not exist a few decades ago. Hogg and Abrams argue that people tend to create social groups based on their membership within these categories.

Hogg and Abrams assume that humans seek to impose order upon potential chaos. This is why we categorize. Categorization simplifies our world. It also creates connections between things in our minds. At times when these categories are apparent, the connections are accentuated. For example, if we are sorting objects by size, we pay more attention to size than if we were sorting them by color. The same is true for people. We pay more attention to gender when we are discussing anything that we associate with gender categorization, and so on. Hogg and Abrams argue that abundant evidence shows that those who place greater importance on a particular categorization tend to stereotype more extremely than others do. Prejudice is a form of rigid focus on categorization, usually by race, gender, religion and so on.

People derive their identity or self-concept in large part from the social categories to which they belong. Hogg and Abrams argue that there is no innate self. This totally separates their Social Identity Theory from Allport's Convergence Theory. Allport seemed to believe that the self is almost totally innate and unconscious. Hogg and Abrams' conception of the self is much more compatible with Miller and Dollard's Learning Theory, which placed so much emphasis on the learned nature of human response.

According to Hogg and Abrams, our self-concept is a composite of our personal identity and our social identity. *Personal identifications* are idiosyncratic descriptions of our self which emerge from interpersonal relationships. *Social identifications* are based entirely on category membership. For example, "brave" is a personal identity. "Fireman" is a social identity. "Brave fireman" is a self-concept based on personal and social identifications. Collective behavior may occur any time social identity becomes more important than personal identity. Members of the crowd think of themselves as "crowd members," and act accordingly. Category membership (the social identity) becomes more salient than personal identifications to crowd members who, for example, are being treated as a mass by police. Their collective identity leads them to engage in collective actions.

Hogg and Abrams define "collective behavior" as people cooperating to achieve a goal, in the same place at the same time, by acting as a group. A crowd is just a type of social group. The same processes of self-categorization and self-identification that drive individual behavior determine crowd action. In other words, as soon as the members of a crowd categorize and identify themselves as members of a crowd, they will consciously behave in ways that they believe are appropriate for members of that crowd. *Referent informational influence* takes place. All members of a group learn the norms and *critical attributes* necessary for group membership, and then try to fit that model of an ideal crowd member. Hogg and Abrams go on to state that categorization often occurs *prior* to crowd formation. People decide to become members of the crowd before it forms. Similar people gather (converge) in particular times and places because they are interested in similar things. Football fans converge at football games, and so on. The O.J. Simpson trial provided an interesting example: people who were deeply concerned about the trial and hoping for a particular verdict gathered in restaurants and bars across the United States to watch the verdict among like-minded people. Hogg and Abrams argue that there are often distinctive or opposing groups already present in many situations. For example, audience members and security guards at a concert venue comprise two distinct categories, as do students and police officers at a college protest.

These factors (common interest, common social category membership) encourage identification with one's group, and make referent informational influence possible. As soon as any factor (idea, emotion, behavior, etc.) becomes a criterion for crowd membership, those who identify with the crowd assimilate the criterion. Crowd behavior is therefore driven by the creation of a new identity: "crowd member." Individual differences become less important to crowd members' social identity. They consciously choose to behave the same because they all want to act the way a crowd member is supposed to behave. Conformity to group norms is driven by conformity to one's self-definition. Interpersonal pressure is relatively unimportant. It is internal individual pressure that each person puts on him- or herself that creates unanimous crowd behavior (see Figure 6.3).

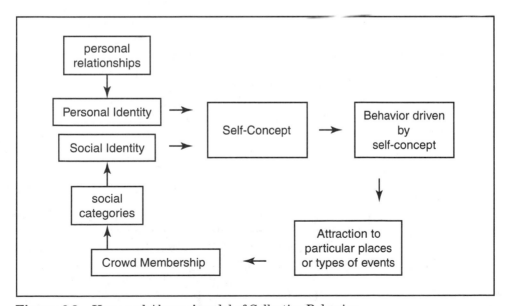

Figure 6.3   Hogg and Abrams' model of Collective Behavior

Summary

Hogg and Abrams' view collective behavior as an attempt by all crowd members to fit the category of crowd member. In this sense, their approach is individualist despite their protests that social forces are important to their theory. Social forces do nothing more than allow circumstances to come about whereby individuals feel compelled to fit the new identity. Further, Hogg and Abrams clearly accept the basic premise of Convergence Theory when they emphasize the importance of the fact that similar people often gather in the same place and time. Allport argues that these people shared common innate internal tendencies. Miller and Dollard argue that crowd members share common learned behavioral tendencies. Hogg and Abrams argue that they share common identifications, which lead them to common behavioral tendencies.

Discussion

Overall, individualist theories of collective behavior have had mixed success. Convergence Theory and Learning Theory never really led to much empirical research in sociology because the outcome is already decided before the research begins: the event occurred because of the internal tendencies of the crowd members. However, the basic idea that individual people are somehow responsible for their collective behavior appeals tremendously to those outside of social science. McPhail argues that the convergence perspective "probably has been the most pervasive and influential explanation of human behavior in the twentieth century" (1991: 226). This is because the general public latched onto the convergence perspective as a simple explanation for a complex phenomenon. It is much easier for most people to believe that "those people" (whoever they may be) are more violent or more irrational or more aggressive or more gullible than the rest of us.

Most other theories of collective behavior argue that circumstances alone drive otherwise normal people to do things that they would never do. Convergence Theory, Learning Theory, and Social Identity Theory all argue that circumstances simply allow people to do things that they want to do or were willing to do anyway. Therefore, the people in the crowd are to be held personally responsible for their actions. Even more importantly, such events are avoidable in the future if we simply try to prevent "those people" from forming large groups. The danger is believed to exist within particular people, not within social circumstances.

This argument seems blatantly false when one views American news clips and political speeches from the early 1970s. News anchors, politicians, and even the President of the United States all condemned "those college students" as a bunch of radical, spoiled, violent, and dangerous people. They were basing these descriptions on an individualistic approach to collective behavior. However, many of those who were active in the violent anti-war protests and race riots of the time are important leaders in U.S. business and politics today. Yesterday's "violent, spoiled, dangerous" revolutionaries are literally today's leaders, yet American business and society do not seem to be led by radical, spoiled, violent and dangerous people. Clearly, one cannot judge participants by their behavior within the context of collective behavior episodes.

Core Assumptions

Individualist theorists assume that there are always people with anti-social tendencies walking around. The potential for collective behavior exists whenever like-minded individuals converge. If the behavior is violent, individualist theorists assume that crowd members shared the potential for violent behavior. They also assume that the crowd encourages or enhances particular internal tendencies over others. Convergence Theory and Learning Theory both assume that a group of people is nothing more than an aggregate, that a group is nothing more than the sum of individuals. Social Identity Theory does assume that groups are more than just aggregates because they allow the creation of a whole new identity: group member. However, Social Identity Theory, like the other individualist theories, still assumes that individuals who attempt to fulfill some inner drive create the collective behavior. They even imply that those drives, the drive to fit into a group and the drive to fill a social identity as closely as possible, are innate (as stated by Argyle, 1957).

Evaluation

Ultimately, the individualist theories of collective behavior have lost most of their earlier popularity. Despite the efforts of Hogg, Abrams, and others (see Abrams and Brown 1989), the more structural/situational theories have won acceptance within the social sciences. Many have realized that theories based on internal predispositions and drives cannot explain why truly spectacular collective behavior occurs so rarely, nor why collective behavior does not occur every time people with similar dispositions gather in crowds.

The greatest problem lies in the concept of predispositions. It is inherently circular to assume that individual predispositions are revealed by crowd behavior. Allport, Miller and Dollard, and to a certain extent Hogg and Abrams all rely upon the same logical tautology: if a person behaves violently, it is because they have a predisposition toward violence. Allport specifically argues that the presence of the predisposition can only be revealed through behavior. There is no other way to successfully test for a predisposition. This means the so-called effect (the behavior) always has to show itself to us *before* the so-called cause (predisposition) can be apparent. This nonscientific approach to human behavior always leads to the conclusion that any crowd behavior reveals the innate or learned tendencies of the crowd members.

The other factor that has led to the relative unpopularity of individualist theories of collective behavior is the potential for snobbery or bigotry. Although none of the theorists discussed in this chapter ever use such language nor express such ideas, one can easily see how theories like Convergence Theory can be used by prejudiced individuals to support their own bigotry: collective behavior reveals inner drives, therefore those who take part in collective behavior are bad people. If a group of poor individuals riot, then poor people must be inherently violent. If members of a particular race are seen looting, then obviously "those people" will steal any chance they get. Such reasoning can go on and on, and only those who find themselves in crowd situations during collective behavior can disagree. However, the entire argument is based on the logical errors discussed above. The idea that crowd behavior reveals individual motivations and drives can lead directly to the condemnation of crowd members, and ultimately to all members of the same social categories as participants. This is exactly the same flawed thinking that would lead someone to conclude that all men are potential dangerous criminals, since prisons are full of men who committed violent criminal acts. Such reasoning is inherently illogical and ultimately does nothing to help those who seek to understand and predict collective behavior.

Chapter 7

General Categories of Collective Behavior

This chapter describes some of the different types of collective behavior. It is not meant to be an exhaustive list of all possible forms of collective behavior, but will give the reader a look at the range of collective behavior that occurs in society today. As discussed in Chapter 1, collective behavior occurs whenever a group of people does something unusual, unexpected, and unplanned. There are many different types of collective behavior. Some are harmful to participants or to others. Others are harmless or even silly. Some last for a very short period of time, others last for weeks or months.

Most of the events discussed below are classic (highly publicized) episodes of collective behavior. Some are recent, some are not, but many are the best known or the most extreme example of that particular category of collective behavior. These different forms of collective behavior can be ordered into three general categories: *violent/destructive collective behavior,* *consumer behavior,* and *hysterias.*

Violent/Destructive Collective Behavior

Some types of collective behavior are extremely destructive and can be deadly. Although they are not necessarily the most common types of collective behavior, they do tend to gain the most attention from researchers, journalists, and the general population. There are several different kinds of violent collective behavior, including mass suicides, mobs and lynchings, and riots. All of these have the potential for the destruction of property, injury, and/or death for participants, victims, or bystanders.

Mass Suicides

A *mass suicide* is exactly what it sounds like; a group of people commits suicide at the same time for the same reason. They are also usually in the same place, but physical proximity is not necessary. People kill themselves every day, but the act is usually an individual one. When a group of people all engage in self-destruction for the same group reason, it is collective behavior. The motivation for the suicide comes from the dynamics of the group itself. Group members who did not participate often talk about feeling guilt over not having "joined" the others. Like all other forms of collective behavior, a mass suicide occurs within a particular context that makes the behavior seem acceptable or inevitable to the participants.

There is no precise number that determines when a suicide becomes a "mass" suicide. However, most of the well-known examples involve dozens or even hundreds of people. One of the most heavily publicized mass suicides took place in California in the late 1990s.

Heaven's Gate

On March 30, 1997, thirty-nine members of a group calling themselves Heaven's Gate were found dead in their rented mansion in Rancho Santa Fe, California. The members of the cult followed a man named Marshall Applewhite who claimed to be both the incarnation of Jesus and a higher alien life form occupying a human "shell." Applewhite's followers set up a business running websites for local companies in the Rancho Santa Fe area in order to support themselves (Hedges and Streisand 1997).

Applewhite and his followers believed that a spacecraft from "the Level Above Human" was using the Hale-Bopp comet as a shield. By leaving their "containers" (their physical bodies), they would be able to join the spaceship which would take them to "their world" (heaven, which is populated by aliens). They believed that the only way to get to heaven is on a spaceship. Applewhite's followers also believed that they themselves were aliens planted here by a UFO (Hedges and Streisand 1997).

The Heaven's Gate website claimed that Hale-Bopp's approach was the marker that they had been waiting for. They were set to "graduate" from the Human Evolutionary Level to the Level Above Human. On a webpage entitled "OUR POSITION AGAINST SUICIDE," members of Heaven's Gate claimed that they would be boarding the craft in their physical bodies. The website made a vague reference to the mass suicide "at Masada around 73 A.D.," but claimed that "this act certainly does not need serious consideration

Thirty-nine members of Heaven's Gate were found dressed in identical outfits and covered with purple shrouds. They calmly committed suicide together.

at this time, and hopefully will not in the future" (www.heavensgate.com, 4/30/1997). Although this seemed to indicate that they did not intend to kill themselves, the last paragraph of that page defined suicide as "turning against the Next Level when it is being offered" (ibid).

These messages were posted only days prior to the mass suicide. Sometime during March of 1997, Applewhite apparently decided that they would have to leave their physical containers in order to board the spaceship. Members of the group killed themselves willingly, and looked forward to the event they had so carefully planned. Videotapes were prepared as an attempt to explain to their relatives why they had chosen to leave this life. They all dressed in new clothes, including identical brand-new shoes, watches, and gold wedding bands. Each had a five-dollar bill and several quarters in his or her pocket (Hedges and Streisand 1997). Applewhite and all thirty-eight members of the group ate pudding they laced with Phenobarbital, drank some vodka, put plastic bags over their heads, and died.

The mass suicide was a major news story, featured on every network and in every newsmagazine in the United States. Journalists could not understand why an entire group of healthy people would kill themselves. They interviewed psychologists and psychiatrists, many of whom talked about cult dynamics and brainwashing. Everyone wanted to know what was wrong with the victims. No one seemed to believe that "normal" people could engage in such behavior.

In the case of Heaven's Gate, participants all willingly gave up their lives because of important religious beliefs that they shared. They believed that Applewhite was from the Level Above Human. They believed that they were aliens placed on Earth. They believed that a spaceship following the Hale-Bopp Comet was going to take them back to Heaven. They believed that killing themselves would set their souls free to join the ship. They believed that they would graduate and move up to the Level Above Human. All of these beliefs allowed a group of thirty-nine intelligent adults to kill themselves calmly and willingly.

The Heaven's Gate suicide was not the first mass suicide in American history, and is unlikely to be the last. Whenever a group of people decides that their physical death is important, unavoidable, or necessary, they are likely to destroy themselves. Mass suicides are relatively rare, though. Other types of violent collective behavior are more damaging to outsiders than to the participants themselves. Mob violence and riots also occur much more often than mass suicides.

Mob Violence

The term *mob violence* describes any event where crowds of normally nonviolent people attack individuals in an attempt to injure or kill them. Sometimes the mob is driven by fear, sometimes by hatred, and sometimes by anger. Many mobs probably contain all three. Lynchings are one form of mob violence.

As Smelser (1962) and Tolnay and Beck (1998) point out, lynchings can often be carried out in an orderly and planned fashion. When organized lynchings take place, they are often part of a larger effort to resist some sort of social change (see Chapter 13). It has also been argued that lynchings were sometimes carried out in some places just to provide excitement and entertainment for spectators and members of the mob (Young 1927). However, many lynchings are unorganized and chaotic. They are what Smelser (1962) calls "a genuine hostile outburst." In such outbursts, participants only want to hurt or kill someone. A violent mob attacks helpless individuals or small groups. Such events truly represent mob violence at its worst. They are more common than most people would like to think.

Mob Violence in Crown Heights

Crown Heights is a neighborhood in the center of Brooklyn, New York, with a population of over 200,000. It is comprised of three distinct groups: African-Americans, Caribbean-Americans, and orthodox Lubavitch Hasidim Jews. Tension has existed between these groups since the 1960s (Girgenti 1993).

On August 19, 1991, a Hasidic Jew in Crown Heights accidentally struck two black children with his car, killing seven-year-old Gavin Cato and seriously wounding Gavin's cousin Angela. Yosef Lifsh was driving the last car in a police-led procession for Rebbe Menachem Schneerson. Schneerson is the spiritual leader of the Lubavitch sect, including the Jewish community in Crown Heights. His status within the community is akin to that of the Pope for Catholics, and he always travels with a procession of followers. Lifsh's car ran a red light, struck another car, and swerved onto the sidewalk where Gavin and Angela were playing (Girgenti 1993, Smith 1993).

Residents of Crown Heights attacked each other and (as this photo shows) clashed with police over a period of several days. Many people were injured and one man was killed.

News of the accident spread throughout Crown Heights, and looting and burning broke out all over the racially divided neighborhood less than an hour after the accident (Girgenti 1993). Crowds of residents roamed through the streets, demanding the arrest of the driver. Angry blacks chanted "Jew-Jew-Jew" and "Die, Bitch, die!!" and attacked any Hasidim that they could find on the streets. Isaac Bitton, a Hasidic Jew, was hit with bricks and pieces of concrete thrown by angry blacks who attacked him and his son in the street. When a black man interfered with the beating, an angry woman with a heavy Caribbean accent asked him "Why you help de Jew-man, boy?" (Noel 1992a: 11). Bitton was eventually rescued by the police.

Approximately three hours after the accident, a mob of black youths randomly attacked Yankel Rosenbaum. Rosenbaum, a twenty-nine-year-old Hasidic history professor from Australia, was stabbed. He died in the same hospital that Gavin Cato was taken to (Girgenti 1993, Noel 1992b, Smith 1993). By the end of the evening, groups of black and Jewish teens were screaming insults at each other.

Throughout the following days, blacks and Jews taunted each other. Groups of blacks attacked any lone Jews they could find. Jewish "patrol" groups did the same to lone blacks (Girgenti 1993, Noel 1992a, Smith 1993). Roving bands of mob participants attacked their victims with no apparent regard for their own safety, the lives of others, or the chance of getting caught by authorities (Girgenti 1993). They only wanted to injure or kill any individual they could find who happened to fit a particular social category (Noel 1992a, 1992b; Smith 1993).

Bitton, who was beaten, and Rosenbaum, who was stabbed, had no personal involvement with the accident. They were attacked because of what they were, not what they had done. The violence was directed at any person who fit the right social category (black or Jewish) for mob participants, not at individuals who were guilty of any particular behavior. The violence at Crown Heights was different from a typical riot for two reasons. First, it was directed at specific segments of the population. People did not strike out at those nearest to them; they sought targets with specific characteristics. Second, there were a high number of injuries relative to the level of material destruction (Girgenti 1993). In a typical riot, there is a tremendous level of destruction of physical objects such as stores, buildings, and especially windows. In Crown Heights, such vandalism was relatively limited. Participants sought human targets for their attacks. The violence was not blind or random: It was calculated and focused.

Violent mobs often take out their anger and frustration on any individuals who symbolically represent the focus of their rage. Rosenbaum died because he was Jewish, despite having had nothing at all to do with the accident that killed Gavin Cato. Many other blacks and Jews were attacked and injured simply because of their race. The black mobs did not believe that they were punishing the specific individuals who caused the death of Gavin Cato, and the Jewish mobs did not believe that they had caught the specific individuals who killed Yankel Rosenbaum. They all believed that punishing *any* member of the other group would suffice. Mob violence can be focused on anyone who happens to have the wrong social characteristics who crosses the mob's path.

Riots

A *riot* is a sudden outbreak of collective violence. Riots are more generalized than mob violence. Participants vent their feelings in a less focused manner than violent mobs. Rather than attacking individuals, riot participants expend a great deal of energy smashing windows and destroying cars. In any riot, crowds of people engage in destructive and dangerous behavior. Injuries are common, property destruction almost always occurs, and deaths are not unusual. Deadly riots (examined in Chapter 8) are the worst-case riot scenario. They feature vicious and intentional attacks on other participants or on outsiders. Deadly riots are usually characterized by large crowds of people physically attacking each other. In a deadly riot, large mobs attack each other, as well as anyone who happens to wander by. Death tolls can be high, and the number of injuries can be staggering. With mob violence, there are many personal injuries but not dramatic property destruction. In a deadly riot, both the death toll and the level of destruction are high.

However, not all riots are intentionally dangerous for participants. There are also *celebration riots*. These riots usually involve the destruction of property but the participants do not intentionally hurt other participants and generally only try to fight with police or other authorities if those forces attempt to interfere with their celebratory activities. Most celebration riots result in a great deal of superficial property damage but far fewer deaths and injuries than a deadly riot or mob violence. People literally go on a frenzy of celebration, which may include the destruction of property and accidental injury or killing of participants or spectators. They riot to express their joy, not anger (Lewis and Dugan 1986).

The "May Day" Celebration Riots in Akron, Ohio

Throughout the 1980s and 1990s, the University of Akron in Akron, Ohio, hosted an end-of-the-semester celebration every May. This official daytime celebration, called "May Day," consisted of various carnival-like amusements. There were games, prizes, cookouts, and so on. Students and other local residents began to hold their own, unofficial May Day parties in the evening. These parties sometimes became rowdy as crowds of intoxicated young men and women gathered in the streets at night.

In 1990, fifty-eight people were arrested for setting fires, public intoxication, and other, similar charges (Kuehner 1995). On May 7, 1994, students lit a bonfire in the middle of the street. They threw couches, tables, and anything else they could find into the fire until the flames reached two stories high. When the fire department showed up just after midnight to put out the fire, partygoers cut the fire hoses. Police arrived shortly after and were showered with rocks and bottles. Four officers' helmets were cracked. About five hundred people, mostly drunken students, were involved. The disturbance was quelled after about thirty minutes, and seven people were arrested. University officials insisted that the party was not part of the sanctioned May Day celebration and that the troublemakers were not University of Akron students (McCarty 1994).

May Day riots occurred sporadically throughout the 1990s. Partygoers were arrested again on May 6, 1995 by Akron police, after the officers were showered with rocks and bottles thrown by attendees. Dressed in full riot gear, the officers used tear gas and smoke bombs to disperse the crowd of about three hundred (Kuehner 1995).

The disturbances, characterized as riots by everyone but police and university officials, were clear examples of celebratory crowds getting out of hand. Few fights were reported and injuries were minor and accidental. The students and other young people were intent on destroying only their own property. The bonfires were built using people's own belongings, in the middle of the street where they would be unlikely to ignite a house fire. When the authorities showed up, participants became angry but only to the extent that they resisted the police and fire department's efforts to end the party. The violence was aimed at those authority figures, and the students were intent on continuing their celebration.

In the spring of 2000, the University of Akron cancelled all official May Day festivities. As a result, most unofficial May Day parties were cancelled, and some students left town. No bonfires were lit, and no rioting broke out.

Although the official, daytime May Day events and the unofficial, nighttime May Day parties took place every year throughout the 1980s and 1990s, riots only flared up in 1990, 1994, and 1995. From 1996 until 1999, Akron police assumed that such riots would continue to occur and prepared for them. Arrests were made, but no major episode of destruction occurred. With the official May Day celebration now cancelled, the unofficial May Day parties will likely fade away, and the May Day celebration riots may never happen again.

Sports Celebration Riots

On June 13, 1997, the Chicago Bulls basketball team won their second straight NBA championship. Joyous fans poured into the streets of Chicago, shooting guns, lighting fireworks, overturning cars, and smashing windows. Property damage was in the millions, and there were numerous injuries.

Similar celebration riots following sports victories have occurred in San Francisco in 1982, Detroit in 1984 and 1990, Chicago in 1992 and 1993, Montreal in 1986 and 1993, Dallas in 1993, Denver in 1998 and 1999, and Los Angeles in 2000. All of these riots occurred after a local team won a major professional sport championship. Two people were killed by stray gunfire in the Chicago celebration of 1993, and three children and five adults were killed in Detroit in 1990 following the Pistons' second title win (Burns 1998, Lewis and Dugan 1986). It can be argued that such riots are becoming so common that the behavior is an expected ritual following any major sports victory.

Celebrating can get out of hand and quickly turn into mayhem. It is important to remember that none of these riots occurred because of anger, and none of the participants apparently intended to injure or kill others. Partici-

Chicago Bulls fans celebrated the Bulls winning the NBA Championship in 1992 by going on a violent spree. Cars were overturned, windows smashed, and many people were injured.

pants caught on film all have looks of joy and excitement on their faces, and most chanted things like "We're number one!" Celebration riots are examples of wild enthusiasm and extreme excitement overcoming people's judgement. People may go on a rampage of vandalism out of euphoria, not just anger. Participants smash, trample, and knock things down to express their ecstasy (Lewis and Dugan 1986). Celebration riots are an orgy of gleeful destruction.

Consumers and Collective Behavior

Most collective behavior is not deadly or destructive. Some types of collective behavior relate to relatively mundane behavior, including buying, investing, and spending habits. We all buy things. Sometimes we buy things because we want them, and sometimes we buy things as an investment for the future. When buying is based on collective greed, panic, or the desire to have something because "everyone else has it," collective behavior ensues.

Crazes and Panics

A *craze* occurs when people purchase or invest in something that they know little or nothing about simply because they believe that the item's resale value is going to increase dramatically in the near future. Craze participants buy for the sole purpose of making a quick and hefty profit. The people making these "investments" believe that someone else will later buy the same item from them for an even more inflated price.

A financial *panic* is the exact opposite of a craze: People try to sell something as fast as they can, certain that the longer they hold on to it the more its value will drop and the more money they will lose. They also believe that the value will continue to drop until it becomes worthless, and will never recover.

Crazes and panics are both driven by the fear of missing out. Craze participants believe that they must buy immediately or else miss out on the opportunity to make a lot of money. Panic participants believe that they must sell immediately or else lose everything. Greed and excitement drive craze participants; greed and terror drive participants in a panic.

The Beer Can Collecting Craze

In the 1970s, people all over the United States started collecting beer cans. According to the Beer Can Collectors of America (BCCA) website, the hobby officially began in 1970 when the BCCA formed in St. Louis, Missouri. By the end of the 1970s, "nearly every grade school and high school in the USA had students who were collecting beer cans and membership grew by over 1000% in the first part of the decade alone" (www.bcca.com, 7/25/2000). Thousands of people bought *The Beer Can Collector's Bible*, a price guide, and spent hun-

Joseph Veselsky poses with his collection of beer cans and para-
phernalia. Such collections were all the rage for a brief time in
the 1970s during the beer can collecting craze, and millions
took part.

dreds or even thousands of dollars "investing" in beer cans. They were confident that the value of rare cans would continue to rise at a rapid pace. Small
breweries began churning out new can designs intended to get collectors to
buy inexpensive beer at premium prices in order to get the cans (Flanagan
1976).

Kenn Flemmons, the current president of the BCCA, agrees that some
dealers got into the hobby to make money off of all the youths and teenagers
who were suddenly collecting. During the craze some beer cans sold for astronomical prices, and many of those same cans were worthless a year or two
later (personal interview, author's files).

Like most crazes, the beer can-collecting craze ended as abruptly as it
started. The price of many cans dropped to almost nothing, and the vast majority of "investors" dropped out of the hobby. Many collections were thrown
away or recycled, or are still gathering dust in a box or bag somewhere. Flemmons states that beer can collecting was actually better for serious hobbyists
after the "quick-buck artists and the kids" stopped buying and selling cans.
Less than four-thousand people throughout the world today belong to the
BCCA, and to get that many members the organization has expanded its
scope to include all "breweriana," any beer-related item such as antique signs
and advertisements (www.bcca.com, 7/25/2000).

Not everyone who bought a beer can during the early 1970s was in the
grips of a craze, but most were. There were small numbers people who had
been collecting them for years and who were interested in preserving the old-
est and rarest cans. These people were engaged in a hobby. The craze participants were the ones who quickly jumped into the hobby, were interested only

in the perceived future value of a can, and intended to make money off of their investments. As with many crazes, a few people continue to collect the cans, but those seeking a quick, sure profit gave it up completely. The hobby remains, but the craze ended abruptly.

The Chain Letter Craze

The beer can-collecting craze may seem odd, but at least participants were actually purchasing a tangible item. In 1935, millions of Americans paid nickels and dimes for "chain letters." A person was supposed to put five names on a letter and add their own at the bottom. They then sent out five copies of the letter. The letter asked each recipient to mail a dime to the name at the top, strike it from the list, put his or her own name at the bottom, and send out five more copies of the letter. If no one broke the "chain," the first person to start it would eventually receive 15,625 letters with dimes included. This would create a profit of $1,562.50 at a time when the country was in the grips of a tremendous depression and many people did not earn that much money in a year (Sann 1967).

Wild rumors circulated about people whose lives were changed for the better with all the "free money" they received, as well as the misfortunes that befell those who broke the chains. Frenzied people ran through the streets of Denver, Colorado, and Springfield, Missouri, desperately buying all the letters that they could find. The entire craze eventually collapsed and the post office was left with two to three million dead letters, some with no address on them. People had mailed the letters with no thought to whom they would go, or where the "riches" would come from (Sann 1967).

The idea behind the chain letter craze was that each person receiving the letter would get rich. It never seemed to occur to participants that the money was coming from the other people receiving the letters. In other words, the last person to receive the letter would get nothing. The entire episode was based on faulty logic, poor math, and greed. Participants claimed to believe that the letter could keep circulating forever, and therefore every person in the chain would get rich. This belief is clearly illogical: Money wasn't being generated, it was being taken from others. Participants quickly ran out of people to send the letter to, and the entire fraud was exposed as a type of pyramid scheme with people willingly ripping off their own friends, neighbors, and co-workers. When the craze was over, people had to face the fact that they had been involved in a scam (Sann 1967).

The Stock Market Panic and Crash of 1929

The New York Stock Market Crash of 1929 is probably the most well-known financial panic in U.S. history. Stock prices had been steadily rising for five years, and many people who knew nothing about stocks or about the companies they were investing in began to buy, expecting to sell the stock for a much higher price in the future. The entire country was caught up in the excitement and ease of getting wealthy through the stock market. Newspapers that had never reported stock prices began to feature them daily. People urged their friends and relatives to get involved with trading, and thousands who had never invested before suddenly got involved. The Dow-Jones industrial average went from 191 in early 1928 to a peak of 381 in September of 1929. Some executives even publicly stated that shares of their corporations were selling for too much money (Kindleberger 1975, Patterson 1965, White 1990).

Prices began to dip in October of 1929. On "Black Thursday," October 24, 1929, over thirteen thousand transactions took place on the New York Stock Exchange. This was more than three times the previous record. At that time, stock prices could only be tracked with a "ticker tape" machine, which printed out the selling prices of stocks on a long, thin piece of paper. The ticker tape machines fell behind the price of stocks due to the extremely heavy trading. This left stockowners with no way of knowing if prices were falling, holding, or rising. Worried that prices might be dropping rapidly, stockholders panicked and began to sell. Further, many stocks had been purchased with "stop-loss orders"; if the price of a stock fell below a certain point, it would automatically be sold by the broker. Stop-loss orders were intended to protect the investor from losing money on a stock, but the result was that every time the price of a stock fell, more shares of the same stock were automatically dumped, driving the selling price of the stock even lower (Patterson 1965, White 1990).

Prices remained stable but shaky during trading on Friday and Saturday, but when the market opened on Monday, October 28, trading was heavy, and prices were again in a downward spiral. People panicked and tried to sell every stock they owned as quickly as they could, for whatever price they could get. On "Black Tuesday," October 29, 1929, over 16,400,000 shares were traded, more than four times the rate of normal trading days and far beyond the capacity of the ticker-tape machines (Kindleberger 1975). Panic gripped investors and brokers: "The hysteria was contagious, and it blocked the critical faculties" (Patterson 1965:122). By Wednesday, October 30, blue chip stocks had fallen to 50 percent of their price the week before. Investment trusts, similar to today's mutual funds, were popular investments at the time. Many of the investment trust stocks completely lost their value. The Dow-Jones had fallen to 198 (Kindleberger 1975, Patterson 1965). People's expectations about future profits had changed, and this produced a panicked rush to sell everything as quickly as possible (Galbraith 1961, White 1990).

Many investors had purchased their shares on credit with a 10 percent down payment. They assumed that they could pay back the loans once they sold their shares at a healthy profit. When the prices dropped, these investors suddenly owed several times as much money as they had started with (Patterson 1965). Many investors lost everything they had. Prices continued to drop for three more years (Kindleberger 1975). Chrysler Corporation stock dropped from $135 in 1929 to $5 in 1932, General Motors from $91¾ in 1929 to $7⅝ in 1932. Although it is not true that brokers threw themselves out of windows onto Wall Street, people did commit suicide once they realized that their entire fortune was lost (Patterson 1965).

It took years for the market to recover. It was not until the 1990s that many ordinary people began to trust the market enough to invest en masse in stocks. The stock market investment craze of the 1920s led to the panic of 1929 and the Great Depression of the 1930s. As Patterson put it, "Those who wondered where this wealth had gone might well have wondered also where it had come from ..." (1965:147). It came from the collective belief that prices could continue to rapidly rise indefinitely.

Fads

A *fad* occurs whenever large numbers of people enthusiastically embrace some pattern of behavior for a short period of time and then quickly drop it. Fads can appear similar to crazes when they involve buying something. However, fad participants who buy something don't do so out of greed or plans to make a profit, they buy the item because they want it. They want the item because everybody else wants it.

Not all fads involve purchases; they can be related to activities as well. For example, dance fads such as the Macarena, the Twist, and breakdancing have all come and gone. Streaking and bungee jumping were also activity fads. Ultimately, the fads that catch the most attention in modern American society are the ones that generate money. Although toy fads (Chapter 11) may seem new, they actually have a long history.

Wham-O sold over 25 million Hula-Hoops™ in 1958. The Hula-Hoop was one of the largest toy fads in American history, but by 1959 the fad was over and most people just didn't care anymore.

Davey Crockett

In 1954 the children's show "Davey Crockett" was the most popular show on television. Its theme song, the "Ballad of Davey Crockett," sold over four million copies. Davey Crockett books sold over fourteen-million copies. Davey, played by Fess Parker on the wildly popular TV show, wore a "coonskin cap." A coonskin cap is a hat made out of raccoon fur, with the tail hanging down the back of the wearer's head. Children all over the United States wanted a cap like Davey's. The hats sold so well that the wholesale price of raccoon tails went from twenty-five cents a pound to as much as eight dollars a pound.

Approximately $100 million worth of Davey Crockett merchandise was sold from 1954 to 1955, almost all of it bought by parents for their young children (Sann 1967). Based on calculations derived from the Consumer Price Index, $100 million in 1954 is roughly equivalent to $641 million today. However, by the end of 1955 the fad was over, and it was impossible to sell any Davey Crockett merchandise, even the coonskin hats. The fad ended as quickly as it began, and retailers learned that children can be a powerful influence on their parents' spending habits, but they also have fickle taste (Sann 1967). Never before had so much money been spent on something so frivolous. The Davey Crockett fad may have been the first major fad in the United States driven by television. Toy manufacturers learned that Americans were willing to spend practically any amount of money to keep their children satisfied. Hot toy fads like the coonskin cap, the Cabbage Patch Dolls, and Furby seem common today, but in 1955 the entire nation was taken by surprise by what seemed to be a new phenomenon.

Davey Crocket merchandise, particularly the "coonskin cap" (shown here) earned over 100 million dollars for companies willing to exploit parents of children who loved the TV character. It was the first major fad in the United States driven by a television show.

Hysterias

The most basic definition of collective hysteria is a situation in which a group of people believes that something is happening when it is not. This can include:

- Believing things that are not true

  ("The Government is putting toxic waste in our drinking water to get rid of it.")

- Acting as if something is happening that is not

  ("Run for your lives—we're being invaded by Martians!")

- Exhibiting physical symptoms that have no physiological cause

  (Breaking out in a rash, believing it is caused by a non-existent "gas".)

The most basic kind of hysteria involves accepting false rumors.

Rumors

A *rumor* is any piece of information that is not or can not be verified. If the person who hears the new information accepts it as true and does not attempt to verify it him- or herself, it remains a rumor. Chapter 10 will examine rumors in depth, focusing on one of the more persistent rumors in recent history. Rumors have been called the lowest, or most basic form of collective behavior (Smelser 1962, Turner and Killian 1957, 1987). Although rumors tend to change over time, many people still believe they are true even when evidence is presented to change their minds. This can make it extremely difficult to defuse or refute a rumor.

McDonald's Wormburgers

In late 1978, a rumor spread throughout the United States that McDonald's restaurants were adding earthworms to their beef in order to keep their hamburger prices low. The original rumor claimed that Wendy's Restaurants were using the worms, but a press conference by Wendy's officials apparently killed the rumor before it could spread nationwide. From that point on, the rumor focused on McDonald's (Koenig 1985).

This rumor spread and was reported in church bulletins, community newsletters, and newspapers all over the United States. Sales fell by 30 percent in some areas. McDonald's produced advertisements emphasizing that they sold only "100 percent beef," but the rumor persisted. Finally, a spokesman for the McDonald's corporation pointed out that worms cost, at that time, five to eight dollars per pound, several times the cost of beef. His argument was simple: Why would McDonald's spend extra money to put worms into hamburgers when beef is so much cheaper? The rumor died down. However, there were still some people who, years later, believed that McDonald's sold "wormburgers" (Koenig 1985, Rice 1981).

Physical Hysteria

Sometimes people believe something so fervently that they actually exhibit physical symptoms. In most other types of collective behavior, people engage in some activity. They lynch someone, they run from something, or they buy something that they think will gain value. In a physical hysteria, something physiological happens *to* people (Kerckhoff and Back 1968). Participants exhibit physical symptoms for which there is no logical, medical explanation. Doctors call this "conversion hysteria," but most sociologists simply call it physical hysteria, mass hysteria or a hysterical epidemic (Bartholomew and Wessely 1999).

The physical symptoms are real. They most commonly include hyperventilation, nausea, dizziness, fainting, abdominal pain, spasms, headache, and weakness (Bartholomew and Wessely 1999). However, the "cause" of these symptoms is purely social-psychological and is usually passed around via rumors. Those experiencing the symptoms may believe that they have food poisoning, that they have been exposed to a harmful chemical, or that a poisonous bug has bitten them. However, in such cases the food tested turns out to be fine, the "chemicals" are harmless, or the bug doesn't seem to exist. Participants literally make themselves sick with worry.

The June Bug

The infamous "June Bug" incident is one of the most publicized examples of a physical hysteria. In June of 1962, a worker at a Southern textile mill broke out in a rash and complained of stomach pains and dizziness. Several other people reported similar symptoms within the next few days. A rumor spread amongst the workers that their illness had been caused by bites from "foreign bugs" in a shipment of fabric from England. Some described the bug as black, others as white. Some said the bug bit them; others claimed it stung them and left behind a stinger (Kerckhoff and Back 1968).

More than sixty workers complained of similar symptoms over the course of a few days, with 95 percent of the "bites" occurring over a four-day period. Officials looked for any insect, chemical or substance within the plant that could have caused the workers' illness. None were found. The mill was sprayed for bugs several times. Workers then returned to their jobs, and no more "bites" were reported (Kerckhoff and Back 1968).

It might seem that the physical symptoms prove that a strange bug was, in fact, biting the workers. However, health officials from the mill and from the Communicable Disease Center found only two kinds of biting insects in the entire mill, neither of which could have caused the symptoms described by the workers. In fact, there is no known bug that causes the precise symptoms the workers experienced. Even more importantly, the symptoms of illness tended to spread through people who knew each other, *not* people who worked in the same parts of the mill. Almost all of those affected worked on the first shift; there were only three "victims" from the second and third shift combined. All three of them knew people on the first shift who were "bitten" and displayed the symptoms. People working right next to those who displayed the symptoms were unaffected (Kerckhoff and Back 1968). Perhaps more importantly, descriptions of the bug varied from report to report, and symptoms were also different from one victim to the next.

Rash, dizziness, fainting, nausea, vomiting, blisters or sores, shaking or convulsing, numbness and partial or total temporary paralysis are all physical symptoms that can be caused by the mind alone (Johnson 1945). Fainting is the most common, and many of the June Bug victims fainted (Kerckhoff and Back 1968).

A physical hysteria like the June Bug incident starts when one person exhibits physical symptoms such as fainting, dizziness, or vomiting. Other participants develop an explanation for those symptoms. If the explanation applies to all of them ("It's the fumes!"), others will exhibit the same symptoms. The emotional excitement, anxiety, stress, or dread actually causes the physical symptoms, but participants view those same symptoms as *confirmation* of their group belief ("I feel dizzy, too!"). An entire room full of people may become ill because of a harmless or imaginary menace. Once the perceived cause of the symptoms is removed, the symptoms themselves disappear. In the case of the June Bug episode, the first few "victims" had a previous history of fainting and nervousness (Kerckhoff and Back 1968). Spraying the mill with bug spray was enough to convince workers that the "bugs" were dead, and no more bites were reported.

Millenarian Groups

Members of *millenarian groups* or *millennial movements* believe that the world is coming to an end sometime soon. They usually believe that some prophecy or sign accurately predicts the coming of the millennium and a catastrophic end of the world as we know it. Sometimes they focus on a specific date, but the prediction is often less precise.

Utopian millenarian groups believe that the event will bring peace, salvation, or utopia to the planet. In Western cultures, this idea comes from the biblical millennium, a thousand-year period of peace on earth. Utopian millenarian groups believe that all the civilizations of the world will be completely restructured into perfect societies.

Catastrophic millenarian groups believe that the entire planet will be destroyed, that only the few chosen ones will be saved, or that we must all suffer and die. This idea, oddly enough, also has roots in biblical prophecy. Some catastrophists believe that existing civilization must be violently destroyed by disaster before the new, perfect society can take its place (Barkun 1974). Other catastrophists are more apocalyptic or doom-oriented and do not expect any salvation for the world. They often believe that technology, warfare, or some other folly of humankind will cause the end of life as we know it.

Whether they are utopian or catastrophic, members of millenarian groups convince each other that the world is going to come to an end sometime soon. Millenarians are all opposed to the current social order. Only those who hate the world the way it is would so fervently want it to end. Members of millenarian groups often engage in behavior intended to prepare themselves for either the trials (disasters) or the rapture (being taken to heaven).

As you might have guessed, millenarian groups are usually religious in nature. However, Chapter 12 will examine a catastrophic millenarianism that was based as much on the here-and-now as the hereafter, the "Y2K" hysteria. The paranoia surrounding January 1, 2000, may have seemed unique to many readers, but such periods of hysteria are not uncommon. In fact, the history of the United States is filled with millenarian groups. They have created widespread dread several times in the last few hundred years. One of the best known of these was a group called the Millerites.

William Miller and the Millerites

In 1831, a Baptist preacher in upstate New York named William Miller became convinced that he had discovered the key to interpreting prophetic and apocalyptic passages in the Old and New Testaments of the Bible. He declared that Christ would return and the world was going to end sometime between March 21, 1843 and March 21, 1844. As many as 100,000 followers waited anxiously during those twelve months. They became excited when a comet appeared in February of 1843 (Melton 1986), but no other sign of the return was apparent and the end did not come. Miller then recalculated and announced that it would take place on October 22, 1844 (Schwartz 1970).

Readers might be inclined to think that the Millerites would have been upset that the world was about to end. Like all members of millenarian groups, they were actually quite pleased. Miller's followers were edgy, but also watchful, busy, and secure: watchful for signs of the desired event, busy preparing for their salvation, and secure in the knowledge that they were the only ones who would be spared. Miller convinced them that they were the only righteous ones, the only ones whom Jesus would take from the Earth upon his arrival. They were happy to be among the privileged few who would be lifted up to heaven (Martin 1986).

With a precise date to focus on, believers were excited again. Most sold their property and gave away all their possessions. Believers clothed in nothing but white sheets spent their days and nights praying for their souls while anxiously awaiting Christ's return. A Boston newspaper article of the time claimed that one could hear the frenzied screams of the faithful coming from inside the church where they prayed (Kruh 1999).

Unfortunately for the Millerites, nothing unusual happened on October 22, 1844. They were so upset that the world did not end that the date is known as "the Great Disappointment" (Schwartz 1970). They prayed all night long, and when morning arrived they wept in anguish that the world was still intact. As one Millerite wrote, "Our fondest hopes and expectations were blasted" (Abanes 1999). They did not fear the end; they yearned for it. This is typical among millenarian groups.

Although most of Miller's followers had stayed faithful after the first set of failed predictions, the Great Disappointment was too much for most to bear and many left the group to return to their previous lives (Martin 1986, Melton 1993, Schwartz 1970). However, some of them did remain faithful to the millennial premise and formed various groups of their own. A woman named Ellen White stepped in and took control of Miller's remaining followers. Eventually, she formed the Seventh-Day Adventist Church (Martin 1986). The Jehovah's Witnesses also rose from among the former Millerites. There are literally hundreds of small splinter sects in the United States who trace their beginnings back to the Millerites, including the Branch Davidians who perished in a fiery standoff with the federal government in Waco, Texas, on April 19, 1993 (Melton 1986, 1993). All of these groups believe that Christ will return to Earth sometime soon to herald The End, lifting the faithful to heaven and leaving the rest of us to suffer and perish.

Sightings and Miracles

Sighting is a generic label for any hysteria in which people believe that they are seeing something that is not actually there. Sightings can be divided into several subcategories. *Religious apparitions* occur when people believe that a religious figure such as Jesus, the Virgin Mary, and angel, a Hindu god, etc., will actually appear at a particular time and place.

The Apparition at Sabana Grande

On May 25, 1953, a crowd estimated between 100,000 to 150,000 people gathered in Sabana Grande, Puerto Rico to witness the appearance of the Virgin Mary. She was expected to appear above a well at 11:00 A.M., as predicted by ten schoolchildren who had regularly communicated with her. Special busses and a train brought thousands of pilgrims into an area of about ten square acres. They came from Puerto Rico, Haiti, the Dominican Republic, Cuba, and the United States (Tumin and Feldman 1955).

Everyone focused their attention on the well, and from time to time one of the children prayed. The mayor of the nearby town called upon the members of the crowd to follow in prayer and duplicate the gestures of the children (Tumin and Feldman 1955).

In the last fifteen minutes before 11:00 A.M., people in the crowd began to report various miracles: the rain turned colors on the garments of the children; the Virgin appeared silhouetted in the clouds; rings of color appeared around the sun; and people who had been sick for years suddenly felt well. Just after 11:00 A.M. the crowd excitedly misidentified an elderly woman dressed in black and a young woman dressed in white as the Virgin. They were disappointed to discover that both women were ordinary members of the crowd. People stayed for hours, looking at the sky and the well. Finally, at around 5:00 P.M., the crowd began to disperse. Pilgrims continued to arrive at the well at a rate of about two hundred per day and as many as three thousand on Sundays for at least a year after the event (Tumin and Feldman 1955).

Although the researchers who went to Sabana Grande treated the event as unique, such apparition events occur all over the world every year. There have been several in the United States within the last decade (see Chapter 9). The pattern is always the same: An individual or small group of people claims to have received a message from a religious figure, they announce the next appearance, and people gather to see it.

Religious apparitions are not the only hysteria related to sightings. *UFO (Unidentified Flying Object) sightings* are another form. People have always looked into the sky and seen things that they cannot explain. However, it wasn't until 1947 that they began to assume that any object in the sky must be a spaceship from another planet. In fact, a rather large UFO sighting hysteria occurred in the late 1800s, and the explanation given was quite different from a modern UFO sighting. Still, the sightings share many similarities to modern "alien spaceship" UFO reports.

The Airship Sightings of 1896 to 1897

Between November of 1896 and May of 1897, at least 100,000 people all across the United States reported seeing a "great airship." Many individuals

100,000 Americans reported seeing this "airship" in late 1896 and early 1897.

even claimed to have spoken to the pilot or pilots of the craft. The airship was generally described as cigar-shaped, with flapping wings and/or propellers, and an attached undercarriage. These descriptions resemble the "flying machine" illustrations that appeared in newspapers, science fiction magazines and so-called scientific magazines of the time.

However, the Wright Brothers did not fly until 1903, and no ship like the one described by all of the "witnesses" could have flown at that time. It would be decades before any craft could fly for days or weeks at a time, as the airship supposedly did. Even more importantly, most of the sightings occurred at night. Air travel in darkness would not be possible until instruments for navigation and landing were invented several years later (Bartholomew 1997, Gibbs-Smith quoted in Clark and Coleman 1975). In short, it is absolutely impossible that the people saw what they believed they saw. There was no airship.

The airship hysteria began when the Michigan *Detroit Free Press* ran a story on November 1, 1896 reporting that a New York inventor would construct and fly an "aerial torpedo boat." Sixteen days later, the California *Sacramento Bee* printed a telegram from a New York man claiming that he and his two friends would fly his invention to California within the next two days. That night, hundreds of witnesses in Sacramento reported sighting an airship. The sightings were then reported in newspapers in nearly every state (Bartholomew 1997).

Notice that the first sightings occurred in Sacramento, where the story ran, and not in New York, where the airship was supposed to be flying that evening. The sightings that occurred over the next year often occurred in areas that were hundreds or thousands of miles from other sightings, and sometimes on the same night. Newspapers all over the country ran stories speculating about when the ship would finally land in public (Bartholomew 1997).

The sightings ended almost as abruptly as they began. On April 30, 1897, the great airship was reportedly spotted over Yonkers, New York, headed out to sea. At that point, the whole episode ended (Bartholomew 1997). In spite of the fact that entire cities and towns had "seen" the airship in the night sky, the story and reported sightings just faded away. Various individual sightings were reported over the next few years, but no more mass sightings occurred, no more newspaper stories ran, and the entire hysteria came to an end.

Conclusion

This chapter is not an exhaustive list of every possible variation of collective behavior. There are other types of collective behavior, but mass suicides, mobs and lynchings, riots, crazes and panics, fads, rumors and hysterical epidemics, millenarian groups, and various kinds of sightings are the most common. Social movements, a variation of collective behavior, will be discussed in depth in the last section of this book.

There are certain things that are true for all types of collective behavior: People accept beliefs that seem strange, illogical or silly to outsiders. They engage in behavior that seems odd, outlandish, or even inconceivable to those not caught up in the episode. Afterward, even participants may think that the event was peculiar, shocking, or mystifying. No one plans to take part in an episode of collective behavior, and participants don't realize that is what they are doing. In fact, many collective behavior participants remain convinced that the explanation they accepted at the time is the correct one, and that the rest of the world is mistaken. "Victims" of the June Bug still believed years later that a bug bite caused their symptoms. Many of the airship "witnesses" also believed that they had actually seen the craft. There are still pockets of people who believe that McDonald's uses worms in their hamburgers.

Collective behavior can be as baffling as it is fascinating. Chapters 2 to 6 examined some of the attempts to explain the bizarre things that crowds of people sometimes do. The next several chapters will look at some recent examples of collective behavior. Each chapter will include an application of one or more of the theories. They are intended to help the reader understand how the events occurred and how the various theories might be used to examine actual collective behavior. The analyses are not intended to provide a perfect explanation for the events, but to give the reader an understanding of how some of the theories can help make sense of seemingly senseless behavior. This section begins with Chapter 8, which looks at one of the most studied forms of collective behavior: riots.

Chapter 8

Deadly Riots: The Los Angeles Riot of 1992

In August of 1965 and in April and May of 1992, the city of Los Angeles, California, was torn apart by violent riots that lasted for several days. Miami, Florida, was the location for similar brutal and bloody events in August of 1968 and December of 1980. Prior to the Miami riot of 1980, the Los Angeles Watts riot of 1965 had been the largest, costliest, and most deadly riot in the United States in the twentieth century (Porter and Dunn 1984). The Los Angeles riot of 1992 was even larger, costlier, and more deadly. The conditions that sparked all of these horrific riots are similar. In fact, all deadly riots have certain characteristics in common. It is the job of the sociologist to recognize the common factors, to understand them, and to explain what caused the social explosions to occur in the first place.

A riot is a violent and emotional social eruption. Most riots result in the destruction of property and sometimes the injury of people. There are different types of riots, some of which are less dangerous than others (see Chapter 7). A riot can be classified as a "deadly riot" when participants attack and attempt to injure or kill each other as well as bystanders. Unfortunately, these events are not unusual in our society. A small riot between Plymouth Pilgrims and Massachusetts Bay Colony Puritans took two lives in 1634. Since then, violent and deadly riots have occurred in every major city and many smaller towns throughout the United States. Riots in the United States have been fought over issues relating to religion, politics, economics, and the

Figure 8.1 A Partial List of Race Riots* in the United States

Providence, RI	1831	Ellenton, SC	1876	Detroit, MI	1943
Cincinnati, OH	1841	Wilmington, VA	1898	Mobile, AL	1943
New York, NY	1863	Atlanta, GA	1906	New York, NY	1943
New Orleans, LA	1866	Springfield, IL	1908	Los Angeles, CA	1943
Camilla, GA	1868	Houston, TX	1917	Athens, AL	1946
Laurens, SC	1870	East St. Louis, IL	1917	Cicero, IL	1951
Eutaw, AL	1870	Philadelphia, PA	1918	New York, NY	1964
Meridian, MS	1871	Chicago, IL	1919	Los Angeles, CA	1965
Grant Parish, LA	1873	Washington, DC	1919	Detroit, MI	1967
Vicksburg, VA	1874	Ocoe, FL	1920	Newark, NJ	1967
Eufala, AL	1874	Tulsa, OK	1921	150 U.S. Cities	1968
Clinton, MA	1875	New York, NY	1935	Miami, FL	1980
Hamburg, SC	1876	Detroit, MI	1942	11 U.S. Cities	1992
				St. Petersburg, FL	1996

*Violent conflicts between different racial groups or between minority citizens and white police officers.

Sources: Jet, The New York Times, Boskin 1969, Hofstadter and Wallace 1970, Smelser 1962, Tolnay and Beck 1998, Turner and Killian 1957.

law. The most violent and destructive riots of the twentieth century have been attached in one way or another to issues of race and social class. These "race riots" were particularly common in the periods between 1917 to 1921 and 1965 to 1972, and 1992 (see Figure 8.1). In 1968, more than 150 cities in the United States experienced riots after the assasination of Martin Luther King, Jr. Eleven cities in the United States, including Atlanta, parts of New York, Las Vegas, and Seattle were home to riots following the not guilty verdicts in the Rodney King vs. LAPD trial.

On Wednesday, April 29, 1992, American television viewers witnessed the beginning of the most destructive and costly riot in modern U.S. history. This chapter will analyze the South-Central Los Angeles Riot (sometimes called the "Rodney King Riot") of 1992 using Smelser's Value-added perspective.

The Los Angeles Riot of 1992

The most deadly riot in our violent society's recent history cost at least 51 people their lives. Another 2,383 were were injured, and at least one billion dollars in property damage occured. Over 700 businesses burned (Webster 1992). The burning, shooting, and looting lasted for about three days. When it was over, South-Central Los Angeles looked as if a major earthquake and several tornadoes had hit. A smoldering twenty-five square-block area was almost totally destroyed. Every single building sustained damage, and most were reduced to burned-out shells or rubble. Nothing remained untouched by the violence that exploded immediately after the announcement of the verdicts in the case against Los Angeles Police officers accused of beating Rodney King.

The Trial and Verdict

On March 3, 1991, Rodney G. King led members of the Los Angeles Police department on a high-speed chase that allegedly reached speeds of 115 miles per hour. When the chase ended and Mr. King emerged from his car, police officers shot him with a 50,000-volt stun gun. Several white LAPD officers then hit him with their batons and kicked him at least fifty-six times, causing multiple skull fractures, nerve damage, a crushed cheekbone, and a broken ankle. Doctors feared that King would suffer permanent brain damage.

George Holliday, a plumbing supplier, lived in an apartment that overlooked the stretch of road where the chase ended. He had recently purchased a video camera and happened to be trying it out when the beating occured. He captured the entire event on videotape. Although there were several eyewitnesses to the brutal beating, it was Mr. Holliday's videotape recording that made national and international headlines. Police officers in the United States are frequently accused of brutality. Department of Justice officials state that their civil rights division has about two-thousand open investigations of police brutality at any one time. The videotape made this case different. Millions of television viewers throughout the United States saw the minute of violence over and over, watching four officers brutally kick and hit Mr. King repeatedly while nineteen other officers stood nearby, watching but doing nothing to stop the beating. There was little doubt in the minds of most Americans that the officers were guilty of police brutality. Tom Bradley, mayor of Los Angeles, immediately called on Chief Daryl Gates to step down. Gates refused.

In July of 1991, a commission investigating the incident recommended that Chief Gates retire and called for multiple changes within the LAPD. Gates announced that he would retire in April of 1992, but later stated that he might stay on until June or July. The State Second District Court of Appeals granted a change of venue for the four officers' trial. This moved the trial from Los Angeles to Simi Valley. The suburban Ventura County community is 98 percent white. Los Angeles is 10 percent black and more than 40 percent Latino. To most commentators, the change of venue appeared to be a move to ensure a mostly white jury.

On March 4, 1992, the trial for the four officers accused of brutality began. It was almost exactly one year since the beating occurred. Ten of the jurors were white, one was Hispanic, and one was Asian. The trial itself was not televised, so newspapers and television stations were reduced to telling viewers what had occured each day. Arguments in the trial closed on April 23, and the jury went into deliberation. On Wednesday, April 29, at 3:15 P.M.,

Figure 8.2 The LAPD Trial

March, 1991:

Rodney King was beaten and kicked by white LAPD officers.

Sgt. Stacey Koon and officers Laurence Powell, Theodore Briseno, and Timothy Wind were indicted on charges of assault with a deadly weapon, excessive use of force as a police officer, filing a false report and acting as an accessory after the fact. All four pled not guilty on all charges.

United States Attorney General Dick Thornburgh ordered a review of brutality complaints against the LAPD over the past six years.

April, 1991:

Los Angeles Mayor Tom Bradley appointed a commission to investigate the police department.

Mayor Bradley called on Chief Darryl Gates to step down.

The Police Commission, whose members were appointed by the mayor, suspended Chief Gates with pay for sixty days.

A judge reinstated Chief Gates while the case was being heard in court.

May, 1991:

Gates dismissed Officer Timothy Wind; Sergeant Koon and officers Powell and Briseno were suspended without pay.

Rodney King and his wife filed a federal civil rights lawsuit against the city.

The grand jury announced that it would not indict the nineteen officers who were bystanders at the beating.

Judge Ronald Sohigian of the Los Angeles Superior Court voided the suspension of Chief Gates. The four police commissioners who voted to place him on leave resigned.

July, 1991:

The Christopher Commission released its report. It recommended that Chief Gates retire, and that the LAPD make a variety of changes. The panel concluded that the LAPD suffered from a "siege mentality" and that a relatively small number of officers frequently used excessive force but remained unpunished.

Chief Gates announced that he would retire in April of 1992. He later hinted that he might stay on through June or July 1992.

The State Second District Court of Appeal granted a change of venue.

August, 1991:

The Second District Court of Appeal removed Judge Bernard Kamins from the beating case, citing improper private communication between the judge and prosecutors.

November, 1991:

Judge Stanley Weisberg, who replaced Judge Kamins, chose Simi Valley as the new venue for the trial.

March 4, 1992:

The trial began. Officer Briseno's lawyer revealed that his client would implicate the other three defendants.

April 23, 1992:

Mayor Bradley announced that he has chosen Willie Williams, chief of police in Philadelphia, to succeed Chief Gates.

Argument in the trial ended, and the case went to jury.

Sources: The New York Times, Associated Press, *The Los Angeles Times*, Webster 1992, Bergesen and Herman 1998.

the jury announced their verdicts: Except for a hung verdict on one count against Laurence Powell, they found all defendants not guilty on all charges. (see Figure 8.2).

Outrage

The verdict was broadcast live on radio and television stations across the country. Within minutes, most Americans knew that the police had been found innocent of all charges. Many were stunned. Having seen the videotape over and over, many assumed all along that the officers would be found guilty.

There was immediate outrage and anger in Los Angeles. Supporters of the police and supporters of Rodney King began shoving each other outside the courtroom before the officers had even left the building. Network affiliate TV stations suspended their regular programming to report on the developments of the case.

The verdict was announced in the afternoon. Small crowds gathered on street corners throughout the city. A crowd of several hundred black, white, Asian, and Hispanic men and women of all ages gathered outside of police headquarters. They stood in the parking lot, which is also adjacent to city hall. People talked to each other and shouted at the police. A news commentator covering the gathering frequently mentioned that the group was racially mixed and covered a wide range of ages. He also noted that the entire crowd seemed restless. Everybody was demanding something, but they didn't seem sure what they really expected to happen. Then, a window was broken in the guardhouse at the entrance to the parking lot. There were too many people packed into the space to see clearly. Despite live satellite coverage, people could not see well enough to determine if the window had been broken purposely or if it had been an accident.

These three demonstrators got into a minor scuffle outside Parker Center immediately after the verdicts were announced, but the actual rioting broke out in South-Central Los Angeles, not the location of the trial.

The sound of the breaking glass caught the attention of many members of the crowd. Within seconds, the entire guardhouse had been knocked over and set on fire. Some people ran away, but many others surged to join the action. The largest riot in American history had officially begun. Within minutes, a fire had been set in city hall and the criminal court building had been trashed. Meanwhile, small groups of angry individuals, mostly young men, had begun to throw rocks, bricks, and bottles at passing cars. Several busy intersections were tranformed into dangerous territory. As news helicopters hovered overhead and America watched on live TV, Reginald Denny was pulled from his truck and brutally beaten by four black men. They left him lying in the road after trying to crush his head with a brick.

It can be argued that what really occurred in Los Angeles in April and May of 1992 was not just one riot, but more like a series of riots that occured simultaneously throughout the Los Angeles area. Burning and looting began in South-Central, spread up to Hollywood, south to Long Beach, west to Culver City, and north to the San Fernando Valley. Most of these riots had merged into one large conflict by the first night. It took over seventy-two hours for the rioting to slow down, and pockets of violence and looting still lingered four days after it had begun. By the time police and National Guardsmen had gained tentative control of the area, there was virtually nothing left to protect (see Figure 8.3).

The 1992 Los Angeles riot did not seem terribly unusual at first. Violent and deadly riots have occurred all over the United States throughout the twentieth century. Thirty-four people were killed in the Watts riot in a nearby section of south-central Los Angeles in August of 1965. The parallels seem almost eerie at first glance: a black motorcyclist was pulled over by white LAPD officers, a struggle broke out, and six days of rioting began. One-thousand buildings were damaged or destroyed, and forty million dollars in damage occurred. However, there was one important difference. In the "race riots" that occurred across the United States from 1965 to 1972, almost every single individual killed was a rioter shot by the police or National Guard. It wasn't until the Miami riot of 1980 that participants began to attack and kill bystanders and other participants. Those who watched the news coverage of the 1992 riot could not help but notice that the rioters themselves had become dangerous. The 1965 Watts riot terrified many Americans, but it was the riot participants who were killed. In the 1992 South Central riot, anyone who wandered into the outburst was likely to be attacked and injured or killed. Reporters, police officers, and unwary motorists were all shot at and had objects thrown at them.

Although the riot was referred to as a "black race riot" in media, analysis of photographs of the event reveal that the majority of participants were not black. Hispanics and whites outnumbered blacks on most blocks, and there were Asian rioters as well. The crowd that destroyed the guardhouse and attacked the police headquarters, city hall, and criminal court building was comprised of whites and blacks in approximately equal numbers, with a smaller number of Hispanics and some Asians present.

Figure 8.3   The 1992 Los Angeles Riot

April 29, 1992 (Wednesday):

The jury announced a hung verdict on one count against Laurence Powell and not-guilty verdicts on all other charges. The verdict was broadcast live throughout Los Angeles and the United States. Angry crowds gathered in several areas near the courthouse and police headquarters. Chief Gates was attending a political fund-raising party and did not return to Los Angeles until after 9:00 P.M.

By nightfall, Mayor Bradley had declared a state of emergency, and Governor Pete Wilson said he would send in the National Guard. At least 120 fires were intentionally started. The first deaths had already occurred.

Shortly after 11 P.M., Bradley announced that the scattered disturbances had been brought under control.

April 30, 1992 (Thursday):

Twenty-four hundred National Guardsmembers arrived in the riot zone, mid-afternoon. At least twenty-three people had already been killed, nine hundred injured, and five hundred arrested. A dusk-to-dawn curfew was declared.

May 1, 1992 (Friday):

President George Bush sent 4,500 federal troops (marines, soldiers, and federal law officers) into Los Angeles to help restore order. The Justice Department announced that a grand jury had been reviewing evidence and issuing subpoenas to determine whether the four officers should be charged under federal civil rights laws.

At least 3,767 building fires had occured, 38 people had been killed, 1,419 people had been reported injured, and more than 4,000 had been arrested.

Violence flared in Atlanta, Seattle, Miami, Los Vegas, San Francisco, and at least six other U.S. cities.

Rodney King appeared on live television and asked for an end to the violence. He concludes with his now-famous appeal, "Can't we all just get along?"

May 2, 1992 (Saturday):

Thirteen thousand police and troops patrolled the street of Los Angeles. 4,500 Army and Marine troops gathered at nearby bases in case of further trouble. There were still occasional fires and gunshots. At least 44 people had been killed, 1,765 injured, and 6,345 arrested.

May 3, 1992 (Sunday):

The streets finally reached a state of calm. Cleanup began, and many grocery stores and gas stations reopened. Officials announced that public schools would reopen on Monday.

Mayor Bradley publicly criticized Chief Gates again, suggesting that Gates' "personal ego" might have kept him from accepting federal help sooner.

National Guardsmembers shot Victor Rivas. His was the last death attributed to the riot.

May 4, 1992 (Monday):

Life returned to normal for those outside the riot areas, and the process of cleaning and rebuilding begins in those areas devastated by the violence.

Sources: The New York Times, Associated Press, *The Los Angeles Times*, Webster 1992. Bergesen and Herman 1998.

Although the official death toll was fifty-one, fifty-four deaths were eventually linked to the riot. Forty-eight were killed by riot participants. Louis Watson, an eighteen-year-old black man, was the first to die in the outburst. He was struck by a random bullet Wednesday evening. Eleven of those killed were white, twenty-two were black, eighteen Hispanic, two Asian, and one man was so badly burned that his identity and race are unknown. Six women died, including an eighty-nine-year-old woman who suffered a heart attack when rioting began in her neighborhood. The other forty-eight victims of the violence were male. Five were shot and killed by police. Victor Rivas, Hispanic, twenty-five, was the last known victim of the riot. He was shot and killed by the National Guard troops Sunday evening.

Analysis

Value-Added Theory

This analysis uses Smelser's model to order and explain the facts of the Los Angeles riot of 1992. The analysis begins with structural conduciveness.

Structural Conduciveness

What conditions generated by the social structure facilitated the violent outburst? When examining any hostile outburst, Smelser points out that three specific factors are important to structural conduciveness: the structure of responsibility, the presence of channels for expressing grievances, and the possibility of communication among the aggrieved.

Structure of Responsibility   Whenever conditions exists that people do not like, they expect official action to rectify the situation. In the beginning of a hostile outburst, this means that the crowd must agree that a particular individual, group, or institution should take control of the situation and fix it. One system of roles proposed by Lewis (1972) typifies a crowd as made of an active core, cheerleaders who act in verbal support of the core, and spectators or observers. The latter create an arena for the action of the active core. Those who comprise the active core demand that those they perceive as responsible for the problem act to amend it. If no official action is taken, or if the action is deemed insufficient, then the crowd may decide that it is up to them to do something. Faced with what appears to be an absence of structured responsibility, they put themselves in charge of fixing the problem.

The California court system carried the primary responsibility for dealing with the police brutality in this case. There was no hostile outburst in March of 1991, when the beating occurred and the videotape first aired. People held their aggression and outrage in check. Many citizens took comfort in the thought that the official channels would produce justice. Civic leaders encouraged patience. Most people believed that the videotape would guarantee a guilty verdict. When the verdicts of not guilty were announced, potential riot participants felt as if those responsible for bringing justice had failed.

Participants wanted legitimate authorities to punish the officers. They did not want the legal skill and cunning of the defense attorneys to outweigh the one piece of evidence that they had seen on TV over and over again. Once the verdicts were announced, there were no more expectations that responsible authorities would do anything to amend the situation.

Channels for Expressing Grievances   Angry crowds want to air their grievances. If there are no legitimate means for the crowd to make their discontent known, or if those means are blocked or perceived as ineffective, the crowd will experience strain. The presence of legitimate and effective channels for expressing grievances reduces the structural conduciveness for hostile outbursts because they tend to reduce the buildup of strain. The absence of such channels increases structural conduciveness and leads to a buildup of strain.

In the case of the Los Angeles riot, many people gathered in public places to share their anger with each other. What they lacked was a legitimate channel to express that anger to anyone except each other. There were no court officials, police officers, or city politicians present. It is unlikely that their presence would have convinced the angry crowds that their demands would have been met. The participants felt as if they had patiently waited for their will to be carried out, and it had been a total failure. Now they felt shocked, angry, and let down. There were no more legitimate channels for them to express their grievances. They perceived violent action as their only channel to effectively express their rage.

Communication Among the Aggrieved   The presence or absence of channels of communication among the aggrieved is crucial to the potential development of a hostile outburst. The more direct and rapid the channels of communication among the aggrieved, the more quickly and easily they can share their feelings with each other. This leads to the rapid development of group sentiments and makes the outburst possible.

In the case of the Los Angeles riot, the participants found it easy to communicate with each other: They had gathered in open, public areas. If the weather had been particularly cold or unpleasant, many of them would probably have stayed at home. Likewise, if the events leading to the trial had occured in an area where the population is thinly spread out over large areas, they would have found it difficult to congregate in such large numbers. As it was, hundreds of angry and disappointed individuals easily shared their outrage with each other. This instant and open communication made it possible for all of the participants to realize just how many people shared their feelings. It also made it easy for them to gain some sense of consensus that the trial was unjust, and what should be done about it.

Radio and television stations also provided an early means of communication among potential participants. Television reporters flashed bulletins, giving updates about the gathering crowds. Some radio stations opened up their lines to callers expressing their emotional outrage over the outcome of the trial. This provided potential participants with information about where to gather to be amongst like-minded people, and broadcast the growing generalized beliefs to anyone with their radio on.

Other Factors   Physical factors are also important for the forming of a riot. In this case, thousands of people gathered in large groups throughout an urban area. The terrain itself made the riot more likely and more satisfying to participants. Crowded city streets provide ammunition, cover, plentiful targets, and alluring loot. Bottles, bricks, and pieces of metal all make for effective weapons. Although they may seem quite brazen at times, most rioters spend a great deal of their time ducking under cover and hiding from police. The staggering number of closely packed buildings in south-central LA provided countless alleys, doorways, and walls to duck under or behind. While it is possible for individuals to take out their rage by impotently attacking a target that cannot be damaged, creating genuine destruction is much more satisfying. Glass windows are particularly vulnerable. The streets of Los Angeles are lined with businesses. Almost all of these targets had large glass windows. Finally, once the initial rage subsides, there has to be something that holds people's attention enough to keep the riot going. Otherwise, the outburst quickly flares and then ends. Los Angeles became a giant shopping center, with looters taking absolutely anything that could be moved. Although looting began within hours after the outbreak of rioting, close attention to accounts of the rioters' activities shows that it became the central focus of the riot on the second day. The first few hours were focused on symbolic targets such as the police headquarters and court buildings. Once the rage had somewhat dissipated, participants turned their attention to more vulnerable and more profitable targets.

The weather was warm and clear. No popular events competed for participants' attention. The rioting on Wednesday started in the late afternoon and early evening, when those with jobs were done for the day. Businesses throughout Los Angeles stayed closed on Thursday, Friday, and Saturday. This freed many people from their work schedules and gave them free time to take part in the activities. Overall, conditions were ideal for anyone who wanted to take part in a riot.

Riots occur when the right circumstances and conditions fall together. Just as a fire needs fuel and oxygen, a riot needs an angry group of people and a setting that provides them with the means to act out on their anger. The trial and acquittal of the officers who beat Rodney King produced the necessary anger and outrage. The location and terrain gave them plenty of places to congregate and plenty of targets for their hostility. The weather made staying outside pleasant, and the relatively early sunset each night gave them cover of darkness. Many participants were unemployed, but even those with full-time jobs found themselves with time off because of all the closings throughout the city. In hindsight, it seems almost as if the riot had been carefully planned. The reality is that these ideal physical conditions are often present in any major city throughout the world. When the social conditions also become conducive to an outburst, it is as if a box of oily rags have been placed close to a source of heat: A fire might not break out, but no one should be surprised if it does.

Structural Strain

The sources of structural strain are not difficult to find in the case of the 1992 Los Angeles riot. The not guilty verdicts for the officers were, of course, the primary source of strain for many participants. However, the explosiveness of the riot might seem out of proportion for those who do not understand the history of city. Social conditions within Los Angeles have been tense for decades. Poverty, government neglect, racism, high unemployment, and conflict between residents and the police are all factors that contributed to the unhappiness of many residents of the second-largest city in the United States. Los Angeles has had tenuous race relations for over a century. The city was home to an anti-Chinese riot in 1871, anti-Mexican "Zoot-Suit" riots in 1943, and the infamous Watts "race riot" of 1965. These are just three specific examples of incidents that were large enough to attract national media attention. Conflicts between whites, blacks, Asians, and Hispanics have been an ongoing and frequent problem throughout the history of the city.

In March of 1991, the same month that Rodney King was beaten, a black teenager named Latasha Harlins was shot in the back of the head by a Korean storeowner. The shooting was captured on store surveillance videotape. Although the jury found Soon Ja Du guilty of voluntary manslaughter, Judge Joyce Karlin let Ms. Du off with probation on the grounds that her actions resulted from social conditions that left her justifiably fearful. Most blacks saw this as a slap in the face, and the feelings were still fresh in April. Many rioters shouted Latasha's name, and blacks attacking Korean-owned businesses wrought the most severe destruction. Tension between blacks and Asians was at an all-time high by the time the Rodney King trial had ended.

There was also tremendous strain between blacks and Latinos, who now outnumber blacks in South-Central. Fernando Oaxaca, a prominent Latino businessman, was quoted as saying "They [Hispanics] have not thrown up their arms and said 'feed me' the way so many blacks have" (Suro 1998: 321). This, unfortunately, seems to be representative of the state of relations between the two minority groups in Los Angeles: Many Latinos believe that blacks are dependent and lazy, and many blacks believe that Latinos are taking over their neighborhoods and driving them out (Morrison and Lowry 1994).

There have also been many conflicts between residents of all races and the police. For at least one-hundred years, there have been constant complaints of excessive force against the Los Angeles Police Department. In 1950, Chief William Parker developed a model for the LAPD designed to cut off interaction between officers and civilians. This was intended to reduce corruption. It dramatically increased tension between residents and the police force. Chief Gates continued these policies, investing a great deal of time and money in high-tech helicopters and very little in community relations. Poor minorities were on the receiving end of what Gates called a "kiss the cement" policy of aggressively overwhelming any suspect. He had also been quoted as saying that Latino police officers were "lazy."

Ironically, another source of strain within the poor and minority neighborhoods was the lack of police response when called. In essence, many residents felt that the LAPD was a hostile occupying force in their own community, while others felt that the LAPD could not be relied upon for protection. Those most likely to be victimized by crime, poor minorities, were also most likely to be at odds with the force charged with protecting them. Violent crime had surged in the 1980s. In the neighborhood of Vermont and Vernon, the heart of the rioting, there was about one murder every other day of 1991, 655 robberies, and 255 rapes. Poor, law-abiding residents felt helpless and abandoned by the LAPD.

Charges of police racism, excessive force, and brutality against minorities and the poor have appeared in the headlines over and over again. Many residents, particularly minorities and those living in poverty, believed that such beatings were a frequent, unprovoked and unjustified occurrence. Many lived in fear of being pulled over or being arrested. This long history of racial conflict and tense relations between police and poor residents was a force of tremendous strain for many residents.

The trial itself was an opportunity for the state of California and the city of Los Angeles to show citizens that the old ways were dead, that brutal or racist officers would not be tolerated. Millions of residents of Los Angeles County were hoping that this trial would be different from all that had come before it, because of the videotape. They fully expected the officers to be found guilty and punished. The actual verdicts were perceived as yet another letdown in a long history of bias, racism, and suppression.

In March of 1992, Los Angeles was a city with a long history of conflict between blacks, whites, Latinos, and Asians. Each of these groups had violently clashed with each of the others at least once in the last sixty years. All had clashed with the police. Recent events, including the shooting of Latasha Harlins, the beating of Rodney King, and the lack of punishment in both cases, magnified and intensified those conflicts until the strain was simply too great to hold in or hold back. The explosion that resulted seems inevitable in hindsight.

Generalized Belief

Several different generalized beliefs operated separately and together to produce the massive outburst of 1992. Most, if not all, participants obviously believed that the trial verdicts were unjust, unfair, and incorrect. However, many nonparticipants agreed. Clearly, there were other related beliefs also at work.

Many participants believed that true justice would never be achieved through official, legitimate channels. They believed that the legal system had failed, that the verdict had been decided before the trial had even begun, and that nothing would ever change unless change was forced. Some also believed that an outpouring of violence would bring attention to their plight and produce action on their behalf. Indeed, the federal government did jump into action within twenty-four hours of the onset of the rioting. By the third day of the rioting, the president of the United States had announced that the federal government would take further legal action. Reporters from all over the country poured into Los Angeles in the wake of the riot, all wanting to know what people were feeling and what they wanted to change. Politicians made bold promises, and some seemed to actually listen to the cries of the people, at least for a while.

It is not difficult to understand how the growth and spread of these generalized beliefs occured. Media, particularly television, played a huge role in the building and spreading of the riot.

As already mentioned, the videotape of Rodney King being brutally beaten was shown over and over again on local, regional, and national television news reports. What almost no one realized at the time was that they were seeing an edited tape. KTLA, the local Los Angeles television station that first acquired the videotape from Mr. Holliday, edited out the first few seconds of the video because it was blurry. Most reporters, together with the general public, saw only the edited, sixty-eight-second version of the video. They were not aware of the missing thirteen seconds, which apparently showed Rodney King charging at the police officers. The vast majority of Americans who saw the televised video believed that the beating had been totally unprovoked and that the officers were therefore guilty. The untelevised thirteen seconds were enough to convince many jurors that the beating was at least partially provoked. Legally, they believed the beating was excessive but not sufficient grounds for conviction in court of law.

The videotape created a presumption throughout the country that the officers would be found guilty. Mayor Bradley (who is black) repeatedly criticized Chief Gates (who is white) and the LAPD in general for being racist, violent, and "out of control." He backed protestors' demands for Gates's resignation. A *Time* article about the trial begins with the phrase "It seemed impossible that any jury could acquit the four officers . . ." (Lacayo 1992).

Immediately after the verdicts were announced, Bradley declared them "senseless" and stated, "Today the system failed us." In a press conference, he declared "The jury's verdict will never blind us to what we saw on that videotape. The men who beat Rodney King do not deserve to wear the uniform of the LAPD" (*New York Times* 4/30/92: A1). Prosecutor Terry White said that the verdicts "sends out a message that whatever you saw on that tape was reasonable conduct" (ibid). Steve Lerman, Rodney King's lawyer, said "It may be that 12 white jurors aren't going to convict four white cops for beating a black man—it may be as simple as that" (*Newsweek* 5/11/92: 33). Councilwoman Patricia Moore, standing on the steps of the courthouse minutes after the verdicts were announced, called the results of the trial "a modern day lynching" (ibid). Then-governor of Arkansas and Democratic Presidential Nominee Bill Clinton said, "Like most Americans I saw the tape of the beatings several times, and it certainly looks excessive to me so I don't understand the verdict" (*New York Times* 4/30/92: D22). Although he had originally declared that "the court system has worked" when the verdicts were first announced, then-President Bush announced on national television two days later that he was "stunned" by the verdicts.

All of these statements by legitimate authority figures who seemed to share outrage with potential riot participants only fueled the belief that the verdicts were unfounded. Numerous authority figures unwittingly gave participants all the proof they needed that the verdicts were indeed unjust. The generalized beliefs were powerfully confirmed.

This is not to say that everyone was wrong in their belief that the beating was excessive. Even Chief Gates, who was vilified as the emblem of all that was wrong with the LAPD, stated later that "Rodney King should never have been hit fifty-six times . . ." (*Newsweek* 5/11/92: 39). However, what many observers seemed to forget is that the legal distinctions between "excessive" and "illegal" can be strictly drawn. None of the jurors in the case has ever publicly claimed that the beating was deserved. Rather, several stated that they found that they could not vote to convict the officers under the strict requirements of the law given the somewhat inadequate evidence offered by the prosecutors. Given the evidence that they were offered, they made what they believed to be the correct *legal* decision. Those who were not present in the courtroom throughout the weeks of testimony believed the jury had blindly voted to acquit based on their racist and pro-police views.

The decision to move the trial to Simi Valley also contributed to the generalized belief that the trial was biased and the verdicts unjust. Much was made of the fact that there were no blacks on the jury. Everyone, including national leaders, local politicians, and the rioters themselves, were certain that a black jury would have convicted the officers. Jerome Skolnick, a law professor at the University of California, Berkeley, said, "The jury wanted to acquit, despite the fact that the evidence was very clear. They could not see putting those nice, white policemen in jail" (Lacayo 1992: 32).

However, juries in Ventura County (where Simi Valley is located) had decided against the police in three of the five police-brutality cases tried there since 1986. This indicates that the residents that the jury was drawn from were not the pro-police patsies that many media sources depicted them to be.

Further, the defense presented forty-nine witnesses, almost all of whom were police officers or experts on law enforcement who claimed that the defendants' conduct fell within LAPD guidelines. They actively attacked King's character and argued that he was a dangerous man. Terry White and Alan

Yochelson, the prosecutor and assistant prosecutor in the case, only presented six witnesses, and never allowed Rodney King to testify. They also did not call a single civilian witness to the beating. There were thirty civilian witnesses available who could have refuted claims by the defense that Mr. King was not badly injured, that he was actively fighting during the beating, and that he had forced the police into such extreme and violent actions. The prosecution behaved as if the videotape guaranteed guilty verdicts and no further legal proof was needed. John Burton, an attorney representing one of the other men in King's car the night of the beating, argues that "From the way it was tried, I can't believe that the D.A.'s office actually wanted a conviction in this case." At the time the riots were beginning, no one blamed the prosecutors; most blamed the jury and the system itself. The generalized belief throughout much of the country and shared by the rioters was that guilty verdicts could not have been reached, no matter what. Participants believed that legal justice was beyond their reach, but revenge was right at hand.

These beliefs were shared by thousands, perhaps millions, of people in Los Angeles County immediately prior to the outbreak of the riot. Of those people, some were experiencing enough strain to feel compelled to act on those beliefs. They added the belief that violence could change or possibly even destroy the system that produced such injustices.

As any riot progresses, the reasons why the rioting continues may evolve and change. This is certainly true in the case of the Los Angeles riot. As mentioned earlier, rioters first focused their rage on symbols of authority in Los Angeles: police stations, court buildings, and government property. These participants were white, black, Latino, and Asian. Almost simultaneously, young black men began to specifically attack white motorists. By that evening, they had turned their attention to Korean-owned businesses. By the end of the first night, Latino rioters outnumbered blacks, and attention had turned to looting and general destruction. Each of these groups operated under different, but related, generalized beliefs. This explains why a riot that began over a specific trial verdict transformed into a shopping spree in less than twenty-four hours. Generalized beliefs are not necessarily rigid. They can change and evolve constantly as circumstances change and as different participants rotate in and out of the action.

Mobilization of Participants

Other than some shoving that briefly broke out in the courtroom immediately after the verdicts were announced, no rioting occurred in Simi Valley. The epicenter of the riot was within the area loosely defined as South-Central Los Angeles, but the burning and looting spread to Koreatown, Hollywood, and the fringes of Westside. Like most riots, this one had two general focal points: specific targets relating to the generalized belief, and anything easily accessible. The first centered on symbols of authority. In this case, such symbols of authority were specifically and consciously attacked. The second general area to undergo tremendous violent attack was not necessarily chosen for its symbolic meaning, but for access. Rioting occurred most heavily close to where participants lived. This seemed illogical to many observers. Many commentators discussed the irrational nature of destroying one's own neighborhood. They overlooked two important factors. First of all, those were the areas that rioters had access to. Second, they were the areas where the rioters felt most secure, and where they could most easily reach safety if the police showed up. Gang leaders wandered throughout the rioters, urging them not to trash their own neighborhoods but to attack richer turf to the west. Such thinking may seem logical, but being on familiar turf is more important than the promise of slightly better loot elsewhere. As one researcher noted, "People tend to engage in riot activity close to where they live" (Bergesen and Herman 1998:139).

Mass media also unwittingly assisted the rioters' mobilization. Television and radio reporters gave up-to-the-minute reports on the whereabouts of the police, directions to the best looting spots, and provided an audience for participants. They created the arena in which the events took place. News helicopters hovered over the areas where looting took place. Several local TV reporters described the exact locations of looting and emphasized the fact that police were doing little to stop it.

Different people were seen encouraging or directing the rioters at various times, but no one emerged as a leader for the participants. Most people followed the directions of the radio and television reporters, or simply surged to wherever the most action seemed to be.

Although the mild and pleasant weather can be considered a factor of structural conduciveness (above), it also contributed to the mobilization of participants. The large crowd that gathered outside of police headquarters was able to do so partially because the weather allowed them to walk and stand without difficulty or hardship. Many of those who later became riot participants initially travelled to the scene by bus. The city of Los Angeles literally provided transportation. Still, the greatest factor in the mobilization of participants was the location of the riot itself. Hundreds of thousands of people lived within walking distance of the riot, allowing thousands to travel by foot to the scene once the event began. This also allowed looters to roam freely throughout the area without the difficulties associated with transporting stolen goods over long distances. Reports indicate that people drove into the area to take part in the looting, and videotapes clearly show small crowds of people walking or running to join the looting. Encouragement from various individuals, including unwitting media figures, surely added fuel to the fire, but physical access to the event was at least as important for participants.

Social Control

The local police are primary agents of social control in any urban riot situation. In this case, the LAPD so totally underestimated the potential for violent outburst that they actually accommodated the riot. Chief Daryl Gates left Los Angeles after the verdicts were announced in order to attend a fundraising party in nearby affluent Brentwood. He did not return to the city until 9:00 P.M., hours after the rioting began, and resisted the assistance of the National Guard until 11:00 P.M. It would be a dramatic understatement to say the police were slow to react to the outbreak of violence. They did not enter the South-Central area until hours after the burning and looting began, long after motorists were being dragged from their cars and beaten. Police actually pulled out of areas when rioting broke out, moving back to safer positions and leaving helpless citizens stranded within the melee. There were numerous accounts of hopelessly outnumbered officers helplessly watching the burning and looting. The first contingent of twenty-four hundred guardspersons and one hundred military police was not deployed on the streets until mid-afternoon, Thursday, April 30, the day after rioting broke out. By that time, at least twenty-three people were dead, nine hundred injured, and hundreds of buildings had been burned.

Everyone involved, including Chief Gates and Mayor Bradley, underestimated the tremendous potential for violence. The two political rivals had not spoken to each other in the fourteen months since the beating of Rodney King occurred. Neither the city nor the LAPD took any steps to prepare for a riot. Two-thirds of the LAPD's captains were out of town at a training seminar. At 2:30 P.M., about an hour before the verdict was announced, one thousand officers were taken off duty to save on overtime pay. There were barely enough officers on hand to prevent the downtown police headquarters from being overrun. All of this indecision and innaction on the part of local authorities created a situation in which riot participants could act freely with little or no fear of arrest. Clint Bolick, Vice President and Director of Litigation for the Institute of Justice in Washington, D.C., happened to be in South-Central when the riot broke out. He called the actions of the police ". . . one of the most brazen derelictions of duty that I have ever witnessed" (Bolick 1997:391).

State and federal authorities were not asked to help until after 11:00 P.M., Wednesday, and they were still slow to react. President Bush did not dispatch federal troops to the scene until the worst of the rioting was over. Thirty-eight people had already died, and entire sections of Los Angeles were reduced to smoldering ruins.

Social control agents utterly failed to prevent the strain from building to the point of explosion. They did nothing to limit the structural conduciveness or mobilization within the situation. They actually contributed to the generalized beliefs. Those in charge completely failed to prepare for any kind of outburst. The officers, hopelessly outnumbered and virtually without command, retreated. This allowed the event to explode with a sudden fury that caught the entire nation off-guard. By pulling out of troubled areas, the police actually accommodated the event. National Guardmembers and federal troops did manage to deter the behavior, but only after it had gone on for three days and nights. It is possible that the rioters would have simply stopped at that point even without the intervention of the troops. After all, there was little left to burn, destroy, or steal. The Los Angeles riot of 1992 is an extraordinary example of the complete failure and breakdown of social control agents in the face of civil disturbance.

Conclusion

Researchers agree that riots, particularly large and deadly ones, are clear-cut examples of collective behavior. Seemingly average people take part in behavior that is violent and destructive, often with no clear motives. We as a society pay a great deal of attention to such events when they occur. They scare us because of their force but also because they seem impossible to understand or predict.

The South-Central Los Angeles riot of 1992 is the bloodiest, deadliest, most destructive riot in modern American history. Smelser's model allows us to examine distinct forces that lead to such an explosive outburst. Many of the factors that led to the South-Central riot had been present for years. It was only when the determinants of structural conduciveness and strain came together with the generalized belief that an outburst occurred. Social control forces are rarely adequate to cope with such an outpouring of anger, but were particularly unprepared and inadequate in this case. The riot was carried out by those participants who most sharply experienced the strain and who most fully accepted the generalized beliefs that made rioting seem acceptable.

Classification of Partipants

Smelser's model gives us a precise and complex tool for analyzing the social forces that drive a deadly riot. Turner and Killian (Chapter 3) give us a typology that allows the classification of different participants within the same event. This schema can be combined with an explanatory model like Smelser's to allow researchers to classify variations of behavior within a riot. The five categories of participants are labeled ego-involved, concerned, insecure, curious spectators, and ego-detached exploiters. Although this typology was not created specifically for use in conjunction with the Value-Added Theory, it is adaptable to the model. Turner and Killian do not make any references to Smelser's concepts, but we can say that each category of participant may be operating under a different generalized belief, and possibly even a different set of structural strains.

Ego-Involved

Ego-involved participants feel a deep connection to the concerns expressed. In Los Angeles, the ego-involved participants were the ones who felt the most empathy for Rodney King, the most hatred for the LAPD, and the most outrage over the verdicts. They fully accepted the generalized beliefs and believed that it was up to them to do something. These individuals placed themselves into the position of responsibility. They threw bricks or started fires because they believed that doing so would produce real change, and that their violent actions were the only way to produce that change. Ego-involved participants actually started the riot. Anger, outrage and disappointment drove their actions. They believed that those actions were necessary, desirable, or unavoidable.

Concerned

Concerned riot participants are not so personally involved. They have a more general interest in the event. The concerned participants were those who took part in the rioting, but who focused their attention on following the lead of others. They accepted the generalized belief and engaged in riotous actions, but they did so as much out of empathy with the other rioters as empathy for Rodney King. These individuals helped the ego-involved start fires, break windows, and so on. Under only slightly different circumstances, they could just as easily have followed leaders in a peaceful march. In Los Angeles, the concerned participants were acting out of hatred of the system or of authority in general. They followed the lead of the ego-involved, but did not choose the course of action themselves.

Insecure

Insecure participants just want to be a part of something, or are afraid of missing out. They may not have any understanding of the riot's causes. In this sense, they may get confused. They see others throwing objects and smashing windows, and they engage in the same behavior themselves. However, it could be that the ego-involved and concerned participants are all attacking a particular building because of what it represents, while the insecure simply smash whatever is handy. Insecure riot participants revel in the power that they feel by taking part, and seek safety in numbers.

In the South-Central riot, the insecure participants went along with the actions of the others because it made them feel powerful. They were standing up to authority, spitting in the eye of society, and all from the relative safety of a large and anonymous crowd. Individuals who would never think of talking back to a police officer suddenly felt secure enough to throw rocks at them. The meek became powerful, the tame became dangerous. These participants turned the violence away from symbols of authority and toward anyone or anything that stood in the path of the crowd.

Spectators

In any form of collective behavior, there may be those who want to watch the actions of participants, but do not wish to get directly involved. Photographs and videotaped segments of the Los Angeles riots frequently reveal more people standing around watching the action than participants. There were many more people watching the attack on Reginald Denny than there were actually hitting him. For spectators, the riot was simply an exciting form of entertainment.

Spectators are important for several reasons. In a deadly riot, they can frequently become targets for the hostile participants. They may also get caught up in the excitement and decide to join the action. They may take the side of participants against police. Sometimes social control agents force them into action. Social control agents usually do not attempt to distinguish between spectators and active participants. Circumstances often make it impossible for them to do so. In Los Angeles many spectators joined in the looting, and the police, soldiers, and guardsmen made no real attempt to distinguish between active participants and spectators. Everyone on the streets not wearing a uniform was perceived as a riot participant, and treated accordingly. This sort of treatment sometimes outrages spectators to the extent that they become active in resisting social control.

Ego-detached Exploiters

The ego-detached participant does not care about the issues that drive a riot. They do not accept the generalized belief shared by many other participants. They might not even know why the riot started in the first place. None of these issues matter to the ego-detached. They only want to exploit the conditions created by the riot for their own personal gain. An individual who throws a brick at a policeman might be driven by outrage over the verdicts (ego-involved), by a general hatred of the police (concerned), or by a sense of power and group identity (insecure). An individual who throws a brick at a store window in order steal a television is driven by the desire for a free TV. Looting is an act of exploitation by those who are detached from the strain and generalized belief of the riot. Looters use the circumstances created by the riot to gather as many material goods as possible for themselves. No deep sense of outrage over a legal injustice drives an individual to steal a freezer. The exploiter uses the chaos, confusion, and temporary lack of social control to acquire commercial goods for free. They carry out their own personal agendas under cover of the collective episode.

The Los Angeles riot was literally taken over by exploiters. The pattern of destruction reveals that the targets changed within the first few hours. Rioters first attacked buildings that symbolized authority or individuals who, through their race, symbolized those with authority. By nightfall, however, they started attacking liquor stores. Before long, any business was fair game. If it could be moved, it was stolen. If it couldn't be moved, it was destroyed. The actions of the exploiters are not difficult to pick out in Los Angeles: they removed any object with any potential value before setting fire to each building. This is not the action of social revolutionaries, it is the action of greedy individuals looking to score. The passion of the ego-involved and concerned participants may fade out within a brief period of time, but the greed of the exploiters does not go away. Only the return of effective social control or the absence of anything to steal ends looting.

Conclusion

By the time a riot as big as the South-Central riot has begun, the ego-involved participants may be dramatically outnumbered by those from other categories. This may make the entire event seem pointless or illogical to outside observers. "If they are so mad at the LAPD, why are they burning down their own houses?" was a common question asked by many Americans during the 1992 riot. These critics were overlooking the simple fact that many of the riot participants were not deeply concerned with the issues that caused the riot in the first place. Insecure participants blindly following the crowd and exploiters using the breakdown of social order for their own material gain can vastly outnumber those who actually care about the issues that caused the riot to begin in the first place. Spectators might outnumber all participants combined. At any minute, they may choose to join in the beating of an individual, the looting of a store, or the throwing of rocks. Using Turner and Killian's typology along with Smelser's model allows us to distinguish between different types of participants by looking not just at their behavior but also at their motives and beliefs.

Discussion

Although it was bigger, more destructive, and more deadly than any other riot in recent United States' history, the 1992 L.A. Riot is not bizarre or baffling. The violent outburst was driven by the same forces that drove many riots throughout the United States before and since. News sources consistently refer to the 1992 Los Angeles riot as some sort of black uprising against white authority. Obviously, the forces surrounding the police brutality trail were attached to issues of race. However, it is important to note that the rioters were not overwhelmingly black, the victims were not overwhelmingly white, and the issues that drove the violence were not one-dimensional. Analysis of photographs and eyewitness accounts of the rioting reveal that black participants were often outnumbered by Latino participants, and that there were many white rioters as well. The death toll shows that blacks were more likely to die at the hand of other rioters than any other race. The Los Angeles riot was about power, hopelessness, and anger. In other words, it was about social strain. The strain existed between each of the racial enclaves of Los Angeles, between all of them and the police, between the police and virtually all residents of Los Angeles, and even between different political leaders in Los Angeles. The South-Central riot was not a race riot, it was an explosive release of tremendous tensions, some of which were related to race and some of which were not. To call it a "race riot" is to ignore the majority of rioters and blame the destruction on just one social group. There is only one thing that we can call the riot with certainty: deadly.

Although this chapter focuses on one particular riot, the principles of the analysis apply to all violent and deadly riots. Each of the determinants must be present in order for any violent or hostile outburst to occur. The factors that make up each determinant may vary, but the overall pattern is the same. Whenever structural conduciveness is present and coincides with structural strain, a generalized belief grows and spreads, and participants can easily mobilize, an outburst becomes virtually inevitable. It can only be prevented or deterred by careful action on the part of social control agents. This explosive situation exists in many cities many times throughout each year. As police Sergeant Mick Schott of North Richmond, California, put it: "Our cities are . . . like a slow fuse burning all the time. Daily there are race crimes: shootings, beatings and violence. L.A.'s flame just got higher. People noticed. But believe me, it's ongoing everywhere. Day and night" (Hackworth 1992: 33). When the strain becomes too much, when participants feel cut off from legitimate means of coping with their complaints, and when social control fails, riots occur. The only surprise is that it does not happen more often.

Most collective episodes are not as horrifying as deadly riots. The next few chapters look at milder and much less dangerous forms of collective behavior. Chapter 9 focuses on religious image sightings.

Chapter 9

Images, Miracles, and Apparitions:
The Soybean Savior and Our Lady of Clearwater

As discussed in Chapter 7, images, miracles, and apparitions are a common form of collective behavior. Participants in these events do things that are considered bizarre by outsiders and spectators. They often gather in an undistinguished location such as a muddy field or a dank basement, weeping and praying. Many participants bear gifts (flowers, money, medallions, and so on), which they leave at the site. Some image, miracle, and apparition events include fainting, speaking in tongues, spontaneous healing, and other behaviors that are considered unacceptable in a public setting and which are only expected in certain religious ceremonies or services. In an image, miracle, or apparition episode, these behaviors take part in a secular, public setting. Participants collectively convince themselves that some sort of miraculous event is taking place. They develop elaborate explanations to justify why such an important occurrence is taking place in such an odd or mundane location. Although all three types of collective episodes share the common thread of religious sentiment, they are different and distinct events.

Images

An image episode occurs when a group of individuals come to believe that the likeness of a holy figure such as Jesus, the Virgin Mary, or an angel has spontaneously appeared on the surface of an ordinary object. These images appear frequently in the United States and throughout the world. A mundane object or location such as a door or wall is transformed into a holy place of pilgrimage by people who gather from the local community and sometimes from hundreds or thousands of miles away to view the image.

Images of this sort have appeared in a variety of unusual locations. For example, the face of Jesus has appeared on automobile body parts, tabletops, billboards, windows, trees, and storage tanks in Texas, Georgia, New York, throughout New England, and Ohio. The image, silhouette, or shadow of the Virgin Mary has appeared on windows, frying pans, pine trees, refrigerator doors, and apartment building walls in Florida, Kentucky, Tennessee, and Illinois. The outline of an angel appeared on a house in Ohio. Jesus, Mary, a flock of angels, and a dove all simultaneously appeared on a bathroom door in Phoenix, Arizona (see Figure 9.1).

The above examples all occurred between 1985 and 1997 in the United States, and I discovered most of them through simple Internet searches of newspapers and newsmagazines sources. Many smaller image events are never reported in regional or national news sources. This makes it almost impossible for us to know how many small, localized image events occur every year. If regional or national media does not pick up the story, the news must spread through word-of-mouth. As a result, only those who live near the image or have social connections to participants are aware that it occurs. Those images that are reported in the media attract people from all over the country and, if it lasts long enough, the world.

Image events typically follow a similar pattern. In each, an individual notices the image, identifies it as the likeness of a religious figure, interprets it as a miracle, and tells his/her friends about it. The event is initially contained within a particular social circle or organization. The next step is often an official announcement to the media that the image of a religious figure has miraculously appeared. Once this announcement is made, local or regional newspapers and television stations looking for a human-interest story may pick up the story. People outside of the initial social group become aware of the image. Many make a pilgrimage of hundreds or even thousands of miles in order to view the image.

Most of these images appear and disappear within a few weeks or months. Occasionally, as is the case in Clearwater, Florida, the image may be durable enough to last for years. Those images that last over time tend to draw more people, but participation in the event still tends to peak within a few weeks.

Except in rare cases of a suspected hoax, the image itself is usually determined to be the result of a naturally occurring phenomenon such as the accumulation of dirt, rust, mold, or fungus. It is the resemblance to a religious figure that makes it significant. For those who believe that the image is divine, this natural origin is considered evidence that the image is not manmade and is therefore divine. For those who do not believe, it is proof that the image has mundane origins and is a fluke rather than a miracle.

Figure 9.1 A Partial List of Recent Images, Miracles, and Apparitions in the United States

IMAGES:

Where:	When:	Details:
Loraine, OH	1986	Not known (Virgin Mary, apparently)
Fostoria, OH	Aug.–Sept. 1986	Images of Jesus on soybean oil tank
New England	1992	Jesus in three trees for three months (fungi)
Cold Spring, KY	1992	Silhouette of Mary in a pine tree
Elsa, TX	1993	Face of Virgin Mary appeared on the hood and/or rear fender of a 1981 Chevy Camaro
New York, NY	1993	Jesus on bathroom window in Manhattan
Clearwater, FL	Dec. 1996–present	Image of Virgin Mary on finance company window
Clearwater	Dec. 1996	A local man also had a rusted cast-iron frying pan with the image of "a manger"
Phoenix, AZ	1996	Mary, Jesus, flock of angels, and a dove on a bathroom door
Bretton Station, TX	1995	Jesus on a Formica table in a junkyard
Stone Mountain, GA	1996	Jesus in a Pizza Hut pasta ad in Atlanta area. The image was dubbed "the Spaghetti Savior"
New York, NY	1996	Jesus appeared on fifth floor apartment window in the rain
Chicago, IL	1997	Virgin Mary shadow appears nightly on the brick wall of a Hanover Park apartment building
Wareham, MA	Feb. 1999	Face of Jesus appeared in the grain of a small wooden door that was being stained in Episcopalian Church

MIRACLES:

Where:	When:	Details:
Lake Ridge, VA	1992–present	Fiberglass Virgin Mary statue weeps when in the presence of a priest who bleeds the stigmata wounds
Brooklyn, NY	March–April 1994	Weeping Virgin Mary icon in a Bensonhurst apartment
Brooklyn, NY	1994	Weeping Virgin Mary icon in Bensonhurst Coptic Church of St. George
Barberton, OH	1992	Weeping Mary painting in a small church
Lewis, KS	Dec. 1996	Weeping Virgin Mary statuette
Troy, MI	March 1998	Weeping Virgin Mary and Christ child figures
Cicero, IL	1997	Weeping Virgin Mary icon
Corpus Christi, TX	June 1998	Moving Virgin Mary statue
Chicago, IL	1984	Wooden Mary statue in John of God church shed tears

(continued)

Figure 9.1 *Continued*

MIRACLES (*cont.*):

Chicago, IL	Dec. 6, 1986	Painting of Mary began to weep at St. Nicholas Albanian Orthodox Church
Chicago, IL	April 1987	Weeping Mary/Jesus painting in apartment of a retired tailor
Hillside, IL	July 1991	Crucifix at Queen of Heaven Cemetery bled
St. Charles, IL	1994	Mary statues at a religious gift store moved
Los Angeles, CA	Spring 1998–present	Photo of Shirley MacLaine that weeps tears and heals in Beta Temple/Black Jewish Synagogue

APPARITIONS:

Eaton Township, OH	1985–1996	Virgin Mary talks to a woman (image seen in clouds)
Conyers, GA	Oct. 1990–Oct. 1998	Virgin Mary and Jesus appeared to Nancy Fowler on thirteenth of every month behind a farm. Nancy announced the final appearance ahead of time (it was covered by CNN). Mary's final message mentioned the coming of the millennium as a time of danger.
Marlboro, NJ	1992–1998	Virgin Mary (apparition)—police try to stop Karen and Vincent Bove from distributing a newsletter publicizing the appearances, citing too much traffic as their primary concern.

Images Miracles, and Apparitions outside the United States

IMAGES:

Where:	When:	Details:
Mexico City, MX	Summer 1997	Image of Virgin Mary appeared in a rain puddle in a busy subway station, and remained after the puddle evaporated. Authorities moved the stone bearing the image to an alcove within the station

MIRACLES:

Trinidad & Topango	1996	Weeping Virgin Mary Statue
Cyprus, Greece	Feb. 1997	Weeping 400-year-old Virgin Mary and baby Jesus icon in a monastery in Kykko Mountain, Cyprus

APPARITIONS:

Fatima, Portugal	1917–present	Virgin Mary appeared to three small children, has been working miracles ever since.
Medjugorje, Bosnia	1981–present	Virgin Mary makes frequent appearances, gives messages to six visionaries (20,000,000 visitors as of 1997)

Figure 9.1   *Continued*

APPARITIONS (*cont.*):

Mellaray, Ireland	Aug. 1985	Virgin Mary apparition
Yankalilla, Australia	July 1994–present	Virgin Mary, in an Anglican church
Marmora, Ontario (190km NE of Toronto)	1997	Mary (apparition) appears on farm of John and Shelah Greensides

Virgin Mary apparitions are often accompanied by "The Miracle of the Sun": the sun dances, pulses, changes color, splits in half, falls to the Earth, and so on. This spectacular effect was first noted in 1917 in Fatima, Portugal, the most famous of all Mary apparition sites. Somehow, only those believers who are present at the apparition can see the sun doing these gymnastics: There has never been any astronomical confirmation of any kind. These dramatic events have never been witnessed by anyone who is not present at the site of an apparition. Believers cannot explain why others throughout the world do not also see the sun performing these dramatic actions.

Sources: Associated Press, Lexis/Nexis, EbscoHost

When analyzing these events, the perceptions and behaviors of the individual participants matter most. The image itself is only important to the extent that a number of participants accept it as holy. It does not matter if the image is the result of rust, spray paint, or mold, as long as participants believe that it is caused by divine intervention.

Miracles

Miracles are similar to image episodes: There is a tangible physical object that is easily viewed and which participants can easily locate. Typical miracles include religious paintings or statues that cry, bleed, or move. Although a few of these events have drawn fairly large crowds within the last five years, they have a somewhat different character than image events. Miracles may attract more devout pilgrims, but far fewer skeptics or observers bother to take part in the event. This is partly because nonparticipants tend to view the event itself as less plausible. People in general are more accepting of the idea that the likeness of a holy figure has appeared (by divine intervention or coincidence) than they are to believe that a concrete statue moves or cries. Another reason why miracles may draw less participants than images is their denomination-specific nature. While images often appear outdoors, miracles almost always occur indoors. This may inhibit many potential participants from taking part.

Miracle events occur almost as often as images. For example, Virgin Mary statues or paintings that seem to spontaneously begin weeping tears of water, oil, and/or blood, were numerously reported in Virginia, New York,

Kansas, Michigan, Illinois, Ohio, and Texas just between 1996 and 1998. A statue of Mary in a Corpus Christi, Texas home was reputed to move her arms from time to time. Moving or weeping statues and icons are the most common form of miracle events in the United States. These miracles are often accompanied by the spontaneous healing of believers (see Figure 9.1).

Images are often visually ambiguous, whereas miracles are visually straightforward. There is no doubt that a statue of Mary is a statue of Mary. There is not doubt that there are tear-like streaks on her face. The only question is whether one believes the tears are real, and what they might mean. Anyone who sees a picture of the object in the newspaper or on TV has essentially witnessed the miracle. Most can decide from this information if they believe it is real. This cut-and-dry character means that only believers are likely to go view the object. Far fewer skeptics are curious enough to take part in the event.

Images, on the other hand, draw a large number of people who are undecided or uncertain about the possibility of such an occurrence. Many participants want to view the image in person before they make up their minds. Pictures just don't convey the necessary information. Often, even after viewing an image repeatedly, some participants will still be undecided as to whether or not it is divine.

Apparitions

Apparitions center around the appearance of some figure. Ghost sightings could be considered a form of apparition. In the United States, Jesus, Mary, or an angel appearing in person and talking to an individual, are the most common apparition events. They are so common that they have become the topic of books, magazines, and talk shows in the last few years. The apparitions often deliver urgent, important messages to the individuals who experience them.

Although they may seem at first glance to be similar to images and miracles, apparitions are fundamentally different. Examples of apparitions include the women in Texas and in Georgia who claim to have regular conversations with the Virgin Mary. Those who gather to take part in such events are faced with either believing or disbelieving the words of one individual. As a result, these events all center on the perceived credibility of the individual who claims to have seen the apparition in the first place. These mediators become the focus of the event. If participants do not believe that the mediator is honest or sane, then the event loses all meaning for them.

The individuals who claim to speak to the apparition often begin to take on some characteristics of cult or religious leaders. They arouse the suspicions of authorities and other religious leaders. It is difficult or impossible for sociologists to determine which aspects of such events are driven by the personal agendas of the mediators. Most participants do not actually see anything. They may "feel" or "sense" a "presence," but they have to rely on the mediator to define and direct the event. Spectators and researchers do not see anything but the crowd.

Unlike apparitions, images and miracles provide the participants and researchers with something easily observable that relies solely on their own perception and interpretation to evaluate. Participants often decide beforehand whether or not they believe that a statue can cry real tears or if an individual who speaks to angels is sincere. Images, the most visually ambiguous, are sometimes striking enough to require careful observation and evaluation. Often, those who claim they do not believe it is divine still agree that the image does indeed resemble the religious figure in question. The uncertainty of the participants shifts subtly away from the possibility or probability of divine intervention. Instead, they focus their attention on whether or not the image looks real. This slight misdirection of attention allows many participants to experience the episode without directly facing questions about the likelihood of the event being divine.

We can use collective behavior theory to analyze all of these events because they involve groups of people engaging in behavior that is neither normal nor routine. Participants faced with a rusted oil tank or a stained painting behave as if they are in the presence of a sacred relic. They do things that they would normally never do in public. People pray, weep, shout, bow their heads, leave five-dollar bills on the ground, and/or throw away their canes. While standing, sitting, or kneeling in a basement, garage, or parking lot they behave as if they are in a cathedral. Images, miracles, and apparitions typically draw hundreds of people to the scene, and sometimes draw thousands or even hundreds of thousands.

This chapter will analyze two of the largest and most publicized image episodes in the United States within recent history. Both drew tens of thousands of participants and spectators within a short period of time, both were located in widely visible places near heavily traveled public roads, and both were extensively reported in national and international media. Smelser's Value-Added theory will be applied to both, and Turner and Killian's classification schema for participants will be applied to the second.

The Soybean Savior: Jesus on an Oil Tank

Fostoria, Ohio, 1986

On a warm night in July of 1986, a fifty-eight-year-old widow named Rita Ratchen was driving her new Ford Taurus east on State Route 12 into Fostoria, Ohio. When she rounded the bend by the Hi-Lo gas station the soybean oil storage tank in the ADM (Archer Daniels Midland) compound to her left appeared different to her. Yellow sodium vapor security lights were illuminating the three large, white, soybean oil storage tanks on the north side of the road. She was about one-quarter mile from the tanks when she realized that the shadows cast on the side of the closest of three tanks looked to her like the figure of Jesus. The image was about twenty feet high. It resembled a man with long hair, a beard, and a robe. Ms. Ratchen pulled over to the side of the road. "My hands came off the wheel. I just crossed my arms over my heart, and I said, 'Oh, my Lord, my God'" (*Time* 9/29/86: 8).

She did not tell anyone about her experience at first, because she was afraid that people would think that she was crazy: "I didn't want to be put away" (ibid). About three days later, she drove her friend Dorothy to the spot, and asked her what she saw. Dorothy ". . . saw it immediately. So I said, 'Oh boy, two kooks now!'" (ibid). The next night Rita and Dorothy told another friend, who also agreed that the image was Jesus.

Only those within Mrs. Ratchen's circle of friends were aware of the image for the first few days. Rita then decided that the media should be notified. Although the local newspaper editor ignored the story at first, more and more people began to call the offices of the Fostoria *Review Times* asking about the image. Within days, the story had hit local, regional, and national media. By the time those outside of Fostoria were aware of the image, the figure of a small child was said to have appeared beside Jesus. Within a few days, participants also reported that a full face had appeared on the east side of the tank.

Fostoria is a town of about 16,000 in Western Seneca County, Ohio. It is about 40 miles southeast of Toledo, and about 110 miles west of Akron. Within days of the news about the image, at least 1,500 cars and trucks were slowly driving past the tank every night. Although estimates vary, the police claim that there were sometimes as many as 2,000 cars in a single night, and most of those vehicles contained at least two people.

ADM company spokespeople, the police, and participants all agreed that the image was caused by combination of rust, paint, and shadows caused by the lights that came on at dusk and went back out at dawn. The tank had been repaired that summer, and the unpainted welds had quickly rusted.

The public event went on for almost exactly two weeks. Participation had only begun to peak, and there were no signs that the event would be over any time soon. Once the sun went down, it took over two hours to drive about one mile on the main route in and out of Fostoria because of the traffic. A local fireman tired of the nightly traffic jams threw balloons full of paint onto the tanks, effectively obscuring the images. Once the images were no longer visible, participation immediately dropped down to a few hundred people per day. By the end of the week, ADM repainted the white tank, and the event ended.

Although articles and books about these types of religious episodes are relatively common, most have been written from the perspective of believers or are straight journalistic reports of information. There are virtually no theoretical analyses of such image events. This book will apply Smelser's Value-Added Theory of collective behavior to analyze this particular event. The details vary from image to image, but this analysis also applies in a general sense to any image event that has occurred in the United States in recent decades.

Analysis

The Value-Added Theory

As discussed in earlier chapters, Smelser's model of collective behavior sets forth a set of concepts and propositions that can be used to order all variations in collective behavior. The five determinants of collective behavior are labeled Structural Conduciveness, Structural Strain, Generalized Belief, Mobilization for Action, and Social Control.

Structural Conduciveness

Structural conduciveness refers to any social and/or physical factors that contribute to the likelihood of a particular episode of collective behavior. Fostoria is a deeply religious, almost exclusively Christian community. There are a high percentage of Catholic residents, and virtually every denomination of Christianity is represented. As Reverand Thomas Hoppe put it, "We live in a Christian country—if there is anyone who means the most to people, it's Christ" (*The* [Fostoria] *Review Times* 8/23/86: 1). Although images, miracles, and apparitions are not restricted to Christian cultures, individuals only see those religious figures that have meaning within their culture. The more religiosity exists in a particular area, the more people there are who are willing to believe in such an image. Similarly, the more devout an individual is, the more likely he or she is to believe that a miracle has occurred. The participants and spectators that I interviewed all agreed that Fostoria contained a high percentage of religiously devout individuals. The local phone book listed thirty-five churches at that time, and many of the people I interviewed indicated that there were smaller places of worship that were not listed at all. This was confirmed in interviews with the chief of police and the editor of the local newspaper.

The depth of religious beliefs among the local population may be the single-most important social factor of structural conduciveness for this type of event. However, physical factors also play an important part in the relative success or size of an image event. Fostoria drew more participants in a shorter time span than almost any other image in the United States. Structural conduciveness largely contributed to this success.

The image could really only be seen at night, between dusk and dawn when the security lights were on. Further, the ideal viewing position was from the road at least several hundred yards from the tank. Participants did not have to leave the comfort and relative privacy of their vehicles. Because Fostoria has no public transportation, residents all either owned a vehicle or knew someone who did.

August is vacation time for many working people. School was still out for summer vacation. Fostoria in 1986 did not have cable television available, and at that time television networks showed only reruns in August. There were few sources of entertainment competing for the attention of the local residents. The image could be seen any time after dark, so that even those individuals with work demands could view it. No matter what shift an individual might work, there was a convenient time before or after work when the image would be visible. The weather had been hot and dry, creating beautiful warm summer nights. Most individuals could have a leisurely dinner with their family, relax for a couple of hours, and then drive out to the tank. Restaurants and local frozen custard stands experienced dramatic increases in their business during the event, suggesting that many participants made an evening out of the viewing.

Route 12 serves as the main artery through Fostoria. In order to travel west from Fostoria, drivers are forced to use Route 12. This meant that every single resident in the area knew where the site was and how to get there. Further, since it is a state route, Route 12 appears on Ohio and U.S. maps, and it is easily accessible from other state highways as well as a state turnpike. It was easy to find, easy to get to, and had plenty of room for thousands of people at once. What could possibly be more convenient than a miracle that can be viewed in the summer, on a major road, after dark, all night every night?

The location of the image is particularly important. Had the image of Jesus appeared on a lesser-known road, or in a less wide-open space, it is doubtful that out-of-town visitors and journalists would have been able to find it so easily. The drive-through nature of the event may be even more significant than the easy access, though. Similar images have appeared indoors, where participants must find a place to park, walk to the site, and then stand in line to view the image. None of these events have ever drawn anywhere near the number of participants as the Fostoria image.

Convenience can never be overlooked as a major factor in the success and duration of a collective behavior episode of any type, including those that are apparently tied to religious fervor. Only extremely devout participants will endure hardship and inconvenience to experience a divine event. Most people are not so dedicated. Those who are skeptical, who are curious about the image, or who merely want to see what all the excitement is all about have to decide to go where the image is. If the effort seems too great, they might engage in some other form of entertainment instead. Few are willing to walk long distances or stand for a long time just to satisfy their curiosity. If the image is not in a convenient location, only the most devout participate in the event. The Fostoria image was in an exceptionally convenient location.

Structural Strain

At first glance, Fostoria seems to be a peaceful and perhaps even idyllic town. Many out-of-town reporters called it a "village," implying a close-knit and old-fashioned community where everyone watches out for everyone else. Unfortunately, this quaint image of Fostoria was an illusion.

According to the local police department's own figures, Fostoria had an abnormally high crime rate. According to the chief of police in Fostoria, the per capita crime rate in 1986 was higher than for Toledo, a much larger city in the same region. Further, in the late summer of 1986 the entire country was experiencing a major economic recession. This recession hit blue-collar, working-class communities like Fostoria the hardest. Ohio had the highest rate of unemployment in the country, and Northwestern Ohio had the highest rate of unemployment in the state. To reporters from other parts of the country, Fostoria may have looked charming, but residents were in serious financial trouble. The crime rate, the unemployment rate, and the severe economic difficulties in the area created considerable stress for most residents.

In addition, there is also yearly conflict between the overwhelmingly white residents and the Hispanic migrant workers that corporate farmers bring into the area late every summer. Companies like Hunts and Heinz bring in hundreds of workers to harvest the tomatoes and cucumbers to be used for ketchup, pickles, and relish. Most of these workers originally come from Mexico, and the local residents perceive them to be illegal immigrants. Frequent bar fights, assaults, and acts of vandalism occur. Police and reporters in Fostoria note this tension and conflict was intensified in August of 1986 by the hard economic times. Local residents felt that "those people" were taking their jobs.

The major employer in the area, Ford Motor Company, had shut down an entire production plant that year. Many residents were suddenly laid off with no hopes of getting their jobs back. Even those who were lucky enough to hold onto their jobs with Ford had to drive over an hour to perform their old job at the nearest operating plant. They were leaving home an hour earlier each morning, getting back an hour later each night, buying far more gas than ever before, putting hundreds of miles per week on their cars and trucks, and still bringing home the same-size paycheck that they had previously received for working just down the road.

As if these problems were not enough, the weather had been hot and dry for weeks. As mentioned above, this created pleasant weather at night. Unfortunately, most of the homes in the Fostoria area were not air-conditioned in 1986. Residents told me that the heat itself became a source of irritation and strain during the day. They also stated that it contributed to their economic strain, as well. Many of the local residents depend on Hunts and Heinz for seasonal employment. Although the hot spell did not turn into a damaging drought, many shared realistic concerns in August that the commercial crops would be damaged or destroyed. This would have created even more financial loss for those employed by the commercial agricultural operations in the area, the largest remaining local employer after the closing of the Ford plant.

Generalized Belief

Looking back on the factors of conduciveness and strain that were present in the area at the time, it may seem almost inevitable for this event to have occurred. Indeed, the Value-added perspective suggests that such intense strain will inevitably to lead to some sort of collective behavior episode. The generalized belief determines what type of episode will occur, and what characteristics the event will adopt. In the case of Fostoria, there were really four variations of the same generalized belief. All of these variations were tied to the primary belief that an image that might look like Jesus had appeared just west of town.

Although virtually everyone believed that an image existed and an event was taking place, four distinctly different definitions of what that image meant were available. These four different definitions then led to different approaches to the event itself. Local residents can be divided into four categories determined by these beliefs: Devout Believers, Devout Skeptics, Doubting Participants, and Nonbelievers.

Devout Believers   Devout Believers were deeply religious and firmly believed that the image was a divine manifestation of Jesus Christ. As is common for these events, the participants often attributed specific meanings to the image. As Rita Ratchen, the first to witness the image, said, "It is caused by the lights and the rust, but I believe the Lord permitted it to happen. Just as I believe the Lord permits things to happen in our lives . . . in order to bring us closer together" (*Time* 9/29/86: 14). "He lives. He walks with us, we have not to fear" (*The Akron Beacon Journal* 8/21/86: A16).

Several participants offered similar definitions of the event. "I think it is Jesus," Dulcie Haycook told a reporter from the *Daily Sentinel Times,* "I think he's telling people the time is right [for the Day of Judgement]. I think it will make more people believe in him." Mecaela Garcia: "I see God—Jesus Christ is there! He has a little boy. He says something about children" (*Akron Beacon Journal* 8/21/86: A1). Bernadine Drool: "I think the Lord is trying to tell us something. He wants everybody to draw nearer to Him" (ibid). "He is letting us know . . . He is reality" (Jeff Hurlbut, *The Daily Chief-Union* 8/22/86: 1).

It is not unusual at these types of events for participants to state their generalized belief and to openly justify why they believe the image is divine. Fostoria is no exception to this pattern: "It's a miracle. Just look at the people. Everybody needs a miracle" (*Daily Sentinel Times* 8/28/86). When asked "why Fostoria?" by a reporter, one participant quipped, "Bethlehem was a small city, too" (*Daily Chief-Union*: 1).

Devout Skeptics   Devout Skeptics were deeply religious, believed in the possibility that the image was truly a miracle, but upon viewing the image they found themselves unconvinced. As one woman told a reporter, "Forget all the scientific stuff about explaining this. If you want to believe it's some kind of spiritual message, you can. If you want to believe it's just some freak of nature, you can believe that, too" (*The Daily Chief-Union* 8/22/86: 1).

Most of the devout skeptics were not willing to rule out the possibility that the image was divine, they simply weren't convinced beyond a shadow of a doubt. "If the Lord were doing something—that's a big if, O.K.?—the Lord would do it that way; naturally. It would get the people to come back to the faith" (John Broski, quoted in *Time* 9/29/86: 14). "I believe there is *something* there" (Tanya Walker, quoted in *Akron Beacon Journal* 8/21/86: A16).

Ironically, this category of participants often includes clergy. It is probably safe to assume that most clergy possess sufficient faith to believe that a miracle may occur. However, they often remain guarded and skeptical when asked to apply that faith to the door of an appliance, the side of an oil tank, or some other odd location:

Rev. Anthony Wade: "I did see what *appeared* to be Christ and a little child" (personal interview, emphasis added).

Rev. Thomas Hoppe: "The Lord says his word is enough, but people still want a verification of their faith" (*Review Times* 8/23/86: 1).

Rev. James Bacik: "People look for it in wild and crazy ways" (*Daily Sentinel Tribune* 8/22/86).

Doubting Participants   Religious images often draw those who can best be classified as Doubting Participants. They want to see the image itself. In this sense, they are participants rather than spectators. However, they lack the religious conviction to make a miracle seem likely. They do not talk about Jesus or God, but about the image itself. Prolonged media attention frequently brings out the doubting participants. "I heard so much about it," O. H. Hammer told a reporter, "It's been on Toledo TV" (*Beacon Journal* 8/21/86: A16). These participants are taking part in the primary activity of the event: viewing the image. However, most are doing so out of curiosity rather than faith. This category of participant is probably unique to religious-based events, particularly image events.

Nonbelievers   The Nonbelievers held the fourth variation of generalized belief in this particular event. These were the only local residents who completely avoided viewing the image. At first glance, it may appear that these people are simply nonparticipants. They seem to have an absence of generalized belief. However, these individuals actually had specific beliefs about the event: The image was not a miracle, the believers were fools, and the spectators were nosy. They all believed that the image existed, and possessed the ability to get to it, but chose not to. Although this may seem confusing to the reader, they chose not to view the image for the same reason that the other three categories of participants choose to view it: They held a specific belief about the image, and acted accordingly. As one unnamed ADM employee said, "It's just rust on the tank. You can make it be anything you want it to be" (*Daily Sentinel Times* 8/28/86).

These individuals did not simply fail to take part in the event, they actively avoided viewing the image at all costs. In a strange way, they were participants in their own, much smaller event which involved avoiding an area to which everyone else flocked.

In an event of this size in a community this small, it is not uncommon for there to be friction between the nonbelievers and other participants. According to sources interviewed, this was the case in Fostoria. When the fireman (a nonbeliever) destroyed the image, many townspeople demanded that he be fired, prosecuted, and forced to leave town. Nonbelievers argued that this was wildly inappropriate. A compromise was reached, in which he was placed on probation, sent home for a month, and convicted of a misdemeanor. Disagreement over these actions lingered for years after the event.

Mobilization of Participants

According to all sources, individuals strongly urged people to go to the site. Everyone I interviewed replied that it simply wasn't necessary, since the turnout was so massive and immediate.

Police and media accounts estimate attendance at roughly 2,000 vehicles per night, and point out that many contained three or more passengers. Using conservative figures based on a rate of 1,500 vehicles per night and two people per vehicle (figures which fall well below all estimates), at least 40,000 people drove past the tank within two weeks. This number is about three times the population of Fostoria in 1986 and would surely have been higher if the event had been allowed to continue until people lost interest. Attendance had yet to peak when the tank was defaced and could easily have topped 100,000.

The police officers in charge of crowd control throughout the entire episode told me that the crowds of participants and spectators represented all religious, ethnic, and gender percentages within the local population. Women were apparently slightly overrepresented during the daytime, but all sources agree that this can be traced to the large proportion of women not employed outside of the household at that time. Police and media sources reported vehicles with license plates from all over the United States, but most of the participants were from Ohio and nearby Indiana.

The biggest factor in mobilization of participants is probably the massive media coverage of the event. August of 1986 was a particularly slow time for news. There were no new wars, no political scandals, and no major catastrophes. For all of these reasons, *Time Magazine; USA Today,* local and regional newspapers, AP (Associated Press), UPI (United Press International), and Reuters wire services; and network television newscasts all gave the story an unusual amount of attention. All three network affiliate stations in Toledo and Cleveland ran multiple reports on the image.

The news director for a Cleveland network affiliate told me that there was "nothing even close to an important news story" that week. He treated the Fostoria image as a fallback story, and was glad to have something regional to fill the time. The *Time* story about the event refers sarcastically to the fact that there was a media "stampede" to Fostoria, caused by the lack of hard news events that August. The reporter apparently didn't consider himself a member of that stampede.

The actual behavior of the participants was fairly typical for an image event. Devout believers prayed, wept, and generally behaved as if in church or at a prayer meeting. Devout skeptics and the curious participants behaved as if they were at a formal event. Even those who merely wanted to see the crowds or the television crews behaved with decorum. There were no fights, no one turned up their radios loud enough to annoy others, and litter was minimal considering the number of people. The police described the atmosphere as being like that in a museum.

Social Control

The first reaction of the local authorities was to try to deter the event. Initially, the police asked ADM to paint over the image or to turn off the lights in order to eliminate the massive traffic jams that occurred nightly. Fearing negative publicity and a local backlash, the company refused. Bowing to the same pressures, the authorities also decided to accommodate the event. It was the relatively orderly nature of the crowds that led the town to decide that the event was essentially harmless. Their role became one of traffic control. Police and volunteers tried to keep vehicles moving at least a little, and would not allow people out of their vehicles unless they had pulled completely off the road. By making sure that everyone kept moving they not only accommodated the event, they enabled it. More people were able to view the image each night thanks to the efforts of the police. Local authorities viewed the entire event as benign, and local merchants saw it as a potential gold mine.

There was no private residential property on either side of the road, and the image was best viewed from a distance. These factors both made the potential harm of the event seem minimal, which in turn shaped authorities' perception of the event. The wide-open setting acted not only as a factor of structural conduciveness, but helped shape the reaction of social control agents as well.

Conclusion

When analyzing any event, the question that researchers ultimately have to answer is "Was this an episode of collective behavior?" This becomes trickier when we are looking at what many individuals believe is a divine event or religious miracle. For any image, miracle, or apparition that does not appear to have been an intentional hoax, there are two possible conclusions. Either it was a divine event, or an episode of collective behavior. If the image really was put there by the hand of God, then the beliefs and behavior of the participants were natural; they were showing proper deference to the manifestation of a deity. If the image appeared by coincidence, then people were praying to a rust stain in the middle of a barren field for no particular reason other than their own delusion.

We can never say with certainty that Jesus did not choose to appear on the side of a soybean oil storage tank in the form of rust and shadows. Some people are still convinced that the image in Fostoria was divine. Many more are still undecided or uncertain. However, if we look closely at the event, there are strong indicators that the "miracle" actually took place in the eyes and minds of the participants. The most striking of these is the fact that there were *no counter-interpretations of the image*. Participants all agreed that the image did look like a man with a beard: "I see His whole face. I see His mouth is open. I see His beard. He's got a big robe on" (Marge Parker, *Akron Beacon Journal* 8/21/86: A16). What is telling is that they then believed that the man with the beard must be Jesus Christ. No one believed that Santa Claus had appeared on the tank, no one argued that it looked like Jerry Garcia, and no one stated that it looked more like their grandfather than Jesus. In other words, they believed that any image of a bearded man that appears on its own *must* be Jesus. These types of belief remain firm even when mundane causes are discovered.

Participants knew all along that shadows and rust created the Fostoria image and welding repairs made to the tank earlier that summer caused the rust. In spite of the fact that the image was caused by human activity and natural corrosion, they still held onto the belief that the image was holy. The fact that no human had intentionally created the image filled their criterion of evidence that the image was divine in origin. This is one of the factors that make images slightly different than miracles or apparitions. Images act as a sort of inkblot association test for entire communities. Participants look at rust or chemical deposits but see a miracle.

The Fostoria image existed for at least a few weeks or months before anyone noticed it and attributed its appearance to Jesus. The rust was not brand-new, and the lights had been there as long as the tanks. Hundreds of cars drove past it every night, but it took Rita Ratchen to define it as a religious miracle. The next example that we are going to examine also existed for some time, within sight of a heavily traveled road, before it was defined as a divine image.

Although the details are different, the overall nature of the event is virtually identical to the Fostoria image. Just as the Fostoria image is a typical model for all image events, the participants in the Clearwater event can be used as a typical model for participants in such events. The Clearwater image has endured long enough for the distinctions between the different types of participants to be more obvious than they may be in shorter-lived image events. This makes the analysis both easier to perform and simpler to understand.

Our Lady of Clearwater: The Virgin Mary on a Bank

Clearwater, Florida, 1996 to 2001

On Tuesday, December 17, 1996, a customer of the Seminole Finance loan company saw something on a glass exterior wall that she had never noticed before. She called WTSP Channel 10, a local television station, to report that the image of the Virgin Mary had appeared on the side of the building. At noon, the station broadcast pictures of the rainbow-colored image throughout the area.

By midnight, 500 people had gathered in the parking lot of the building to look at the image, pray, and weep. Within days, the numbers had reached the thousands. Police estimate that there were 500,000 visitors (including repeat visitors) to the site within the first two months of its reported appearance. This is four times the population of the city of Clearwater.

Within weeks a shrine, complete with benches, a collection box, and a wooden kneeler, was erected in the parking lot. The fence erected around the property was decorated with silk flowers and photographs of families, loved ones, and pets. The parking lot itself was littered with votive candles, paper images of Jesus, poinsettias, rosaries, and trinkets. Police installed six portable bathrooms and placed officers in the parking lot to maintain order. They had to remove two individuals, a Baptist minister and a radio station employee, each of whom separately mocked the crowds. In both instances, the crowd reacted with hostility to the criticism. No such confrontations were reported after December 22, 1996.

The image itself faces northbound traffic. About twenty-five feet tall, it takes up an entire two-and-a-half-story wall. The rainbow-colored image is

A family gathers at the altar placed in the parking lot of a former finance company building in Clearwater, Florida. The rainbow colors on the glass wall are said by believers to resemble the Virgin Mary.

said to resemble the head and shoulders of a woman wearing a shroud. Although the "face" is a blank oval, the tilt of the "head" and the presence of the "shroud" all resemble popular depictions of the Virgin Mary. Though most believers claim that the image appeared sometime just after Thanksgiving of 1996, Florida Department of Transportation photographs reveal that the image existed and was clearly visible at least as early as 1994.

The building has stood just north of Drew Street on U.S. 19 since 1980 and is clearly visible from the road, a major four-lane route. According to the Florida Department of Transportation, approximately 65,000 to 75,000 cars travel past that intersection on U.S. 19 every day. U.S. 19 is the main artery for anyone traveling north or south of Clearwater.

The exterior walls of the building are constructed entirely of glass panels. Most of the panels have discolored, many with the rainbow colors of the Mary image. The south wall is the only such area on the building that resembles a holy figure, however.

Several different chemists and glass analysts have studied the discoloration of the glass and all agree that it is caused by the chemical reaction and corrosion of metallic elements in the glass coating. Water from lawn sprinklers corroded the glass, and the resulting discoloration creates a rainbow appearance. The discoloration is brightest when viewed in direct sunlight, but is clearly visible at night if there is sufficient light. Since the beginning of the episode, lights have been left on overnight to keep the image visible.

Unlike the Fostoria image, no one has destroyed or defaced the Clearwater image. The image and surrounding property have been turned into a shrine and an outdoor church. Security cameras were installed, and a fence has been erected around the image to prevent vandalism. Although it seems to have faded and changed colors somewhat since 1997, the image is still clearly visible. Glass experts believe that it will probably last for several more years.

The building itself has changed hands twice since 1996. The Ugly Duckling Corporation bought the building from the Seminole Finance Corporation in 1997. In July of 1998, a group from Ohio calling themselves the Shepherds of Christ Ministries leased the building. Although the Shepherds of Christ call themselves a Catholic ministry, the Catholic Diocese of St. Petersburg has no record of the group. The Shepherds are turning the building into a chapel, and hope to raise two million dollars to buy the building. They have converted the interior of the building into a gift shop and shrine, and they plan to remodel it into a cathedral. The portion of the parking lot facing the image contains neat rows of chairs, an altar, a public address system, and an information table where literature is passed out. Services are regularly held in the parking lot, with the Mary image as the focus of attention. They have officially named Her "Our Lady of Clearwater."

Further, the group includes a "Catholic visionary" named Rita Ring who is frequently visited by Mary and Jesus in her sleep. They provide her with messages on an almost daily basis, many of which are directly related to the image itself. Visitors to the site are given free books, pamphlets, cards, and audiocassette recordings. All of these materials relay the words of God, Jesus, and Mary as received by Rita.

Analysis

The Value-Added Theory

The episode surrounding to the Clearwater image is similar to the Fostoria event. An in-depth value-added analysis would be redundant. A quick run-through of the five determinants should be enough to demonstrate the striking similarities.

Structural Conduciveness

Like the Fostoria Jesus, the Clearwater Mary appeared in an area that is heavily Christian. At least 23 percent of Hillsborough county residents are over the age of fifty, based on U.S. Census data. Those who are retired have few competing demands for their time. Although not quite as easily viewed as the Fostoria image, Mary is still visible from the heavily traveled, well-known main route. For best viewing, participants must pull off the road into a parking lot, but may still choose to remain in their car if they prefer. Although the image actually existed for at least two years, the announced "appearance" occurred just before Christmas, when many people were on vacation and many schools closed for several days. Religious sentiment runs high as the holiday draws near. Participants could visit any time, day or night, and still view the image.

Structural Strain

The sources of strain are not the same as those in Fostoria in 1986, and are more difficult to pick out. Participants quoted in newspapers of the time tended to make vague references to the confusion and turmoil of modern life. One participant talked of having cancer, another of having lost custody of her son. Some of those quoted in the next section seem to be suffering personal hardships, some simply believe that "the End" is near. Several commentators have suggested that the looming of the year 2000 was a possible factor. Indeed, a widespread belief among many Christians was that January 1, 2000 would mark the beginning of the Judgement (Junod 1999).

Some specific events are cited as causing residents of the Florida Bay Area anxiety. First, ValueJet flight 592 crashed and sank into the Florida Everglades in May of 1996. There was extensive media coverage of the event, which claimed the lives of all 110 on board the plane. In fact, *Newsweek* dubbed 1996 "the year of fear" for travelers. Florida's economic reliance on tourism may have contributed to stress within the entire state.

The ValueJet crash may have created strain throughout the state of Florida, but residents in the Clearwater area expressed anxiety over riots that occurred that autumn. In October of 1996, a white police officer shot and killed a young black man. Rumors quickly spread that the killing was unjustified. Rioting occurred in St. Petersburg, which escalated to the extent that the National Guard was called in to restore order. Much more extensive rioting broke out again in November, when the grand jury exonerated the officer of all wrongdoing. Two police officers were shot, scores were injured, and initial estimates claimed at least five million dollars in property damage. This rioting was caused by the racial tension already present in the Clearwater/St. Petersburg area, and it dramatically magnified that tension. Area newspapers were full of articles about the riots, their effects, and the potential for future violence. Two weeks later, Mary was "discovered" on the Seminole building.

Most importantly, one source of strain in Clearwater in 1996 directly relates to religion. The Church of Scientology, led by L. Ron Hubbard, began purchasing millions of dollars of property in Clearwater in the early 1990s. The group moved their national headquarters from Dallas to Clearwater in 1994. Nobody seemed to notice until late 1995. That December, Lisa McPherson died of malnutrition and dehydration while under the care of Scientology "professionals." Her relatives accused the church of killing their daughter in order to keep her from leaving the group. This caused a huge scandal in the Clearwater area, and put the Church of Scientology on the news and in the papers for months to follow.

In April of 1996, stories in the *Tampa Tribune* stated how much property the Church of Scientology already owned in Clearwater (twenty-eight million dollars in property) and reported that the group had purchased three more motels. Stories were also reported about the legal battles between the city of Clearwater and the Church of Scientology. Many residents believed that the Scientologists were trying to take over the city government, and a Scientology magazine laid out plans to "clear" the entire world, starting with Clearwater. As these stories reached regional and national media, the entire country became aware that a battle was occurring in Clearwater.

Although Scientology focuses most of their attention on attacking therapists, psychologists, and psychiatrists, they are legally a tax-exempt religious organization and members do not attend any other religious services. To the older, religiously devout population of Clearwater, this dangerous "cult" represented a threat to their beliefs, their city, and their way of life. Letters to the editor of local newspapers and residents that I spoke to indicated that citizens of all denominations and beliefs were united in their fear and hatred of the Scientologists.

Generalized Belief

As is often true with these types of collective behavior episodes, the generalized belief is not as simple as "the Virgin Mary appeared on the side of a building in Clearwater." It is particularly important to remember that over two hundred people had been working in that building and they, along with any customer who parked in the lot, had seen the image every day for at more than two years. However, it was not until the anonymous woman first defined it as Mary that they began to see it as such. As Kam Garnes put it, after the customer pointed it out to them, "It was so obvious. I'd never seen it like that before" (*St. Petersburg Times* 12/18/96: 1B). As with the Fostoria image, a natural cause for the odd discoloration was easily discovered. And just like Fostoria, believers took this as an endorsement: "The culprit seems to be the sprinkler. The issue is, is the culprit that good an artist, or did it have any [divine] help?" (Michael Krizmanich, owner of the building, *St. Petersburg Times* 12/20/96: 1B).

As with the Fostoria image, some initial disagreement took place as to what the image actually meant (all quotes from the *St. Petersburg Times* 12/18/96: 1B):

Gloria LaRosa: "She's come to tell everyone to pray. That's all she asks of people is to pray."

Dick Oliver: "I think it's the face of Jesus. There are too many non-believers, and he's a little mad about that."

Kam Garnes: [It is a reminder] " . . . that there are bigger and better things beyond us."

Mary Stewart: "I believe it is here to get people's attention that we are living in the last days . . . to get ready to meet the soon-coming king."

Annette Mullin: "It shows you how close we really are to seeing Jesus."

Anna Burkett: "I know [her recently deceased 12-year-old grandson] is up There now."

Over the first few days of an image event, the competing interpretations get blended together and those that don't fit (such as the idea that this particular image is Jesus, not Mary) are rejected. Within a week or two, there is much more agreement among participants. In the case of the Clearwater Mary image, one particular group of believers has leased the building and therefore leased the image itself. This allows the Shepherds of Christ Ministries to control the event and enforce their own specific interpretation of the image's meaning.

Mobilization of Participants

Media obviously contributed to the massive mobilization of participants in the Clearwater event. Local television, radio, and newspapers all ran stories on what was thought at the time to be the "sudden" appearance of the image. All of these stories mentioned the location, and often included directions or a map. The story may have received wider exposure because it was so close to

Christmas. Many news sources emphasize religious stories during the holiday season. Joe Mannion, a spokesman for the Catholic Diocese of St. Petersburg, said the event suggested "the power of television" more than the power of religion (*St. Petersburg Times* 12/19/96: 1A).

Like Fostoria, most residents in Clearwater also had easy access to transportation. U.S. 19 is an extremely well-known and heavily traveled highway that cuts through much of the state of Florida. As a result, virtually everyone within range of the radio and television stations knew how to get to the image. As one participant put it, "What's remarkable is that this came to a place where you can get so much access to it" (*St. Petersburg Times* 12/20/96: 1B). It probably never occurred to her that similar images were languishing in much less convenient locations, and that this particular episode might never have happened if the image had appeared somewhere more obscure.

Social Control

As in the Fostoria event, the official reaction of the police was traffic and crowd control, with an emphasis on the safety of the participants. Just like Fostoria, the Clearwater police made an initial effort to deter the event, and when unsuccessful they simply accommodated it. They focused on maintaining traffic flow as much as possible on U.S. 19, and on pedestrian safety. Officers were posted in the parking lot around the clock during the attendance peak of the event, which lasted about two months.

Although the image in Clearwater is still clearly visible and individuals still trickle in to view it, the episode is essentially over. Visitors dwindled from the thousands to virtually nothing. Crowds are now so small that no formal social control is necessary.

Classification of Crowd Participants

If Smelser's Value-Added Theory best describes the conditions necessary for collective behavior to occur, then perhaps Turner and Killian's Emergent Norm Theory best illustrates the attitude and motivations of the individuals participating in collective behavior. As we discussed in earlier chapters, Turner and Killian's typology for participants can be used to classify all of the variations of behavior associated with an episode of collective behavior. The five categories of participants are labeled Ego-Involved, Concerned, Insecure, Curious Spectators, and Exploiters.

Ego-Involved

The ego-involved participant feels a strong personal commitment to the event. In an image event such as the Clearwater Mary, the ego-involved participants are the devout believers. They are the first to initiate pilgrimage behavior, and may be most active in organizing other participants. This category would include those who first declared the image to be that of Mary, and anyone who genuinely believed that the image could work miracles. Carmen Albuerne of Sarasota, who brought her daughter, Elena Plavko, twenty-six, who had been undergoing treatment for cancer since August, told a reporter "If this is a miracle, I expect to have a miracle, too" (*St. Petersburg Times* 12/19/96: 1A). She was staunch in her belief that Mary would cure her daughter. Isabelle Perri of Tampa led the crowd in prayer on Wednesday, December 18, then shouted the Hail Mary over the noise of news helicopters and urged the crowd to fight abortion. Richard Levin, who was Jewish, talked of looking into the sun and seeing the gates of heaven with Mary waving them inside. "This makes a believer of me, I believe this is a miracle" (*St. Petersburg Times* 12/19/96: 1A). Rose Giamburro also saw Mary, Jesus, and the gates of Heaven in Polaroid photos of the sun that she took in the parking lot. "I have such faith in the Blessed Mother," she said, "The Blessed Mother watches over me" (*St. Petersburg Times* 12/19/96: 1A). "You can feel the power" (Teresa Huffman, ibid). "I stepped out of my car and the presence of God just almost drew me to my knees" (Mary Stewart, pastor of the Campaigning for Jesus Christian Center in Tampa, *St. Petersburg Times* 12/18/96: 1B). "It's real" (Paul Rush, pastor of the Shepherds of Christ Ministries, *St. Petersburg Times* 7/8/98: 1). All of these individuals are ego-involved. They experience the image as real and the episode as emotionally moving.

Perhaps the best examples of ego-involved, devout believers would be Paul Rush (quoted above) and Rita Ring. Rita, who lives in Ohio, is the "visionary" who receives frequent messages from Mary, Jesus, and God. Paul, who moved to Florida when he read about the image's appearance, is the organizational leader of the activities in Clearwater. After most of the other participants have forgotten about the image, Rita is still channeling messages pertaining to it, and Paul is still spending his days providing visitors with information and materials. They have literally shaped their lives around the image.

Concerned

The concerned participant has a more general interest in the event. These may include friends or companions of the ego-involved. The concerned also include those who are personally touched by the image but do not feel compelled to take action other than viewing it themselves. The concerned are unlikely to lead others, but are likely to follow the lead of others. This would include devout skeptics and curious participants: those who want to view the image, but somehow fail to make the leap of faith to become devout believers.

These individuals do have a religious experience in the sense that the image makes them feel more connected to their faith. However, they are not compelled to become an active part of the event in the way that the ego-involved are. "I believe that it is a natural phenomenon, but the message is there just the same: peace, good will" (Geraldine Soboleski, *St. Petersburg Times* 12/20/96: 1B).

Church officials often occupy the role of concerned, rather than ego-involved. The Catholic Diocese of St. Petersburg urged caution and skepticism and never officially sanctioned the image as divine. They also never officially condemned it. The official reaction of religious leaders to images is often one of cautious disbelief, accompanied by the attitude that the event will probably do no harm and may bring some participants closer to God.

Insecure

In any collective behavior episode there are some participants who simply want to belong to any group that will provide them with a sense of purpose or importance. They might not understand what the group is actually hoping to achieve or why they are engaging in a particular behavior. Taking part in an episode of collective behavior gives them a sense of direction and identity. They achieve a sense of importance because they are involved in something bigger than themselves.

Religious episodes such as image events probably magnify this appeal. They make it possible for an individual to seem to be in the presence of a holy figure. These individuals do not believe that the image is real, they believe that others believe it is real. Like the college student who takes part in a protest march in order to feel "in," these individuals miss the whole point of the event. It is the crowd that draws them, not the image itself.

Unfortunately we can't readily identify these participants unless they are open and honest about their motivation for participation. If they claim to see visions (like Richard Levin and Rose Giamburro) but do not actually believe what they are saying, then they are insecure while appearing to be ego-involved. It is more likely that an insecure participant will attempt to "blend in" with true believers rather than seek publicity or attention. They are often much more in touch with the behavior of the crowd than they are with the generalized belief held by the ego-involved and concerned.

Spectators

Curious spectators want to watch the crowds and are not interested in the image itself. They focus on the other participants. The curious spectators don't want to see an image of Jesus or Mary; they want to see the people who do. They want to see the reporters and cameras. They want to be able to tell their friends what the event was like. The image is only of minor, secondary concern.

Media attention dramatically increases the number of spectators at any event. In Clearwater, many spectators simply drove slowly by the parking lot, taking a quick look at the crowd gathered there. Others parked their cars and stood on the fringes, watching. These individuals focused their attention on the reporters, photographers, and participants. Participants, by contrast, focus their attention on the image itself, and may seem oblivious to the activity around them. Spectators quickly tire of an event, and their numbers diminish rapidly after the first few days of an image episode.

Exploiters

Ego-detached exploiters do not care about the event itself, nor are they interested in the participants. They wish to exploit the event for their own personal gain. In religious image episodes there are frequently individuals selling items such as T-shirts, mugs, photographs, and so on. These individuals have no emotional involvement with the event or with other participants and are only interested in making a profit.

Although they might not be happy about being labeled as such, reporters, correspondents, and professional photographers who congregate at a religious image are also ego-detached exploiters. They are not there because they accept the generalized belief, and they do not undergo personal religious experiences. Instead, they use the event as a means of furthering their own careers, boosting ratings for their channel or station, or making money. A local radio station employee who dressed as Santa and carried a derogatory sign about the Virgin Mary on December 19, 1996, was most likely motivated by the possibility of gaining publicity. This would classify him as an exploiter.

Any researchers on the scene (including myself) could also be classified as ego-detached. A researcher whose primary interest is in furthering his or her own personal goals by observing and recording the behavior of participants is using the event to profit. The "profit" might be in the form of scientific knowledge and understanding, but it is profit nonetheless. They are not there to witness a miraculous image, but to study an episode of collective behavior.

The most obvious ego-detached exploiters are the actual vendors who sell mementos at image events. At both Fostoria and Clearwater, individuals set up booths selling mugs, T-shirts, and cheap religious paraphernalia within thirty-six hours of the first public announcement of the images' appearance. Their numbers were dramatically larger in Clearwater than in Fostoria, and more participants and observers openly labeled them as mercenary.

By December 20, 1996, police announced that they would prohibit anyone from selling T-shirts, photographs, or religious mementos without proper permits and permission from property owners. In early January of 1997, the city of Clearwater stopped distributing temporary vendor permits to those selling items at the site of the image. They cited traffic tie-ups and concerns about the safety of those who might wander into traffic to buy the trinkets.

This made it illegal to sell items at or near the site of the image and effectively ended participation by those exploiters selling merchandise.

Although Paul Rush seems quite sincere in personal interviews, it cannot be left unsaid that if he or Ms. Ring were not devout believers, they would be classified as exploiters. Rita has essentially become the spiritual leader of a rapidly growing organization. Her words are taken as divine. Short of subjecting her to interrogation, a polygraph, and psychological analysis, there is no certain way to ascertain her sincerity. A cynical observer could easily argue that she is simply using the image to bolster her own credibility among believers. She now occupies a position of great power and respect within the Shepherds of Christ organization. Her words are published in books, pamphlets, and cassette recordings.

Similarly, Mr. Rush states that he was hoping for a little spiritual uplift, and ". . . ended up getting a full-time job out of it" (personal interview, author's notes). He seems completely sincere and devout. However, if he were cynically using the image as an excuse to move to Florida (which he states he was looking for a reason to do) and to acquire a comfortable and enjoyable job, he would clearly be an exploiter. There is no evidence to indicate that Mr. Rush and Ms. Ring are not devout believers, but the possibility exists that anyone occupying their positions may use those roles for personal gain.

It is not the behavior of participants that marks them as ego-involved or exploiters; it is their motivation that matters. Their acceptance or rejection of the generalized belief is crucial to making the distinction. If an individual claims to accept the belief that the image is divine, there is no way to determine whether they are being honest and truthful. Although an ego-involved participant might personally gain from his or her participation, and exploiter *only* takes part for the sake of such gain. Exploiters use the event to further a personal agenda. They remain ego-detached, cynical, and aloof from the events around them.

Conclusion

Like most religious image episodes, Our Lady of Clearwater shows evidence of participation by all five of Turner and Killian's categories. What makes this particular image so fascinating is the timing of the event. It is a photographically documented and irrefutable fact that the image was present in its current form for at least two years before anyone interpreted it as divine. Further, it still remains today, years after the event peaked in participation and dwindled down to virtually nothing. The episode began long after the image appeared, and ended long before the image disappeared. This makes it possible for us to look at the social forces that work to create and end such an event.

Discussion

The Fostoria Jesus and Clearwater Mary events are typical exemplars of religious image events in general. There is nothing peculiar or unique about the Fostoria or Clearwater images other than the large number of participants and the amount of media attention that they attracted.

What principles can one derive from these case histories? Two general points should be noted. When looking at the determinants of structural conduciveness and strain, it seems reasonable to conclude that these conditions are often present throughout the United States. Thus, the likelihood of such events is fairly high. Indeed, such events do tend to occur fairly often, and are large enough to attract regional media attention at least several times every year.

Given the prevalence of structural conduciveness for such events and the frequent presence of structural strain in our society, the determinant of generalized belief becomes extremely important. This sort of image is reported fairly often, but only occasionally does the belief of a small group of individuals become generalized outside of their own social circle. In Fostoria a small network of friends initially shared the belief but all sources agree that within the first days of the mass pilgrimage, believers represented most of the Christian denominations. Likewise, Clearwater was never specific to any one denomination. There are some Christian denominations that do not believe that Mary is a divine figure, and they generally refused to accept the generalized belief. They represent the minority of Christians in many parts of the United States. Both of these images appeared in secular, mundane locations. This provided them with a more broad-based appeal than one that occurs in a particular church or other religious location.

Participants in the images, miracles, and apparitions that I have been able to find information about all attribute the episode to helpful figures who bring advice and good fortune or, at worst, scary but ultimately helpful warnings. There are almost always what Smelser labels wish-fulfillment beliefs attributed to the image events.

Many outsiders tend to point to the people in these events as some sort of overzealous fanatics. However, the frequent occurrence of such image events and the large number of participants from all over the country tend to contradict this assumption. Likewise, it can never be proven that the images are not divine, a fact that many believers like to point out. The reader should also remember to distinguish images from apparitions, in which religious zealotry plays a much stronger role.

Images as a form of collective behavior, although fairly common, have been virtually ignored by sociological researchers. Smelser's model provides a framework with which past episodes can be understood, and future ones may be anticipated. Turner and Killian's schema allows us to separate and distinguish the different participants in terms of their motives, beliefs, and behavior. Together, they provide us with a complete model of religious image events. As you read this, someone somewhere is praying to a stain or mark on a tree, a door, a table, etc. When sufficient structural conduciveness and strain coincide with the right generalized beliefs and mobilization factors, the tiny event becomes a major episode of collective behavior.

Chapter 10 looks at persistent rumors. Turner and Killian's Emergent Norm Perspective will be applied to a particularly durable (and unfounded) rumor. This will allow the reader to see how explanations other than the Value-Added Theory may be applied to a particular episode of collective behavior.

Chapter 10

Rumors, Urban Myths, and Urban Legends: Procter & Gamble, the Devil, and Amway

As discussed in Chapter 7, a *rumor* is unconfirmed information that is often passed through informal social communication. The person who hears it cannot or does not verify the information. It may be quite simple to find out if a rumor is true or false, but most who hear the rumor don't bother to do so. A person hears or reads a rumor and accepts it as factual without any further investigation. They believe the rumor is true and repeat it to others. Some rumors eventually turn out to be true, but most are false.

Rumors tell us something about the people who tell rumors and about those who believe them. *Tellers* consider the information important or interesting and feel a need to pass the rumor on to others. Tellers do not always believe the rumors are true. In fact, research seems to indicate that social outsiders repeat rumors when they are in an awkward social situation (Koenig 1985). They tell the rumor to gain attention, to gain status, or simply to provide some entertainment and excitement.

Believers consider the information plausible and accept it as fact. People accept rumors that fit their world view and reject those that do not. We tend to decide whether or not we believe a rumor based on our own beliefs, knowledge, and any existing information that we may have about the subject. Rumors are accepted as fact when they confirm what is already believed on some level.

There is something about popular rumors that appeals to people, and looking at which rumors spread gives us clues about the beliefs, hopes, fears, etc., of the people who spread and believe them. People do not repeat a rumor that is boring, so we know that the tellers find something interesting about the rumor that they pass along to others. Likewise, people do not believe rumors that go against ideas and beliefs that are important to them, so we indirectly learn what believers think about the world from the rumors that they accept as true.

Enduring Rumors: Urban Myths and Urban Legends

Some rumors get passed around for so long that hundreds or even thousands of people accept them as fact. These persistent, enduring rumors can be called *urban myths* or *urban legends*. The Urban Legends Resource Centre defines an urban legend as

> a story that has had a wide audience, is circulated spontaneously, has been told in several forms, and which many have chosen to believe (whether actively or passively) despite the lack of actual evidence to substantiate the story (Wells 2000).

There are several websites on the internet devoted exclusively to debunking urban legends that have been reported as fact by some "reliable" source. Urban myths and legends are sometimes reported in newspapers and on radio or television newscasts as if they were true.

Urban legends are told in the form of a story. They give specific details about an event that has supposedly occurred. For example, there is a legend about a man who wakes up in a bathtub full of ice. He finds a note left by the attractive woman he met at a party or bar the night before. She has purportedly stolen his kidney, and the note says "dial 911 or you will die." This urban legend gives specific details (that may change every time the story is told) about a particular event that is alleged to have occurred.

Urban myths do not recount a specific event. Instead, they give general information pertaining to a specific "fact." They outline something that is either supposed to be happening over and over, or something "unknown" about some person or group of people. For example, the rumor that a tooth left in a glass of cola will dissolve overnight is an urban myth. It persistently spreads throughout American society, is believed by thousands of people, and is simply not true. Unlike a legend, however, it does not recount the actions of any people. Instead of recounting an event, a myth supposedly reveals a "truth."

Urban myths and urban legends often support each other. The biggest difference lies in whether a person believes that something is true (a myth) or they believe that a specific, detailed incident took place (a legend). Though slightly different in format, urban myths and urban legends are both forms of persistent, enduring rumors.

Examples of Urban Myths

One example of a persistent rumor that has grown into a myth claims that a vast web of organized "Satanic cults" abduct and sacrifice thousands of babies and young children every year in the United States. Thousands of fundamentalist Christians believe this myth. Numerous books and websites "reveal" the horrific statistics. There is only one problem: It isn't true. The FBI (Federal Bureau of Investigations) classifies it as an unfounded, untrue story.

The FBI spent years investigating these allegations and never found one single case of a child abducted or killed by members of any organized satanic cult. Perhaps most telling of all, the number of children supposedly abducted and killed by these cults every year is significantly higher than the total number of children reported missing (Wells 2000). Despite this, many still believe in an "organized network of Satanic cults" and their "sacrifices."

Who would persistently believe this rumor even after legitimate authorities spent years seriously investigating it and found it to be unfounded? There are certain related "facts" that a person must believe in order to accept this rumor. A person must believe that large numbers of people in the United States worship Satan. The person must believe that satanic cult members kill young children and babies. The person must believe that thousands of children go missing every year and vanish without a trace. The person must believe that society has become so decadent, evil, or chaotic that effective law enforcement is virtually impossible. The individual must believe that mainstream popular media sources are covering up the stories of these families and the disappearances. Finally, the individual must believe that law enforcement officials at the state and federal levels are either corrupt, too inept to uncover the baby killers, or covering up the "truth" for some reason.

Another example of an enduring rumor that has achieved urban myth status is being spread almost entirely by e-mail. The message claims that feminine hygiene pads and tampons contain asbestos. The message alleges that manufacturers know that the asbestos makes women bleed more during their period; therefore, the asbestos is used to increase the sale of the products. Further, the message asserts that the U.S. FDA (Food and Drug Administration) and the manufacturers know that this causes cervical cancer and "womb tumors," but they don't care because "the powers that be" don't consider the products worth regulating because they are not ingested orally.

This myth is also absolutely false. The FDA has received so many calls about the story that their webpage (www.fda.gov) contains a detailed explanation and denial. Asbestos is not a component, trace or otherwise, in any feminine hygiene product. It is illegal to include it in any such product. Further, neither the FDA nor the makers of feminine hygiene products are willing to allow women to be subjected to carcinogenic ingredients that will make them bleed. If such a story were true, major corporations would be liable to massive lawsuits that would quickly bankrupt them.

So why would someone spread this story if it is obviously not true? The anonymous version of the e-mail that I received contained specific information on how to order "cotton tampon alternatives," including 1-800 telephone numbers for Organic Essentials and Terra Femme, as well as "catalog sales" internet addresses for GreenMarketplace.com and Botanical.com (authors' files). Neither Organic Essentials, Terra Femme, nor GreenMarketplace.com claim that tampons and feminine pads are toxic. However, the webpage for Botanical.com (which is a "news" site, not a catalog sales address) does contain an article about asbestos and other toxic ingredients in tampons and pads (www.botanical.com, 9/27/00). In the article, the operators of the site claim to have spoken to someone at Johnson & Johnson and the FDA. Although the story notes that both sources denied the story, it then goes on to argue that neither source is reliable, and provides information about using organic cotton pads and tampons.

The e-mail message also included specific instructions like "buy and use only organic cotton pads and tampons," and phrases such as "we are being manipulated by this industry and the government." It is currently impossible to determine if this myth is being perpetuated by someone who works for or runs the companies that make or sell the alternative products. No one at the companies I called was willing to admit starting the rumor. However, it is a distinct possibility that someone who sells the organic products is using the myth to promote sales of these company's own products. Competitors often turn out to be the sources of negative rumors related to businesses (Keonig 1985).

In order to believe this myth about feminine hygiene products, a person must believe that the federal government and hygiene industry do not care about women, are willing to intentionally kill their own customers, and that lawmakers are so inept or corrupt that they are unwilling to do anything about it. Many urban myths related to "dangerous" products rely on similar beliefs.

Examples of Urban Legends

Urban legends, though more specific in detail than urban myths, can endure just as long. For decades, many people in the United States have believed that a teenaged babysitter on drugs actually roasted an infant. The legend, as it is usually told, says that a "hippie girl" showed up at the parents' home acting a bit spacey. The parents, while out to dinner, called home to make sure everything was okay. The girl answered that "everything is fine and the turkey will be ready soon." When they returned to their house, they found that the babysitter, in a drug-induced state, mistook the baby for a turkey and roasted the infant in the oven. You may have heard this story at least once. It apparently started in the early 1970s, but it is often told as if it took place within the last few years (Brunvand 1981, Wells 2000).

In order to believe this legend, people must also believe several things. They must believe that "hippies" are untrustworthy, that drugs are dangerous, that society is changing in bad ways, and that young people are "different" from themselves. They have to believe that drugs could make it possible for someone to confuse a live infant with a frozen turkey. The story, like most urban legends, carries moral lessons: Don't take drugs, don't trust hippies, and don't trust teenagers. Some might also add "and don't go out to dinner when you should be at home taking care of your own children."

Another example: Authorities discovered the charred remains of a scuba diver in a tree in the middle of a burned-out forest fire. The deceased was wearing a full wetsuit, scuba tank, snorkel, and so on. An autopsy revealed that the man did not burn to death, but died of massive internal injuries. Authorities were able to identify the body through dental records. They discovered that he had been scuba diving off the coast of California (or France, depending on which version one hears) over twenty miles away. Authorities then realized what happened: a fire-fighting helicopter carrying a giant bucket scooped up the diver, along with plenty of water, and dumped him over the raging flames. Sound familiar?

Like the babysitter tale, this legend is totally false. No scuba-diver's body has ever been found in the middle of a charred forest in California or France, or anywhere else. Fire-fighting helicopters do not drop their buckets into the ocean, nor do they scoop up water in areas where people are swimming, diving, or boating. No person has ever been accidentally picked up by a helicopter with a bucket attached to it. Still, the story has been revived several times since it first appeared in the late 1980s (www.snopes.com 9/17/2000, Brunvand 1989).

The remainder of this chapter is dedicated to examining a specific example of a persistent rumor about a major corporation and its alleged ties to the Church of Satan. It is probably the longest-lasting, most publicized, and most expensive rumor in recent American history. The event will be described and then analyzed utilizing Turner and Killian's Emergent Norm Perspective.

Procter & Gamble, the Devil, and Amway

The Birth of a Rumor

In 1980, Procter & Gamble began to receive phone calls and letters from Minnesota about the company's ties to satanic causes. The company was able to trace this rumor to three sources. Paul Martin, director of the high school club division of a Youth for Christ Office in Willmar, Minnesota, claimed that the Procter & Gamble logo could be found on a "Satanic church" in St. Paul. The "Satanic church" was actually a bookstore, and the logo above their door was a simple crescent moon, not the elaborate man-in-the-moon and stars of the Procter & Gamble logo. The second source was Jim Peters, a St. Paul fun-

The rumors about Procter & Gamble and the Church of Satan all began because someone claimed that the company's Man in the Moon logo contained satanic elements.

damentalist Christian crusader against rock music. Peters claimed that the company logo appeared in a book called *Amulets and Superstitions* (Budge 1978). It does not. Both men admitted to making these allegations, and backed down when confronted by representatives from Procter & Gamble. A Minnesota minister named Wynn Worley admitted telling people that the Procter & Gamble logo symbolizes witchcraft. He maintained his belief despite denials from Procter & Gamble (Koenig 1985).

The Rumor Grows

Once the connection between the Church of Satan and Procter & Gamble was made in peoples' minds, word began to spread. The rumor was fully formed into an urban legend by October of 1981. A story spread amongst fundamentalist Christians throughout the Midwest that "the owner of Procter & Gamble" appeared on *The Phil Donahue Show* and admitted giving 20 percent of the corporation's profit to the Church of Satan (Asher 1999, Drought 1999, Koenig 1985). Some versions of the rumor added the fact that he admitted making a pact with Satan and gave all credit for his success to the Devil (Koenig 1985). In fact, Durk Jager, the CEO of Procter & Gamble from 1970 until July of 2000, had *never* been a guest on *any* television show prior to October of 1981 (Koenig 1985).

Even those who believe that Satan exists and that He makes pacts with businessmen should have found the story difficult to believe because the same exact rumor had circulated in 1977, with Ray Kroc of McDonald's as the villain. Kroc was alleged to have appeared either on *The Tonight Show with Johnny Carson, 60 Minutes, 20/20, Phil Donahue, Merv Griffin, Tom Snyder,* or *The Today Show* (depending on who you asked) and announced that he was giving 35 percent of his earnings to the Church of Satan. Most of those who claimed to have seen the show themselves backed down when confronted by company representatives. However, many who admitted that they did not see it still believed that it had actually occurred. The rumor only died when it was replaced by the worm contamination rumor discussed in Chapter 7 (Koenig 1985).

By 1982, the Procter & Gamble rumor was spreading throughout the southern United States. Like the McDonald's–Satan rumor, it was spread primarily by clergymen who did not bother trying to confirm the rumor before spreading it. Church newsletters all over the country called for parishioners to boycott Procter & Gamble. Around that time, reports also began to claim that "666" ("the mark of the Beast," a sign that something is of or for Satan) could be found in two places within the company logo. Procter & Gamble began to receive five hundred inquiries per day, forcing them to hire four employees just to deal with the letters and phone calls (Koenig 1985).

Because the primary source of the false information was fundamentalist Christian newsletters and clergy, nationally known fundamentalist ministers Jerry Falwell, Billy Graham, and Donald Wildman were enlisted to help fight the false rumor. They distributed letters and other materials to their followers, members of the Moral Majority, and others, categorically denying any link between Procter & Gamble and the Church of Satan. Ann Landers and "Dear Abby" both ran letters about the rumor with strong responses, calling the rumors ridiculous. *Christianity Today* ran a story about the rumor, disclaiming it. Each of these sources not only explained that the rumor was false, but also chastised people for spreading unfounded rumors in the first place (Koenig 1985).

On July 1, 1982, Procter & Gamble held a press conference and announced that they would pursue lawsuits against anyone intentionally spreading the rumor. By the spring of 1982, calls about the rumor to the company had dropped to a couple hundred a month. However, the rumor resurfaced again in 1984. Procter & Gamble received three thousand calls in the month of October alone. This time, the rumor seemed to be spread primarily through Catholic, rather than fundamentalist, networks. Further, the rumor picked up a new detail: Reports now claimed that "the head of Procter and Gamble" stated on television that "there aren't enough Christians left for me to worry about a boycott" (Koenig 1985).

As a result of the ongoing nuisance and expense dealing with the rumor, Procter & Gamble pulled the logo off of all their retail products. The logo remains on the company stationary, but it can no longer be found on store shelves (Asher 1999, Koenig 1985).

Charismatic Capitalism and Corporate Competition

The dramatic rise, spread, and revival of the Church of Satan story alone would make the persistent Procter & Gamble rumor a fascinating case study. However, the saga continues and there is another twist: Procter & Gamble traced the resurgence of the rumor throughout the 1990s to several Amway distributors (Asher 1999, Neff 1995, Staff 1990). Amway is a direct-marketing company that manufactures and sells many products that compete directly with Procter & Gamble: soaps, shampoos, detergents, and so on. Amway bills itself as a Christian-based company with a "mission to do good" that offers not just a job but a lifestyle. The company emphasizes a powerful sense of renewal, purpose, and fellowship. They call this approach, which supposedly emphasizes humans over profit, "charismatic capitalism" (Anderson 1993).

Many Amway distributors work by selling to or recruiting salespeople within their workplace. Distributors often make more money signing up new salespeople than from selling the products themselves. They also focus specifically on church congregations. In fact, in 1994 the Reverend Tom Logan, of Abbotsford Parish, in Clydebank, Scotland, resigned his ministry when ordered by his superiors in the Dumbarton Presbytery to stop trying to sell to his parishioners, several of whom had complained (Drought 1999).

In 1990, Procter & Gamble filed a lawsuit again James and Linda Newton of Parsons, Kansas, for promoting the Church of Satan rumor in order to boost their own sales of Amway products (Staff 1990). The couple circulated a flyer repeating the rumor and offering information about "alternative [Amway] products." Eventually, the Amway Corporation was added to the lawsuits. Procter & Gamble alleged that the large number of distributors circulating the rumor were actually following suggestions from corporate management to encourage boycotts of Procter & Gamble products (Asher 1999, Neff 1995, Staff 1990).

Amway, which has never denied that the distributors spread the rumor but claims that the company tried to keep it from happening, also had other legal problems. They were sued in 1996 by eleven major record labels for copyright infringement (Horak 1996), and the company was convicted of defrauding the Canadian government out of millions of dollars in customs fees (Schmertz and Meier 2000). However, the Procter & Gamble lawsuits against Amway were dismissed for lack of evidence. Procter & Gamble attorneys were able to prove that several Amway distributors were responsible for spreading the rumor, but they could not prove that the company endorsed the technique nor that they intended malice (Olgeirson 1999, Staff 1999, Tedford 1999).

There are still thousands of people who believe that Procter & Gamble gives money to satanic causes. One of my own students recently insisted that he, himself, had seen "the head executives from Procter & Gamble" announce on Oprah Winfrey's talk show that "they belong to a coven of witches and give all their money to satanic causes." The next time that student came to class, he insisted that it was his wife who told him *she* had seen the show. A week later, he said that his wife's sister told her about it, and he acknowledged that it might not be true. (No one from Procter & Gamble has ever appeared on *Oprah*.) Why does this rumor linger? Why do so many people believe the bizarre story when they hear it? Even if Amway did intentionally boost the rumor, it had spread like wildfire throughout the United States at least twice without any intentional assistance. Perhaps the Emergent Norm perspective can shed some light on the phenomenon.

Analysis

The Emergent Norm Perspective

Turner and Killian's Emergent Norm Perspective, discussed in Chapter 3, argues that collective behavior occurs when people conform to new, emerging norms within an unusual situation. The theory enables a researcher to understand why people might engage in behavior that seems odd or unusual. Collective behavior participants follow situational norms that may be totally at odds with those of the dominant culture.

As the reader will see, the Emergent Norm Perspective does not apply to a diffuse situation like a persistent rumor as easily as crowds of people who gather in the same place and time. Chapter 11 will apply the same theory to more traditional crowd behavior.

Tuner and Killian argue that the factors leading to any type of collective behavior are Uncertainty, Urgency, Communication of Mood and Imagery, Constraint, Selective Individual Suggestibility, and Permissiveness. This analysis begins with *uncertainty*.

Uncertainty

The key to the Emergent Norm Perspective is confusion or *uncertainty*. Confusion creates doubt, and doubt makes people likely to follow others who seem to know what to do. In the case of a rumor, the uncertainty has to do with the truth of the rumor itself. A person hears new information, and is uncertain as to whether or not it is true. Many people in this situation ask someone they know and trust if they have heard the rumor, not necessarily asking if it is true (Koenig 1985). This act effectively spreads the rumor. Many people, uncertain as to whether or not the Procter & Gamble rumor might be true, also told other people about it "just in case it were true" (Koenig 1985). In other words, even if they weren't certain that the rumor was true, they told other people about it both to restore their sense of security and to find out what other, trusted people thought of the rumor.

Gordon Allport and Postman (1946) call the people who care about a rumor, both tellers and believers, a "rumor public." Members of the rumor public are unsure about something, and the rumor seems to give them some concrete information. However, most of the people who spread the rumor about Procter & Gamble and the Church of Satan did *not* seem uncertain at all. Early tellers like Paul Martin, Jim Peters, and Wynn Worley were all quite certain that they were correct (Koenig 1985). Even when confronted by representatives from Procter & Gamble, Worley stood by his belief that the logo was indeed satanic in nature. Those who spread the fully-formed version of the rumor also seemed to be quite certain that the information was true. At first glance the Emergent Norm perspective does not seem to account for this apparent certainty.

However, as Koenig (1985) suggests, the uncertainty may lie between those who believe the rumor and their relationship with the rest of society. Most of those doing the spreading were at odds with mainstream American culture. They believe that the country has lost its way, is decadent and decaying, and has abandoned the conservative Christian values that they themselves hold dear. In times of such uncertainty and fear about what is happening in one's society, a rumor about a major corporation working on behalf of the Devil may actually help an individual make sense out of the perceived rise of evil. The uncertainty is generated by distaste for the present and fear and trepidation about the future.

Urgency

Along with uncertainty, collective behavior participants must experience a sense of *urgency*. They have to feel as if something must be done, soon. In the case of the Procter & Gamble rumor, those who spread the story did so with a great sense of urgency. Newsletters and flyers all indicated that the "Satanic conspiracy" was a great danger to all of society, and if decent Christians did not act quickly (by boycotting Procter & Gamble products), the Devil would win another victory and America would be lost (Koenig 1985). Tellers didn't just believe that the rumor was interesting, they believed that it was extremely important, worth sharing, and required immediate action.

This urgency was probably magnified by the historical conditions of the early 1980s. The economy was in a sharp decline while unemployment and crime rates were going up. News stories constantly focused on stories about drugs and crime. Politicians, celebrities, and news anchors talked incessantly about "crack babies," "welfare dependency," and the dangers posed by the Soviet Union. Although the actual social conditions were not as bad as many believed, the fact that they *believed* the country was rapidly falling apart gave those spreading the Procter & Gamble rumor a greater sense that things were spiraling out of control. The rumor provided not only a way to make sense of this perceived decline, but a quick course of action to reverse it through product boycotts.

Communication of Mood and Imagery

When there is uncertainty and urgency, the communication that does occur within the crowd begins to focus. Crowd members (the *rumor public*) talk about little besides what they think is happening, what is likely to happen next, and what actions and attitudes are important. Participants are able to reach a common understanding and definition of the situation.

In this case, word of mouth seems to have played a secondary role. The primary source of communication of this particular rumor involved church newsletters and direct-mail flyers (Koenig 1985). There was remarkable consistency in these printed reports, all of which repeated the story about the alleged television appearance, and then followed with a suggestion for action. Ironically, the list of products to boycott usually contained just a few items, while Procter & Gamble manufactures literally thousands of household products. In addition to the soaps and shampoos often listed (such as Prell, Pert, Ivory, and Coast), Procter & Gamble also manufactures such items as Charmin, Puffs, and White Cloud bathroom tissue, Clearasil, Cover Girl, and Max Factor cosmetics, Crest toothpaste and Scope mouthwash, Pringles chips, Sunny Delight and Hawaiian Punch beverages, and a host of other food products. They also make and sell prescription drugs, colognes and perfumes, laundry detergents, and various other household items. The list goes on and on. Anyone trying to eliminate Procter & Gamble from their home would have to go to extraordinary lengths to do so. The people spreading the rumor seemed unaware of this fact. The boycott lists were usually short and limited to soaps and detergents, products that Amway also produces.

The rumor spread from one geographic region to the next, starting in Minnesota, and traveled almost exclusively through fundamentalist Christians in the South in the first wave, Catholics in the second (Koenig 1985), and still travels mostly in fundamentalist Christian and Southern Baptist circles (Asher 1999, Neff 1995). The rumor travels through people who already share a view of the world that makes the rumor seem plausible. The rumor public includes people who believe in a literal Satan who has many humans helping him in his work to destroy American society. As Koenig said, ". . . for many fundamentalist religious groups, the rumor about Satan and his followers helps explain what is happening better than anything else" (1985:28). The Procter & Gamble rumor justifies and verifies beliefs already held. Believing and spreading the rumor gives them something tangible to fight against and makes them feel like better, more righteous people by comparison to those who do nothing and particularly in relation to those who "work for" Satan. The mood is panicky, the imagery is stark, and the suggested action is relatively simple and painless. What could be more satisfying than defeating Satan's minions by simply repeating some information and throwing out one's shampoo?

Constraint

Once uncertainty and urgency are present and a mood has begun to form, members of the rumor public begin to feel a sense of *constraint*. They feel as if they should go along with the norms of the crowd. In this case, it might seem un-Christian to scoff at the rumor. If one's loved ones all seem to believe that the rumor is true, it could be construed as somehow sinful to question it. Those with doubts might feel constrained to keep those thoughts to themselves. When a preacher, minister, or priest is rallying about the evils of satanic corporations, few people would stand up and suggest that it's all just a silly rumor. When newsletters, telephone messages, letters, and (more recently) e-mails arrive from friends, relatives, or religious leaders urging an immediate boycott, few people ignore the message. The rumor passed most quickly through tight-knit religious groups (Koenig 1985), where people were less likely to contradict each other. More importantly, to argue against a boycott could potentially be construed as arguing *for* the Devil and the Church of Satan, and *against* God and the Church. Many versions of the rumor contained phrases like "all decent Christians must . . ." and "to battle evil we have to . . ." (Koenig 1985). This places a great deal of constraint on anyone who is a part of such a tight-knit community, discouraging them from doing anything to stop the spread of the false rumor. Given a choice between appearing to accept a questionable rumor or alienating and angering friends and relatives, many members of the rumor public chose to keep all doubts to themselves.

Selective Individual Suggestibility

As the rumor public develops a common definition of the situation, members become more and more polarized. They become increasingly likely to accept any information, belief, or behavioral cue that fits the established beliefs of the crowd. One can see this pattern of development in the growth of the rumor. In 1980, the only specific allegations focused on the Procter & Gamble logo. It was suggested by three sources (Martin, Peters, and Worley) that the logo was satanic or contained satanic elements. Less than a year later, this belief had grown into a detailed story about the head of Procter & Gamble announcing allegiance with the Devil. Not too long after that, calls for boycotts went out along with descriptions of an incident that never actually took place (Koenig 1985). Each level of the rumor set the stage for the more detailed versions that followed.

It may be tempting to assume that "selective individual suggestibility" means "gullible." Indeed, when a rumor seems preposterous, we tend to think that only a fool could believe such a thing. However, the basic premise of the Emergent Norm perspective is that people who are *not* particularly gullible or mindless will take part in collective behavior under the right circumstances. In this case, the suggestibility does not have to do with a generally gullible personality. Most of the people who believed this rumor do not believe everything that they hear. Other people who laughed at this rumor probably believed some other tale that was circulating at the same time: perhaps "the engine that runs on water" (which "they" won't produce because then "they" won't be able to sell oil anymore), the "hippie babysitter" legend discussed earlier, or the "McDonald's wormburgers" rumor discussed in Chapter 7. It is not general gullibility that matters; it is the individual's susceptibility to rumors pertaining to certain specific topics that matters. Some people are more likely to believe in satanic cult conspiracies than others. Some are more likely to believe that major corporations knowingly produce poisonous products, or that people in big cities will steal kidneys from strangers. The people who spread the Procter & Gamble rumor during the first few waves were more likely to believe such tales than the general population because of their religious and cultural beliefs. Those beliefs created a selective suggestibility among them.

Permissiveness

The last component that contributes to collective behavior in the Emergent Norm Perspective is *permissiveness*. Crowd members feel a sense of freedom in relationship to certain urges or tendencies that they normally keep hidden for fear of social rejection. In the case of the Procter & Gamble rumor, normally constrained people were able to talk openly about the idea that big business people were succeeding because of their cooperation with the Devil. They could openly discuss the decline and fall of American society, because now they had proof. Not only was a major corporation giving money to the Church of Satan, but most people did not seem to care and (in a later version of the theory) the Satanists did not believe that real Christians were numerous enough or powerful enough to worry about.

All of these beliefs combined to produce a situation where distributing a flyer accusing people of collusion with the forces of evil seemed perfectly acceptable behavior for hundreds of people across the United States. In normal daily life, people do not publicly accuse businessmen of working for the Devil. Product distributors do not say untrue things about a competing company, and religious leaders do not commit liable or slander. Concerned Christians do not sabotage the operation of law-abiding corporations. However, the Satan rumor permitted people to do all of these things with a clear conscience. Not only did feel guilt-free about their behavior, they actually felt righteous and holy for their efforts on behalf of the Lord (Koenig 1985). Imagine the freedom of being able to spread malicious tales *and* feel morally superior to those who scoff at the rumor.

Conclusion

The Emergent Norm Perspective seems to explain the growth and durability of the rumor about Procter & Gamble and the Church of Satan. To really test the theory one would have to find and interview a number of people who had heard the rumor. This should include those who believed the rumor and those who did not, as well as those who passed the rumor on and those who did not. This would allow a researcher to determine if those who spread and/or believed the rumor did in fact experience more uncertainty, urgency, and so forth. The literature does not contain such specific data. Most of the research done on this particular rumor focuses on the reasons for individual suggestibility, and the communication of mood and imagery. Still, this application should illustrate how the Emergent Norm Perspective is used and give the reader some indication of its usefulness.

There is nothing peculiar or unique about the rumor about Procter & Gamble and the Church of Satan, except the active participation by Amway distributors. It is a fairly typical example of a common category of collective behavior in the United States. Such rumors do not circulate constantly, but they do occur frequently and are likely to circulate again in the near future. The Emergent Norm perspective gives a specific pattern to look for: A large number of people feel uncertain or uneasy about something. They believe that time is running out or that something is happening at a rapid pace. As long as they can develop a belief that seems to alleviate or explain the situation and communicate it to others who feel the same way, the rumor can grow and spread.

If they feel constrained by their associates from questioning the rumor, doubts will be kept quiet. If there is a rumor public with sufficient suggestibility, the rumor is likely to spread and grow. This creates a level of permissiveness within the crowd that allows people to say and do things they would never say or do under normal circumstances. The rumor takes on a life of its own only if it captures the attention and imagination of enough people. Those who find the rumor interesting are likely to repeat it, and those who find it plausible are likely to believe it. The result can be harmless, but it can also result in millions of dollars being wasted by a company to fight a story that has no basis in fact. Worst of all, the nature of the rumor may make denials worthless: If people believe that you are in league with the Devil, they have no reason to believe anything that you say and no reason to worry about any harm that they may do to you.

Discussion

The Internet has contributed more to the spread of rumors in the last ten years than anyone could have ever imagined. People constantly e-mail each other "warnings," "updates," and other urgent messages that are totally untrue. They are so common that the dire warnings are referred to as "scare-mail." What is important is that few people bother to check the story to find out if it is true or false. They might receive an e-mail stating that a dying little boy in a hospital in Philadelphia wants to receive bottle caps. Rather than contact the hospital and verify the story, they forward the message to hundreds of other people. Their bank newsletter contains an "urgent warning" that gang members are shooting people who flash their headlights at night. Rather than call the police and ask if there have been any motorist shootings lately, they repeat the story at social gatherings and mutter about "kids today" or "the gang problem."

The reasons why most people don't take the extra time to check out a story before passing it is simple: They believe it is true. If the story sounds true and the source seems credible, most people see no reason to check any further. If a person believes that gangs are increasing in size and violence, then the story about flashing headlights seems possible, plausible, and likely to them. If someone believes that Satan and his organized followers are destroying American society, then it seems quite likely that they are also killing small children by the thousands and/or running major corporations. A person who believes that the world is much more violent and dangerous than it used to be is likely to fall for any rumor that confirms that belief. If the rumor also comes from a source that is credible and trusted in the eyes of the person receiving the information, they may never stop to question the story or doubt its truth.

As Koenig (1985) points out, people may accept a rumor or hearsay specifically because it supports a point they wish to make. We all decide whether or not to believe everything that we hear. In the absence of hard evidence, we have to use our own judgement. That means that we must weigh the new message in light of what we already know and believe. If a rumor fits what we already think we know ("gangs are an increasing problem," "society is falling apart," etc.) then it seems more credible to us. If it also confirms some opinion or fact that is important to us, then we are likely to not only accept the rumor as fact, but to repeat it to others.

Rumors are the most basic form of collective behavior. Sometimes they do not require any action other than repeating the story to others. Chapter 11 will apply the Emergent Norm Perspective to a much more action-oriented type of collective behavior: fads.

Chapter 11

Fads and Crazes:
The Furby Frenzy

Fads

Fads can take a wide variety of forms. However, almost all fads have a common pattern. They always appear quickly. They seem to come from nowhere and suddenly occupy the attention of virtually everyone. Then as quick as they came they fade from popularity. Many fads are related to physical activities, such as miniature golf in the 1930s and streaking in the 1970s. The most common type of activity fad may be the various dances that quickly come into style and just as quickly disappear. The Mashed Potato, the Hustle, and the Macarena were all wildly popular for a brief period of time and then virtually disappeared from popular culture.

Some fads resurface from time to time. Skateboarding is a good example of a recurring fad. A relatively small number of individuals have been actively riding skateboards since their introduction into American culture in the 1960s. However, at least once in the 1960s, twice in the 1970s, and again in the 1990s, skateboarding suddenly became so popular that skate shops appeared all over the country and magazines dedicated to skateboarding equipment, technique, and accessories popped up. The rise and fall of skateboarding as a fad can be traced by monitoring the rise and fall of these magazines. Each time the fad dies down, only a few dedicated hobbyists are left.

Types of Fads

Turner and Killian (1987) list a wide variety of fads. There are fads relating to beliefs, such as flying saucers in the 1950s or astrology in the 1960s. There are fads relating to activities, such as bungee jumping or skateboarding. Some fads relate to amusements like discos, light shows, or music festivals. Fears and/or moods may be fad-like, such as the fear of the Black Panthers in the 1960s, the "Red scares" of the 1920s and 1950s, and the witch hunts of the 1600s. Behavior contrary to norms, like streaking and panty raids, can suddenly become extremely popular and then fade quickly. Turner and Killian argue that even the emulation of comic book or movie characters can be a fad. How many people said "Is that your final answer?" after seeing the television show "Who Wants to Be a Millionaire?" These various types of fads all relate to ideas, actions, products, or fashions and most of them can be placed into one of three general categories: activity fads, product fads, and fashion or apparel fads.

Activity fads center on some leisure activity like breakdancing or rollerblading. People suddenly feel excited about taking part in an activity that has never seemed appealing before. Prior to the 1950s, nobody felt the urge to stuff themselves into a phone booth with a large number of other people, and few have done it since then. However, it was all the rage for several years in the 1950s. Disco dancing came and (thankfully) went. Manufacturers often capitalize on these fads by producing a range of accessories to go with the activity. Often, music and movies that relate to the activity are rushed into production in an attempt to cash in on the fad before it ends. The song "The Streak," by Ray Stevens and the film *Wheels* (a skateboarding film) are both good examples of attempts to make money from fad participants.

Useful product fads center on the acquisition of products that serve some purpose, however unimportant. In late 1998, "onion-bloom machines" suddenly became popular. Millions of Americans bought this kitchen tool designed to cut a large onion into a ready-to-fry "bloom" similar to the popular fried "onion blooms" served in restaurants. They were advertised on television almost every night. Stores quickly sold out their supply of the devices. The product itself is relatively useful, or at least serves some function. In this case, it makes a kind of variation of onion-rings. However, the product is neither particularly necessary nor terribly important. The vast majority of onion-bloom machines are probably gathering dust in kitchen cabinets and closets all over the United States. Like many products at the center of these fads, onion bloom machines remain on the market but prices and demand dropped dramatically once the initial excitement wore off and people no longer felt the need for such a product in their lives.

Frivolous product fads may be the most interesting of all. People may stand in line for hours, fight with each other, and spend hundreds or thousands of dollars just so they can own something that is useless. The Pet Rock is the ideal example of this type of fad. In late 1975, an entrepreneur marketed a plain rock in a cardboard box called "the Pet Rock" and sold over one million at five dollars each (Marum & Parise 1984). The Pet Rock was not decorated, nor did it do anything. It was, in fact, an ordinary rock. Today it may seem difficult to understand why one million Americans would pay five dollars for a stone, particularly in 1975 when five dollars could buy a meal or two tickets to the movies. Such is the nature of useless product fads. They are always difficult to explain or understand after they end.

Fashion fads may or may not involve the purchase of a particular item, and therefore sometimes overlap with frivolous product fads. For example, millions of American women purchased and wore "leg warmers" in the 1980s. These wooly socks without feet were worn over pants or stockings and were used for their look, rather than practical function. Other fashion-related fads may not involve buying anything. In late 1999, at the University of Missouri in Columbia, Missouri, hundreds of young women on campus began wearing their hair loosely gathered into a small ponytail that stuck straight up from the top of their head. The only accessory required was a rubber band. No products were purchased. The rapid adoption of the unflattering look and its relatively rapid disappearance would categorize the hairstyle as a fad.

Fashion has a slow cycle of acceptance. There is a sort of "flow" from one fashion to the next. Fashion-oriented fads, however, appear quickly with no precursor and then just as quickly vanish from favor with no new look having grown out of it. Fashion evolves, while fads appear and disappear.

Crazes

Crazes are slightly different than fads, although the behavior may appear similar at first glance. Crazes always involve the purchase of, or investment in, something for the sole purpose of making a profit. Craze participants only want to own the product because they believe that it will quickly increase in value (see Chapter 7). There is a "bigger fool" mentality at work (as in "I might be a fool to pay this much, but a bigger fool will come along tomorrow and give me twice as much").

Crazes can be distinguished from the legitimate rise in the value of some product or commodity. Crazes often center around something that has little or no use value, such as swampland in Florida or tulip bulbs. Even if the product or object does have some genuine value, the price during a craze is dramatically higher than any objective measure determines that it should be. These ridiculous prices are only maintained as long as craze participants believed that prices will continue to rise. They frequently have no idea what they are buying, nor do they care.

The easiest way to determine if speculation or price inflation is driven by a craze is to wait. Crazes always end, sometimes quite suddenly. Products or objects that have some genuine value can lose some desirability, but they do not become worthless overnight. The subject of speculative crazes do. Once the illusion of the bigger fool goes away, there is no reason to own the craze item. Craze victims are often left with thousands of dollars invested in something with absolutely no resale value.

Toy Fads

The remainder of this chapter is going to focus on recent fads. A curious fad cycle has appeared repeatedly in the United States in the last few decades that centers on the "hot" Christmas toy. Seemingly every year there is some toy that every child reportedly wants for Christmas and, therefore, every parent wants to buy. These fads do not actually occur every year, but they do come with alarming regularity (see Figure 11.1). When a Christmas toy fad occurs, parents line up outside of stores in sometimes-freezing temperatures at midnight, 2:00 A.M., or even 4:00 A.M. They stand in line for hours. They pay three or four times retail price. They push, shove, yell, and fight each other. All just to get the hot toy that they "must have" that Christmas.

Tickle-Me-Elmo, Beanie Babies, and The Furby Frenzy

The most recent examples of this behavior occurred in late 1996 and late 1998 with Tyko Toys' "Tickle-Me-Elmo" and Hasbro's "Furby." Beanie Babies, which were a Christmas toy fad in 1997, have since gone on to become the center of a speculative craze that only recently peaked and has not yet ended. Elmo and Furby, however, have followed the traditional path for a Christmas toy fad: massive media exposure and tremendous consumer demand that all but disappear the day after Christmas. Tickle-Me-Elmos and Furbies are still available at stores nationwide, but sales, publicity, and excitement have dropped dramatically compared to the first holiday shopping season of their introduction.

Figure 11.1   A Partial List of Christmas Toy Fads since 1983

1983 Cabbage Patch Dolls	1994 Mighty Morphin Power Rangers
1984 Trivial Pursuit	1995 Holiday Barbie and Nintendo
1985 Teddy Ruxpin	1996 Tickle-Me-Elmo
1986 Lazer Tag	1997 Beanie Babies
1987 Pictionary	1998 Furby
1988 Teenage Mutant Ninja Turtles figures	

There were no major Christmas toy fads in 1989 to 1993 or in 1999. Sony Playstation 2 and scooters were both very popular Christmas 2000 gifts, but the cost of the former and the easy availability of the latter kept either from reaching a frenzy state.

Sources: *Milwaukee Journal Sentinel, Washington Post*

Furby, an electronically animated toy, was declared the "hot toy of 1998" long before Christmas shopping season ever began. The toy itself was not available until October of 1998.

Furby

A Furby is an animatronic toy manufactured by Tiger Electronics. Computer chips allow it to speak about two hundred words and eight hundred phrases in English and its native "Furbish" tongue. The Furby can also respond to external stimuli, creating the illusion that the toy is actually alive (Crum et al., 1998). Small, furry and resembling the creatures from the movie *Gremlins,* the Furby became the "must-have" toy of the 1998 Christmas shopping season. It was reported that no two Furbies would have the same personality or react to stimuli in the same way. Described metaphorically as "Cabbage Patch dolls with artificial intelligence" and "Tickle-Me-Elmos that could influence one another," the Furby was expected to be the season's number-one toy before it ever reached the market. In fact, at an annual toy fair in February of 1998, Wal-Mart committed to buying one third of Tiger's entire production run (Minneapolis *Star Tribune* 12/26/1998). The buyer was absolutely confident that Furby would be the "must-have" toy the following Christmas.

Parents' struggle to purchase a Furby in time for Christmas of 1998 was particularly spectacular. It was a relief to many observers that a similar fad did not occur in 1999 or 2000. There are popular toys every holiday shopping season, but only true fads generate behavior such as this:

Parents, grandparents, and scalpers gathered all over the country and stood in line for hours in the hopes of buying a Furby.

November, 1998

Two women suffered minor injuries as shoppers stormed into the O'Fallon, Illinois Wal-Mart store at midnight in search of Furbies. (*St. Louis Dispatch* 11/28/98)

Customers waiting outside of a Wal-Mart in Tewksbury, Massachusetts became unruly while waiting for a 6 A.M. opening time. Police were called to restore order. (*Los Angeles Times* 11/28/98)

At a Wal-Mart store in Cerritos, California, shoppers started lining up at 1 A.M. for a 6 A.M. opening. Two thousand people arrived. There were 115 Furbies available. (*USA Today* 11/30/98)

December, 1998

Fury erupted when Wal-Mart employees in Lynn, Massachusetts announced to waiting shoppers that only 30 Furbies were available. (*Arizona Republic* 12/5/98)

Two women began fistfighting over Furbies at New York's F.A.O. Schwartz toy store. (*Buffalo News* 12/8/98)

A 76-year-old woman and her grandson were knocked to the ground as people dashed into a Wal-Mart in Battavia, New York. (*Buffalo News* 12/8/98)

A clerk at a Sacramento, California store suffered a loose tooth when he was punched in the mouth by a customer angry that he was too late to buy a Furby. (*Washington Post* 11/13/98)

Fighting broke out at a suburban Milwaukee, Wisconsin Toys-R-Us. (*Milwaukee Journal Sentinel* 12/20/98)

Riot Police were brought in to calm crowds at a Los Angeles mall. (*Milwaukee Journal Sentinel* 12/20/98)

Shoppers knocked over displays and trampled bystanders near Denver. (*Arizona Republic* 12/5/98)

Furby shoppers bit each other at a Wal-Mart in Mississippi (Milwaukee Journal Sentinal 12/20/1998)

Police said Furby rage at a Wal-Mart in New Smyrna Beach, Florida had customers "banging, hitting and fighting." (*Buffalo News* 12/8/98)

Shoppers waiting in line outside of a Hill's department store in Buffalo, New York were verbally abusive to the customer service person and spread rumors throughout the waiting crowd when it was announced that only customers over the age of 18 would be able to purchase a Furby. (*Buffalo News* 12/8/98)

As with Tickle-Me-Elmo in 1996, newscasts all over the United States ran stories about Furby and the behavior of those trying to purchase one. Stores quickly sold out every time Furbies went for sale. Tiger Electronics, the company that actually manufactured Furbies, shipped approximately three million units (*Buffalo News* 12/8/1998) which was not nearly enough to meet demand.

The Furby was heavily publicized before it even went on sale. This is often the case with toy fads. Hasbro purchased Tiger Electronics in February of 1998 for $335 million, partly because they expected the then-secret Furby to make a lot of money for them (*Star Tribune* 12/26/1998). Hasbro announced in August of 1998 that they would spend $5 million on a "TV push" to create a demand for the toy that was supposed to reach the market in September. *Wired,* a popular magazine that focuses on high-tech electronics, ran a behind-the-scenes feature story about the creation of Furby. The Cartoon Network also engaged in heavy Furby promotion, airing a series of games and contests related to Furbies. The Furby was supposed to arrive in stores in September with a retail price of twenty-five dollars. The toy did not actually reach stores until October 2, 1998, when a launch party at F.A.O. Schwartz in New York was broadcast live on "The Today Show" *(The Boston Herald* 1/21/1999). By December, the suggested retail price was thirty dollars, and several stores were selling it for about forty dollars.

Most reporters were less-than-sympathetic to the plight of the Furby shoppers. Articles with titles like "Fanatics Camp Outside of Store for Chance to Buy" became common in newspapers across the United States. Editorial letters and articles began to appear by December condemning the shoppers and, in some cases, the toy itself. By January, most had decided that the entire "Furby Derby," as some called it, had been shameful. These reporters and letter-writers were not participants in the fad. In any fad, including the Furby frenzy, the behavior of participants seems irrational or illogical to outsiders. They often ridicule or condemn fad participants. Ironically, it was the constant reporting of Furby-related stories in the newspapers and on television and radio news broadcasts that helped keep the fad alive. Reporters perpetuated and condemned the fad at the same time.

Analysis

The Emergent Norm Perspective

Turner and Killian's Emergent Norm perspective of collective behavior sets forth a set of concepts and propositions that can be used to order all variations in collective behavior. The factors leading to collective behavior are labeled Uncertainty, Urgency, Communication of Mood and Imagery, Constraint, Selective Individual Suggestibility, and Permissiveness. These factors make it possible for a crowd to form. These crowds are not guided by the norms of society. They develop new norms that may be totally at odds with the norms of the dominant culture. This analysis uses Turner and Killian's model to order and explain the facts of the Furby fad of Christmas 1998. Although the factors do not have to appear in precisely this order, this analysis will follow the order given. The analysis begins with Uncertainty.

Uncertainty

The key to the Emergent Norm Perspective is confusion or *uncertainty*. What conditions made people uncertain about appropriate or acceptable behaviors? People must be convinced that the situation makes normal behavior inappropriate or ineffective before they will take part in unusual behavior. Confusion creates doubt, and doubt makes people likely to follow others who seem to know what to do.

In the case of the Furby fad, there was a great deal of uncertainty. People who had never been to a toy store knew that the Furby was supposed to be the hottest toy of the year and that it would be difficult to acquire because supplies were scarce. Television news broadcasts made it clear that no one could expect to shop for a Furby the way they would normally shop for a Christmas toy. "Each new incident of Furby-frenzied crowds lining up outside store entrances [was] gleefully recounted by TV anchors . . ." (Shaffer 1998:11). Television, radio, newspapers, and newsmagazines all made it clear that buying a Furby was by no means a certain, simple, or casual affair. People were bombarded by messages that all boiled down to "the normal rules of shopping do not apply to the Furby."

Urgency

Along with uncertainty, collective behavior participants must experience a sense of *urgency*. They have to feel as if something must be done, soon. "People wanted it because they think everybody wanted to have it. They were willing to do anything to get it" (Szymanski quoted in *The Boston Herald* 1/21/1999: 49). In other words, many people believed that time was quickly running out and that other shoppers would snatch up all available Furbies if they did not act quickly. There were also rumors circulating that Furby was going to be totally redesigned because of a lawsuit. This led some participants to believe that it would be pulled from shelves until after Christmas. Anyone who wanted a Furby (or knew someone who did) and who believed these rumors would feel a compelling sense of urgency. They believed that the limited supply could disappear overnight.

Store owners, employees, and company executives were also frequently quoted in various media as saying that the Furby was going to be impossible to find (see, for example, *USA Today* 11/30/1998: 5A). "Parents panic, remembering that in past years the hot-toy shelves were picked clean by Thanksgiving. The media cheerfully report the latest shortages. The buzz ratchets up another notch" (*Milwaukee Journal Sentinel* 12/20/1998: 1). Memories of recent toy fads filled parents with the dread of simply being too late to get the hot toy for their child in time for Christmas. For most parents, even one day after Christmas would be too late. This unchangeable deadline heavily underlined and reinforced the urgency that these people experienced.

Communication of Mood and Imagery

When there is uncertainty and urgency within a crowd, the communication that does occur within the crowd begins to focus on the situation at hand. Crowd members talk about little besides what they think is happening, what is likely to happen next, and what actions and attitudes are important. Through rumor and milling the crowd participants are able to reach a common understanding and definition of the situation. People tell each other what they think is going on and what they think is going to happen next. They attempt to find out if other crowd members agree with them. In essence, they create new norms to fit the new circumstances they find themselves in.

News sources also repeated plenty of mood-related information. They quoted shoppers, store employees, and company representatives who repeated the rumors and reinforced the idea that the quest for a Furby had become a first-come, first-serve, free for all. "People just seemed crazed. There's [already] enough stress and tension around Christmas" (Flamburis, quoted in *Boston Herald* 1/21/1999: 49). "The message is you do a lot of things for your kids" (Zamparelli, ibid). Newscasters and reporters frequently referred to the Furby as the year's biggest toy. "Suddenly, the toy pops up on hot-toy lists, on the "Rosie O'Donnell Show," on "Good Morning America," in *USA Today* articles" (*Milwaukee Journal Sentinel* 12/20/1998: 1). All of these quotes refer to the fact that people were being bombarded with messages that reinforced the confusion and urgency of potential fad participants. Even if no shopper had spoken to any other shopper, media sources alone would have sufficiently communicated a mood of tension, urgency, and importance.

However, the reality is that most of those shoppers did speak directly to others. In the most dramatic Furby-related mob scenes, hundreds of shoppers stood around and waited for hours before finally being allowed into the store. During this period of milling, there was plenty of time for rumor sharing, for discussion of motives and planned actions, and for observing the mood and intention of other crowd members. Store managers unwittingly created the perfect setting for emergent norms. They forced hundreds of like-minded individuals to mill in an uncomfortable and isolated setting. Speculation about how many Furbies might be available and how many each individual might be able to purchase was rampant at all of these sights. Wal-Mart, by intentionally placing their few available Furbies at the far corner of the store, particularly created a situation in which pushing, shoving, and running were most likely to occur and, therefore, most likely to be perceived as acceptable by all members of the crowd. They also announced specific times at which the toys would be sold and intentionally withheld all information about how many would be available. As popular as the Furby was that year, Wal-Mart could have sold every single available Furby by quietly placing them on shelves during normal operating hours. Instead, they actually created a situation where a crowd was formed, given little or no information, allowed to mill for several hours, and then released into the store like horses shooting out of the gate at the beginning of a horse race. This extended period of milling allowed participants to communicate to each other what was likely to happen once the doors were opened.

Constraint

Once uncertainty and urgency are present and a mood has begun to form, members of the crowd begin to feel a sense of *constraint*. They feel as if they should go along with the norms of the crowd. They may even feel as if they have no choice. Social pressure takes two different forms. Normative influence makes people feel as if they have to go along with the crowd (Asch 1951). Informational influence occurs when people believe that those around them are doing the right thing and they should do it as well (Sherif 1936). When some people aren't sure what to do (*uncertainty*), they tend to do what others around them are doing. Once the crowd begins to engage in this behavior, even those who disagree feel compelled to join in (*constraint*).

In the case of a fad like the Furby frenzy, otherwise normal people feel as if they must take part in the waiting, pushing, shoving, and gloating that takes place when a "hot toy" is for sale. Those who would prefer to show up at the store at a reasonable hour, quietly wait for the chance to buy a toy, and do so calmly are made to feel that this simply will not do. They feel pressured by those around them to take part in the frenzy and they feel constrained from doing or saying anything about it at the time. Store employees reported that many Furby seekers were verbally abusive to employees, and violence occurred at more than one store. In other words, outspoken and brutish behavior was clearly displayed within the crowds of gathered shoppers. This created a situation in which calmer, quieter people with more reasonable ideas would be unlikely to express their opinions.

People rarely speak out in a crowd situation to express their disagreement. It can be scary and may even be perceived as physically dangerous. As a result, even if the majority of crowd members do not want to push and shove, they feel as if they have to and are afraid to express doubts or concerns. A false sense of crowd unity is created and everyone feels as if they are the only person who believes differently. Calm and reasonable people believe that they have to engage in running, pushing and shoving in order to achieve their goal. Even those few who disagree feel constrained by the crowd and therefore go along and keep their doubts to themselves.

Selective Individual Suggestibility

As the crowd develops a common definition of the situation, members become more and more polarized. They become increasingly likely to accept any information, belief, or behavioral cue that fits the established mood and imagery of the crowd. In other words, they become more and more inclined to accept new, emergent group norms. While waiting in line for hours outside of a store, people had plenty of time to see what others were doing and to hear what they were saying. Many shoppers were shocked to see how many people were waiting in line when they arrived. The mere presence of so many other shoppers, all there for the same specific toy, created a sense that it was going to be more difficult to get than they had believed.

As a result, ordinary people came to believe that it is acceptable, appropriate, and necessary to behave in an uncivilized manner. "I could see the other woman making her move to get to that darn Furby, and I thought, 'No way, lady'" (*Milwaukee Journal Sentinel* 12/20/1998: 1). Individuals who would show up at 4:00 A.M. to wait in line for hours in the cold and dark to buy a toy for their child or grandchild are more likely to feel a sense of urgency about getting a Furby. Gather several hundred such people into the same place, and you have an entire crowd of people likely to accept any suggestion that seems to make getting the toy more likely. As time slowly passes and milling takes place, they become more and more likely to feel this way.

Permissiveness

The last component that contributes to collective behavior in the Emergent Norm Perspective is *permissiveness*. Some members of the crowd develop the feeling that behaviors and attitudes that are normally socially rejected are acceptable within this situation. It is as if the entire crowd says "It's okay;

you can do it." Crowd members feel a sense of freedom in relationship to certain urges or tendencies that they normally keep hidden for fear of social rejection. Not all participants felt pressured to act the way they did. Some would act that way more often if social circumstances permitted it. As one shopper said, "There was so much pushing and shoving. I know I ran past at least two people in front of me. But it was really fun" (*Buffalo News* 12/8/1998: 1C). The idea that running through a store, pushing and shoving others out of the way, and fighting over the few items on the shelves is "fun" reveals something important: Not all of the participants in the Furby fad were acting out of character. Some of them were acting out their inner urges for the first time.

There are people who might push and shove all the time if it were socially acceptable. The Furby fad, like all other Christmas toy fads, permitted them to act in ways that would be socially condemned under normal circumstances. The mood of the crowd allowed normally restrained people to act as out of control as they liked.

Classification of Participants

As discussed in several other chapters, Turner and Killian include a schema for the classification of participants along with their Emergent Norm explanation for collective behavior. This schema helps the researcher to understand why different behavior patterns exist within the same event.

Turner and Killian classify the attitudes and motivations of the individuals participating in collective behavior into five separate categories. This typology can be used to classify all of the variations of behavior associated with an episode of collective behavior. The five categories of participants are labeled as Ego-involved/Committed, Concerned, Insecure, Curious Spectators and Ego-detached/Exploiters.

Ego-involved/Committed

The ego-involved participant feels a strong personal commitment to the event. In the case of the Furby fad, this would include all of those people who felt as if they *had* to get a Furby for their child or grandchild. These are the people who got up at (or stayed up until) four or five in the morning and stood in line for hours in freezing temperatures just for the chance to purchase one specific toy. Personal greed or selfishness did not motivate them. It was some sort of drive to satisfy their child's desires that led to such determined behavior. "All my kids made clear this is the only toy they want. This becomes their whole world. You want to fulfill all their wishes" (*The Boston Globe* 11/28/1998: B1). These are the words of a man who is emotionally evolved in the event and has a strong personal desire to successfully purchase a Furby. In other words, he is ego-involved.

Concerned

The concerned participant has a more general interest in the event. This group may include friends or companions of the ego-involved. The concerned take part out of concern for other participants rather than a great deal of personal and emotional involvement.

The concerned participants in the Furby fad are those who knew someone (often a grown son or daughter) who desperately wanted to get a Furby for their own child or grandchild. They did not personally want a Furby for themselves, nor did they feel a powerful drive to get one as a Christmas present for someone. Instead, they were attempting to get a Furby for someone who would then in turn give it to their child or grandchild as a present. Because they were one step removed from the direct pressure to succeed, they were less likely to take extreme measures to acquire a Furby.

Insecure

Some people simply want to belong to any group or crowd that will provide them with a sense of purpose, importance, or belonging. They might not have any personal interest in the goals of the ego-involved or the concerned. Taking part in the event simply gives them a sense of direction and identity. They feel important because they take part in what they interpret as important events.

In the case of the Furby fad, it may be difficult to identify any insecure participants. If anyone took part in the mad dash for Furbies simply because they didn't want to be the only one without one, we could classify them as an insecure participant. Anyone who wanted to get a Furby just because everyone else seemed to want one, even if his or her children did not particularly care, was an insecure participant. Less likely, but also possible, would be someone who took part in the actual mob scenes just to be a part of the group.

Curious Spectators

Curious spectators just watch the participants. They do not have any interest in the event itself. Instead, they are interested in the actions of those caught up in the event. In the case of the Furby fad, this would include any shoppers who gathered just to see what was causing noise or commotion. In many cases, store employees stood by to watch the shoppers race and struggle to get a Furby. They were spectators interested in the actions of participants, not in the goals of the participants. It could be argued that news camera crews who showed up to film and interview those waiting in line were also spectators. They weren't interested in Furbies; they were interested in the crowd.

Spectators are much more likely to be present under conditions that make it easy or pleasant to do so. Spectators were much more likely to satisfy their curiosity about the Furby fad in warm climates than in cold regions. And they were unlikely to get up before dawn just to see what was going on. As a result, some of the Furby scuffles took place in front of hundreds of witnesses while others occurred with no one but store employees looking on. Eyewitness reports from a wide variety of sources all make references to a few dozen people running, fighting, and so on. Others present were spectators.

Ego-detached Exploiters

Exploiters are totally ego-detached participants. They are there to use the episode for their own personal gain. They do not care about the event itself, nor are they particularly interested in watching other participants. Instead, they look out for their own personal interests.

Exploiters are easy to spot in toy fads like the Furby fad. There are several different types of exploiters. All of them are driven by profit.

Counterfeiters produce or sell cheap imitations of the real toy. This is easier with some toys than others, but factories interested in ripping off the American public can crudely duplicate virtually any toy. These toys don't sell themselves; they are sold by individuals who exploit the high demand for their own personal financial gain.

Bootleggers are another type of exploiter. They manage to somehow import the real toy from other countries. For example, Beanie Babies are manufactured in China and are readily available there. Some individuals may have the ability to purchase the real toy directly from factories or distributors, smuggle them into the United States, and sell them at a profit.

Pirates may steal the toy from stores, warehouses, trucks, factories, or individuals. They then sell the toy to desperate parents who don't ask too many questions.

Scalpers purchase the product from a legitimate retailer in order to resell the product to others at what may be a dramatic profit. Recently, it has become common on online auctions such as eBay for people to resell brand-new products, which were inexpensive or even free, to collectors who want them enough to pay inflated prices. Every single toy listed in Figure 11.1 also showed up in classified advertisements for resale at dramatically inflated prices.

Exploiters usually do not make too much of an effort to hide their motives and interests. Ever since the Cabbage Patch frenzy of 1983, every Christmas toy fad has seen its share of profiteers who attempt to resell the toy to more desperate shoppers. In the case of the Furby, newspaper advertisements listed them for sale for prices as high as two and three hundred dollars. Such speculative greed drives exploiters to undergo all of the steps necessary to acquire a Furby, only to turn around and offer it for sale to other, less lucky, shoppers. This isn't the same as participating in a craze, however, because the exploiters do not believe that the item is actually worth the money they are asking and because they knew that the product will lose

some or all of its black-market value the day after Christmas. Craze participants believe that they are making a long-term investment. Toy fad exploiters simply think that they can rip someone off for a quick profit.

A father who had already purchased two Furbies the day after Thanksgiving offered fifty dollars to other customers for theirs but was turned down.
Two teenagers offered to sell him one for over one hundred dollars. He
turned it down, saying it was too much money. As one shopper said in December, "I'm in line watching a little 10-year-old boy get his Furby, and he
turns around and yells 'First $50 takes it!' I thought, boy, they learn young
nowadays, don't they?" (*Buffalo News* 12/8/1998: 1C). A seller in Schederville,
Indiana, auctioned off two Furbies that had never been out of their boxes on
eBay for $262. Diane Leoncini of Batavia, New York, ran a newspaper ad of-
fering her "Midnight Black Furby, brand new, in box" for two hundred dollars. She argued that two hundred dollars was not too much to ask because
she got in line at 4:00 A.M. outside of a Wal-Mart the day after Thanksgiving
in order to purchase it. By Christmas day, there were reports of people who
"demanded as much as $800" for their Furby (*The Boston Herald* 1/21/1999:
49) and of "scalpers getting as much as $1,000" (*The Washington Post*
12/13/1998: H1).

These profiteers were a part of the Furby frenzy, but not in the same
way as the ego-involved and concerned. Although selfish motives may have
played a part in all of the participants' behavior, the exploiters were driven
almost entirely by greed. They did not want a Furby, they did not know any-
body who wanted a Furby; they simply wanted to make money off of those
who did. They make it increasingly difficult for other participants to purchase the toy legitimately by snapping up available stock. Exploiters make it
seem increasingly important to get one and create a sense of the toy's worth
that is far beyond what manufacturers and retailers set as the value. They
become one more group of people pushing, shoving, and spreading rumors in
the quest to purchase what has become a scarce item.

Conclusion

Like most fads, the Furby Derby shows evidence of participation by all five of
Turner and Killian's categories. This particular fad is similar to all of the
Christmas toy fads of the last few decades and, presumably, like the ones
that are bound to occur in future holiday shopping seasons. There is nothing
peculiar or unique about the Furby or Tickle-Me-Elmo fads. They are recent
examples of fads that occur frequently and are likely to occur again in the
near future. If this happened every single year it could become institutionalized behavior. The fact that they occur sporadically keeps the behavior unexpected, unwanted, and relatively spontaneous.

Turner and Killian argue that collective behavior participants behave
the way they do because of the circumstances they find themselves in. They
are following the norms of the crowd, just as they always do. The ego-

involved, the concerned and the insecure collectively create a new or different definition of acceptable behavior. Their definition of the situation may lead to norms that call for unusual behavior. Once the situation makes collective behavior possible, other categories of participants such as spectators and exploiters join in.

In the case of the Furby fad, individuals found themselves in situations where things were not working as usual. Stores usually have an adequate supply of items. In toy fads, they frequently do not. Stores generally open at the same time every day, and although some shoppers like to get up early and enter as soon as possible, it is usually possible to go much later and still find desired items. This would not work if the shopper desired a Furby in late 1998. Retail stores do not typically announce ahead of time precisely when a particular item will be placed on the shelf for sale. With Tickle-Me-Elmos and Furbies (and nearly every other fad toy), they did. Television and radio news programs do not normally run daily stories about toys, their desirability, and their availability. During toy fads, they do. In other words, the typical business of going to a store and buying a toy is suspended when it comes to Christmas toy fads. The usual ways of going about daily life are suddenly inadequate. Many in society turn their attention to the current popularity, availability, and desirability of one specific toy. Even people who have no children, do not celebrate Christmas, or do not care about toys are bombarded with constant information about the latest fad. All of this adds up to a situation in which the societal norms do not seem to apply and newly emerged group norms dictate acceptable and necessary behavior.

Discussion

Fads usually seem strange or even ridiculous in hindsight. Looking back, it is hard to believe that hundreds, thousands, or even millions of Americans took part in such bizarre fads as pole sitting, phone booth stuffing, breakdancing, and so on. What drives otherwise normal people to pay money for a rock, to jump from a bridge or crane attached to a bungee cord, or to stand in freezing weather for hours in order to run, push, shove, and fight over a thirty-dollar toy? Turner and Killian's answer is clear: The circumstances leading to the behavior. There is nothing wrong with the participants. Most of them are ordinary people. The situation is abnormal. Once confusion and uncertainty set in, people can potentially be led into unusual behavior. If the uncertainty is accompanied by a sense of desperation or urgency, it becomes possible for new group norms to emerge and for collective behavior to occur.

The circumstances leading to an activity fad are not the same as those that create a product fad, but the basic principle is the same. People find themselves questioning their normal patterns of behavior. They feel as if they are missing out on something important. They receive information about the activity, including the idea that it is fun or exciting or important. They feel actively encouraged to take part, maybe even ashamed of not joining in. Finally, the new definition of the situation makes the behavior acceptable, possibly even liberating. Any time people find themselves in such circumstances they are likely to participate in a fad.

The implications for future toy fads are clear. The next time a new toy is introduced and heavy publicity captures the attention of children or parents, a potential Christmas toy fad exists. If the supply of the toy turns out to be less than the demand, the fad becomes likely. If media sources begin to run constant stories about the desirability and unavailability of the toy, including detailed descriptions of desperate crowd behavior across the country, the fad is almost a certainty. The lure of that toy, coupled with the knowledge that there won't be enough for everyone, is enough to make a crowd of reasonable adults run and fight like savages. If the store creates a situation where an interested crowd forms and is given no information but plenty of time to mill, such frenzies are almost unavoidable. It would be shocking to discover a crowd under these circumstances that did not take part in such activities. On the other hand, if the stores provide ample information and create some tolerable method of distributing the toy through a lottery system or other means before people arrive and form a large crowd, then the frenzy is unlikely. People take part in the behavior, but manufacturers, advertisers, and store managers create the situations that make the crowd unstable.

Chapter 12 looks closely at an even more recent episode of collective behavior, the Y2K hysteria. Unlike Chapters 8, 9, 10, and 11, several different theories of collective behavior will be applied to the same event. This allows direct comparison and contrast of the different approaches to collective behavior.

Chapter 12

Millennialism: Y2K and the End of the World as We Know It

The late 1990s were fascinating for anyone interested in doomsday groups. As discussed in Chapter 7, participants in apocalyptic millennial hysteria believe that the world is going to end sometime soon. This is often rooted in religious beliefs. However, the end of the twentieth century generated a slightly different variation of the doomsday scenario. Although many of those who were most frightened did attach their fears and fantasies to apocalyptic religious beliefs, there were many secular millenarians who truly believed that the world as we know it would end with the coming of the year 2000. All of these beliefs focused on what became known as "the Y2K bug," "the Y2K problem," "Y2k" and "Y2K."

This chapter examines the entire range of hysteria related to Y2K. It begins with a general discussion of the Y2K beliefs that were circulating throughout 1998 and 1999. This is followed by an outline of the various beliefs people held about Y2K, the meanings they attributed to it, and the consequences they expected Y2K to bring. Next comes a description of what actually happened when 2000 arrived, followed by an examination and general analysis of Y2K issues. The chapter concludes with a look at Y2K hysteria from each of the major collective behavior perspectives.

Y2K

"Y2K" (for "Year 2k," the year 2000) refers to the problem that some older computers had when recognizing dates after January 1, 2000. Many of the programming languages created in the 1960s, '70s, and '80s are still in use today. Space was at a premium when these codes were created because computers were much less powerful than they are now. Because of this, programming codes used two digits to indicate the year in programming scripts. For example, "98" equals 1998 and "99" equals 1999. This created a potential problem whereby "00" could be interpreted by a computer as "1900" instead of "2000."

Therefore, any calculation that relied upon accurate date information could be wildly inaccurate once the calendar rolled over from 1999 to 2000: Billing records might show that a mortgage payment had not been made in 100 years, automated medical records might indicate that treatment had not occurred for over 100 years, and so on. Many people came to believe that inaccurate interpretation of the year could cause problems with most or all computers. People calling themselves Y2K "experts" announced that entire networks of computers throughout the world would either shut down or go haywire. They made dire predictions of disruptions in the delivery of food, fuel, electricity, water, sanitation, and so on. Virtually all of these "experts" agreed that the world would be plunged into darkness. The only disagreement seemed to be over how much chaos would ensue, how terrible it would be, and how long it would last.

What Was Supposed to Happen

Many of the Y2K predictions taken seriously in the late 1990s may sound ridiculous today. It is important to remember that few people were absolutely certain how widespread Y2K-related failures might be. This created an opening for alarmists who sought to convince the general population that Y2K was a major problem and that its effects would be a major disaster.

Individuals identified as "Y2K experts" such as Peter de Jager (an author, motivational speaker, and consultant), Edward Yardeni (Chief Economist for Duetsche Morgan Grenfell), Paloma O'Reilly (director of the Cassandra Project, "a not-for-profit organization dedicated to disseminating information on the role of the individual and the community in Y2K preparedness"), and Michael Hyatt (author of *The Millennium Bug*) were repeatedly interviewed by mainstream newspaper, newsmagazine, and television reporters. All of these "experts" spouted alarmist predictions about the chaos and potential destruction that Y2K would bring. After a while, they began to refer to each other's predictions as evidence that something terrible would, indeed, happen. This created a spiral of excitement, with Y2K alarmists growing increasingly bold with their frightening predictions.

News reports claimed late-model cars probably would not run after January 1, 2000, that elevators would all go to the basement or the top floor and refuse to budge, and that home appliances would probably malfunction, all because these items contained embedded computer chips. Respected news sources reported that whole communities could lose their electricity, water, sewer, and waste management services. The telephones might not work. The entire world could possibly experience a blackout. Airplanes might fall from the sky, or crash into each other. Financial records could be lost. Banks might collapse. Food, clothing, and fuel could become difficult or impossible to acquire. People living in cold climates might freeze to death. ATMs probably would not work. Credit cards could become useless because computers would read them all as expired. Home computers might become useless. Electronic records would be lost. Hospital equipment might malfunction. Emergency systems and 911 could fail. In short, everything that makes modern life in the United States possible was potentially going to malfunction, shut down, or go haywire because these systems all depended upon computers in one way or another.

Survival guides (available at bookstores and grocery stores throughout the United States) ran articles with titles like "Which Gun Is Right For You?," "When Water Becomes Precious," "The Threat is Real," and so on. Advertisements for survival supplies declared "Y2K is less than 12 months away!" and "Prepare for the worst . . . with the best." These guides were made to look like reliable and credible purveyors of information. The fact that they were placed on newsstands next to more respected news magazines only enhanced the illusion.

The Y2K experts gave interviews for countless newspaper and magazine articles and made frequent appearances on mainstream television and radio programs. Most predicted that all of the failures mentioned above were possible, and many said that some failures were guaranteed to take place. It was never clearly established what, precisely, qualified someone as an expert on a phenomenon that had never happened before. Most were not experienced computer programmers, manufacturers, or engineers. Some were economists, some were authors or political commentators, and some had limited experience with computer software or hardware. At least one author stated, "I have never claimed to be a computer expert, and, quite frankly, I'm proud of that. . . ." (Hyatt 1998: xii). Journalists all over the country actively sought out these self-proclaimed Y2K experts. Throughout it all, the idea that nothing at all might happen was never seriously discussed. Y2K experts scoffed at skeptics, arguing that those who failed to prepare were irresponsible or in denial. Truly knowledgeable people who disagreed with the alarmists were rarely heard from until the fall of 1999.

Too Much Information

It is often difficult for a researcher to gather enough information about collective behavior when an episode occurs. Most of the analyses in this book are based upon newspaper articles and a few interviews with participants or witnesses. However, the hysteria surrounding Y2K lasted for a few years. The biggest problem encountered while writing this chapter was dealing with too much information. Books dedicated to the idea that Y2K was going to cause major problems for the world were available in bookstores, department stores, grocery stores, gas stations; virtually anywhere one looked. The Internet, in particular, yielded a bewildering mass of materials. A Webcrawler search of the Internet for "Y2K" and "the end of the world" on March 9, 1999 yielded 1,343 hits. The same search yielded 4,230 hits on December 29, 1999. The information in this chapter comes from hundreds of newspaper and magazine articles, dozens of Internet sites and e-mail alerts, books, magazines, pamphlets, newsletters, television and radio news broadcasts, and personal interviews with journalists, computer programmers, and people involved with Y2K preparation.

Different Levels of Fear, Different Courses of Action

Several different levels of fear were related to Y2K, and therefore several different levels of participation were involved. Most Americans did not take drastic action to prepare for the predicted catastrophe, but thousands did. Hundreds of thousands of people bought books, videos, and magazines to help them prepare and survive. Millions watched the New Year roll in around the world, anxiously waiting to see if the lights would go out in underprepared or unprepared nations. The most extreme participants tried to convince everyone around them that the world (or at least modern civilization) was about to end. This viewpoint will probably be characterized in years to come as representative of the entire Y2K hysteria. However, it is important to remember that millions of people did not believe the extreme doomsday scenarios, but *did* take part in preparations for what they believed was going to be a real problem throughout the world. Each of the various levels of panic must be addressed separately before we can discuss the entire event in a coherent manner. It is also important to remember that Y2K was a genuine problem. Thousands of computer systems had to be fixed to rectify the year discrepancy. The hysteria, though, centered around rumors that were never be true in the first place (falling airplanes, stranded cars, etc.), the belief that the problem could never be fixed in time, and in making extensive preparations for a social shutdown that never came. People who addressed their software problems were working to solve a problem; people who stocked up on supplies and braced themselves for catastrophe were taking part in the largest episode of millennial hysteria in recent Western history.

There were different beliefs about the size, nature, and severity of the Y2K problem. Consequently, there were different levels of action in preparation for the New Year. At the most extreme were those who truly believed that the world would come to an end or that modern civilization would collapse. These individuals published books and articles urging everyone to prepare for life in the dark ages. They built survival shelters in the wilderness and prepared for life "off the grid" (independent of electricity, telephones, and so on). The majority of these *hardcore Y2K Believers* were already involved with anti-government, anti-technology, or anti-society beliefs and actions before they ever heard of Y2K.

One step down from this were the people who thought that society would be thrown into chaos by all of the disruptions, but not into permanent meltdown. These *softcore Y2K Believers* tended to stockpile a few months' or years' worth of supplies, along with plenty of weapons and ammunition to protect themselves from the hordes of hungry city-dwellers. Some mild Believers expected society to experience many and possibly lengthy disruptions that would make daily life challenging, but also expected society to overcome these problems. They stockpiled food, along with generators, lanterns, and so forth. However, they were less likely to emphasize a need for weapons and did not expect the total breakdown of social order.

Cautious participants were slightly less panicked. They believed there would be sporadic problems, with some systems failing totally, but that daily life would continue as usual for most people. They spent most of their time checking everything (their own cars, appliances, computers, etc., along with their local bank's and utilities' level of preparedness) to make certain their fears would not come to be realized.

The least extreme level of participants were the millions of Americans who worried about possible problems but did not take drastic measures to prepare. The *Worriers* filled up their gas tanks, took extra cash out of their bank accounts, and spent New Year's Eve at home, anxiously watching television for signs of breakdown throughout the world. These millions of "normal" people who scared themselves and their friends make up the bulk of Y2K hysteria participants.

Not all Americans fell prey to the hysteria. There were *Skeptics* who, for various reasons, were absolutely confident that nothing at all would happen when the calendar rolled over to 2000. Some Skeptics had no more technical knowledge than those who did panic. They made their judgments using the same available information, but filtered that information through different social, political, or religious beliefs. Other Skeptics possessed sufficient understanding of computer technology to know that the most extreme predictions were impossible and/or illogical.

Official statements and actions by state and federal government officials tended to reinforce the beliefs of each of these groups. However, most officials seemed to believe that it was better to encourage preparation for a nonproblem than to risk failures and an unprepared public. Therefore, the government response can be viewed as leaning toward hysteria.

Hardcore Y2K Believers

The most extreme of all the Y2K hysterics were those who truly believed that January 1, 2000, would bring the destruction of modern civilization. Some of these individuals believed that various biblical prophecies would come to pass because the year 2000 was the logical end of times, or because we had angered God. Some simply argued that we had become too "soft" and reliant on technology. Others believed that aliens or secret government groups would use the coming Y2K chaos as a cover for their own covert actions. All agreed on one thing: life as we know it would come to an end.

The End of the World as We Know It

Hardcore Y2K Believers coined a phrase to sum up their vision of the end-times: "TEOTWAWKI" (The End Of The World As We Know It). TEOT-WAWKI Believers were firmly convinced that the collapse of modern civilization would begin in January of the year 2000.

Hardcore TEOTWAWKI Believers were certain the entire grid of computers throughout the world would shut down. They believed that this would lead to rioting and looting in every city throughout the world. This, in turn, would precipitate the collapse of civilized society. Only those who were prepared for such chaos would survive. One author argued that disasters tend to destroy societies at their peak, and this could be America's peak. He claimed that many people throughout the Western world would die because of Y2K meltdown. The same author also claimed that "preparing" is not "being afraid," and therefore preparing for Y2K was not a sign of fear (http://Y2Ksurvival.com/#top 3/8/99). Most Hardcore Y2K Believers based their outlook on apocalyptic Christian or antisocial Luddite beliefs.

Christian Millenarians   Many of the hardcore Y2K Believers accepted the TEOTWAWKI position for religious reasons. There were thousands of Christians across the country who believed that Y2K would end the world. Many believed that 2000 would mark the return of Christ, the reign of Satan, or the literal end of the world. Either way, life as we know it would be over.

The idea that something as momentous as a new calendar century and millennium could be insignificant or meaningless did not fit their belief system. The reality that our Gregorian calendar has been wildly inaccurate and readjusted several times in the past did not trouble them. The fact that the year 2000 was actually the last year of the twentieth century and second millennium, not the first year of the twenty-first century and third millennium, seemed to completely escape them as well.

Most Christian millenarians believed that God would end the world, and the computer was just His chosen tool. Some argued that God was angry because "we" (modern society) had replaced Him with the computer. Many considered doubting Y2K destruction to be akin to doubting their Christian faith (Junod 1999). Others believed that computers were actually the tools of Satan. Articles with titles such as "Would God Judge America?" and "Y2K Opportunity for Antichrist" indicate the general slant of the Christian millenarians: We have lost our way, fallen from grace, and angered God. We are at the mercy of evil and now we will be punished. Before God could renew our society, He would destroy and humble us. "God will not bring his revival to America, except on a platter of ruin" (quoted in Junod 1999:98). God simply chose the computer as His tool of destruction.

Luddite Survivalists   Not all of the TEOTWAWKI Believers based their hysteria on religious beliefs. A number of secular individuals attributed the coming end to purely social and technological causes. Their logic was equally simple: Mankind has become too weak, too dependent upon others, and too dependent upon machines. The machines will fail, and everything else will collapse along with it. Humanity will be plunged back into the Dark Ages, but those with the proper survival skills, knowledge, and equipment will persevere.

They did not attribute our predicament to spiritual decline but to something more closely resembling weakness. Luddites are opposed to technological change in principle. They believe that technology itself is inherently dehumanizing, degrading, or weakening of humanity. Modern societies in general, and high technology in particular, are considered inherently suspicious. The Luddite survivalists view electricity, running water, computers, video games, and other conveniences of modern life as crutches that undermine our independence, ruggedness, and self-reliance. This outlook was well-represented in many of the Y2K survival guides published throughout 1998 and 1999. Many of the Luddites seemed to look forward to Y2K as a time to teach "them" (us) a lesson. *U.S. News & World Report* ran a story about a man who moved to a farm in rural Virginia, armed himself with six AK-47 machine guns, built a bunker, and had all of his teeth pulled so that he wouldn't need dentists anymore (Longman 1999). He and his wife were stockpiling supplies and patiently waiting for Y2K to create havoc and destruction in every city throughout the United States.

It is particularly ironic that many of these anti-technology people had websites on the Internet. They used computers to spread the message that computers would destroy society. Gary North emerged as the self-appointed spokesman for hardcore Believers during the late 1990s. He created one of the largest Y2K-oriented websites on the internet (www.garynorth.com). Many other Believers deferred to North as the leading expert and compiler of Y2K-related materials.

A long-time spreader of doom and apocalyptic beliefs, North latched onto Y2K as the sure-fire trigger to end civilization. His blend of apocalyptic Christian beliefs and Luddite survivalism endeared him to many different brands of Believer. In an editorial ("The Year 2000 Problem: The Year the Earth Stands Still") posted on his website in June of 1998, North wrote:

> At 12 midnight on January 1, 2000 (a Saturday morning), most of the world's mainframe computers will either shut down or begin spewing out bad data . . . This will create a nightmare for every area of life, in every region of the industrialized world.
>
> Months before January 1, 2000, the world's stock markets will have crashed . . . A worldwide run on the banks will create havoc in the investment markets . . . How will you even get paid? How will your employer get paid? How will governments get paid?
>
> Everything is tied together by computers. If computers go down or can no longer be trusted, everything falls apart (http://www.garynorth.com/ 3/9/99).

He concluded the same article by stating, "I'm not a programmer. My Ph.D. is in history" (ibid). The fact that many of these predictions had already failed by late 1999 apparently did not deter North. "I maintain that the y2k problem is systemic. It cannot be fixed. . . . There are not enough programmers to fix it. . . . We are facing the breakdown of civilization . . ." (http://www.garynorth.com/ 11/8/99). With that, he urged everyone to move out of the cities, preferably to Northern Arkansas. North and others like him are excellent examples of people who spread the hysteria and provided many other hardcore TEOTWAWKI Believers with rationales for their odd theories.

Both the apocalyptic Christians and the Luddite survivalists always claimed to be hitting the "logical middle between two extremes." As the Virginia survivalist mentioned above said, "We're not survivalist nut cases" (Longman 1999:47), to which the reader might logically wonder "then who is?" The apocalyptic Christians and Luddite survivalists never considered the possibility that nothing at all might happen. The "middle ground" they hit fell between mild hysteria and extreme panic, creating the illusion of a middle-of-the-road perspective. The constant presence of hardcore TEOTWAWKI viewpoints and the absence of skeptical rebuttals in the popular media created a situation where not participating in the hysteria seemed like an "extreme response" to many. This allowed Believers to depict skepticism as extremism. Clearly, the hardcore Believers' response to Y2K uncertainty went far beyond what most would consider reasonable preparation.

Softcore Believers

There were also thousands of less extreme individuals who nonetheless believed that society would be seriously harmed and possibly destroyed by Y2K-related problems. These softcore Believers often ridiculed the hardcore TEOTWAWKI Believers as "survivalists" and "conspiracy theorists." Such remarks made the softcore Believers seem reasonable and rational by comparison. However, they were still preaching a similar message: The world will not be the same after January 2000. One softcore author even referred to the idea that nothing at all would happen as a "nonscenario," an impossibility. The only "legitimate" scenarios in his book were:

1. "Brownout"—isolated failures and interruptions, collapse of the IRS, and severe economic recession lasting several weeks or months.
2. "Blackout"—multiple, simultaneous failures, widespread looting and rioting, collapse of sanitation, transportation, etc., and massive economic depression lasting for several months or years.
3. "Meltdown"—total collapse of American society and economy, widespread starvation, and a "new dark age" that would last between four and ten years (Hyatt 1998).

As one seller of survival supplies put it, "Our food supply is fragile. . . . Cities where food can't be delivered will eventually be gutted, looted, and evacuated and likely burned to the ground . . . You need to start stocking food" (www.y2ksupply.com/index.asp? PageID=Food 11/3/00). Another softcore Believer wrote, "Start considering alternate transportation . . . horses and carts might be an option" (O'Riley 1998:88).

At first glance, this may seem no different from the hardcore Y2K Believers' outlook, but the key difference is in emphasis: They agreed that meltdown *could* occur, but *expected* a milder brownout or blackout scenario. Most softcore Believers focused on economic disaster. Life and death survival could potentially be a problem, but economic recession and/or depression were considered a certainty. For example: "I'm taking all my money out of the bank. They can promise all they want, but I just don't trust it" (Chris Cook, *The Joplin Globe* 9/12/99: Y2K-3). Said Edward Yourdon in "My Y2K Outlook: A Year of Disruptions, a Decade of Depression":

> . . . it will be difficult (if not impossible) to maintain the level of productivity and efficiency that many of us are accustomed to . . . I believe that Y2K will be equivalent to throwing a million monkey wrenches into the 'engine' of the global economy, and that it will lead to a depression similar in severity and duration to the Great Depression (http://www.yourdon.com/articles/y2koutlook.html 2/17/99 and 1/3/00).

The softcore Believers tended to fall into two camps. They either believed that computer breakdown would cause economic chaos, or they believed that Y2K panic would be the catalyst that would unleash hoarding and violence. Either way, social life would be disrupted. They seemed convinced that theirs was the only reasonable response.

> If they can't find you, they can't hurt you. *While one should avoid an alarmist mentality,* the fact is that no one in an urban, or even suburban area can be certain of what will happen should serious social disorder arise with the new millennium. Many programmers dealing with the year 2000 bug have already purchased and developed remote tracts of land in the midwest. Some have highly advanced security systems to assure the safety of their families and possessions, should the situation become so desperate that those in the crumbling cities seek them out. (http://home.earthlink.net/~aaronb17/sanc.html 3/9/99 and 1/24/00, emphasis added.)

Hardcore and softcore Y2K Believers frequently repeated the "fact" that many computer programmers had already given up and built high-tech bunkers somewhere isolated and remote. However, this information was impossible to confirm and is likely a fabrication or rumor.

The softcore Believers could not accept the idea that others' lack of concern could possibly be reasonable, and therefore dismissed it as a sign of faulty reasoning. They depicted TEOTWAWKI advocates as lunatics and referred to skeptics as being in denial (see, for example, Davidson and McLaughlin 1998).

Softcore Believers spent most of their time writing about the potential collapse of social order. One of the best examples of this perspective is the *Y2K Citizen's Action Guide*: *Preparing yourself, your family, and your neighborhood for the year 2000 computer problem and beyond*. This booklet was mailed, free of charge, to all subscribers of *Utne Reader* magazine in November of 1998. The booklet, available at bookstores and online, was recommended by a number of Y2K websites. The first two pages are quotes from various sources, including: "This is not a prediction, it is a certainty—there will be a serious disruption in the world's financial services industry. . . . It's going to be ugly." (attributed to *The Sunday Times,* London) and "We're concerned about the potential disruption of power grids, telecommunications, and banking services." (attributed to Sherry Burns, CIA). None of these quotes came with a date, many did not list a specific author or speaker, and none of them explained the context in which the quote first appeared. All were used to create the impression that a lot of important people were worried about Y2K.

Another example of the softcore Believer perspective can be found in *The Millennium Bug*: *How to Survive the Coming Chaos* by Michael Hyatt (1998). The front cover of the book boldly displays these phrases:

12:01am [sic] January 1, 2000
- Your electricity goes off.
- Phones aren't working.
- The computer at your local bank crashes.
- Police and 911 are nowhere to be found.
- The illusion of social stability is about to be shattered . . . and nothing can be done to stop it.
- Can you protect yourself, your family, and everything you have worked for?

The book argues that everything we take for granted in modern life is going to fail us, that this will cause widespread chaos, and, ultimately, only those who prepare beforehand will come out with their lives intact. He does not claim that the world will end or that civilization will collapse. Like Utne,

O'Riley, and the other writers in *Y2K Citizen's Action Guide,* Hyatt preaches the softcore litany of failures, disruptions, and possible civil breakdown. Interestingly, the back cover of the book jacket also repeats the untrue tale that "computers ordered the destruction of tons of corned beef" under the heading "warning signs" (see The Role of Mainstream Media, below). Apparently, like many authors, journalists, and "experts," Hyatt never bothered to call Marks and Spencer, the site of the alleged destruction, to find out what really happened.

Softcore Believer articles, interviews, and websites all made bold statements about impending failure. For example: ". . . the probability of substantial failure [throughout society] is sufficiently great" (Halpern 1998:10). "It's inevitable, and it's going to be terribly ugly when it happens" (Hyatt 1998:3). "Indeed, I believe that it is inevitable that it [Y2K] could disrupt the entire global economy in several ways" (Edward Yardeni, Chief Economist for Duetsche Morgan Grenfell, a global investment firm, opening remarks in testimony before the Senate Banking, Housing, and Urban Affairs Committee, Nov. 4, 1997; quoted in Hyatt 1998:233). "By the time you read this there will be little more than a year to prepare for what I have come to believe will be the social equivalent of a worldwide earthquake" (Utne 1998:13). Those statements would come to haunt them once January arrived.

The Cautious and the Worried: Panic, Just in Case

The next level of participants did not believe they were actually involved in any unusual activity. Their perspective can best be summed up like so: "No one can say what will happen. The world probably won't go into meltdown. Preparing will help if it does, and won't hurt anything if it doesn't. I am going to prepare for the worst, just in case it happens." This was often contrasted with "irrational" beliefs (hardcore and softcore Believers), and depicted as being similar to buying an insurance policy to be covered for an accident that might never happen. Said one citizen, "I think it's probably not going to happen, but I'd rather be safe than sorry. I'm taking my money out of the bank" (Angie O'Dell, *The Joplin Globe* 9/12/99: Y2K-4). These participants accepted a belief that preparing for disaster was the only prudent course of action to take.

Prepare for the Worst, Hope for the Best

Cautious participants did not believe that society would collapse or that civilization would disappear. They did not expect martial law to be declared or the United Nations to take over the United States. They believed that the country would be just fine and that our lives would not be in danger. However, they also assumed that Y2K would cause major problems with various services. They reasoned that electricity, telephones, personal computers, billing services, shipping services, and other vital components of modern society would experience disruptions and cause a major slow-down of life as usual.

All of this led to a slightly less extreme variation of the softcore Believ-ers' vision for 2000: There might be rioting in the streets, but it would be spo-radic. There might be looting and hoarding, but it would not be catastrophic. There might be serious disruptions in electricity, water, and so on, but the properly prepared individual would pull through just fine. Those who took the "panic, just in case" approach often argued that to *not* prepare would be irresponsible. Over and over they indicated that these things would only come to pass if too many people failed to prepare. *Those people* would be pan-icked. *Those people* would be rioting and looting. *Those people* would realize, too late, that they should have prepared just in case. "If all does not go well and martial law is put into effect, we are all going to find out the true mean-ing of the words 'hard times'" (community activist Amy Smiley quoted in spe-cial section of the *Kansas City Star*). "If I prepare for the worst and nothing happens, what am I out? Some money? But if all hell breaks loose and *you* haven't done anything, you're dead" (survivalist quoted in Giese 1999:120).

Cross Your Fingers and Hope for the Best

The Worried were an even milder variation. They kept actual preparations to a minimum, but double-checked everything before the end of December to make certain everything would be okay. Then, they put extra gas into their automobiles, pulled extra cash out of the bank, and sat at home anxiously waiting to see if the power would go out.

Y2K Skeptics

Not everyone in the United States fell prey to Y2K hysteria. By November of 1999, Y2K had become a joke for many. McDonald's began to run "FrY-2K" commercials, depicting people stockpiling mounds of McDonald's french-fries. Some Skeptics went out of their way to convince others that there was no real problem, but many ignored the entire issue and went about their daily lives unaffected by the hysteria. Skeptical newspaper articles were few and far be-tween. Further, they tended to blend in with all of the more hysterical Y2K articles because even the fairly extreme Believers claimed to be using ratio-nal thought and a common-sense approach to the issue. Most Skeptics fell into one of two general categories: Those who believed Y2K would cause only insignificant problems, and those who believed that it would cause absolutely no problems at all.

Speedbumps and Hiccups

The most common skeptical articles characterized Y2K as a "speedbump" or "bump in the road." They argued that there would probably be some isolated, mild computer failures or "hiccups" caused by Y2K, but these would be no

As this photograph from late 1999 shows, many people reacted to Y2K hysteria with a sense of humor.

more disruptive to daily life than driving over a speedbump disrupts a trip. We would notice the failures, fix them, and then move on. For example: "I think we'll be without power for a few days. My friends will probably unplug their computers at midnight . . . " (Teresa Brown, *The Joplin Globe* 9/12/99: Y2K-3); "I think the banks are probably squared away, but I don't know how things like Social Security checks will be. Some things might be a problem" (Mike Qualls, *The Joplin Globe* 9/12/99: Y2K-4).

In August of 1999 "Dear Abby" ran a letter from Carl Schutte, "a computer operations manager for a large company." Schutte assured the public that most of the things predicted would not occur, and those few things that did happen would be quickly and easily dealt with. He pointed out that everyone had been without electricity at least once in his or her life, and they did not perish, so why would it be such a huge catastrophe if it were to happen on January 1?

There Is No Problem

A far less common perspective, but one that could be found if one looked hard enough, stated that nothing unusual would happen on January 1. There would be no shutdowns, no blackouts, no disruptions, and no real problems. Two people interviewed for a special Y2K section of *The Joplin Globe* expressed this view in simple terms: "I don't think anything is going to go wrong" (Gilbert McHone, *The Joplin Globe* 9/12/99: Y2K-3), "I think it will be [just] another year. I don't think it will be any kind of problem at all." (ibid: Y2K-10).

Throughout 1999, it became clear that most people who were paying any attention to Y2K were convinced that the "no problem" perspective was either naïve, delusional, or just plain incorrect. Most individuals who believed that

Y2K was not going to cause problems (or who didn't know enough about it to care in the first place) didn't bother to set up websites or to write books and articles. Consequently, this perspective is underrepresented within the written record. Some journalists managed to interview one skeptic among all the believers, but many did not. The idea that Y2K would be an insignificant event almost never appeared in newspaper and magazine articles. Instead, journalists focused on alarmist individuals and began to describe the elaborate preparations being made by various people and institutions.

At least one well-known computer software expert told me that reporters called frequently asking for quotes throughout the year but were less insistent when told the quote would downplay Y2K as a problem. Some skeptics avoided talking to reporters in the first place from fear of being misquoted or of contributing to the hysteria. As a result, most news articles in 1999 lacked the Skeptic perspective.

A few articles did manage to convey the idea that Y2K would be a dud. In January of 1999, James Gleick wrote a column for the *New York Times* titled "Fast Forward—Doomsday Machines." Wrote Gleick:

> [Those who look back on Y2K hysteria will conclude that] ". . . we are a silly species, easily confused and given to sudden fits of hysteria. . . . We [members of news media] have been co-conspirators of an army of people with a vested interest in seeing money spent on the [Y2K] problem: consultants, hardware manufacturers, corporate and government information-technology managers, plaintiff's lawyers, and more.
>
> A confession: the first *New York Times* account of the year 2000 problem appeared in this column, back in June 1996. I'm sorry.
>
> The amount of time that you, a dutiful citizen of the modern world, should spend worrying about Y2K is zero" (1/24/99:6.16).

He then goes through a list of reasons why one should not expect anything horrible to happen January 1, 2000. He argued that many of the failures being harped on by alarmists either happen all the time or wouldn't happen at all, and those failures that might occur would be meaningless and insignificant. Although a number of articles appeared throughout 1999 pleading for a calm and rational approach to Y2K, Gleick was one of the few journalists who went so far as to state that Y2K was not a real problem.

In a February 1999 interview for *Working Woman Magazine,* Nancy Leveson, full professor of aeronautics and astronautics at the Massachusetts Institute of Technology (MIT) and the world's leading expert in air safety computer software, dismissed Y2K as a trivial issue. She did not say that there was no such problem, only that its effects would be miniscule and extremely easy to fix.

Marilyn Vos Savant, who writes a weekly answer column for *Parade* magazine, also argued in May of 1999 that Y2K was not a problem. She stated that the only reason people noticed it was because it happened to coincide with the year 2000 (which seemed significant because it was such a big, round number). She then argued that over-reporting by journalists was creating needless anxiety over such a small problem. "These reports are causing concern disproportionate to the threat involved. . . . But I currently believe that, other than scaring half of us half to death, any serious consequences will be scattered and only temporary" (1999:19). It is a difficult argument to refute, particularly with the benefit of hindsight.

Because so many of the hardcore TEOTWAWKI Believers were apocalyptic Christians, it may come as a surprise to learn that many Christians were also among the most skeptical. *Charisma & Christian Life,* a magazine dedicated to the same evangelical, charismatic Christianity that many of the most extreme apocalyptic Believers follow, ran an entire issue in July of 1999 dedicated to convincing readers that devout Christians should not expect, hope for, or prepare for the end of the world. The lead editorial, "Silly Rumors, Crazy Fears" set the tone for articles with titles such as "Why We Must Reject Millennium Madness" and "Why I'm Not Afraid of Y2K." The writers and editors took care to check out some of the false tales being circulated (see The Role of Mainstream Media, below) and discovered that all of them were false, wildly exaggerated, or had nothing at all to do with Y2K computer failures.

The articles pointed out that many ". . . Christians . . . embraced kooky predictions about the end of the world," (Grady 1999:6) pushed by ". . . prophecy peddlers who are promising Christ's return" (Abanes 1999:42). One author pointed out that these predictions had always been wrong in the past. For example, in 1988 a book announcing the world would end in 1989 sold 4.5 *million* copies. The same book has been rereleased every year since then as a "Final" report. Many in the evangelical Christian world saw Y2K hysteria as yet another example of hucksters and alarmists making a great deal of money by scaring the weak with their false prophecies.

The Official Government Position: Leaning Toward Hysteria

Most federal government officials maintained an air that can best be described as "leaning toward hysteria." Public statements prior to 1999 ranged from wildly inflammatory to mildly paranoid. For example, Arthur Gross, Chief Information Officer for the IRS was quoted as saying "Failure to achieve compliance with the year 2000 will jeopardize our way of life on this planet for some time to come." Senator Robert Bennett, Chairman of the Senate's Special Committee on the Year 2000 Problem weighed in with a milder ". . . I am generally concerned about the possibility of power shortages . . . Don't panic, but don't spend too much time sleeping, either" (both quoted in the *Utne Reader Y2K Citizen's Action Guide*: 4–5). The federal government of the United States issued a Y2K survival guide containing the following statements:

> Computers not able to properly recognize the year 2000 date may produce incorrect data or shut down . . . the large number and inter-connectivity of computers we depend upon every day make Y2K a serious challenge.

Organizations taking a wait and see approach to the Y2K issue are placing themselves—and the people they serve—at a greater risk of experiencing difficulties related to the date change. (4)

With those words, the federal government officially declared a) the Y2K problem is a real threat, and b) failure to prepare would be dangerous and irresponsible.

FEMA (the Federal Emergency Management Agency) spokesman Marc Wolfson stated that the agency would prepare exactly as they had for Hurricane Floyd, and NASA (National Aeronautics and Space Administration) powered down everything they could shut off. A fourteen-person "civil disturbance team" was kept on standby in the city of Joplin, Missouri, (population 40,000) in case riots broke out at midnight. The entire city of Grants Pass, Oregon, stockpiled supplies at the urging of the mayor. The city of North Kansas City, with a population of just over 4,000, spent nearly $347,000 on a 1,200-amp generator for the water-treatment plant and pump stations. These official city, state, and federal actions lent credibility to the "panic, just in case" approach.

On March 2, 1999, the U.S. Senate Special Committee on the Year 2000 Technology Problem released "Investigating the Impact of the Year 2000 Problem." The report, dated February 24, concluded that society would not collapse, but there might be civil unrest. They did not predict any catastrophes, but stated that there could be serious glitches. All of this, the release stated, was unlikely to last for more than a few days. It was apparently never suggested that Y2K would cause no significant problems at all. This report also set the tone that most U.S. officials would adhere to for the rest of the year: Prepare as you would for a severe winter storm.

A Three-day Storm

The official U.S. government *Y2K Guide* suggested that people keep at least a three-day supply of food and water in their houses. Federal officials gradually adopted the position that all Americans should prepare as they would for "a three-day storm." While members of the federal government went out of their way to assure citizens that the world would not be plunged into darkness and martial law would not be declared, they also encouraged all Americans to prepare for a temporary crisis and to expect lingering problems with financial transactions, billing, and records.

Issue #1 of *Y2K Bulletin: Preparedness Guide*, published by FEMA in early 1999, contains the following paragraph under the heading "Know Your Risks":

Whether or not any of these projections come true, we need to prepare. We need to take the same approach we use with hurricanes, tornadoes, floods and other natural disasters. *Plan for the worst and hope for the best* (1: emphasis in original).

FEMA's support for preparing as a form of insurance against the unlikely gave credence to those pushing survivalist stockpiling.

Most government agencies and officials did all they could to quell TEOT-WAWKI beliefs, but simultaneously gave support to the milder forms of hysteria. The myth of the "three-day storm" lent legitimacy to the Cautious/Worrier outlook.

Changing Tunes

By the end of 1999, public officials began to take a more calm and measured approach. Although most still advocated the "three-day storm" level of preparation, federal officials seemed to be directly concerned with stifling hysteria. For example, on June 29, 1999, the FAA (the Federal Aviation Administration, which oversees all air travel in the United States) announced that there would be absolutely no Y2K problems and the FDIC (the Federal Deposit Insurance Corporation) announced that 98 percent of all U.S. banks had been Y2K tested twice, and ATMs would still work. This unified approach to calmly refuting extreme Y2K rumors and beliefs may have helped calm many people down, and at least removed the government from the long list of sources adding to the hysteria. To his credit, Alan Greenspan (director of the Federal Reserve and, by many accounts, the single individual most responsible for investor confidence in the United States today) publicly announced that Y2K would not harm the U.S. economy. By November of 1999, then-President Clinton announced that there would be no major disruptions on January 1 because all major areas had been brought into Y2K compliance. Jane Garvey, administrator of the FAA, announced that she would be flying in a commercial airliner as midnight struck. However, the U.S. government also spent fifty million dollars to create a year 2000 crisis center to "track glitches." Believers took this as confirmation that their fears and worries were reasonable.

Chain of Beliefs

People had to accept a chain of beliefs, all related, in order to believe that January 1, 2000 might really bring catastrophe. Hardcore Believers, softcore Believers, and Worriers all accepted at least one of the following ideas: the "Domino Effect," panic as a typical response to disaster, danger from outside the United States, and the possibility that Y2K fears might trigger social chaos before January 1 even arrived.

The Domino Effect

The term "domino effect" began to appear more and more toward the end of 1999. Sometimes referred to as "cascading failures" or a "cascading effect," the reasoning behind the domino effect held that any one computer with a Y2K problem would, in turn, give false data or no data at all to any other computers it was linked to. This would cause all interconnected computers to fail or malfunction, thereby increasing the size of the problem exponentially and passing it along to other computers or systems. One non-compliant computer could literally cause the collapse of entire systems, and one collapsed system could cause the collapse of several other systems (see Halpern 1998, Hyatt 1998, etc.). Participants who accepted this hypothesis seemed to believe that most of the world's computers constantly exchange data with each other.

Proponents of the domino effect argued that this made it impossible for society to prepare for Y2K effectively because any one computer could take all the others down with it. Since it is impossible to fix every single computer, all of the computers would fail. It is not a question of "if" things will stop working, but "how soon?" and "for how long?": "*When the clock strikes midnight on January 1, 2000, computer systems all over the world will begin spewing out bad data—or stop working altogether!*" (Hyatt 1998:3, italics in original). Bills would be lost, accounts would be wiped out, and banks would collapse all over the world: "**have a couple year's worth of rent socked away in cash** . . . the banking system is in grave danger" (www.prepare4Y2K.com/myadvice. htm 3/3/99 and 1/3/00; emphasis in original).

Civil Disorder and Riots in the Streets

Y2K hysteria participants also discussed the almost certain possibility of looting and rioting. They seemed to believe that disaster always leads to chaos and violence. In fact, people tend to pull together in a disaster, working long and hard to help total strangers survive the situation that they have found themselves in. When massive floods displaced hundreds of thousands in the Midwestern United States in 1992, National Guardsmen reported no looting and no fighting (personal interview, author's files). Y2K Believers didn't know this. They all believed that once people lost electricity, running water, or access to gasoline and groceries, civil disorder and chaos would quickly follow. They expected riots to break out in every major city across the country, and desperate (unprepared) people to engage in looting for the supplies they would need to stay alive. Your neighbors might become your enemies. The advice was simple: Move to an isolated, rural area and don't tell your neighbors that you have food and fuel in your basement.

Those Damn Foreigners: International Dependence and Terrorism

It became clear toward the end of 1999 that most of the major utilities and industries in the United States would handle the rollover just fine. Hardcore Believers disregarded any such information as "propaganda," but less-extreme participants generally accepted the good news as legitimate. However, they did not back away from their gloomy stance. Instead, they decided that the *real* Y2K threat was from overseas. Proponents of the domino effect simply expanded the concept beyond the borders of the United States: *We* might be prepared for Y2K, but *they* (various foreign nations with whom the United States trades goods and services) are not ready. When foreign nations' systems go down, they would take our nation's systems down with them. Or, their societies would collapse into chaos and this would leave us without a supply of (for example) oil. As one softcore Believer so delicately put it, "Do you trust the people in charge of Saudi Arabia, Iraq, Iran, and Kuwait with your life?" (www.y2ksupply.com/index.asp?PageID=Food 11/3/00). Without oil, we can't function properly. A depression will hit after all. Stepanek wrote an article entitled "Hold the Bubbly, For Now: Y2K will effect everyone, from the ready to the clueless" for *Business Week* magazine (October 1999), in which she specifically named Indonesia, China, and Venezuela as potential problems because they failed to take Y2K seriously as a threat. Other writers echoed these sentiments, but focused on China and Russia as the biggest "problem areas."

There was another threat from outside the United States that many, including government officials, accepted as gospel: foreign terrorists would use Y2K for their own evil purposes. Major cities like Seattle, Washington, cancelled public celebrations, confident that anti-American forces would use Y2K for their own evil purposes. They believed that bad people from all over the world would take advantage of Y2K failures (or Y2K hysteria) to wreak havoc on our society.

The Only Thing to Fear Is Fear Itself

Some Y2K Believers, Cautious, and Worried participants feared social chaos that would take place before any computer disruptions actually occurred. They argued that panic, hoarding, and selfishness within the American population would cause major problems even if computer failures were not a direct threat. In fact, they expected the problems to begin before January 1, 2000 even arrived.

Grossman (1998) argued computer failure itself might not be a major problem; the real problems might occur in December when panicked mobs began to fight over the last supplies in town. Those who feared Y2K panic predicted bank runs and hoarding, which they believed would lead to shortages of critical supplies, creating more panic and, in turn, more hoarding. This cycle would end with major riots and disturbances caused by panicky and unprepared citizens. As one interviewee put it, "I thought it was possible that all those people who bought guns to 'be prepared' might end up shooting friends and loved ones by accident. . . . It is my experience that it is usually the 'demon you know' who causes you problems, i.e., stupid people doing stupid things" (author's files). Another said, "I do agree with one prediction that I've heard, is that the most serious concern about Y2K is the panic. I am concerned about that" (author's files).

All of these beliefs made social chaos seem unavoidable to those who accepted them. Most of the softcore Believers accepted all of them, while Cautious and Worried participants accepted one or two. Whether or not a
potential participant accepted or rejected these beliefs determined their level
of hysteria.

Accepting or Rejecting Rumors and Beliefs

As discussed in Chapter 10, accepting a rumor frequently depends upon one's
existing knowledge and beliefs. Many of the Y2K rumors circulating required
the believer to *not* know much about the technology involved. A lack of knowledge often equates to a willingness to accept bad information. This was certainly true in the case of Y2K. Most of those who were leading the hysteria
knew a little about computers, but not much. This is why they accepted beliefs that seemed clearly illogical to those who better understood computer
technology and the nature of the software problem. For example, only someone who does not understand the role of computer chips in a modern automobile would believe that it might not start after January 1, 2000.

Many of those pushing panic had impressive-sounding credentials that
seemed to establish them as authorities. However, a Ph.D. in history or economics does absolutely nothing to help one understand the nature of a computer software problem. Being the head of a large corporation does not give
one any special understanding of society or human nature. Many of the "experts" seemed almost willfully ignorant, being careful to only seek information that would support what they already believed.

As is often the case in our information-saturated society, a great deal of
conflicting information was being disseminated. When faced with such situations, people must choose what to believe. This choice is most likely based
on our perception of the credibility of the source (Is it someone we trust or
respect?) and on our perception of the credibility of the information (Does it
fit what we already know?). Our own personal beliefs and prior knowledge
heavily influence each of these judgements. Pessimists and those with the
most distrust of the social status quo were most likely to fall for the Y2K hysteria. Optimists with thorough working knowledge of computers and/or a
basic faith in the government, society, and humanity were the least likely to
fall for it.

The Role of Mainstream Media

Intense, credible media coverage plays a role in spreading false beliefs in
many collective delusions (Bartholomew and Wessely 1999). This was certainly true for the Y2K hysteria. For example, the lead article for a special
Y2K section of *The Joplin Globe* began with this line: "It was discovered several years ago that some computer systems were designed to self-destruct, to
cease functioning when the language they are governed by can no longer read

the date" (9/12/99:2). This is not true. No computer systems were "designed to self-destruct" or to cease functioning, and the only problem that Y2K ever posed was that computers might make incorrect calculations if they interpreted "00" as "1900" rather than "2000."

Mainstream media sources circulated numerous false rumors of "Y2K failures" that had supposedly already occurred. It was constantly reported that sewage systems, electrical systems, financial and school records, and a variety of other systems had shut down completely or wildly malfunctioned when tested for Y2K compliance.

The June 2, 1997 cover story for *Newsweek Magazine,* "The Day the World Shuts Down" probably did more to legitimize Y2K fears than any other source because *Newsweek* is a respected, mainstream publication. In that story, it was reported that, "In Britain computers at the Marks & Spencer company have already mistakenly ordered the destruction of tons of corned beef, believing they were more than 100 years old" (Levy et al. 1997). However, a quick look at various British newspaper articles (readily available through Internet services such as EbscoHost and Lexis/Nexis) reveals that this never happened. No food was destroyed, and the "company" was actually a grocery store. A computerized scanner at the store misread the expiration date on some cans of corned beef, rejected them, and the beef was sent back to the distributor. The mistake was quickly discovered and easily corrected (*The Observer* 10/20/96, *The Daily Telegraph* 12/31/96). The story, however, intensified each time it was retold: a "rejected can of corned beef" (October 1996) became "rejected tins of corned beef" in December, "disposed consignment of corned beef" by January of 1997, then finally "tons of destroyed corned beef" in June of 1997.

Once the tale had been printed in *Newsweek,* it was accepted as fact and repeated endlessly by American magazines, newspapers, and websites. Virtually no one bothered to check the story out. When asked about having repeated the untrue tale in his own article, a business reporter for a regional newspaper in the Midwest said, "It happens. It's regrettable, unfortunate. If somebody [in the media] makes a mistake, it goes everywhere. My goal was to tell readers that things could happen to them. To warn them" (author's files). The author of the original *Newsweek* article said ". . . everyone talked about elevators [failing], so we had to find some elevators that didn't work when they did a [Y2K] test. . . . we just went and tried to find people who did tests and found they didn't work" (author's files). In other words, journalists actively sought out examples of malfunctions that could be blamed on Y2K. They did not write articles listing systems that had successfully passed Y2K tests, and the fact that the reported glitches had occurred in 1997 or 1998 did not seem to deter people from thinking of them as "Y2K failures." Any Y2K tale, no matter how improbable, was repeated endlessly once it hit the wire services. Journalists were too busy, too pressed for time, or too indifferent to bother confirming the stories before repeating them in their own articles. Half-true and untrue rumors of "Y2K events" spread throughout American society through newspapers, magazines, newsletters, and the Internet.

In December of 1998, a group of "international Y2K crisis managers" met at the United Nations to devise ways to soothe public panic. They drafted a formal resolution asking Hollywood not to produce any Y2K disaster films (Stepanek 1999). NBC did not heed this call and aired *Y2K, The Movie* in November of 1999. In the film, cars don't run, coffeemakers and telephones malfunction, a fighter jet crashes, ATMs don't work, there are massive blackouts, medical equipment fail, nuclear power plant workers die, prison door locks fail, and airports shut down. Y2K Skeptics were depicted as fools in denial. One has to wonder how many people watched the movie and took it to heart as a warning about how bad things might just become on January 1? It may have raised people's edginess from skeptical to mildly worried. More likely, Skeptics disregarded it while various levels of Believers took is as confirmation that they were right.

Y2K News Coverage 1997 to 2000

News stories about Y2K and its possible consequences ran constantly throughout 1998 and 1999. There were even a few printed in 2000. All of them discussed the terrible things that might happen. Most of the news stories did mention that Y2K would probably not be catastrophic. However, almost none of them stated that January 1 might come and go without a noticeable glitch. They saw no need to mention the possibility that Y2K might have no negative effects at all. As one reporter put it, "we tried to, as best we can at that point in time, try to be realistic about what the worst case was, and what the likely case was." When asked why his article did not include any "best case" scenarios, he replied "Well, that's obvious: nothing. It's an unstated assumption" (author's notes).

The focus of the stories often shifted from Y2K itself to the people who were preparing for it. "Year 2000 bug has some preparing for societal chaos" (San Jose *Mercury News* 3/9/99), a typical example of such stories, focused on interview snippets from a variety of frightened people and survivalists discussing "a return to a pre-1900 lifestyle." Many such articles included a statement or two from a skeptic, often talking about the dynamics of panic or fear. Respected, mainstream media sources provided a platform for a variety of survivalists, millenarians, and hucksters. They did so in such a manner as to dramatically outnumber the occasional skeptic, and to make the sources all appear equally credible. After all, doesn't being quoted in several articles for major news publications qualify one as an expert?

Most mainstream journalists seemed to take the "panic, just in case" or "leaning toward panic" outlook. That is, they almost all stated that the terrible things they wrote about were unlikely to occur, but always maintained an air of "it *could* happen" and *never* explicitly stated that absolutely nothing at all might occur. The fact that they tended to hedge and include words such as "might," "could," and "probably will not" does not change the fact that they provided a credible forum for people who were peddling hysteria and helped to give legitimacy to those hysterical beliefs.

"NBC Nightly News with Tom Brokaw" ran a story July 16, 1999 implying it was reasonable to fear losing all of the money in one's bank account, then went on to say that the "real worry" is a run on banks caused by panicking depositors. Brokaw is a trusted news anchor, and "Nightly News" is a major national news program. Announcing on a national newscast that people might panic and drain banks of their deposits could potentially lead to that very thing actually occurring.

When an article states that "growing numbers of Americans" are preparing for Armageddon, that "people" are buying huge amounts of grain, or that "reasonable citizens" are arming themselves in preparation for riots that could make the 1992 Los Angeles riots seem like "child's play," it is difficult to argue that the tone of the article is neutral. Even seemingly skeptical articles such as one in *Scientific American* (Grossman 1998) labeled Skeptics as "in denial." Alarmist hardcore and softcore Y2K Believers constantly referred to these mainstream media stories to show that other people supported their views and that Y2K was a problem that legitimate, mainstream sources were taking seriously.

Prophet Motives

Most of the Y2K hysteria participants were genuinely frightened, worried, or confused. However, many of those who generated the hysteria in the first place (the self-proclaimed "experts") also seem to have gained personally from the entire episode. It is difficult or impossible to know someone's ulterior motives, but there are at least three obvious ways in which the alarmists benefited: monetary profit, notoriety, and attempts to actually make their wishes come true.

Prophets and Profits   The profit motive of many Y2K experts is easy to spot. None of them went broke in 1999. Peter de Jager, one of the first to dedicate himself to sounding the Y2K alarm, tried to sell his "www.year2000.com" domain name on eBay, an online auction site, in January of 2000. He apparently expected to receive something in the range of one million dollars. The bidding was sabotaged by false bids and the sale was called off, but the entire event clearly indicates that de Jager expected to make a huge sum of money by selling something (access to Y2K information) that he himself created the demand for. Perhaps he believed that it would acquire value as a curiosity in the same way that the Ryder truck used to carry contested presidential election ballots to the Supreme Court in Florida did.

All of Gary North's Y2K publications strongly recommended buying more of his publications. Christian leaders like Jerry Falwell and Jack Van Impe sold thousands of books and videos with titles like *Y2K: A Christian's*

Survival Guide to the Millennium Bug. Pat Robertson, head of the Christian Broadcasting Network, held a Y2K conference in 1998. Over 200 people paid hundreds of dollars to attend (Junod 1999). Peter de Jager was one of the paid speakers at the conference.

Consultants got paid to consult for firms on how to fix their Y2K problems. Authors sold books. Freelance writers got articles published. Speakers were paid to speak, and many were booked solid throughout 1999. Merchants sold far more survival-related supplies than they do under normal circumstances. Every day Oliver North ran commercials on his radio show urging his listeners to spend all of their money buying gold and silver. Unscrupulous commodity companies bombarded potential investors with the message that precious metal was the only "safe" investment, because it would hold its value even if Y2K destroyed the economy.

Most of the TEOTWAWKI proponents sold newsletters, videos, books, pamphlets, and sometimes the survival supplies themselves (generators, grain, water purifiers, first-aid kits, guns and knives, and so forth). One peddler who stated "You need to start stocking food now" recommended buying his Y2K guide and a $389 supply of survival food, as well as paying to join his online "preparedness community." The organizer of a Y2K "Preparedness Expo," owner of a business selling survival supplies, stated that his business had doubled since Y2K concerns had cropped up. Eight thousand people paid $8 admission to get into the exposition (Bullers and Hayes 1999). It is extremely difficult to find any source of hardcore or softcore Y2K hysteria that did not include alarming advertisements encouraging people to purchase products or services.

Fame and Attention   There was another, slightly less obvious motivation for many of the experts and prophets loudly sounding the Y2K alarm: attention. Daytime talk shows have shown us that many people are willing to do just about anything to get themselves on television. National reporters for major newspapers, magazines, radio, and television news broadcasts interviewed many of the Y2K experts. That kind of fame and attention does not fall into someone's lap. They pursued it. At least one national reporter that I spoke to told of being phoned, faxed, e-mailed, and written to constantly throughout 1998 and 1999 by people who wanted him to write a Y2K story about them. He stated that this was particularly true for those with something to sell. Fame, glory, and profit are not mutually exclusive. Most Y2K alarmists did not attempt to remain anonymous; they fought for their moment in the spotlight. The Virginia stockbroker-turned-survivalist mentioned earlier in this chapter stated that he was giving "lots" of interviews (Giese 1999). Y2K gave him national attention, which he used to tell the whole world how smart and self-reliant he and his wife were.

Making Dreams Come True: Wish Fulfillment and Y2K Beliefs   Grossman (1998) pointed out that many Y2K Believers apparently felt great self-satisfaction because they made up the in-group that would survive Y2K chaos; they were smarter and tougher than the rest of us. She calls these self-satisfied doomsayers "Cassandras." The label is particularly ironic since Paloma O'Riley's website was called "The Cassandra Project." The term generally refers to anyone whose warnings of misfortune are disregarded by foolish skeptics.

This tone of superiority toward non-believers is easy to discern in many of the Believer writings. Some of the most extreme sources seemed to relish the moment at which the rest of the country (or world) would come crawling to them for food and they would be able to shoot us instead. The less extreme sources simply believed that people would get what they deserved, whether good or bad.

Even the apocalyptic writers who seemed so pessimistic about the future relished the coming of the Y2K the same way the Millerites relished the end of the world in the 1840s (see Chapter 7). Howard Ruff, author of *How to Prosper During the Hard Times Ahead,* argued that Y2K would "attack us where we are weakest, exposing the hidden fault lines in civilization's infrastructure" (quoted in Frick 1999: 28). A reviewer of the book was alarmed because Ruff clearly hoped that American society would be destroyed so that it could be rebuilt in his own, ideal image (Frick 1999).

Many of these people seemed determined to actually make their wishes come true. For instance, it is possible to create panic by bombarding people with the message that there is going to be panic. Convincing people to hoard large quantities of various products can, in fact, create a shortage of those products. Scaring people into taking all of their money out of a bank can cause that bank to collapse. Some of the Y2K prophets may have actually been attempting to bring about the events that they continually warned might occur. They wanted to spread confusion, doubt, and anxiety, either to benefit from it personally or to use it as a tool to achieve changes in society.

After January 1

What Actually Happened

Almost nothing at all actually happened to the world's computers at the turn of the New Year. World markets were unaffected. Indonesia, which took absolutely no actions to prepare, suffered only a few minor glitches. Russia, which was reported by Y2K Believers to be totally unprepared, also fared quite well. No blackouts were reported, and no one lost their supply of food, water, electricity, heat, fuel, or cash.

A few minor glitches occurred in some systems, but more often than not the events reported as "Y2K failures" were actually caused by human error or typical, everyday malfunctions. Thousands of computers that had failed "Y2K readiness tests" worked just fine. Headlines from all over the world announced "No Y2K problems so far" from all over the United States and Canada, as well as Africa, Europe, Asia, the Middle East, and various countries of the former Soviet Union. After such a long and fevered buildup, the Y2K rollover turned out to be no more chaotic than any other New Year's day. The few glitches that did occur caused no harm. This absolute failure of all the gloomy Y2K predictions produced a variety of responses. Most of those responses were defensive.

Responses to Failed Predictions

Those who were deeply concerned about Y2K prior to January 1 did not simply lose interest when nothing went wrong. Although many of the alarmist websites remained unchanged (creating unintentionally humorous juxtapositions), many others were updated December 31 or January 1. Responses tended to fall into one or more of the following categories: disappointment, hedging, backpedaling, and defensive apologetics.

All of these responses can be seen in the extended quote below:

> ... I'll bet you are now joining the leagues that say it [Y2K] was all a hoax from the beginning, and that the whole world did not have to spend all those hundreds of billions of dollars ... I do understand your point, even if I don't understand your way of thinking. First, let me just say that there are a whole lot of us around the world that are definitely STILL talking about this because we are STILL concerned.
>
> Obviously, if at midnight going into 1 January 2000 all the lights went out ... then we would have had the terrible catastrophes we feared most and which some predicted. All the best information available prior to rollover told us there would be significant infrastructure breakdowns in several countries outside the U.S. For some reason, it seems to not have happened anywhere. ... I KNOW, with every fibre of my being that we were right. Nothing can shake me from that belief. ... Is it all over? Of course not. ... Remember that it has ONLY been two weeks ... February 29th must be handled correctly, and then first quarter closings at the end of March. And the systems have to be able to close out 2000 properly. ... But don't think it will end there. We will continue to see some problems throughout 2000. ... It will likely continue over a ten-year period.
>
> We concluded early on that we were not getting all the facts, much less the truth in many cases ... why weren't there daily articles and reports every day in each and every newspaper? ... it's still too early to know [if government systems will crash].
>
> We were right to prepare [for catastrophe]. We did the right thing. ... We had the opportunity to seek out the same sources of information on Year 2000, to listen to whomever we chose to listen to, and to draw our own conclusions.
>
> It's like the whole world was indeed prepared for going to war. We had spent years anticipating the very worst; preparing ourselves to contend with the worst ... Our years of preparation and training for this were about to pay off!
>
> Heavily armed and totally prepared for battle, the troops [believers] were in the trenches and foxholes, and manning their duty stations. On the highest alert, worldwide. Ready for the destruction to begin precisely at midnight.

> There were literally millions of brave soldiers [believers] . . . holding their breath for the first report of that first devastating blow signaling the beginning of the end . . . there was nothing to do now but wait.
> Nothing. . . . There's not going to be a war today!
> Everyone was celebrating. Except the troops who were prepared to fight the war. They were emotionally drained, and not ready to celebrate. [When those who prepared find out the worst would not occur] a great disappointment takes over immediately. A letdown. (Bone 2000).

The author, a typical hardcore Y2K Believer, gives us a fascinating glimpse into the various defensive measures that many end-of-the-world proponents engaged in when virtually nothing went wrong on January 1, 2000. Keep the quote in mind as you read the following descriptions of those defensive postures.

The Second Great Disappointment

When the world failed to end in October of 1844, Millerites were so upset that they labeled the day "the Great Disappointment" (see Chapter 7). Hardcore and softcore Y2K Believers were equally upset when their doomsday prophecies failed on January 1, 2000. After all, their "years of preparation and training for this were about to pay off!" Some were shaken in their beliefs, and admitted to feeling foolish for having spent so much time and effort on an imaginary problem. Others ranted about having been "duped." Many expressed feeling "let down" because they had prepared so thoroughly for a disaster that just didn't come: ". . . a great disappointment takes over immediately. A letdown" (Bone 2000).

Hedging: It Is Happening!

Those who clung stubbornly to their doomsday predictions simply argued that Y2K was happening all around us, we just weren't aware of it—yet. We had not defeated Y2K, but simply postponed the inevitable downfall: ". . . it's still the early days. We'll see what happens" (Mary Kellner, quoted in January 2, 2000 Associated Press story). One could see signs of this softening position beginning in late 1999 on many of the Believer websites. Their focus shifted from a sudden catastrophic shutdown to a gradual, insidious slide to a halt. Even in January they considered the collapse inevitable. Many claimed that it would happen later. Perhaps things would go haywire on Monday, January 3 when banks and businesses turned on their computers for the first time. Or, possibly it would happen in February, when systems managing to toddle along thinking that it was 1900 would be tripped up by the leap year (1900 was not a leap year, 2000 was). "The real tragedy will come in 30 days as invoices start to arrive and people start to get laid off. The day of reckoning is coming" (Bill Merckle, ibid). "It's reasonable to expect that in the coming weeks, we'll see loads of unspectacular but annoying and sometimes costly problems in our systems" (Levy 2000:41). In other words, they didn't accept that they were wrong, and they believed that it would just be a matter of days (or weeks or months or years) until circumstances proved them right.

This hedging often included the idea that Y2K failures were being hidden or covered up by authorities. As an article posted on Yourdon's website in January, 2000 put it:

> Was Y2K really a non-event, or are the problems simply unfolding more slowly and being hidden more cleverly by corporations and government agencies? . . . Suppose . . . that Y2K is just the first of several complex, global, technology-based crises—to be followed by crises involving cyberwarfare, bio-terrorism, ecological crises, or a non-Y2K collapse of the technology-based utility/telecommunications/ banking infrastructure (http://www.yourdon.com/y2kfan/index.html 12/9/00).

Impressive-sounding words and unfamiliar terms should not confuse the reader. Yourdon explicitly argued that Y2K really was causing major problems, but authorities and business leaders were hiding those problems from the public. Further, he claimed there would be other, major crises in the future that would make all of his dire predictions ultimately true. Y2K Believers thought that they were the only ones clever enough to see this obvious truth; everyone else was being fooled.

Backpedaling: I Never Said . . .

Many of those who actively encouraged others to prepare for disaster prior to January almost immediately began to deny their role once Y2K turned out to be a non-event. Backpedaling furiously, they essentially argued that they had never said anything definite in the first place. For example, Michael Hyatt claimed in January of 2000 ". . . Y2K has never been about trying to predict the future" (http://www.michaelhyatt.com 1/3/00). This seems odd coming from the man who wrote "It's inevitable, and it's going to be terribly ugly when it happens" (Hyatt 1998:3). Perhaps the most extreme example of backpedaling comes from Clark, who in 1999 wrote "America *will* go down!," "I am convinced that America will fall as a result of the Year 2000 Computer Problem," and "we are still oblivious of the enormity of the problem" (http://uponair.com/nationaleagle.feature.html 11/11/99). Upon returning to the same webpage in January, 2000, one could find the following: "If you read objectively you will see that I was very careful not to insist that either a Y2K disaster or a nuclear strike would definitely happen on a certain date" (ibid, 1/18/00).

Defensive Y2K Apologetics: You May Thank Us Now
for Causing Panic

Although some Believers were baffled and disappointed or evasive, an even more fascinating (though predictable) response developed: some began to take credit for having saved society by alerting others to the problem in the first place. They argued that since they had spent months or years dutifully alerting everyone to the problem, and the problem had been overcome, it must have been their prompting that helped us all avert disaster. These modern-day would-be Paul Reveres actually took credit for the fact that their predictions did *not* come true. "If you've been sounding the alarm for the past few years, you've been part of the solution" (http://www.michaelhyatt.com 1/3/00). The most obvious case of patting oneself on the back comes from Peter de Jager, who posted "K2Y!—Kudos to You!" on December 31, in which he says "Thanks, if you've done anything to make sure the scenarios used to motivate people to action never took place" (http://www.year2000.com/archive/NFKudos.html, 12/31/99). In other words, those who ran around spouting doomsday scenarios throughout 1998 and 1999 had "motivated" people. Spreading hysteria solved the problem. This attitude is echoed in "Why no Chaos?," posted by de Jager in January: "All the hype, including some of the more ludicrous statements, forced companies to do one thing and one thing only. It forced competent managers around the world to examine their systems . . ." (ibid 1/24/00). Many Believers were quick to take credit for having helped force those in charge to undergo heroic efforts to defeat the Y2K problem.

The Y2K apologetics apparently forgot about all of those nations who did nothing at all to prepare for Y2K and who experienced virtually no problems. They also seemed to think that having scared citizens into spending their life savings on generators and survival rations is insignificant or not worth mentioning. This self-serving attitude might have been easier to accept were it not for the fact that many of the same websites still contained outdated articles from 1998 and 1999 that claimed Y2K would bring major disruptions, business failures, and wild stock market fluctuation in late 1999 and early 2000.

Some Luddite Y2K Believers argued that the hysteria itself was good for us as a nation. "Unless we have the self-reliance to prepare and be ready for emergencies, whatever they are, we are at the mercy of fate" (Gordon Anderson, quoted in AP story 2/2/00). "Some [who prepared for Y2K disaster] have an entirely different opinion about alternative energy, or food stockpiling, or banking relationships . . . and based on that, they're now considering significant changes in their lifestyle" (http://www.yourdon.com/y2kfan/index.html 12/9/00). Taking the time to stockpile food and water, getting in touch with our rugged survivalist or community-oriented sides, and learning not to take modern conveniences for granted had actually made us a better, stronger, and humbler people. We will be better off in the long run. "Money spent to avoid the loss of life is always money well spent" (Levy 2000:41). "Most IT managers are better off post-Y2K because the 'crisis' gave them the excuse they needed to upgrade systems corporate-wide" (Rist 2000:27). Rist went on to point out that the money spent on Y2K would just have gone for skyscrapers and nuclear submarines, which "we [American society] don't need any more of." Y2K hysteria temporarily distracted us from our evil, greedy, and destructive ways.

Anyone familiar with millennial groups should not be surprised by this development. It is a common response to failed prophecy (Weber 1999). It is a nice trick to be able to feel smart because one is wrong. Many of the most alarmist Believers pulled it off nicely.

Analysis

Each of the theoretical perspectives discussed in earlier chapters of this book explains certain elements of the Y2K hysteria. Perhaps because Y2K hysteria was so large, so diffuse, so pervasive, and so long lasting, none of the theories seems to account for every aspect. This chapter will briefly discuss several of the different theoretical perspectives as they apply to Y2K hysteria. This will allow the reader to note the strengths and weaknesses of each approach. Although this chapter takes a fairly general approach in applying each theory to Y2K hysteria, there is certainly information available for students to perform their own, more thorough empirical analysis of the event.

The Emergent Norm Perspective

The Emergent Norm Perspective (Chapter 3) assumes that people take part in collective behavior whenever they experience a combination of confusion and anxiety. *Uncertainty, urgency, communication of mood and imagery, constraint, selective individual suggestibility,* and *permissiveness* make any form of collective behavior likely to occur. Crowd members want to do something, but don't know what. Under these circumstances new social norms emerge to guide individuals' actions. Most crowd members follow the situational norms, just as they do in everyday life.

The Y2K hysteria showed clear evidence of uncertainty, urgency, and the other variables considered important within the Emergent Norm perspective. No one knew for certain what would happen in January. Even genuine computer experts disagreed with each other about how extensive the effects of Y2K might be. One thing that everyone except the skeptics agreed upon, however, was the deadline for fixing the problem. There was a strong sense of urgency among Believers. Everyone felt as if they had important work to do in too short a time. The mood and imagery of Y2K was also unavoidable. Every newspaper, magazine, television network, and cable news channel in the United States ran frequent stories about Y2K. A person would had to have had no television, no radio, no Internet access, no newspapers, and no friends, relatives or co-workers interested in Y2K in order to avoid such imagery. The Believers, Cautious participants, and Skeptics I interviewed all received Y2K information from each of those sources. Once the mood began to spread, many felt constrained from expressing their doubts. They became more likely to notice information supporting their beliefs and actions and to ignore those that contradicted it. Finally, the newly emerging norms allowed them to express negative feelings about technology, modern society, or the government without fear of reprisal. People who, in general, worry about the near future were suddenly free to discuss their worries with other people who shared their anxieties.

The Emergent Norm Perspective seems to do a good job of explaining why so many people harboring anti-social values suddenly placed themselves into the public spotlight. It also seems to account for the millions of Americans who, feeling uncertain and anxious, engaged in what they saw as logical preparation for a disaster that they knew might not happen. If everyone that you know or trust is worried about something, are you not more likely to worry about it as well? If they are providing "information" that seems to confirm certain courses of action as reasonable, doesn't that make you more likely to engage in those actions? It is easy to argue these social connections, combined with group interpretations of Y2K, produced many of the odd behaviors that occurred during 1999. People don't normally take all of their money out of the bank and spend it on guns, generators, or beans, but many did in 1999. People don't normally encourage others to arm themselves against hungry mobs of city dwellers, but many did in 1999. People don't normally huddle in their homes on New Year's Eve, anxiously awaiting the strike of midnight to see if they will still have heat, light, and running water. Millions of Americans did exactly that in 1999. They were responding to the norms that emerged throughout 1998 and 1999. Those who were most uncertain, most anxious, and most immersed in preparationist social groups took the most extreme actions. Those who were the least anxious and least socially attached to the alarmists did little or nothing.

The Value-Added Theory

The Value-Added Theory (Chapter 4) assumes that collective behavior is a sort of "release valve" that allows groups of people to cope with social stress or pressure. Whenever people within a social setting experience the same strain and collectively form or accept a belief that guides action, they are likely to take part in collective behavior in an attempt to alleviate that strain. The collective event can only occur if specific social circumstances exist. Whenever *structural conduciveness, structural strain, generalized belief,* and *mobilization of participants* exist, collective behavior is immanent unless agents of *social control* eliminate one of these components.

The greatest factor of structural conduciveness, ironically, was the Internet itself. The vast majority of Y2K-related information was posted on the Internet. Thousands of websites asserted strident views and provided links to hundreds of other, similar sites.

Expressions of strain seemed to focus on a few issues: the importance attributed to the calendar rollover itself, the tremendous doubt and uncertainty generated by negative and conflicting information, and the fact that it might all happen in the coldest and darkest month of the year. Many people use technology they barely understand. In much the same way that people who have no idea how to fix a car dread breakdowns, the majority of Americans today dread the moment when their TV, VCR, personal computer, or other high-tech electronic device stops working. This creates strain.

A number of different generalized beliefs formed among groups of people experiencing different levels of strain. Most Americans believed that 2000 marked the beginning of the new century and millennium. It was actually the last year of the second millennium, but most did not pay attention to that fact, nor to the fact that the Gregorian calendar has been dramatically readjusted several times in history and therefore does not accurately mark any important date precisely. Our culture's tendency to treat 2000 as a significant year fed this belief. Prior to the 1980s, "the year 2000" was often considered the beginning of the future. Hardcore Y2K Believers adopted beliefs attaching this date to religious or political beliefs that led them to expect great catastrophe. Softcore Believers attached the year 2000 to their social and economic anxieties. They expected recession, depression, and the general breakdown of social order. Cautious participants attached it to their distrust and sense of helplessness in the face of modern technology. They expected confusion, chaos, disruptions, and general inconvenience. Skeptics did not consider 2000 particularly important or monumental, did not accept the belief that social order hangs by a delicate thread, and therefore did not accept any of the Y2K beliefs.

Mobilization was never an issue, because the Internet, mail-order, and a blizzard of Y2K publications made it possible to fully participate in Y2K hysteria without ever leaving one's own home. If that home also happened to be in a rural area, then even the most extreme preparations could be made without interference. Building a survival shelter may be difficult in an apartment building, but is easy if one owns some land and one's nearest neighbors are out of sight.

Social control agents did a fairly good job of dampening the most extreme rumors and beliefs. However, they actually accommodated and encouraged the milder forms of participation by encouraging preparation for a three-day storm that never came.

The Value-Added Theory seems to do a good job of explaining how so many Americans could become so afraid of one specific problem and how so many of them could go to such great lengths to prepare for a disaster that most genuine computer experts did not expect to strike. By the end of 1999, even some alarmists were trying to reassure people that the major problems had been fixed. Believers considered them traitors (see, for example, Junod 1999). They simply disregarded this turn of events and moved on with their preparations. Why? The Value-Added perspective assumes that the participants were driven by strain, and participation was a way of relieving that strain. If we assume that the strain lay, as many Believers indicated, in tension over modern technology, fear of international dependence, and dislike of societal interdependence, then preparing for disaster by turning one's home into a self-sufficient survival shelter would, in fact, be an excellent way to reduce or eliminate that strain. Those who prepared extensively for Y2K not only reassured themselves that everything would be okay for them, they actually created a situation they believe will enable them to survive if society does collapse. This may seem trivial to those unconcerned about the collapse of civilization. However, if you truly do worry about the collapse of social order for religious, political, or psychological reasons, having such preparations at hand would help reduce those fears to a manageable level. Preparing for "The End" allows one to stop worrying about when it will come.

Milder hysteria participants did not go to such great lengths to prepare because their level of strain was much lower and their generalized beliefs were less extreme. People who expected the equivalent of a storm only needed to take limited precautions. Once the threat of Y2K breakdown had passed, they were able to relax and resume their lives. The "new millennium" had come and gone, and was no longer a source of fear or anxiety. The strain passed, and with it the need for relief.

The Individualist Perspective

The individualist perspective (Chapter 6) is a psychological approach to collective behavior. Convergence Theory, Learning Theory, and Social Identity Theory all assume that collective behavior occurs when the right people are in right place at the right time. Participants are driven by their pre-existing tendencies.

Convergence Theory

Allport's Convergence Theory assumes that collective behavior occurs whenever people with innate tendencies toward certain behaviors end up in the same situation and respond in the same way. Individuals' behavior throughout the Y2K hysteria reveals their predispositions. *Approach* and *avoidance* are key to the convergence process: people pay attention to (*approach*) anything that interests them and ignore (*avoid*) anything that does not. Those with innate hysterical tendencies were more likely to panic, and the innately skeptical were less likely to do so. The first group paid attention to negative Y2K information, the second ignored it or focused on the skeptical and reassuring information.

Learning Theory

According to Miller and Dollard, a person must want something (*drive*), notice something (*cue* or *stimuli*), do something (*response*), and get something (*reward*) in order to learn a pattern of behavior. The pattern is likely to be repeated once it is learned. Members of a crowd act the same whenever they have the same responses to their circumstances. Crowd stimuli are stronger and more important when crowd members experience *interstimulation, proximity, numbers, anonymity,* and leaders with a *prestige factor*.

In the case of Y2K hysteria, the drive may have been as simple as surviving. It may have been as self-serving as gaining notoriety and fame through shameless self-promotion and the exploitation of unwitting dupes. Or, it may have been as complex as a desire to return society's respect for knowledge and skills that just aren't important in a post-industrial, information-driven society. In any case, participants all wanted something and taking part in Y2K hysteria helped them get it.

Interstimulation, numbers, and anonymity were provided by the Internet. Chat rooms, e-mail alerts, and literally thousands of websites allowed participants to communicate with other Believers all over the world. Most of the leaders also possessed a certain measure of prestige. Many Y2K leaders possessed a Ph.D., religious title, or an important-sounding position with some organization.

As for patterns of response, Miller and Dollard assume that the cue can be generalized from other, similar stimuli. People all face potential threats and setbacks in their lives. Some worry and prepare constantly, while others relax and "go with the flow." Those who normally prepare for anything bad that might happen were more likely to prepare for Y2K. Those who normally take a skeptical approach to bad news, who cross their fingers and hope for the best, did nothing at all.

Each of these learned patterns has been rewarded in the participants' past. For example, some people carry as much auto insurance as possible, just in case they have an accident. Others carry little or no coverage and hope they never need it. If carrying insurance allows one to drive without worrying, then that person is rewarded for their preparations. If driving with no insurance makes one feel clever and frugal, then that person is rewarded for hoping for the best. These learned patterns of response will then repeat whenever any potential threat, including disasters, storms, or Y2K, comes along. Y2K hysteria behavior revealed people's learned responses to potential threat.

Social Identity Theory

Hogg and Abrams' Social Identity Theory argues that much of what we do is driven by our self-images. People modify and monitor their own behavior within a group in the hopes of achieving or maintaining acceptance from other group members. *Personal identifications* and *social identifications* create a set of guidelines within individuals' minds. Once they self-identify with a particular category or group of people, *referent informational influence* causes them to behave in whatever way they think a member of the group should act. Group identities drive group behavior: People do what the people they identify with do.

Personal identifications are descriptions of our self that emerge from interpersonal relationships. "Wise" and "self-sufficient" are personal identities that would encourage Y2K preparation. To do otherwise would seem unwise. Those with "clever" and "skeptical" personal identities would be likely to wait and see, expecting nothing terrible. To do otherwise would seem foolish or gullible.

Social identifications are based entirely on category membership. Those whose social identities carry responsibility toward others (such as "parent") would be more likely to do whatever it takes to ensure their own safety and the safety of others in the face of a potential problem like Y2K. Those with social identities that do not include responsibility toward others would only take action for more selfish reasons.

Personal and social identifications can be combined, so that one becomes a "responsible father," a "skeptical columnist," a "committed Christian," and so on. These identities guide our actions. Those with identities associated with Y2K skepticism would do nothing, while those with identifications associated with Y2K preparations would take immediate action. To do otherwise would mean admitting to oneself and to others that one cannot live up to the identification.

There is evidence that group identification did occur, at least for some Believers. A Y2K Believer I interviewed stated, "We've looked at fiscal year rollovers, we've looked at September 9 . . . we've looked at a number of different dates . . ." (author's files). In each case, "we" refers to himself and all the other softcore Believers. He does not know these individuals personally, but clearly thinks of them as a group to which he belongs.

As soon as people categorize and identify themselves as members of a group, they will consciously behave in ways that they believe are appropriate for members of that group. All members of a group learn the norms and *critical attributes* necessary for group membership, and then try to fit that model of an ideal crowd member.

People often decide to become members of the crowd before it forms. Similar people gather (converge) at particular times and places because they are interested in similar things. Y2K believers noticed the same information, read many of the same publications and websites, and acted the way they believed their fellow Believers would. They often referred to themselves as a group, and contrasted their "reasonable and responsible" preparations with the "irresponsible" behavior of others.

The individualist theories all assume that collective behavior comes from within the participants themselves. This can be a tempting and seductive perspective. If one is not careful, it leads to the conclusion that collective behavior participants are somehow abnormal. For instance, it may seem logical to argue that Y2K hysteria participants were all gullible, paranoid, or militant before the event ever caught their attention and this is what led them to focus so much attention on it. This may be true for some of the most extreme hardcore believers. Gary North, Lee Clark, and Howard Ruff are among the dozens of people in this country who predict doom and chaos on a regular basis. However, most of the Y2K hysteria participants were not involved with millennial beliefs before Y2K. They were not crazed lunatics, running around the woods pretending they're hiding from the New World Order. Most Y2K hysteria participants were psychologically normal people who simply became convinced that terrible things would happen when the calendar rolled over to 2000. Their lack of ties to other millennial groups casts doubt on the individualist explanation, since it shows that they do not respond to every prediction of disaster with equal interest or activity.

The Sociocybernetic Theory

McPhail's Sociocybernetic Theory (Chapter 5) assumes that people take part in collective behavior in order to reach a desired state. Each participant engages in self-interested behavior. In many ways this perspective is similar to the individualist theories discussed above: people take part in collective behavior because they (as individuals) believe they will get something out of doing so. This forces one to assume that similar people with similar wants are likely to engage in similar behavior. The Sociocybernetic Perspective assumes that those who do not take part in the event also do so out of self-interest; they just have different interests.

People are guided by their *goals and objectives, reference signals,* and *self-instructions*. Whenever their reference signals (standards) tell them that they are not meeting their goals, people give themselves self-instructions intended to restore the desired state. People who have similar goals and develop or adopt similar reference signals are likely to engage in similar behavior. People who have different objectives or different expectations will engage in different behavior.

From this perspective, Y2K hysteria is a case of millions of self-interested people doing what they felt necessary in order to overcome their fear of the unknown and to feel secure. Once they developed or adopted a reference signal that made them feel unsafe, they gave self-instructions to do whatever it took to restore their sense of equilibrium. Those who adopted a reference signal telling them that Y2K was not going to be a problem did not have to do anything at all. Those with a reference signal indicating that Y2K would cause disruptions instructed themselves to do whatever it took to make them feel prepared. A reference signal indicating Y2K meltdown as a distinct possibility required extreme preparations. For many, this included spreading the word as far and wide as possible in order to bring others into the fold. The level of detail contained in many descriptions of Y2K's "likely" effects revealed much more about the individual participants than about Y2K itself.

Like the individualist theories, Sociocybernetic Theory assumes that people's internal beliefs and tendencies drive individual participants. This creates a tempting explanation for Y2K hysteria: those who participated believed that the costs of preparing for unlikely disaster were far outweighed by the costs of failing to prepare for a disaster if it did strike. If someone's primary goal is to survive, then taking precautions for something that probably won't happen does start to seem like a small price to pay for peace of mind. Many of the less extreme Believers expressed precisely this sentiment. However, unnecessary preparations might seem excessively costly to someone with a reference signal that places a high value on dignity and composure. To those people, the odds of looking and feeling like a fool in January 2000 outweighed the extremely slim odds of regretting not having prepared. The first reference signal led to a "panic, just in case" approach; the second, "wait and see" or skepticism.

Conclusion

Similarities and Common Ground

All of the theories of collective behavior discussed in this chapter share certain things in common. Although the terms used by each can be totally different, all of them focus on the definition of the situation, the influence of others, motivated participants, and response to stress.

Definition of the Situation   Although they use different terms to describe it, and place its importance at different levels, every theory discussed in this chapter argues that the way in which a group of individuals interprets and defines the situation influences their behavior within that situation. Turner and Killian call it "common mood or imagery." Smelser calls it "generalized belief." Miller and Dollard call it "cues" or "stimuli." Hogg and Abrams call it "referent informational influence." McPhail uses the term "reference signal." In each theory, participants are assumed to have thought about their situation long enough to decide upon a course of action that seems appropriate. Their group definition may be incorrect in hindsight, but participants accept it at that time and that definition leads them to act as if it is correct.

Social Influence   Each of the theories discussed also argues that the presence of others heightens or dampens feelings and behavior. Being in the presence of others who seem to share one's own feelings makes those feelings seem more legitimate and more powerful. Being in the presence of others who are acting in ways that go against one's feelings can dampen those feelings and inhibit one from expressing them. Each theory places importance on this outside influence, assuming that it can lead to behavior that would not have occurred otherwise. Even Convergence Theory argues that people only act according to their predisposition if or when the situation allows it.

Motivated Participants   All of the theories discussed in this chapter assume that people can do abnormal things because they *want* something. They assume that participants are motivated. People don't take part in collective behavior for no reason at all, they do it to get something. Learning Theory assumes that eliminating or reducing frustration is the primary motive for any non-normative behavior. With Social Identity Theory, it is the desire to fit in, belong, and be accepted. Sociocybernetic Theory is based on the fundamental assumption that people act in whatever way they believe will return them to a desired state. The Emergent Norm Perspective argues that most participants are driven by a desire to resolve their uncertainty and alleviate a sense of urgency. Most participants do whatever seems to be the right thing to do in that situation. They are motivated by the desire to do the correct thing. The Value-Added perspective argues that participants are primarily motivated by their desire to alleviate structural strain. Once a generalized belief forms, actors engage in specific behaviors suggested by the belief. This explains why, for example, people might take part in a lynching when the strain they feel is actually caused by economic conditions: they can't actively change the economy, but if they believe that some social taboo has been violated they can "do something" to keep it from happening again. Each of the theories assumes that people engage in behavior because they believe it will solve some problem or achieve some goal.

Stress   Each of the theories discussed above assumes that collective behavior participants are driven by some sort of strain, tension, frustration, or anxiety. If people do things that seem odd it is only because they are under duress. They find themselves in a situation that *feels* odd. People are blocked from their goals (Learning Theory), worried that they won't fit in or will let themselves and others down (Social Identity Theory), or out of sync with their reference signal (Sociocybernetic Theory). They feel uncertainty, urgency, and anxiety (Emergent Norm Theory) or structural strain (Value-Added Theory). Either way, some sort of internal or external stress helps drive the behavior.

The individualist theories and the Sociocybernetic Theory assume that each participant independently chooses to engage in that behavior, whereas the Emergent Norm and Value-Added theories assume that collective behavior will only happen if the strain or anxiety itself is collective. The individualist theories treat collective behavior as a situation where many people who are under strain choose (through similar learned patterns of response or adopted feedback reference levels, etc.) similar patterns of behavior. The Emergent Norm Theory and the Value-added Theory assume that people choose a common course of behavior not because they are similar people, *but because they experience a common strain or anxiety*. This is the key difference between the perspectives. One branch (individualist, psychological, and Sociocybernetic) assumes collective participants act the same because they individually define the situation the same or because they have similar individual response patterns. The other branch (Emergent Norm and Value-Added) assumes that people will tend to act the same when placed under the same circumstances. This difference might not seem obvious because each of the theories includes many other variables. However, it is a key difference at the root of the theories: either internal factors are the most important, or external ones are. Convergence Theory, Learning Theory, Social Identity Theory, and Sociocybernetic Theory all place slightly more importance on factors within the individuals. The social surroundings simply trigger certain responses. Emergent Norm Theory and Value-Added Theory place more importance on the external, structural conditions. Internal factors only act as a secondary component, as one piece of selective individual suggestibility or permissiveness, or one component of structural conduciveness or generalized belief.

Looking within the individual can help to explain different behavior within the same situation. Looking at the situation can help to explain similar patterns of behavior from different people. For example, only some people exposed to certain rumors choose to believe them. Clearly, not all individuals respond the same to any situation. However, some of those who accept the rumor are old, some young, and so on. Different people sometimes engage in the same behavior.

Neither the individual nor external approach is "right" or "wrong," it depends on what a researcher hopes to explain. If the goal of the researcher is to understand why apparently normal people took part in some episode of collective behavior, Emergent Norm and Value-Added Theory may be most useful. If the goal is to understand why some took part while others in the same place and at the same time did not, then the individualist and Sociocybernetic approaches may help. All of the theories take situational and personal variables into account, but each theory emphasizes the importance of one over the other. Each researcher must decide which is more important.

The greatest strength of the Emergent Norm and Value-Added perspectives lies in their ability to take all of the factors suggested by Convergence, Learning, Social Identity, and Sociocybernetic Theory into account. Convergence Theory essentially says that whenever certain kinds of people come together, certain events are more likely to occur. Each of the other theories takes this as a given, and either builds from it or treats it as a minor detail. Convergence and Learning Theory both fail to describe the conditions that lead up to a collective outburst. Instead, they can only explain what happens once it starts. Social Identity Theory and Sociocybernetic Theory go further, but still fail to describe the *social* conditions that make any collective event likely to take place. Social Identity Theory assumes that a group role has already been defined, but does not explain how this occurs. Sociocybernetic Theory assumes that participants adopt (or arrive) with similar goals and expectations, and once they form an ideal, act in similar ways to achieve those goals. It does not explain why this would happen in the first place. They do not explain why people engage in spectacularly unusual behavior in what appear to be typical situations, nor why people who normally obey social rules might suddenly decide to act against them.

The Emergent Norm Perspective and the Value-Added Theory both attempt to explain these riddles in their own way. The Emergent Norm Perspective argues that temporary social situations cause doubt, confusion, and anxiety, which lead to unusual patterns of behavior within the crowd. The Value-Added Theory argues that conditions within a social structure lead to stress and strain among the populace, and certain factors may combine with this strain to lead people into patterns of behavior that they believe will alleviate or eliminate the strain.

Discussion

Y2K was a once-in-a-millennium event. There will probably never again be a time when so many people are so concerned about the same problem and so convinced that it could cause major disruptions for the entire world. This unique event provided a golden opportunity to observe collective behavior as it developed and unfolded. The sheer size of the Y2K hysteria was unusual, but millennial madness itself is not. There are frequently groups of people somewhere in the world who believe that society is about to collapse, that some disaster is about to strike, or that the world is about to end. Y2K simply created such feelings on an unusually massive scale.

Y2K hysteria also generated more information for the casual observer than one could ever hope to expect from an episode of collective delusion. This is because Y2K came at a time when the Internet had reached millions of homes and offices and when thousands of people had learned how to create their own websites. Huge quantities of Y2K hysteria information were also published in the form of books, pamphlets, and newsletters, because there was money to be made. Researchers can examine those materials for decades to come. Because broadcast and print media have become so pervasive, virtually every single American was bombarded with countless messages about Y2K for a full two years before the arrival of January 2000. All of these factors combined to create what will probably be looked back upon as the greatest folly of the twentieth century.

The next several chapters of this book focus on social movements. This begins with Chapter 13, which defines and discusses social movements as a phenomenon.

Chapter 13

Social Movements

When a group of people organize in an attempt to encourage or resist some kind of social change, they create a *social movement*. People with little or no political power join together in order to acquire some. They hope to influence their community or their society by joining together. Ordinary people decide that "something must be done," that they are the ones to do it, and go about trying to make it happen. Most collective behavior theorists consider social movements a type of collective behavior, but many social movement theorists consider them a separate phenomenon. This chapter will explain each of those positions and look at the similarities and differences between social movements and all other forms of collective behavior.

Social Movements and Social Movement Organizations

A social movement is rarely represented by just one organization. A "movement" includes any individuals or groups working toward some common goal. Most successful social movements are led by one or two large organizations, but there may be dozens of smaller ones as well. For example, the second-wave feminist *movement* that began in the United States in the 1970s included specific feminist *organizations* such as the National Organization for

Women (NOW), the National Women's Political Caucus (NWPC), and the American Association of University Women (AAUW). Each of these organizations is a part of the social movement. Such groups often cooperate with each other and form coalitions to increase their power and visibility.

Some sociologists call social movements "collective action" instead of "collective behavior." They argue that social movements really aren't the same as other kinds of collective behavior. Other sociologists classify social movements as a form of collective behavior. They argue that the similarities outweigh the differences. There are arguments to support both positions.

Ways in which Social Movements Are Like Other Forms of Collective Behavior

Social movement participants do unusual and unexpected things that they would not do if they were not participating in the movement. Social movements alter people's behavior just as much as any other form of collective behavior.

As in all other forms of collective behavior, social movement participants do things that go against social norms and expectations. They engage in non-institutionalized behavior that may be considered odd or deviant. Protests, sit-ins, and petition drives are not a part of everyday life for most people. These things are typical in the daily life of social movement members. They may break laws, challenge authorities, and even publicly denounce powerful people or institutions. These behaviors are not expected of people in normal daily life. It is this perception that participants' behavior is "odd" or "wrong" that links social movements to other types of collective behavior. Like any other form of collective behavior, it is group deviant behavior.

Theorists such as Turner and Killian, and Smelser point out that the behavior of social movement participants is fundamentally different from the behavior of nonparticipants. Fads, crazes, riots, and social movements all entail people acting in ways that they would not act were it not for a common group definition of the situation and social influence from other group members. Participants in fads, crazes, riots, and social movements are all motivated; their participation serves some purpose for them. Finally, participation in any of these forms of collective behavior helps to reduce some anxiety or strain within the situation or society. For all of these reasons, classic collective behavior theorists included social movements in their analyses. They would see no significant difference between, for example, participation in Y2K hysteria and participation in a radical political organization.

Ways in which Social Movements Are Different from Other Forms of Collective Behavior

However, there are also important differences between social movements and the other forms of collective behavior that have been discussed so far. Researchers who specialize in social movements consider these differences more important than the many similarities.

Social movements are different from other forms of collective behavior in three ways: 1) they are organized, 2) they are deliberate, and 3) they are enduring.

Organized

Social movements are *organized*. Most collective behavior is unorganized. Riot participants might cooperate with each other for a short period of time in order to foil the police or gain entry into a store, but the episode is more a of free-for-all than a carefully organized event. Typical collective behavior leadership comes and goes quickly, if it exists at all. Whoever manages to grab a crowd's attention can influence the entire group's behavior.

However, social movement participants are often given specific tasks to perform. There may be a carefully designed strategy. Leaders often create jobs and make careers out of leading specific organizations dedicated to the cause of the movement. Participating in a social movement is in many ways similar to participating in a fad. People consciously choose to stand outside at four in the morning to buy a Furby, and they consciously choose to take part in a march to protest some social injustice. The factor that sets social movements apart is the level of organization.

Deliberate

Social movements are also *deliberate*. Most collective behavior episodes occur without anyone planning them ahead of time. Social movements, on the other hand, are intentionally created and participants carefully decide whether or not to join. There are often pledge drives and membership drives. Social movements seek publicity and attempt to get as many people as possible to support them. This deliberate planning is not present in most other forms of collective behavior.

Enduring

Finally, social movements are long-lasting or *enduring*. Most collective behavior episodes are brief. A riot may last for minutes, hours, or a few days. A fad may last for a few months. However, many social movements exist for years or even decades. The smallest social movements form in order to create or resist one specific change within a particular community. They may only last for a few weeks. Social movements that seek to change an entire society often last for decades. There is a established nature to social movements that is embodied in things like letterhead, post office boxes, and so on that other forms of collective behavior do not have. Their goals are difficult to achieve and long-range in nature so they form with the full knowledge that it may take more than one generation to fully reach their goals. No other form of collective behavior lasts so long. Most are characterized by their brevity.

Because of these differences, many sociologists consider social movements a separate category of phenomenon. These researchers have developed their own theories, to be discussed in Chapter 14.

Types of Social Movements

There are different kinds of social movements. Some movements come about because people are interested in a specific aspect of their community. Some are created out of concern for an entire category of people or an entire group of laws and regulations. Some are intended to completely wipe out and replace the existing social order. Most social movements fall into one of the following four categories: alternative, redemptive, reformative (progressive or reactionary), or revolutionary (Aberle 1966).

Like all alternative social movements, D.A.R.E. (Drug Abuse Resistance Education) seeks to change particular thoughts or behaviors in one specific target audience. In this case, they hope to prevent teens from using drugs or alcohol.

Alternative Social Movements

Alternative social movements want to create change in some people's thoughts or behavior in a specific area. Their goal is to change the way specific groups of people think about a particular behavior or category of behaviors. Alternative social movements are not concerned with topics outside of their stated focus. They are not terribly threatening to established social order because they only want certain people to change and only in one particular way.

For example, organizations such as the Drug Abuse Resistance Education (DARE) Program and Students Against Drugs and Alcohol (SADA) exist to keep young Americans from getting involved with the use of drugs. This entire movement is only aimed at one specific segment of the population (children, teenagers, and young adults) and only seeks to change one particular aspect of their behavior and attitudes, those relating to drug and alcohol use. A typical alternative social movement is not terribly concerned with issues outside of their specific focus. DARE does not try to change people's religious beliefs, dietary habits, or dental care practices. Like most alternative social movements, they have a specific area of interest and that is where their focus stays.

Redemptive Social Movements

Redemptive social movements want to create a more dramatic change, but only in some individuals' lives. Their goal is the complete transformation of certain people. However, the target audience is narrow and specific. They want to totally change the lives of their followers.

Religious revivals, a form of redemptive movement common in the United States, seek to completely transform the lives of a specific target audience. Converts must change every aspect of their life once they have been "saved" by joining the movement.

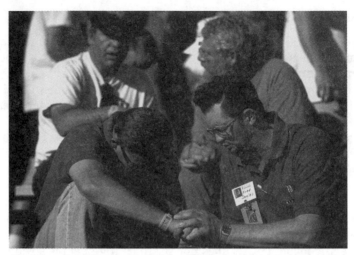

The Promise Keepers, a religious-based, men-only movement, swept the United States in the 1990s. The most recent redemptive movement in U.S. history, it attempted to transform the lives of those men who paid a fee to learn how to be better Christian husbands.

Examples of redemptive social movements would include any religious movements that actively seek converts, such as the Jehovah's Witnesses and certain Christian fundamentalist and Baptist congregations. These groups want to totally transform the lives of the individuals they "save," but the only way to be saved is to join the movement. Those who join are transformed, but the rest of the population of the world remains unchanged. They don't want people to change just one set of attitudes or beliefs, they want them to become a part of the group in every way and to take on evangelizing as a way of life. Members of redemptive social movements see themselves as changing the world one person at a time.

Reformative Social Movements

Reformative social movements want to change an entire community or society, but in a limited way. Their goal is to change society's attitude about a particular topic or issue. Reformative social movements do not want to destroy or replace the existing government; they want the existing government to change in some specific way. Reformative movements are probably the most common category of social movement in American society.

Reformative social movements can be *progressive* (seeking to make a change) or *reactionary* (seeking to resist or reverse a change). Reactionary movements are often called "countermovements" because they usually form immediately after a progressive movement has succeeded in creating changes within society.

The Ku Klux Klan, a reactionary reformative social movement, formed in the South after the Civil War in an attempt to resist social changes that were sweeping the region. They used terrorism and intimidation to effectively block most social change efforts.

The push against drunk driving in the 1980s and 1990s, led by Mothers Against Drunk Driving (MADD), is an example of a progressive reformative social movement. The movement sought the change of laws and the attitudes of law enforcement officials, politicians, and citizens toward drinking and driving. The movement largely succeeded, as authorities and citizens are now much more likely to consider drunk driving a major crime rather than a minor infraction. Other examples of progressive reformative movements would include the suffrage movement, the civil rights movement, and the feminist movement. All of these movements sought the change of society in one relatively specific area such as women's right to vote, racial discrimination and segregation, or gender discrimination.

The white supremacy/white separatist movement, anti-feminist movement, and militant right-wing movements are all examples of reactionary reformative social movements. All formed to fight social change to return society to the way it was before those changes took place. DAMM (Drunks Against Mad Mothers) is a recently formed reactionary movement. DAMM seeks to relax some of the recent drunk driving laws and penalties and to return people's attitudes to be more accepting of drunk drivers. The Ku Klux Klan was created in the South after the Civil War to fight the social changes that were taking place. Both of these movements are typical reactionary reformative social movements because they seek to reverse some specific social change that they oppose.

Whether they are reactionary or progressive, reformative social movements want to create what they call a better society. They believe that one specific change is the key to improving every other aspect of society.

Revolutionary social movements like the current American Militia Movement seeks the complete transformation of their entire society. Many militias actively oppose local, state, and federal authorities in the United States and harbor dreams of revolution.

Revolutionary Social Movements

Revolutionary social movements want to completely destroy the old social order and replace it with a new one. Their goal is the total transformation of society. They want to destroy any existing government and replace all current leaders. Revolutionary social movements are the most threatening to existing social order, authority, and power. Sometimes they have specific goals, sometimes only vague utopian dreams.

There are "militia groups" in the United States that believe the federal government is evil and want to overthrow it. These groups, such as the Montana Freemen, could be considered revolutionary social movements. More obvious examples are those movements that have actually led to real social and political revolutions in their society. Fidel Castro's socialist movement in Cuba, the French anti-monarchist movement in nineteenth-century France, and the Communist Revolution in China all succeeded in completely destroying the existing power structure and replacing it with a new, idealized social order. All of these revolutionary social movements were intended to create a perfect society by replacing the power structure with one based on different principles.

Resistance to Social Movements

Because all social movements want to change something or to keep something from being changed, there are always people who do not want the movement to succeed. The greatest resistance to social movements usually comes from those who benefit if the movement fails. This often includes political or social leaders. If there were no resistance to the proposed change, there would be consensus and no need for a social movement. Society resists social movements in ways not often found with other forms of collective behavior. Revolutionary movements meet the greatest resistance, of course, but society also can be repressive toward some reformative and redemptive movements. The more the goals or ideology of a movement go against the beliefs of society, the more opposition and resistance the movement faces. Several methods are used to resist social movements. The most common are ridicule, co-option, formal social control, and violence (Roberts and Kloss 1979, Zald and McCarthy 1988, Schaeffer and Lamm 1998).

Ridicule

Ridicule can be a terribly effective way of resisting a social movement. Ridiculing a movement's leaders, followers, and/or goals belittles the movement in the eyes of everyone else in a community or society. Talk show hosts, comedians, and political cartoonists and commentators all tend to ridicule social movements that they do not like. If they can succeed in making the leaders of the movement seem like selfish buffoons, they can undermine those leaders' ability to be taken seriously by the public. If they succeed in making the followers of the movement seem like mindless idiots who are being blindly led by conniving outsiders, they can make it difficult or impossible for movement participants to have their concerns seriously addressed. Finally, if they make the goals of the movement seem trivial, foolish, or short-sighted, the entire movement may lose critical social support from outsiders. The use of ridicule is not an accident, it is carefully used to undermine the movement. Constant sniping makes any demand from the movement seem foolish and unimportant.

Ridicule over social issues can be two-way. Movement followers and supporters often ridicule their opponents in an attempt to counter their own loss of face. Leaders and followers of opposing movements often ridicule each other in an attempt to undermine the other side. This is easiest to notice when reading any publication that caters to a particular political orientation. It is particularly prevalent in newsletters published by social movement organizations.

Co-opting

To "co-opt" something means to take something over for one's own purposes or to lure an opponent to one's own side. In the case of a social movement, it refers to an established, relatively powerful group or organization neutralizing a social movement organization through what looks like cooperation. This can be accomplished in at least two ways. First, a group can form an organization that has a similar name to an existing social movement organization

MADD founder Candy Lightner, here standing with President Ronald Reagan and a host of other federal officials, left MADD in 1993 to work for a lobbying firm on behalf of the liquor distilling industry. This represents a serious blow to MADD's credibility and a major coup for the liquor companies attempting to resist tougher drunk driving standards.

and then release press statements. Second, powerful groups can sometimes bribe or otherwise tempt social movement leaders to join them.

Forming organizations with names similar to existing social movement organizations confuses the general public, who believes that the statements are coming from the social movement when in fact they are coming from the opposition. For example, manufacturing industries have formed organizations like the Southern California Air Quality Alliance and the American Crop Protection Association. The Western Fuels Association, a group of electricity and utility companies, formed the Greener Earth Society. The Greener Earth Society is dedicated to furthering the notion that carbon dioxide emissions do not cause global warming and are actually good for the environment. The names of these groups are clearly meant to create the impression that they are part of the environmental movement when in fact they are part of the opposition, the industries that produce pollution.

Another method of co-opting a social movement is to somehow tempt its leaders into joining the opposition. Leaders of social movements may be driven by righteousness, but they might also be seeking personal wealth, fame, or glory. Leaders whose motivations are less than righteous can often be persuaded to join the opposition. They may be offered large sums of money. They might be given high-status jobs within an organization, corporation, or bureaucracy. They may even be convinced that they will be able to do more good working within the system than against it. Either way, that person's credibility is damaged and the reputation of the movement along with it. Once they get comfortable with their new high-paying, high-status position, they often become much more timid about criticizing the powerful forces that pay their wages.

The most notorious recent example of a social movement leader being co-opted occurred when Candy Lightner, the founder and original leader of Mothers Against Drunk Driving, accepted a job for a lobbying firm that worked on behalf of the American Beverage Institute, comprised of every major alcohol distiller in the United States. The American Beverage Institute was MADD's primary enemy in the fight to toughen drunk driving laws throughout the United States. Lightner's job as a lobbyist was to use political pressure in an attempt to keep any state from lowering the legal intoxication limit from .10 to .08 (Griffin 1994). MADD still exists and still enjoys a great deal of support, but the defection of their founder and former leader damaged MADD's credibility in the eyes of the public. The liquor distilling and serving industry essentially bought Lightner's name and reputation. Her defection is still used as ammunition by opponents of MADD who want to depict the group as a bunch of out-of-control radicals who have lost sight of their original purpose.

Formal Social Control

Social movements frequently meet resistance from existing authorities because they want changes that social and political leaders do not want. There are several different ways that formal social control by legitimate authorities can be used against social movements. Generally, they fall into two categories: legitimate force and laws/ordinances.

Legitimate Force

Police officers, National Guard members, and soldiers can all be ordered by their superiors to use *legitimate force* in order to quell any public activity. As long as it stays within reason and the force is not blatantly excessive, most citizens will not question this tactic. This means that social control agents can use force legitimately, but any force on the part of social movement members will be perceived as illegitimate. For example, police officers can physically push protestors out of a public park, but protestors cannot legitimately push the police at all. Authorities' use of force is considered legitimate as long as it stays within certain bounds. This allows elected and appointed officials to use the police and other agents of control, within limits, for their own purposes.

Laws and Ordinances

The most common use of formal social control is not physical. It has to do with over-enforcement of existing *laws and ordinances* and the creation of new ones. Leaders of various social movements throughout history have been

Cities and towns frequently pass laws, ordinances, and codes with the specific intention of preventing public protest, strikes, and picket lines.

arrested for minor crimes that usually would not result in arrest for average citizens. Public nuisance and disturbance laws, noise ordinances, and loitering laws can all be applied selectively to members of any kind of protest or demonstration. Jaywalking laws, rarely enforced in normal life, can be used to ticket people marching down a street. Cities may pass ordinances banning signs in particular areas, limiting the number of people who may walk as a group on sidewalks, or even make it an offense to stand on a corner for more than a few minutes. Obscure fire code violations can be used to justify shutting down a group's headquarters. Some communities allow for the confiscation of any equipment if a noise ordinance is violated. Property can be condemned, cars can be pulled over for safety inspections and impounded, and people can be jailed for littering, loitering, or disturbing the peace.

These are just some of the tactics that can be used against any group or individual at any time. Any social movement that police officers or their commanders do not like will likely find itself the target of all these tactics and more. The more a movement upsets or opposes existing authorities, the more of this type of resistance they are likely to face. The authorities technically do not violate any laws when they use this kind of tactic against a social movement. In fact, they can argue that laws are being vigorously enforced for the "betterment" or "protection of society."

It can be difficult for any movement to maintain momentum when followers have to worry about harassment from law enforcement officers and when every day the organization faces more legal difficulties. None of these minor offences will put anyone behind bars for long, and many of them only amount to a small fine. This harassment can even bring a movement together and fire up their passion. However, if done effectively, constant legal harassment makes it difficult for members of the movement to actually get anything done. The constant cycle of being ticketed or arrested, appearing in court, and paying a fine or serving a short time in jail destroys the group's efficiency. Group members may also become known as criminals. This severely hinders their attempts to build a respectable reputation with outsiders.

Ideally, all groups would receive equal protection under the law. In reality, groups that upset or anger social control agents are likely to receive little or no protection and face a great deal of harassment, resistance, and even imprisonment.

Violence

The most extreme form of resistance to social movements is physical violence. Sometimes violence is a last resort, but all too often it is a first line of defense against social movements. Violence against social movement leaders or followers can come from individuals, from other social movements, or from the government.

When an individual decides that abortion is murder and therefore it is okay to kill a doctor to keep him or her from performing abortions, violence may seem to be a logical next step. In the last twenty years, several pro-life individuals have killed, injured, or attempted to kill doctors and nurses in the United States (Blanchard 1994). Their goal is not just to stop that one individual, but

Blue-collar "hardhats" attacked anti-war protestors in New York City in 1970. This was an attempt by private citizens to use violence as a means of discouraging a social movement.

Lynching was used for decades as an extreme means of intimidation against those seeking racial progress in the South between 1870 and 1954. Notice the air of excitement and celebration on the faces of the participants in this photograph, taken in Indiana. The violence was not an hysterical outburst, but rather a planned and orchestrated event aimed at striking fear into the hearts of would-be opponents.

to scare other doctors and nurses enough to make them stop, too. Violence is aimed at a small number of people but is also intended to intimidate anyone else who may be sympathetic to the cause they represent. This use of violence as intimidation is a typical rationale for those who try to resist social movements through violence. Blacks were often lynched by white mobs in the rural South specifically with the goal of scaring all other blacks in the area into submission to the Jim Crow laws (Tolnay and Beck 1998). Lynchings and assassinations are the most extreme forms of violence against social movement leaders and followers. Beatings and threats are much more common.

Sometimes violence is part of an organized effort of resistance from a countermovement. As mentioned above, the Ku Klux Klan was organized after the Civil War to resist all of the social changes that were being brought by Reconstruction (Boyer et al. 1996, Dobratz and Shanks-Meile 1997). Members of the Klan carefully used terror, beatings, and lynchings to resist the move toward greater freedom and equality by Southern blacks. This technique was used again by racist groups like the Klan and the White Citizens' Council in the 1950s and 1960s to resist the advances of the civil rights movement (Halberstam 1993, Greenberg 1994, Salmond 1997).

Unfortunately, the violence sometimes comes from the same people who are sworn to protect and serve the citizens of the United States. This chapter already mentioned that the police and private security forces sometimes use force in resisting social movements. Sadly, they also sometimes use violence. Far too many individuals working on behalf of the labor movement in the 1920s and '30s and the public action phase of the civil rights movement in the 1950s and '60s were killed by police officers (see, for example, Halberstam

1993, Salmond 1997). Social movement leaders and followers can be victims of brutality and abuse that come from social control agents who are following orders from their superiors. In May of 1970, National Guardsmen shot thirteen anti-war protestors at Kent State University in Kent, Ohio. Four of the protestors died. None of the students were armed and none of them were within fifty feet of the Guardsmen who fired high-powered rifles at them (Hensley and Lewis 1978, Lewis 1972, Tiene 1995).

This kind of violence from authorities is less common in the United States than in some other parts of the world, but it is not as rare as many would like to believe. Any time groups of people are actively engaged in activities that upset or directly threaten the power of authorities, they are in danger of violent retaliation by those authorities. Although video cameras and other communications technology have made it more difficult for social control agents to use violence against movement leaders and followers, it is still an ever-present danger. For example, the murder of Chinese dissidents in Tiananmen Square was recorded in its entirety on videotape. The presence of cameras acting as witnesses could not prevent the violence from taking place.

The goals of individuals, countermovements, and local, state, or federal authorities are always the same when they use violence to resist a social movement: They hope to scare leaders and followers so badly that they abandon their goals. They hope to limit the effectiveness of the movement by removing key leaders or "instigators." They hope to prevent social changes that threaten them in some way.

Why Social Movements Are Important

Social movements can influence the way an entire nation lives. They can alter national government policy. They can change the way that citizens view themselves, their society, or the world around them. They can even destroy a society. Social movements make history.

The Prohibition Movement succeeded in getting alcohol totally outlawed in the United States from 1920 until 1933 (Boyer et al. 1996). The Nazi movement in Germany began as a workers' social movement and led to the destruction of much of Europe (Kornhauser 1959). More recent American social movements like the fight against drunk driving, led by groups like MADD, have changed the way an entire nation views specific behaviors.

People's attitudes and behavior are always influenced by outside factors. When a movement sweeps through society, it tends to influence the judgement and perceptions of many people. Without social movements, social change would only occur when leaders and elites decide that it should. Whenever people with no individual political power join together and form organizations, they create their own power. Their ability to change their own society is increased by several factors. The more organized they are, the more they understand the political and legal system that they operate within, and the more astute and determined they are, the more likely they are to succeed.

All citizens have the right to vote in a democratic society like the United States. However, elected officials do not always do what people want them to do. As the civil rights movement clearly showed, political leaders can be mean-spirited, shortsighted, or just plain stupid. For example, in 1957 the governor of Arkansas lied to the President of the United States and broke federal law for the sake of winning reelection. He told President Eisenhower that he would cooperate with the effort to desegregate Little Rock's Central High School. Instead, he ordered his National Guard troops to block the school doors and refuse protection to the nine black students who were to enter (Greenberg 1994, Halberstam 1993). Countless other city and state officials attempted to skirt federal law and encouraged their constituents to commit acts of violence, all in the name of preserving segregation (Bloom 1987, Greenberg 1994, Halberstam 1993, Salmond 1997, McAdam 1982). Social movements make it possible for citizens to change policies created by elected officials who do not follow their own oaths.

Not all social movements want to create positive change. Anti-immigration movements and white supremacy/white separatist movements have, as their primary goal, the oppression of others (Boyer et al. 1996, Dobratz and Shanks-Meile 1997). Some social movements are trying to better society, some are trying to exclude others from opportunities or liberties, and some just want to change things back to the way they believe they used to be. What all of these social movements have in common is the desire by ordinary citizens to have a say in the operation of their society.

Discussion

As one can see, social movements come in a variety of forms. Some have narrow and specific goals. Others have broad and general goals. Some seek to alter the attitudes or behaviors of a specific group of people. Others seek to alter their entire society. All of them are attempts by ordinary people to influence their lives and their society.

Social movements exist because a group of people wants something. They often meet resistance from those who do not want the same thing. Progressive reformative movements and revolutionary movements meet the most resistance because there are always people who just want to leave things the way they are. The broader their focus is and the more ambitious their goals are, the more resistance a movement is likely to face. The movements that meet the most resistance are those that threaten the power or position of authorities and elites in society. They not only face individuals and groups that oppose their goals, but official resistance as well.

Not all social movements succeed. A lot of them fail, and few achieve all of their goals. However, society is constantly being shaped by the actions of social movements.

There are a variety of theories specifically intended to analyze and explain social movements. The Chapter 14 will examine some of the most well known social movement theories. Chapter 15 will look at a successful social movement (the American Civil Rights movement) and an unsuccessful social movement (the Prostitutes' Rights movement). Chapter 16 will apply social movement theories to two social movements that are currently battling for dominance in the United States, the Pro-Life and Pro-Choice movements.

Chapter 14

Understanding Social Movements

Classic collective behavior theories such as Turner and Killian's Emergent Norm Perspective and Smelser's Value-Added Theory can be applied to social movements just like any other form of collective behavior. The Emergent Norm Perspective, for example, assumes that people join social movements for the same reasons that they take part in any type of collective behavior: Confusion and anxiety lead them to follow the norms within their social situation. If everyone they know seems to be taking part in a social movement, they will, too.

The Value-Added Theory also assumes that social movements arise for the same reasons as any other type of collective behavior: Strain occurs in a conducive social situation, a generalized belief forms, and people join together in an attempt to alleviate the strain. The collective episode takes the form of a social movement because of the generalized belief that grows.

However, as discussed in Chapter 13, social movements are different from other forms of collective behavior. Because of this, there are special theories designed to explain them. These theories tend to focus on the lasting and organized nature of social movements. Most social scientists prefer to use these theories to specifically explain the appearance, formation, and long-term development of social movements. This chapter will describe and discuss some of the classic social movement theories. Chapters 15 and 16 will focus on applying these theories to actual social movements.

Social Movement Theories

Mass Society Theory

In 1959, William Kornhauser published *The Politics of Mass Society*. Kornhauser's Mass Society Theory can be summed up as follows: The organization of a society leads to certain categories of behavior by its members and leaders. Any society with a lot of alienated citizens who have a lot of direct influence over their elites and who, in turn, are unduly influenced by those leaders, has the potential to become a mass society. A mass society creates mass movements. "Mass movements" are anti-democratic and seek to destroy or totally transform their society. The members of the mass movement usually believe that they are creating a perfect society. Instead, they lead to the restriction of personal freedom and make their culture an oppressive and sometimes dangerous one.

"Mass society" is a negative term that carries a connotation similar to a "herd society." A mass society is one in which everyone wants the same material goods, has the same ideas, and pursues the same lifestyles. It is dull, uniform, and mediocre. People in a mass society do not think for themselves. This is the opposite of a "pluralist society," in which a wide variety of different people and organizations all exist together but are independent of each other. The social structure determines whether a society becomes a mass society or a pluralistic society.

Mass Society Theory focuses on *mass movements*, "popular movements that operate outside of and against the social order" (Kornhauser 1959: 5). These mass movements tend to consume an entire society. They can be terribly destructive. A mass society is vulnerable to these destructive political movements which aim to eliminate freedom.

World War II was still a recent memory when *The Politics of Mass Society* was written. Everything that had taken place in Fascist Italy and Nazi Germany during the war had recently become public knowledge. Large parts of Europe were falling under Communist Soviet rule and people were learning of some of the horrors of Stalin's regime. It is from this serious, life-and-death outlook that Kornhauser critiques social structure as a source of a specific type of social movement. Mass Society Theory is intended to explain movements that could and did tear entire societies apart from the inside out. This perspective gives Kornhauser's analysis a certain force.

The mass society has specific characteristics. These characteristics make mass movements more likely to occur.

Atomization

The most important of these characteristics is what Kornhauser calls *atomization*. It refers to people being socially isolated from each other and feeling powerless in their society. Most sociologists today refer to this as "alienation."

It can also be thought of as feeling disconnected. Feeling alienated from others makes people more likely to engage in any behavior that provides meaning for them. Feeling alienated from society makes them more likely to engage in behavior that is intended to destroy, revolutionize, or totally transform their society. Combined, they produce citizens who are searching for meaning and who are willing to destroy their society in order to find it.

Access

Another important factor is the amount of direct influence that citizens have over their leaders. Kornhauser calls this *access*. He argues that too much direct access or influence by citizens creates a situation where elites feel overly compelled to follow the whims of citizens rather than leading them. The problem of access refers to any leaders who can lose their position at any moment if they do something that displeases people. In a society with too much direct influence by citizens, leaders (elected or otherwise) would have to make each and every daily decision based on what the people seem to want. It is as if the people are constantly looking over the official's shoulder, questioning and second-guessing every small decision. The loudest voices are heard the most and taken to be representative of the people. Leaders under these conditions become neurotic and insecure and begin to do whatever "the people" seem to want at that moment. Leadership therefore becomes irrational.

Availability

A third characteristic of mass societies is excessive *availability* of citizens to influence by leaders. Citizens who are too available to leaders are more easily manipulated. There is the potential for manipulation in any society where individual leaders have the ability to sway the attention and activity of the entire population. The potential for mass behavior therefore exists. "Mass society is a social system in which elites are readily accessible to influence by non-elites and non-elites are readily available for mobilization by elites" (Kornhauser 1959: 39). The accessibility of elites and the availability of citizens work hand-in-hand to produce a situation in which the mass rules over the individual. Decisions are not made based on the idea of rights and privileges. Instead, people strive to do and think what they are supposed to do and think. Leaders follow the whims of public opinion, and the public follows the commands of the leaders. The result is an unstable, unpredictable, and repressive society.

Intermediate Groups

Kornhauser consistently argues that a lack of strong, intermediate groups tends to magnify all of these characteristics. Examples of intermediate groups could include community organizations, Parent-Teacher Associations, church groups, local or regional political groups, and so on. The more involved with these kinds of groups an individual is, the more connected they feel to others and to society. The group gives them connections outside of their own family but still grounded to their community. Being more socially connected leads to being more socially active which, in turn, leads to being more socially tolerant.

A mass society, on the other hand, tends to be characterized by individuals who are not involved with any organizations outside the family *or* who are only involved with official, state-run groups. The result is a "mass." Kornhauser defines a mass as "large numbers of people who are not integrated into any broad social groupings" (1959: 14) and "an undifferentiated and amorphous collectivity" (34). A lack of ties to the community or region produces a mass of atomized individuals who are isolated and who may concern themselves too much with matters that do not directly effect them. These people develop "mass personalities." They are attracted to mass movements rather than to independent groups. Therefore, independent, intermediate groups are key to maintaining freedom in any society.

Mass Movements

A society that has the characteristics described above is a mass society. Such a society will tend to spawn "mass movements." It is important to remember that not every social movement is a mass movement. Mass movements are extreme in their goals and may be irrational and violent in their methods. Extremist groups are fundamentally hostile to the social order partially because they are made up of alienated, atomized people. Mass movements have specific characteristics:

1. They pay more attention to national and international events than personal and local events. Members of a mass movement view themselves as part of something much greater than their own lives, communities, or families. They are on a crusade to totally transform their entire society.

2. Response is direct. Mass groups and mass movements tend to favor activism over diplomacy. Strikes and protests are used as a first line of action, rather than a last resort. They don't tolerate discussion. For example, they may disrupt a meeting rather than take part in it. They may try to kill a leader rather than campaign against him or her in the next election. They may use guns or bombs to get their way. They do not want their concerns brought to light for discussion, they want their own "solutions" immediately implemented.

3. They are unstable. Members of mass movements tend to be fickle. They may rapidly shift their attention toward or away from anything at any time. Similarly, the intensity of their response may suddenly increase or decrease dramatically.

4. They are organized around a program with continuity and purpose. Without organization, mass members are just a bunch of isolated people. A purpose gives them a reason to form an actual movement. However, their objectives are usually remote (unlikely to occur) and extreme (unrealistic).

Mass movements favor activist modes of response. This means that they do not want to follow the normal ways of getting things done. Independent thought is discouraged, not encouraged. Disagreement is rarely tolerated and genuine debate is often absent. Everyone is required to agree with the "party line."

A mass behaves like a herd of sheep. They want to be involved with social life and to gain personal meaning for their lives but don't know how. A mass movement, with its focus on grand goals and large themes, provides the illusion of both. The demands and goals of the mass movement may seem irrational to outsiders because they are not based on realistic efforts to better society. Similarly, the techniques used by the mass movement may seem unnecessarily harsh or extreme because they are unwilling to engage in accepted political or social means of being heard. They use force, bullying, threat, and argument in place of diplomacy, discussion, or debate in order to achieve goals that are vague, extreme, and sometimes illogical.

Crisis Politics

Kornhauser states that the mass society perspective is best used to analyze extremist responses to "crisis politics." Mass movements do not occur in healthy societies under normal circumstances. Instead, they occur at times of crisis, when a society is either in chaos or has fallen into a pattern of atomization, access, and availability.

Culture and Personality

Cultural factors and individual personalities are both important to the acceptance and growth of a mass movement because *cultural legitimacy* and *psychological support* give power to ideas and movements. In a mass society, the culture makes mass movements seem legitimate and there are a lot of people who are likely to be attracted to such a movement. The structure of the society creates a mass culture full of people with mass personalities.

Cultural Legitimacy   Mass standards are uniform and can quickly change for no good reason. When a culture values the mass over the individual, people all learn to like the same things and change what they like whenever the opinion of the masses seems to change. This creates too much cultural uniformity. Once a culture comes to value uniformity, it becomes expected of everyone. People start to demand conformity from each other. This anti-democratic approach does not respect individual tastes, preferences, or rights. Mass agreement becomes the only standard of what is right and if everyone agrees on something, it is believed to be good.

Kornhauser uses fads to illustrate how mass standards tend to operate. A fad appears out of nowhere, is wildly popular for a brief period of time, and then vanishes. On the other hand, fashion changes relatively slowly and has continuity over time. New fashions gradually gain acceptance and then gradually fall from popularity. In a fad, everyone is doing, thinking, buying, or wearing exactly the same thing and only because other fad participants are doing the same. In the world of fashion, there is tremendous room for group and individual variation. People may look similar, but no one looks exactly alike. People choose the items that they like from multiple acceptable fashionable choices. From Kornhauser's perspective, fashion is pluralistic but fads are mass-oriented.

Mass standards happen when the concept of "equal rights" is confused with the obliteration of all social differences. Kornhauser argues that diversity of opinions, tastes, and preferences are good. They keep us fresh and open as a society. Mindless conformity to perceived mass standards produces an entire culture of people with no tolerance for individuality or dissent of any kind. The more diverse a culture is, the more tolerant of dissent and individuality members of that culture are. The more uniform a culture is, the more likely it is to spawn mass movements.

Psychological Factors   A lack of intermediate group connections makes people feel unable to participate in their social world. This leads to a poor self-image because the individual feels cut off from society. It makes individuals more eager for activist "solutions" to the anxiety caused by their alienation. As a result, such atomized individuals become highly suggestible. They lose the ability to decide anything for themselves. Instead, they rely on suggestions from others. Eventually, atomized people begin to think of mass opinions, desires, etc. as their own. If something is popular, they like it. At this point they develop mass personalities and become what Kornhauser calls "mass men." These mass people are selfish and unhappy. They do not have close or personal ties to their communities. They have given up their thoughts to those of the mass. Their main focus is personal satisfaction, and they can't find it because they are self-alienated.

Multiple and varied social connections allow people to form distinctive self-images. This produces autonomous people who have respect for themselves and therefore respect others. In a normal society, people feel connected to their community which, in turn, makes them feel connected to society and humanity. They tolerate disagreement and understand that everyone does not have to like the same things or want the same things.

Conclusion

This theory is only intended to explain one particular type of social movement: dangerous, extreme, and potentially destructive movements such as Fascism, Nazism, Stalinism, and McCarthyism. The far more common small-scale, local movements don't fall under this perspective. Neither do most re-form movements, revivalist movements, or grassroots political organizations. Instead, Kornhauser attempts to show how social structure can produce the cultural conditions and personal attitudes that made fascism rise in Italy, Nazism in Germany, and Communism in much of Eastern Europe. Consider-ing that most of these movements were recent when *The Politics of Mass So-ciety* was written, this intense focus on totalitarian and revolutionary movements is understandable. However, a student today might wonder what the practical uses of such a theory are. If the goal is to understand why cer-tain movements catch on in some societies but not others, or to understand why similar kinds of movements tend to appear over and over in the same so-ciety, then Mass Society Theory may be of use. If the goal is to understand various kinds of common social movements, the theory is not useful.

Relative Deprivation Theory

Relative Deprivation Theory is a broader and more general theory than Mass Society Theory. It focuses on the psychological reasoning behind the decision to form or join a social movement. Denton Morrison (1971) argues that there are social conditions that cause relative deprivation within the population in any society. If enough people feel this way, a social movement is likely to form.

Relative Deprivation

The term "relative deprivation" was introduced by Samuel Stouffer (1949) and Robert Merton (1949). It refers to a situation where a person has less than they believe they deserve. A person who does not have enough food, clothing, or shelter is experiencing *absolute* deprivation. A person who *feels* like he or she doesn't have enough clothes because all of his or her friends got brand-new outfits is experiencing *relative* deprivation. Relative deprivation is an important concept because it reveals that people are happiest when their expectations are met. It is the level of expectations that determines the level of contentment. People feel the most discontent when there is something that they want and believe they deserve, but cannot have.

A person can experience relative deprivation no matter how much of something they actually have. A teenager who receives a used Camaro from her parents on her sixteenth birthday may feel terribly deprived if her friends all received new BMWs. Relative deprivation only exists in relation to those who we compare ourselves to. These *reference groups* allow us to decide if we have more than enough, enough, or not enough. A poor reference group makes a person feel wealthy. Comparing oneself to wealthier people gener-ates a feeling of deprivation relative to that reference group.

Morrison identifies two different kinds of relative deprivation that can drive social movements. The first is *decremental deprivation*. This occurs in any situation where people believe that their opportunities have been suddenly reduced. For example, in a financial recession people believe that their chances of landing a great-paying job are suddenly reduced. They experience a blockage of their goals and do not believe that it is their own fault. The second form of relative deprivation is *aspirational deprivation*. This occurs when people's expectations and ambitions rise but their opportunities do not. If a large number of people suddenly decide that they deserve something that they have never had and most of them cannot get, they will feel blocked and discontent.

Decremental deprivation tends to produce conservative and rightist movements intended to change society back to the way it used to be (when the opportunity was more widespread). These can become nationalist or fascist movements. Aspirational deprivation tends to produce liberal and leftist movements intended to change society in new, progressive ways (to provide new opportunity to movement members). These can become revolutionary movements.

Both types of relative deprivation create similar feelings: Something that is desired, expected, and demanded by a large number of people does not seem to be available to them. Whether the problem is caused by new desires or by a reduction in former opportunities, people feel blocked from something that they expect to have access to.

Legitimate Expectations

The key to relative deprivation is the development of what Morrison (1971) calls legitimate expectations. The individuals can't just want something; they have to believe that they have a *right* to expect it, that they *deserve* it. Once people become convinced that their expectations are legitimate, they begin to feel deprived if those expectations are not met. It does not matter if the expectations really are legitimate, as long as they believe they are.

In order for a social movement to form, people must be aware of the group goal, believe that it is desirable, and believe that it is possible to achieve. Morrison argues that this happens most often through social contacts. People may develop these expectations themselves, but then they try to convince others to see things the same way. This can create large numbers of people who desire the same thing.

Blocked Expectations and Discontent

The next step in the process has to do with whether or not those expectations are blocked. If people can get what they want with a little effort, they don't need a social movement. However, if they believe that the path is blocked they will be unhappy and unfulfilled. It does not matter if it really is blocked. As long as the people perceive their fulfillment is being blocked, they will be upset and are likely to try to do something about it.

Morrison (1971) refers to this situation as a "special type of cognitive dissonance." People want something, believe that they have a right to expect it, and believe that they won't get it. This is not a happy situation. People in this situation experience cognitive dissonance, a psychologically upsetting state, over this "injustice" or "inequity." There are four ways that the discontent can be reduced:

1. People can blame themselves for the shortfall. This lowers their expectations and therefore reduces the dissonance. They decide that they are either unlucky or personally inadequate. Either way, they drop their expectations and learn to tolerate their life the way it is.

2. People can psychologically discount the blockages. In other words, they can convince themselves that patience or hard work will allow them to achieve their desired goals. This gives them some positive, concrete path of action to take in order to get what they want. Even if they are wrong, their discontent is reduced because they believe they will eventually reach their goal.

3. People can change their personal situation. For example, people who believe that they will never achieve their ambitions in a small town may move to a big city. People who think that their own country does not allow them adequate opportunity may emigrate to another nation. They feel as if they are doing something that will make their expectations attainable.

4. If people do not engage in any of the first three and they come to believe that their problems are structural rather than personal, they can decide to reduce their relative deprivation by changing the system that they live in. If the society is defined as the problem, then changing the society becomes the solution. This does not immediately reduce the discontent, but it makes people feel as if they are doing something that will eliminate it eventually.

Conditions in a society that cause relative deprivation make social movements more likely to occur. People experience relative deprivation any time they expect something that they can't get. If enough people expect the same thing and believe that society is keeping them from getting it, a social movement will form.

Morrison argues that there are specific structural conditions that make social movements likely to form. First, there must be a large population experiencing relative deprivation. A few people here and there do not make a social movement. The idea of changing society will only catch on if there are enough people with the same expectations to make the problem appear to exist within society itself, not the individuals. For example, if I am out of work but everyone I know is still working, I might feel unlucky. If everyone I know is out of work, we might collectively decide that there is something wrong with the economy. The problem has to be defined as structural before a movement can form.

Second, there must be close interaction, communication, and proximity between people in the same situation. The ideas driving a social movement must be spread and accepted. The more communication there is between people experiencing relative deprivation, the more likely they are to try to change their society to alleviate it.

Third, there must be what Morrison calls "high role and status commonality." This means that a movement requires socially similar people who are all in the same situation. The more alike they are, the more likely they are to join together.

Fourth, social movements are more likely to form in a society that has a rigid and obvious stratification system. In a society where the power differences between different social classes or castes are obvious, people are more likely to believe that their problems come from that social structure. Those who are close to the top of their own social group are most likely to be aware of the differences between their own social group and the one above them. They are also most likely to believe that these differences are unfair and should be eliminated.

The fifth factor in Morrison's list is the high presence of voluntary association activity in the society. He argues that this creates the belief that voluntary group efforts can make a difference in a society. Those who are already active in community activities are more likely to put the same kind of effort and resources into making changes on a societal level. Morrison also mentions that such groups provide a "residue" of leadership and organizational skills.

Conclusion

Morrison and other Relative Deprivation Theorists claim that individual discontent is the driving force behind social movement formation. When a large group of people want something, believe that they deserve it, and believe that their society will not let them achieve it on their own, they are likely to form a social movement in an attempt to change the society. Therefore, two totally different situations can lead to the formation of social movements: 1) the raising of expectations within a society, or 2) the reduction of opportunities in a society. Either of these produces feelings of relative deprivation. If people expect more than they have, they are unhappy.

Morrison argues that the decision to join a movement is a tough one. There are extra costs to the individual and the potential for no rewards at all. People must achieve something like faith in the group solution to a problem that they define as structural.

Although social movements tend to create social change, they also tend to be created by social change. Any time society changes in such a way that opportunities are reduced or expectations rise, relative deprivation increases and so does the likelihood of a social movement forming. As long as things stay exactly the same as they have always been, people are unlikely to feel that they can or should be changed. When the social structure does change in some way people become more likely to want to change it back (decremental deprivation) or change it even further (aspirational deprivation).

Relative Deprivation Theory is perhaps useful in determining what conditions make a social movement likely to form in the first place. No one can deny the logic inherent within the theory: People won't try to change their society unless they are unhappy about something, believe that they can fix it by changing society, and believe that they can succeed at making those changes. However, the theory is also intended to explain why people join the movement once it forms. Many theorists, including the next two to be examined in this chapter, argue that relative deprivation is only one of the factors that create a social movement. For example, research has consistently shown that many movement members do not stand to directly gain from the success of the movement (Oberschall 1973, 1993). Relative Deprivation Theory does little to explain why, for example, Northern whites took part in the United States civil rights movement during the 1950s and '60s or why men get involved in the debate over abortion. Outside support and political factors may be just as important as a sense of deprivation. Not all members of social movements experience relative deprivation and not all people who experience relative deprivation join the movement. There are complex social, economic, and political issues that determine how successful a movement is at producing change. Relative Deprivation Theory does not include these factors and therefore doesn't fit real-life social movements well. The next two theories that we will examine specifically address these issues.

Resource Mobilization Theory

Resource Mobilization Theory first gained prominence with the publication of *Social Conflict and Social Movements* by Anthony Oberschall in 1973. Mass Society Theory was still the dominant perspective in the study of social movements at that time, so Oberschall criticized Kornhauser's theory quite a bit. According to Oberschall, Mass Society Theory fails to account for what really happened in anti-democratic movements such as McCarthyism and the Radical Right in the United States or Nazism in Germany. Research done during the 1960s contradicted many of the assumptions made by Kornhauser in his 1959 book. Like Relative Deprivation Theory, Oberschall's Resource Mobilization Theory is designed to account for the new information that had come to light over the prior decade of research.

Resource Mobilization Theory focuses on the social processes that make it possible for a movement to form and succeed. It pays much more attention to political and economic factors than Mass Society or Relative Deprivation Theory and much less attention to the psychological traits of movement members. The theory makes no assumptions about individual motivations for joining. Individual alienation is considered irrelevant. Resource Mobilization theorists assume that all societies contain enough discontent for social movements to arise at any time. It is the organization and leadership (or lack thereof) that make or break a social movement (McCarthy and Zald 1977, Oberschall 1973, 1993).

"Mobilization" refers to "the process of forming crowds, groups, associations, and organizations for the pursuit of collective goals" (Oberschall 1973: 102). Average people with little or no individual power join together in an attempt to influence regional or national policy. They have to fight legitimate authorities as well as any individuals or groups who benefit from leaving things the way they are.

Resource Mobilization Theory rests on one simple assertion: No matter how upset, outraged, or righteous people feel, without organization and leadership they cannot effectively produce social change. Short-lived protests, riots, etc. may occur, but no lasting changes will come about. It does not matter how upset or deprived people feel, but how effectively they can manage ("mobilize") the resources that they need to gain social acceptance for their cause.

Definitions

Resource Mobilization Theory uses certain terms and concepts in precise ways (see McCarthy and Zald 1977). The term "social movement" refers to the presence of beliefs within a population that support social change. "Countermovement" refers to beliefs in a population opposed to a social movement. A "Social Movement Organization" (often referred to in the literature simply as an SMO) is a complex or formal organization that attempts to carry out the beliefs of a social movement or countermovement. For example, the civil rights movement in the United States is a social movement. It can be loosely defined as the desire for increased racial equality and opportunity for blacks. Within that social movement, there were (and still are) a variety of specific SMOs such as the NAACP (National Association for the Advancement of Colored People), CORE (Congress of Racial Equality), SCLC (Southern Christian Leadership Conference), and so on. Each of these organizations was created with the intention of furthering the goals of the civil rights movement.

Adherents are individuals and groups who believe in the goals of the movement. *Conscience adherents* are people who believe in the goals of the movement even though they personally will not benefit if it succeeds. *Constituents* are adherents who actually provide resources (time, labor, or money) to specific social movement organizations. *Conscience constituents* are people who actually help out SMOs even though they have nothing personal to gain from the group's success. *Bystander publics* are outsiders who don't particularly care about the movement. Those bystanders who personally stand to benefit if the movement succeeds are known as *free-riders*. *Opponents* are outsiders who actively try to block the movement. They often form or join countermovements.

Resources

Any SMO must successfully manage available resources. These range from material resources such as jobs, income, and savings to nonmaterial resources like authority, moral commitment, trust, friendship, skills, and so on. The main resources that any potential social movement organization must manage effectively are labor and money. There are jobs that have to be done. They can be done by volunteers or by paid employees. There are many expenses such as transportation, printing or broadcasting costs, and so on, which must be paid. They can be paid out of the pockets of movement members, donations from outsiders, or some larger organization. Any movement must successfully acquire and manage both labor and money if they are to achieve anything. Good organizational structure and effective leadership make this possible.

The success or failure of the movement depends on how many people join the organization, how determined they are, what sacrifices they are willing to make, and the resistance of their opponents (Oberschall 1993). Bystanders must be convinced to join; otherwise the group cannot grow. Adherents must be convinced to contribute time and/or money; otherwise the group will run out of resources. These decisions are influenced by individual perceptions of what others are doing for the common cause and by expectations of who else will join and what they will contribute (Oberschall 1993). Effective social movement organizations are coordinated to achieve a common goal. Individuals may be enticed by the thought of individual gain, but there must also be shared, group reasons for taking part. Otherwise the group will tend to fall apart before much can be achieved.

Organization and Leadership

Strong, existing groups can easily become mobilized as movements (Oberschall 1973). Oberschall specifies that existing social groups make social movements more likely to form if they are *segmented*. Segmented social groups draw their members from one level of society. For example, if the same people who belong to the Rotary Club also belong to the Preservation Society, the Town Council, and the local country club, then no intermediate social connections exist. Those groups do not provide their members with numerous social connections to a wide variety of different people. Instead, the same small groups of people simply associate with each other in a variety of settings.

The more segmented the group associations are in any society, the more likely those groups are to mobilize into social movement organizations. Members of those groups are alike, so their wants tend to be alike as well.

More importantly, existing groups make the mobilization easier because they already have established communications networks, partially mobilized resources, the presence of members with leadership skills, and a tradition of participation (Oberschall 1973). They also have established leaders, members, meeting places, an activity routine, social bonds, and shared beliefs, symbols, and a common language already in place (Oberschall 1993). Leaders of a social movement organization must focus on problems of mobilization, the manufacture of discontent, tactical choices, and the infrastructure of society and movements necessary for success (McCarthy & Zald 1977). Much of the initial work is already done if they can start within an existing organization, especially if they hold a position of authority within the group. The entire existing group can be recruited as a "bloc" (Oberschall 1973, 1993). This "bloc recruitment" dramatically simplifies the process of conversion.

Leaders of social movement organizations take greater risks than ordinary followers but they also receive greater rewards. As Oberschall puts it, "No one is in a position to disregard where his [or her] next meal is coming from and whether or not he [or she] is going to have a roof over his [or her] head" (1973: 159). Leaders often gain status and authority, and sometimes wealth, from their position within the social movement organization. They become political entrepreneurs, just like politicians. If the movement is successful, they may also acquire a great deal of status within society. Leadership of a movement organization can be a stepping stone to tremendous upward social mobility.

An effective leader brings everyone together within the movement and creates a common loyalty. However, leaders do not "make" a movement in the way that some people believe. Oberschall argues that the leader often has to cater to the wants of the followers. Communication and influence frequently take place in small groups within the movement. In this way, the group has some social control over the leaders just as the leaders have some social control over group members.

In the beginning stages of a successful social movement, the organization is informal and the leaders engage in a lot of face-to-face interaction with potential members. Once the movement begins to build momentum the organization must acquire a more formal structure. Too much formal organization in the beginning reduces the attractiveness of the group for outsiders. Not enough formal organization after formation limits the growth potential and reduces the resource efficiency of the group (Oberschall 1993).

Professional Social Movement Organizations A new form of social movement, the professional social movement organization, has popped up in the United States sometime over the last three decades (Oberschall 1993). This is possible because of the technology, mass media, and political system in the United States today.

In a professional social movement organization, the leaders and primary activists are professional reformers pursuing a career in reform causes. They are not from the group that stands to benefit if the movement succeeds. They tend to move from one cause to the next, applying the same techniques of fundraising, publicity, organization, and leadership in each situation. Most of their funding generally comes from third-party sources such as churches, cor-

porations, or even the government. A small, vocal group of potential beneficiaries are used for public relations purposes and as media representatives of
the movement. A large conscience constituency is accessed through direct-
mail appeals and newsletters.

Oberschall himself points out that many social movement organizations
have some of these qualities, and "professional" movements are not really that
different from others (1993). They are more organized, more structured, and
more formal, but that often leads to the most success in achieving their goals.

Goals

Those who are favored or privileged in any society have a vested interest in
keeping things the way they are. Those who are disadvantaged stand to gain
by changing things. Any social movement organization that seeks social
change will have to battle not just legal or political authorities, but also any
groups or individuals who stand to lose something if the movement succeeds.

Outsiders are crucial to the success of a social movement (McCarthy and
Zald 1977, Oberschall 1973, 1993). Rarely does a social movement succeed by
strong-arm tactics. Instead, they must gradually convince the majority of citizens, or the majority of elites and leaders in a society, that the goals of the
movement are just. The most important people to a social movement organization are those who do not take part and are not directly affected. For example, the civil rights movement succeeded partly because the majority of
American lawmakers were gradually convinced that legal segregation and
discrimination were unconstitutional and the majority of powerful American
citizens were gradually convinced that segregation and discrimination laws
were undesirable.

Resource Mobilization Theory does not focus on the discontent of any
particular group of people in society. Oberschall assumes that no society is
perfect and there are always people who share dissatisfaction. When those
dissatisfied people aim their hostility toward the same target, they come to
see themselves as a group. If they hold those targets responsible for their
grievances, hardship, and suffering, they have a focus for their dissatisfaction. All it then takes is common interest and a sense of a common fate for
them to form a social movement. At that point, the mobilization of resources
(or lack thereof) becomes the only factor that determines whether or not they
achieve their goals.

Oberschall (1993) identifies three major tasks that must be successfully
tackled in order for a movement organization to achieve its goals. The first
task is to turn free-riders into contributors. Most social movements have to
convert these people into members by convincing them that the goal cannot
be reached without their help, by promising them special rewards for taking
part, or though some sort of coercion (either force or guilt). The second task is
to overcome organized opposition. Most social movement organizations face
active resistance from countermovements. Countermovements are organiza-

tions that seek to block the movement from getting the changes it seeks. The organization that seeks to keep things the way they are has momentum on its side, so the organization seeking social change must work much harder in order to succeed. The third task in achieving group goals is to create, acquire, and manage (mobilize) the necessary resources for maintaining the organization and accomplishing some collective action.

Factors Encouraging Mobilization

Strong, repressive social control inhibits mobilization. Loosening social control allows and actually encourages mobilization because the relaxation of formerly rigid rules makes the further desired changes seem even more attainable. Freedom of speech and association make mobilization much easier and therefore more likely in a society. In fact, civil liberties in general are more permissive of social mobilization.

Another factor encouraging mobilization is the presence of what Oberschall (1973) calls "focal points." Focal points are people or places that tend to be watched closely for clues as to what will happen next. For example, many people keep an eye on Washington to see how a particular piece of legislation might go. Their decision as to whether or not they should mobilize may be based entirely on what happens there. Members of the NRA, for instance, take their cues from the leaders of the NRA and from political events in Washington, D.C. In this case, "Washington" and the NRA leaders are focal points for those for and against gun control. Either side may suddenly leap into action because of what happens at these remote focal points.

Oberschall also discusses outside help. He seems to argue that social movements are unlikely to succeed unless they receive assistance and support from groups or individuals who have higher social standing. He even goes so far as to argue that rural movements tend to be unsuccessful without assistance from urban individuals (1973). Urban movements, on the other hand, are unlikely to achieve national success unless they manage to get rural people to do the hard work.

Success

Oberschall argues that the ultimate success for any social movement organization is to be accepted and institutionalized into society. Once a social movement has become a part of everyday political life, they no longer have to struggle to achieve and maintain legitimacy, to win converts, and to raise the material resources necessary for continued existence (Oberschall 1993).

The most deserving social movement with the most just cause is not necessarily the one that succeeds. It really boils down to resources: Any social movement organization which gains sufficient resources to overcome social control forces and opposing social groups will tend to succeed. Any social movement organization that fails to raise, create, and manage sufficient material and nonmaterial resources will fail.

Conclusion

Resource Mobilization Theory seems to fit the pattern of social movement formation much better than Mass Society or Relative Deprivation Theory. Years of research have shown that the most successful social movements in American society do, in fact, tend to be those that organize themselves in specific ways and manage available resources to their maximum efficiency (see discussion in Oberschall 1993). In order for any movement to succeed, the organizations must acquire physical power, political power, or social support from a majority of citizens and/or political leaders. Of the three theories discussed so far, Resource Mobilization Theory focuses most heavily on movements that succeed through the persuasion and conversion. Social support has become the most valued resource for many movements.

A problem with Oberschall's theory is his insistence that massive outside assistance is required for the success of most social movements (1973: 214–215, 220, etc.). Resource Mobilization Theory is known as "elitist" because of statements such as the following:

> In a sense, the [1954 *Brown v. Board of Education*] decision marks the high point of a program of reform-from-above by means of legal and institutionalized channels for bringing about social change sponsored primarily by the progressive elements within the ruling groups and elites that so often is followed by the mass action and confrontation phase of a social movement subsequent to the reform's failure (1973: 215).

One does not have to be a careful reader to conclude that Oberschall is saying that all of the important, legal reforms that took place during the civil rights movement were the work of powerful whites. In fact, as Chapter 15 will show, movement organizations led by black attorneys *forced* the Supreme Court and various national political figures to create these changes. President Eisenhower, for example, regretted appointing Earl Warren to the Supreme Court and hated being forced to enforce the *Brown v. Board of Education* decision (Bloom 1987, Greenberg 1994, McAdam 1982, Salmond 1997). Eisenhower did not carry out those decisions because of any personal conviction; he did so because it was politically expedient (Bloom 1987, McAdam 1982, Salmond 1997). Once the movement organizations had successfully won the *Brown* decision, the president of the United States had little choice but to enforce it (Greenberg 1994). The next theory is an attempt to retain some of the most effective aspects of Resource Mobilization Theory while overcoming Oberschall's elitist political biases.

Political Process Theory

The Political Process Theory of social movements was first fully formulated by Douglas McAdam in his 1982 book *Political Process and the Development of Black Insurgency 1930–1970*. McAdam argued that classic social movement theories such as Mass Society and Relative Deprivation Theory focused too much on the psychological dynamics of movement followers. He also believes that "elitist" perspectives such as Resource Mobilization Theory focused too heavily on material resources and outside assistance and not enough on the political environment that makes movements possible in the first place. Internal and external factors are considered equally important in Political Process Theory. Ideology and beliefs are just as important as material resources, as are political connections and the overall social structure. The theory really is an attempt to combine the best of Mass Society, Relative Deprivation, and Resource Mobilization theories together into a more historical and political perspective.

Political Process Theory is similar to Resource Mobilization Theory in several ways. Like Resource Mobilization, Political Process Theory focuses on the factors that make it possible for a movement to form and to achieve success. Political and economic factors are considered much more important than personal ones. However, Political Process Theory focuses much more on the factors that allow ordinary citizens to form their own social movements in opposition to the dominant society. Some sociologists consider the theory Marxist (Dobratz and Shanks-Meile 1997, McAdam 1982) because of this focus on the potentially revolutionary power of ordinary people and the assumption that society is controlled by a small group of powerful elites.

McAdam (1982) argues that three factors most determine the creation and success of a social movement:

> *Organizational strength,* the level of organization within an aggrieved population. The more organized a particular group of people are, the more likely they are to successfully form a social movement and the more likely that movement is to succeed.
>
> *Cognitive liberation,* the perception of the odds of success within that same population. The more they believe they can be successful, the more likely they are to try.
>
> *Political opportunities,* the alignment of groups within the larger political environment. The more allies a group has in the political arena, the more likely they are to be able to achieve changes in the political system.

Political Process Theory focuses much more on political connections than on material resources. A social movement is viewed as a *political* phenomenon, not a psychological one, and is examined as a continuous *process* from formation to decline, which does not develop in a set of rigid stages. Mcadam (1982) assumes that wealth and power are concentrated in the hands of a few groups in America and most people have little say in the major decisions affecting their lives. Social movements are viewed as rational attempts by excluded groups to gain sufficient political leverage to advance their collective interests. All social movements are a struggle against oppressors for social and political power.

Organizational Strength

As in Resource Mobilization Theory, McAdam's Political Process Theory notes the importance of existing organizations for the formation of new movements. Existing organizations of any kind provide potential members, established structures of "solidary incentives," a communication network, and recognized leaders. McAdam argues that existing social groups provide social and interpersonal motivations for taking part in group activities with other members. This includes taking part in the new movement with them. Group members who do not join the movement with their fellow group members will feel guilty and may be socially shunned or punished, while those who do join will be socially rewarded and feel closer to other members.

Cognitive Liberation

Cognitive liberation is a simple concept. Before they become likely to take part in any social movement, potential members must develop the idea that their current situation is unjust and that the oppressive conditions can be changed through collective action. In other words, they must develop a sense of relative deprivation, believe the deprivation is wrong, decide that their cause is righteous, and believe that the solution to their problem is structural. McAdam never uses the term "relative deprivation," but the idea is the same. Before a movement can start there must be a group of people who want something and who believe that they can get it by acting together.

McAdam also argues that the "powerlessness" of ordinary people is often simply a matter of perception. Workers, for example, can go on strike and bring an entire company to a grinding halt. They always have this power, but only realize and utilize it under certain circumstances. This realization is cognitive liberation.

Political Opportunity

Of the three factors listed above, political opportunity is the most important. As McAdam puts it, "the ongoing exercise of significant political leverage remains the key to the successful development of the movement" (1982: 52). Movement organizations have to acquire and use political power in order to get anything significant accomplished. Social movements do not exist in a vacuum; they are products of their social and political environment. Any changes within the system make social movements possible because they can capitalize on the temporarily unstable situation. Society can become more open and therefore more friendly to social movements, or it can become more restricted and therefore discourage social movement formation. All movements exist within and must successfully navigate the political currents of their social system. The maintenance of organizational resources over time is of utmost importance. As long as there are sufficient material resources to keep the organization afloat, political and social factors are most important in determining if the movement group will succeed.

The Social System   Social movements have to adapt to changing political and economic conditions within their society in order to survive. McAdam (1996) lists four key dimensions of political opportunity that relate directly to the social system the movement exists within:

1. The relative openness or closure of the institutionalized political system.
2. The stability or instability of the various interconnected powerful groups.
3. The presence or absence of allies among society's powerful.
4. The state's capacity for and tendency toward repression.

Each of these factors directly determines how much political opportunity a social movement can have. These factors are all beyond the control of the movement members. To succeed, a movement must exist in a time and place where these factors are favorable and must use them to the fullest advantage if they are to gain any success.

Conclusion

Political Process Theory is similar to Resource Mobilization Theory in many ways, but the fundamental difference lies in the focus. Where Resource Mobilization tends to focus on social support and the movements that successfully acquire it, Political Process Theory focuses more on the acquisition of political power. Popular opinion becomes just one small tool in the quest for power. Social change does not occur because "the people" want it, but because a specific group manages to get enough political clout to make it happen. Social movements are depicted as situations in which common people join together to fight the elite forces that rule society. Social movement members are often portrayed as something like folk heroes in Political Process analyses.

Discussion

Each of these theories has some flaws and each of them has some strengths. Mass Society Theory has been criticized for its exclusive focus on extreme, mass movements. At least one author (Ferber 1998) has argued that undue attention to the most extremist social movements has led to a lack of attention to more mainstream problems and movements. One attempt to analyze the simultaneous formation of several social movement and countermovement organizations in Chicago over the course of a decade of racial tension found that Mass Society did not adequately explain or account for the formation of any of the groups (Berlet 1999).

Research has also failed to support Relative Deprivation Theory. Although the theory appeals to common sense and seems perfectly logical, many social movement organizations are led by individuals who do not experience any deprivation at all (Oberschall 1993). Further, many members of social movements do not stand to personally gain anything if the movement succeeds. Thousands of white Northerners actively contributed to the black civil rights movement in the United States in the 1950s and 1960s (McAdam 1982, Oberschall 1973). None of these individuals were motivated by a sense of personal deprivation, and none of them expected any direct benefits if the movement succeeded. It is not that relative deprivation is unimportant, but rather that there is too much which cannot be explained by relative deprivation alone.

This leaves us with Resource Mobilization Theory and Political Process Theory. Both theories seem to work well in explaining the rise and success or failure of social movements. Both include the relative deprivation experienced by some potential members as a minor but important factor. Both have been applied in research over the years and have fared well. The biggest difference between the two theories is ideological.

Resource Mobilization Theory looks at social movements from a slightly jaded perspective. The cause of the movement is barely noticed and the goals of the movement are not considered important as long as they are realistic and attainable. Resource Mobilization Theory applies to all movements in precisely the same way. This is its strength as an empirical theory; the processes that lead to the success or failure of a movement are exactly the same whether the movement is radical, liberal, conservative, or extremist. However, the emphasis on material resources, outside assistance, and professional leadership has led some to label the Resource Mobilization perspective "elitist" (McAdam 1982). Resource Mobilization Theory pays little or no attention to why a movement forms in the first place and largely ignores values and beliefs within a movement.

In contrast, Political Process Theory paints a picture of social movements as brave collections of powerless individuals joining together to strike out against the powerful elites who run society. This viewpoint is abundantly clear in McAdam's analysis of the civil rights movement in the United States. However, it is important to remember that not all social movements have admirable goals. There is a long history of oppressive, racist, and intolerant movements in American society (see discussion in Dobratz and Shanks-Meile 1997). Political Process Theory seems to indicate that members of these movements should be admired for their courage in standing up to the elite forces that controlled their lives.

However, the theory can be applied without these ideological biases coming into play. The real factor that sets Political Process Theory apart from

Resource Mobilization Theory is the attention paid to outside sociopolitical factors that change over time. Resource Mobilization Theory focuses on the conditions that must exist within an organization for it to succeed. Political Process Theory focuses on the conditions that must exist within a society before any movement can even begin, let alone succeed.

In the Chapter 16, all four of these theories will be applied to competing social movements in the United States today. This should make each theory's strengths and weaknesses more obvious to the reader. Chapter 15 focuses on the characteristics that tend to make a movement likely to fail or succeed in achieving their goals. This includes a look at the civil rights movement and the prostitutes' rights movement in the United States.

Chapter 15

Successful and Unsuccessful Social Movements:
The Civil Rights Movement and the Prostitutes' Rights Movement

This chapter looks at the qualities that tend to make a social movement successful or unsuccessful in achieving the goals of the movement. It begins with a discussion of the qualities that make a movement successful. This will be followed by a look at the civil rights movement. A brief discussion of the qualities that tend to make a movement unsuccessful will then be followed by a look at the prostitutes' rights movement.

This chapter does not provide extensive analyses of these two social movements, but should give the reader enough information to understand why one movement was so successful and why the other failed. The goal is to provide a structural framework that can be used to analyze other social movements and maybe even help predict how successful they are likely to be.

Successful Social Movements

A "successful social movement" leads to institutionalized changes within society and in the lives of its beneficiaries. Successful social movements actually accomplish their stated goals and create a noticeable difference in society. Laws are changed, policies altered, and attitudes shifted. If the goal of the movement is social change, then the success of the movement can be gauged by the significance of change that occurs. If the goal of the movement is to resist or reverse social change, the success of the movement can be gauged by whether or not the undesired change occurs.

Examining numerous successful and unsuccessful social movements in American history reveals certain patterns of organization and behavior. While they are not universal to every successful social movement in history, most successful social movements have these characteristics: *effective leadership, positive image, socially accepted tactics, socially acceptable goals,* and *cultivated financial and political support.*

Leadership

Successful social movements have effective leaders. These individuals understand the legal and political system and operate effectively within them. They are tightly focused on the tasks required to accomplish the goals of the group. They are articulate enough to explain to outsiders what the goals of the group are and why they are reasonable. The most important quality of social movement leaders is the ability to inspire others to act. They have to be able to get people to follow them and to do what must be done. Effective leadership greatly increases the chances that any social movement will succeed in achieving at least some goals.

Image

Successful social movements are respected. They manage to convince bystanders, politicians, and authorities that they are good, honest people who just want what is right. The public image of the group and the groups' leaders is positive. This makes it easier for supporters to make their feelings known and more likely that neutral observers will be convinced that the movement is reasonable or even honorable.

Tactics

Successful social movements use socially acceptable tactics to achieve their goals. Some social movements resort to breaking laws that they want changed or find their methods outlawed by the passage of new laws, ordinances, or regulations, but in general their tactics adhere to the legal and moral guidelines within society. Socially accepted tactics allow the movement to maintain the public respect and positive image they have been so careful to establish.

Goals

Successful social movements convince outsiders that their goals are just, are in the best interest of society, and will not cause harm to others. They persuade bystanders that all of society will benefit if the movement gets what it wants. This persuasion keeps neutral bystanders from turning into opponents and can convince them that they have a positive vested interest in the success of the movement.

Successful social movements also focus more attention and effort on changing laws than on gaining publicity. Groups that succeed in the courtroom enlist legal authorities to their side. Groups that try to change social laws and organizational policies by taking their message directly to the public are far less effective. It is not impossible to change the beliefs of the population, but it is quicker and more efficient to force changes in the law. Protests and marches help get publicity and followers for a movement, but they can also harden opposition to a movement and endanger the group's public image. One successful court decision, particularly at a state or federal level, does more to change the way society operates than any public event ever can.

Successful social movements have specific short-term and long-term goals. They may talk about "making a better society" or "improving life," but their day-to-day efforts all focus on concrete steps toward specific goals. The more those goals fit into the dominant social ideology, the more likely outsiders are to perceive those goals as reasonable and just. For example, if a movement can convince outsiders that their specific political goals are justified by American ideals of freedom, liberty, or equality, they are much more likely to gain approval from bystanders. The general population may support the movement based on a vague sense of "justice" or "democracy."

Support

Successful social movements do not bite the hand that feeds them. Many social movement groups get financial support from a web of other groups, organizations, and institutions. The most successful social movements tailor their message and techniques to avoid alienating financial supporters whenever possible. Unsuccessful social movements, on the other hand, blindly attack anyone who they see as standing in their way. This often leads to the hardening of opposition and the withdrawal of support by those who had formerly been helpful to the group.

The civil rights movement is one of the most successful social movements in recent American history. While not intended to be a complete history of the entire movement, enough information will be provided so that the reader can understand the important forces that existed and the changes that took place in the twentieth century.

The NAACP, LDF, and the Civil Rights Movement

The civil rights movement in the United States really has three distinct phases of action: the legal phase (1910–1954), the public action phase (1954–1968), and the militant phase (1968–1970s).

The covert, *legal* phase of the movement lasted from approximately 1910 until 1954. During that time, public demonstrations were rare. Almost all of the important civil rights victories took place in the courtroom. Other than the members of the civil rights movement itself, only small groups of politicians and attorneys knew what was happening in the courtrooms of America. The general public was completely unaware that a quiet revolution was taking place.

This all dramatically changed in 1954 when the Supreme Court of the United States ruled that all public schools must be racially integrated. Suddenly, the topic of segregation exploded into the national consciousness (Bloom 1987, Halberstam 1993, McAdam 1982). There was tremendous resistance to ending segregation, and the battle grew to involve the governors of several states and the president of the United States. This marked the beginning of the second phase of the movement, the *public action* phase. This is when most Americans first became aware that there was a movement for black civil rights in the United States. From that point on, the movement focused on demonstrations, marches, and public boycotts to increase support and strength and to force various institutions to obey newly changed federal laws (Oberschall 1973, Bloom 1987, Halberstam 1993).

In the late 1960s, the civil rights movement entered into a third, more *militant* phase. Social movement organizations tend to become more moderate as they grow. Radical members become unhappy with leadership, and may split off to form their own, more radical organizations. Young, urban blacks in the 1960s became dissatisfied with the older, established and (in their eyes) conservative civil rights leaders. This led to the creation of various militant organizations such as the Black Panthers. It also led to broader and more revolutionary demands from some segments of the movement. This militancy only increased when leading figures in the movement, like Medgar Evers and Martin Luther King, Jr., were murdered by whites. Ultimately, this militancy and segmentation of the movement created what many writers consider to be the downfall of the movement as a cohesive and effectively organized force (see, for example, Oberschall 1973, Bloom 1987, McAdam 1982, Salmond 1997).

Most analyses focus on the second phase of the movement, the public action phase. This chapter will pay more attention to the covert, legal-oriented phase of the movement. The legal phase of the movement focused on forcing institutionalized changes. Public events and spectacles were avoided. The important decisions won in the Supreme Court turned the struggle into a national one and pitted racist whites against the forces of the U.S. government. Without those decisions, segregation might have continued to be perceived as a "local issue." The majority of whites would never have thought about black civil rights, let alone fought for them.

History

In the first decades of the twentieth century, black citizens were legally denied many of the rights that most Americans now take for granted. The region referred to as "The South" included those confederate states that seceded from the United States prior to or during the Civil War: South Carolina, Mississippi, Florida, Alabama, Georgia, Louisiana, Texas, Virginia, Arkansas, Tennessee, and North Carolina (Boyer et al. 1996). Generally, states like Kentucky, West Virginia, Maryland, Missouri, and Oklahoma were considered "border states" because, although loyal to the Union during the Civil War, their laws and customs were often more southern than northern (Halberstam 1993).

Jim Crow laws, enacted in the late 1800s, made it illegal to treat blacks the same as whites in the South (Bloom 1987, Greenberg 1994, McAdam 1982). Black children were sent to inferior schools or no schools at all. It was difficult or impossible for blacks to buy land. They could not testify against whites in a court of law. They were blocked from voting. Blacks had to sit at the back of public busses, ride in special segregated train cars, could not eat in white restaurants, and could not shop in white stores. They were required to step off of the sidewalk if a white woman approached. Looking white men or women in the eye or calling them by their first name was forbidden. Newspapers refused to use the titles "Mr." or "Mrs.," and instead referred to blacks by their first name or, more often, simply as "a colored man," "the Jones woman," and so on. All of this was *required* under Southern law. Any black who violated any of these rules could be arrested and imprisoned or, far too often, lynched (see Tolnay and Beck 1998). Any white who attempted to treat blacks with respect or humanity would be treated just as harshly. The owner of a restaurant, for example, could be arrested and imprisoned for serving black patrons at the front counter. The system was totally oppressive, completely legal, and firmly entrenched in Southern culture (Bloom 1987, Boyer et al 1996, Greenberg 1994, McAdam 1982, Salmond 1997).

Prior to the 1930s, most efforts to change this system of segregation and discrimination had failed (Salmond 1997). However, the Great Economic Depression of the 1930s and World War II dramatically changed life for everyone in the United States and reshaped political and economic structures throughout the South (Bloom 1987, Greenberg 1994, McAdam 1982, Salmond 1997). The old Southern power structures collapsed and were replaced by new ones.

The Great Depression led to Franklin D. Roosevelt's "New Deal." The New Deal was a set of economic policies and measures that dramatically increased the role of the federal government in business and also dramatically increased transportation, communication, and commerce between the South and the rest of the country (Bloom 1987, McAdam 1982, Salmond 1997). The South was no longer socially isolated from the rest of the United States. It was also much less rural and much more urban than it had been through the 1920s. The New Deal brought industry to the South and permanently changed the economic base. Urban businessmen quickly replaced small farmers as the most important economic force in the South (Bloom 1987, McAdam 1982, Salmond 1997). These business people had contacts reaching outside of the region, which gave them a broader perspective than the provincial farmer.

World War II also led to significant changes. Hundreds of thousands of black men from all over the United States were put into segregated all-black military units where they met men from other parts of the country. Many rural Southern men learned for the first time that brutal segregation and oppression were not universal throughout the United States (Boyer et al. 1996). They came home from the war expecting to be treated with dignity and respect (Greenberg 1994, Salmond 1997). After all, they had fought valiantly for the United States in a war against racism and fascism, and they had won.

World War II also put the United States at the forefront of international relations. U.S. policy had been isolationist before the war, and we had stayed out of foreign affairs as much as possible (Bloom 1987, Greenberg 1994, McAdam 1982). This simply wasn't possible after the war. Further, the Cold War with communist Russia began immediately after World War II. Communist leaders constantly used racism and segregation in the South as a propaganda weapon against the United States (Bloom 1987, McAdam 1982, Greenberg 1994). This forced Presidents Truman and Eisenhower to concern themselves with what had always been considered a "local problem" as Southern segregation drew national and international attention.

All of these factors combined to create a situation, starting in the 1930s, where the entire country and eventually much of the world paid far more attention to the South and to Southern racial policies than ever before. These forces also changed the South itself.

Democratic candidates automatically won virtually every local and state election in the South. Those blacks who could manage to vote only had two choices: vote for the Democratic candidate who was going to win anyway, or vote for the Republican who was going to lose. This made their votes almost meaningless, and most Southern Democrat politicians ignored them. As more and more blacks poured into northern cities, however, this changed. The Democratic and Republican parties were much more closely matched in power and votes in the North. The millions of blacks who poured into cities like Chicago and Cleveland and New York could easily win an election for a Democratic candidate if they voted as a "bloc." Franklin D. Roosevelt was the first national politician to receive such northern black support, and from that point forward any Democrat who wanted to win in the North had to be able to convince black voters that he took their interests to heart (Bloom 1987, Boyer et al. 1996, Greenberg 1994, McAdam 1982).

Blacks living in cities were also much less likely to be victimized by the white violence that was common in rural areas (Bloom 1987, McAdam 1982). The overwhelming majority of lynchings took place in isolated small towns and rural areas in the South (Tolnay and Beck 1998). The simple fact that people lived close to each other in the city meant that it would be difficult or impossible for a small mob to grab any person from their home and drag him or her away to be harmed or killed. Urban blacks felt (and were) much safer from the mob violence that haunted blacks in the rural South.

Changing social, economic, and political conditions also made it possible for many blacks to gain better education, better protection under the law, and access to more information. Every single aspect of the black American experience had changed *except* the segregation, oppression, and discrimination that Southern blacks faced in every facet of daily life (Bloom 1987, Boyer et al. 1996, McAdam 1982, Greenberg 1994, Salmond 1997).

The Birth of the NAACP

The National Association for the Advancement of Colored People (NAACP) was formally incorporated in May of 1910 at a liberal conference of blacks and whites in New York City (McAdam 1982). It remained a mostly northern organization until James Weldon Johnson was appointed field secretary and organizer in 1917. Johnson pushed for growth in the South, and by 1919 the NAACP had grown to 91,203 members (McAdam 1982). Most of these new members lived in the South.

In 1929, Charles Houston became the dean of the Howard University School of Law. Howard University was already the most prestigious black university in the United States. A graduate of the Harvard Law School and a member of the NAACP, Houston turned Howard into the country's top black law school. Houston used Howard as a training school for an entire generation of young black lawyers who, like Houston himself, were determined to use legal means to end segregation in the United States (Greenberg 1994). In 1935, Houston became the legal advisor of the NAACP.

The Margold Plan

In 1930, a small committee directed by Nathan Margold was commissioned by the NAACP to create a report outlining the direction that the organization should take in the courts to end segregation (Greenberg 1994). The report specifically argued that the NAACP should focus most of their attention on legal cases that could be taken to federal court and that directly attacked the constitutionality of the various segregation laws then in existence. This carefully orchestrated legal approach later became known as "the Margold Plan."

The NAACP Legal Defense and Education Fund

The NAACP was considered a political association and therefore could not give tax-exempt status to donations. Many in the organization believed that wealthy donors such as the Rockefeller family would provide sizable contributions if they could deduct those donations from their taxes at the end of the year. The NAACP created the NAACP Legal Defense and Education Fund (LDF) in 1940 to perform the association's legal and educational activities. The LDF avoided propaganda and lobbying activities. This allowed the organization to maintain tax-exempt status, which the NAACP believed would increase overall contributions (Greenberg 1994).

Thurgood Marshall led the LDF throughout the 1940s and 1950s. A firm believer in the Margold plan, he specifically kept the LDF focused on cases that would set legal precedents and would eventually allow for the end of segregation through purely legal channels (Greenberg 1994). Marshall, Houston, and most of the other lawyers working for the NAACP and LDF spent their time pursuing precedent-setting cases.

In 1957, the LDF began to operate independently from the NAACP. From that moment on, most of the important legal battles were fought by the LDF alone while the NAACP focused on political action and public opinion (Greenberg 1994).

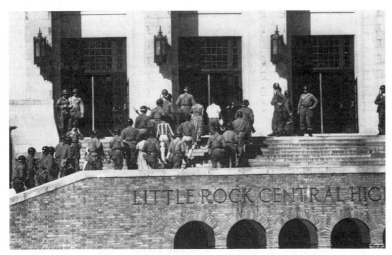

This 1957 photograph shows the federalized National Guard troops escorting black students into Little Rock Central High School. The Brown v. Board of Education decision forced President Eisenhower to take such actions. Orval Faubus, the Governor of Arkansas, had been using the same troops to bar the black students from entering the school.

The NAACP and LDF were highly organized, relatively well funded, and led by some of the most well-educated individuals in the nation (Bloom 1987, Greenberg 1994, McAdam 1982, Oberschall 1973, Salmond 1997). They carefully fought and won cases in the federal supreme court that outlawed segregation and discrimination in transportation, education and, eventually, every aspect of life in the United States.

Many people today do not seem to realize that prior to *Brown et al. v. Board of Education of Topeka, Kansas et al.* (1954) Southern states *required by law* that black children and white children be sent to separate schools. The *Brown* decision made it against federal law to do so. That was a momentous change. It would have been virtually impossible to eliminate school segregation when state law required it. The movement would have had to battle state authorities and politicians. However, to eliminate it in a state when federal law says that it *must* be eliminated is another thing altogether. Suddenly the movement was fighting *with* the federal government of the United States of America, *against* local authorities and politicians who resisted. Whites who fought against desegregation after 1954 were violating federal law and were perceived as criminals. Federal troops were brought in repeatedly to defend and support desegregation, crushing segregationist local forces with higher legal authority, superior force, and greater national public support.

Changes in federal law made presidents Truman, Eisenhower, Kennedy, and Johnson, allies in the fight against old political powers in the South. The federal government forced the Southern states to change their laws and the public action phase of the civil rights movement gradually forced them to change their customs, as well. By the middle of the 1960s not one of the original segregation laws still existed, and it was illegal to racially discriminate in any public institution. The movement succeeded in transforming society by changing federal law. The fact that many Americans were totally unaware of the civil rights movement until after *Brown v. Board of Education* was decided in the Supreme Court is a testimony to the focus and aim of the LDF (and of the NAACP prior to 1957). They attacked the law of the land, not the attitudes of the people who lived in it.

Success of the Civil Rights Movement

Leadership

One of the most important factors in the success of any social movement is effective leadership. The civil rights movement had some of the most determined and intelligent leaders of any movement in American history. People like James Weldon Johnson, Charles Houston, Nathan Margold, and Thurgood Marshall made the legal phase of the movement a smashing success. They did not set out to become celebrities, and they did not waste time doing interviews or chasing publicity. They understood that publicity was not the key to their success. Instead, they carefully followed a strategy designed to institute social change from the top down.

Image

A movement must maintain a positive public image in order to operate effectively in society. Public image was a primary concern of the civil rights movement. Many of the early leaders went out of their way to dress as dapper as possible (Greenberg 1994). The NAACP/LDF worked hard to act and look professional and dignified whenever they appeared in public or in court. When anti-communism swept the United States, the NAACP/LDF ejected any members who appeared to have any communist ties. This was done to maintain the positive image of the movement and to keep it from being associated with socialism or communism (Greenberg 1994).

Tactics

Successful movements have to use socially acceptable tactics in order to maintain their positive image. The civil rights movement used strictly legal and carefully planned tactics throughout the legal phase. The public action phase of 1954 to 1968 sometimes involved breaking local laws, but always in a way that made movement members appear peaceful, dignified, and determined. Civil rights leaders never engaged in personal attacks on their opponents and never used violence. This strict adherence to socially acceptable tactics generated a great deal of sympathy for the movement and admiration of the leaders and followers. The television broadcasts of white policemen and police dogs brutally attacking protestors in the 1950s and 1960s probably

Police turned attack dogs loose on peaceful civil rights protestors in Birmingham, Alabama in 1963. This scene, and many others like it, severely damaged the image of Southern authorities and elevated the civil rights movement in the eyes of most Americans.

Prior to 1968, the Civil Rights Movement used non-confrontational, peaceful tactics typified by this March on Washington, D.C. in 1963. These tactics won the movement support from outsiders.

helped the public action phase of the movement more than anything else could have (Salmond 1997). People who were neutral toward the movement found themselves feeling tremendous sympathy and respect for the individuals who were willing to peacefully take such punishment without fighting back. In contrast, the violent urban riots of the late 1960s turned many people against the same movement.

Goals

A major goal of the early civil rights leaders was to convince the public that their demands were not only reasonable but also fit closely with cherished American values and beliefs. Public speeches tended to emphasize that what the movement wanted was promised by the Declaration of Independence and the Constitution of the United States: freedom and equality, liberty and justice. As a result, their opponents began to look more and more un-American while the movement began to look more and more righteous.

Support

When a social movement has a positive public image and effective leaders, support is relatively easy to acquire. Successful movements carefully maintain that support. When the movement entered its third and most militant phase many liberal and moderate whites withdrew their social and financial support from civil rights organizations. Prior to that, however, civil rights leaders had always been careful not to anger or upset their supporters. For example, they did not point out the hypocrisy of some of the people who donated money or public support but lived segregated lives (Greenberg 1994).

Conclusion

What many theoretical perspectives such as Resource Mobilization Theory and Political Process Theory (discussed in Chapter 14) overlook is the importance of the individual leaders who go about changing the law, the government, and society. Earlier, "classical" theories of collective behavior such as Contagion Theory, the Emergent Norm Perspective, and Value-added Theory all emphasize the importance of individual leaders and instigators. Gustave LeBon dedicated entire sections of *The Crowd* (1982 [1895]) to the role of leaders in social uprisings. Perhaps social movement theorists, in an attempt to distance themselves from collective behavior theory, have gone too far the other direction. Their heavy emphasis on societal factors such as economic and political changes has removed the role of the individual from social movement analysis.

By contrast, historians tend to place much more emphasis on the role of individuals such as Franklin Roosevelt, Charles Houston, Thurgood Marshall, Martin Luther King, Jr., and so on. Greenberg (1994) dedicates an entire book to them.

Resources and organization were central to the continued momentum of the movement throughout the 1950s and 1960s, but individual leadership created the movement. A few brilliant people managed to change the course of an entire society. It was their drive, courage, and intelligence that made the entire movement a success.

A student who truly wants to understand the success of any movement must take many factors into account. As Oberschall (1973, 1993) argues, the ability of an organization to accumulate and efficiently use resources such as money and labor is critical. As McAdam (1982, 1996) argues, political, economic, and social circumstances make it possible for the movement to form and succeed. Every successful organization is guided by a few brilliant individuals who understand their social circumstances enough to create a workable plan. The civil rights movement had all of these qualities. Over time the movement managed to overcome resistance, maintain an image of respectability and honor, and convince virtually all outsiders that their cause was just and right under American principles of liberty and equality. It would be difficult to find any movement that so successfully harnessed the social forces in such a well-planned and productive way. The next movement to be examined has failed on virtually all of these counts.

Unsuccessful Social Movements

Unsuccessful social movements fail to achieve specific goals. They are poorly organized and lack effective leadership. Leaders are either unable to gain the necessary volunteers and resources or unable to use them efficiently. Their public image is negative and their tactics are perceived as illegitimate. This creates a great deal of hostility toward the movement by people who otherwise would not care. They may also run into legal trouble because of their tactics, which brands leaders and followers as "criminals" before the movement can secure a positive public image. Their goals are either too vague to be achieved or are so far from mainstream societal norms that others cannot be convinced of their value. They tend to focus more on public events and spectacles than on making any kind of real, institutionalized changes. Finally, unsuccessful social movements tend to alienate other movement groups, bystanders, and even their own members through criticism, personal attacks, or other behavior that creates hostility and resistance rather than good will and cooperation.

COYOTE and the Prostitutes' Rights Movement

Although most readers may not be aware of it, there has been a movement for "prostitutes' rights" in the United States since the early 1970s. This movement's only stated goal is the full legalization and acceptance of prostitution.

The prostitutes' rights movement has gone through three phases: local political activism, national publicity stunts, and finally, a source of public AIDS education and awareness. The first phase began in 1973 as a local effort to change prostitution laws and enforcement tactics in San Francisco, California. The second phase of the movement began in the mid-1970s with a national publicity campaign. The movement tried to convince American citizens that prostitution is a legitimate occupation that does more good than harm to society. They also tried to link the rights of prostitutes to the women's rights movement. The third phase began in the mid-1980s, when prostitutes' rights organizations began working at the national level to counter assertions that prostitutes spread HIV and the AIDS virus. Throughout all of those phases the movement has failed to achieve any of the main goals of the movement.

History

Earlier social movements related to prostitution in the United States have always been moral crusades attempting to stamp out prostitution altogether. They were generally led by authorities, public health officials, religious figures, and/or citizens concerned about the moral damage done to society by prostitutes (Jenness 1990, 1993, Weitzer 1991). The prostitutes' rights movement is the first organized movement in the United States to fight for increased legal and social acceptance of prostitution.

In 1965, Edwin Schur published a book titled *Crimes Without Victims*. He argued that many things that are illegal in the United States don't actually hurt anyone. He attacked laws against "victimless crimes" such as abortion, homosexuality, and illicit drug use. He argued that such laws do more harm than good, forcing people to engage in private behavior under conditions of secrecy and danger and filling jails and prisons with people who hurt no one except perhaps themselves. The idea that laws could be immoral was picked up by the prostitutes' rights movement and became the central argument for the repeal of all such laws. Prostitution as a "victimless crime" became the mantra of the movement.

The late 1960s and early 1970s were a time of tremendous social conflict and change in the United States. The women's rights movement, also known as the feminist movement, had gained momentum and began to grow in size and effectiveness. The country's first gay rights movement developed in California and was also rapidly gaining constituents and influence. These movements provided the ideological basis for the prostitutes' rights movement. The prostitutes' rights movement essentially extended the arguments put forth by the civil rights, feminist, and gay/lesbian rights movements to include prostitutes. Prostitutes' rights members argued that prostitutes, like blacks, women, gays and lesbians, were being discriminated against and deprived of their constitutional rights (Jenness 1990, 1993, Weitzer 1991). So far the movement has been unsuccessful in convincing citizens or lawmakers that prostitution is a legitimate occupation that should be fully legalized.

The Birth of COYOTE

The modern prostitutes' rights movement began in the early 1973. Margo St. James, who claims to be a former prostitute, received a five-thousand-dollar grant from the Point Foundation at Glide Memorial Church to form a prostitutes' union to prevent the abuse of prostitutes (Jenness 1993). St. James used the money to create Call Off Your Old Tired Ethics (COYOTE) in San Francisco, California. COYOTE, often billed as a "hooker's union" (Jenness 1993, Weitzer 1991), actually acted as a lobby group that hoped to repeal anti-prostitution laws in San Francisco. In its first campaign, COYOTE engaged local law enforcement and municipal government officials in debate over selective and discriminatory enforcement of prostitution laws. During this time St. James became something of a regional celebrity. COYOTE enjoyed popularity among many liberals and intellectuals, and received an additional thousand-dollar grant from the Playboy Foundation (Jenness 1993).

Recruiting working prostitutes into COYOTE proved to be difficult. Some prostitutes were apparently interested in joining, but were afraid that authorities would arrest them if they did join. COYOTE never claimed more than 3 percent of their members were working prostitutes. This did not stop them from portraying themselves as a union of prostitutes, the only organization that actually represented the needs and views of working prostitutes (Jenness 1993, Weitzer 1991). COYOTE failed to generate any changes in the prostitution laws in San Francisco, but did manage to acquire enough publicity and money to take their campaign to the national level.

In the next phase of the movement, COYOTE joined in the feminist debates on violence against women and the right of women to control their bodies. They attempted to link the question of prostitution to the larger issue of women's rights. COYOTE argued that outlawing prostitution deprived women of the right to choose a legitimate and lucrative career. Laws against prostitution were depicted as sexist and discriminatory. COYOTE staged small protests at political conventions. They also formed a "hooker's lobby" and went to Capital Hill to lobby for the federal decriminalization of prostitution (Jenness 1993, Weitzer 1991).

Many prostitutes' rights organizations began to appear all over the United States. Some of them had silly names, like CAT (California Advocates for Trollops), FLOP (Friends and Lovers of Prostitutes), and HUM (Hookers' Union of Maryland). Others had more serious names like NTFP (National Task Force on Prostitution), ASP (Association of Seattle Prostitutes), and PEN (Prostitution Education Network). However, all of these organizations were directly tied to COYOTE, and many of them only had one or a few members (Jenness 1993, Weitzer 1991). The NTFP and PEN are both run by COYOTE. They don't have any members or leaders other than those of COYOTE. However, COYOTE claims to be "affiliated and endorsed" by the NTFP and PEN, and both of those organizations say the same thing about COYOTE (Jenness 1993, Weitzer 1991). The "movement" does not seem to have many constituents or adherents, and most prostitutes have never been actively involved.

The prostitutes' rights movement suffered a serious blow with the emergence of the AIDS crisis in the United States. By the end of the 1980s, the leaders of COYOTE/NPTF/PEN spent almost all of their time fighting the idea that prostitutes spread AIDS throughout society. These organizations now act as a mediator between prostitutes and public health agencies (Jenness 1993). This provides the NPTF and PEN with increased visibility and credibility, but has pulled all of their attention and resources away from the fight for legalization of prostitution (Jenness 1993, Weitzer 1991).

The prostitutes' rights movement suffered another blow when a feminist group called WHISPER (Women Hurt in Systems of Prostitution Engaged in Revolt) emerged in the early 1980s. WHISPER, like COYOTE, advocates the repeal of prostitution laws. However, the ultimate goal of WHISPER is to end all prostitution in the United States. They believe that the laws that exist are helping to keep prostitution underground where it can thrive in secrecy and violence. The ideological opposite of COYOTE, WHISPER further damaged COYOTE's credibility (Jenness 1993, Weitzer 1991).

The prostitutes' rights movement has never had many active constituents. Most "members" never did more than pay a small fee to join. The three most visible prostitutes' rights organizations, COYOTE, the NPTF, and PEN, are led by the same few women, none of whom are professional organization leaders. St. James showed a definite flair for gaining publicity for herself in her reign over COYOTE from 1973 to 1986, but little understanding of what it takes to change laws and attitudes in the United States. She did manage to make a career as the leader of the "movement," but even that was a marginal success. According to the COYOTE website (July 2000), St. James has unsuccessfully run for city council in San Francisco more than once. Although the organizations still exist, the prostitutes' rights movement is effectively over.

Failure of the Prostitutes' Rights Movement

Leadership   Margo St. James admits that she is not a particularly organized person (Jenness 1991). While "leading" COYOTE, the NPTF, and PEN throughout the 1970s and early 1980s she consistently failed to make the kinds of political connections that could have helped the movement. Her public persona and the organizations' overall image were light-hearted, and confrontational. St. James simply never understood how to make real social change occur.

Priscilla Alexander, a feminist educator, and Gloria Locket, a former prostitute, took over leadership of COYOTE in 1986 (Jenness 1993). Like St. James, they spent most of their time, energy, and resources on publicity rather than pursuing legal precedents that could help their cause. They, too, lacked the foresight and ability required to lead a movement for social change. They may be more organized, but their time and resources are totally

Margo St. James (center, wearing a shirt bearing the slogan "MY ASS IS MINE!") led COYOTE in lighthearted public spectacles that generated short-lived public attention but little support for the prostitutes' rights movement.

consumed by the AIDS awareness mission of the groups. Perhaps most importantly, COYOTE has never pursued any precedent-setting cases at the state or national level. Their attempt to change prostitution laws centered entirely on lobbying Congress and holding public protests.

Image American's negative and immoral image of prostitutes worked against the prostitutes' rights movement. However, the gay/lesbian rights movement started out with many of the same social obstacles and managed to achieve much greater success. The biggest difference lies in the way that each movement dealt with their initially negative public image. Gay advocates in the early 1970s went out of their way to convince outsiders that they are good citizens with a legitimate complaint. They also rely on the idea that their legal demands are legitimate even if one does not like the constituents themselves.

In contrast, prostitutes' rights advocates seemed determined to shock and titillate. The use of words like "harlot," "whore," and "hooker" in the official names of many prostitutes' rights organizations made the problem even worse. This inability to overcome their deviant image kept them from being perceived as respectable (Weitzer 1991). This, in turn, kept them from being taken seriously.

Tactics The primary tactics of the prostitutes' rights movement centered on holding press conferences and small protests in prominent locations (Jenness 1993, Weitzer 1991). Although the general public may consider them legitimate tactics, they are not effective ways to change state or federal law. The tactics of COYOTE seem to indicate that leaders never knew what tactics they should use to achieve any of their legal goals.

Goals The stated goals of the prostitutes' rights movement are simple: 1) the repeal of all laws prohibiting or restricting prostitution, 2) the reconstruction of prostitution as a viable service occupation, and 3) labor laws protecting prostitutes as other legitimate service workers are protected (Jenness 1993). However, almost none of the actions of the movement organizations seem to have any direct connection to those goals.

COYOTE and the other prostitutes' rights organizations have always focused the majority of their efforts toward changing the public's perception of prostitution. This is ineffective for at least two reasons. First, public attitudes do not directly influence laws. For example, more Americans condemn pornographic movies than marijuana use, but porn is legal and pot is not (Weitzer 1991). Changing the viewpoints of Americans, even if it were likely, is a terribly ineffective way to change the law. Second, attempting to change the opinion of millions of Americans would require vast resources that COYOTE just never had. A few interviews and talk show appearances are not enough to have a major impact on society. Getting into the courtroom actually requires a lot less time, effort, and personnel than getting into the living rooms of

America. This lack of focus on the goals created an organization that only vaguely knew what it wanted and had no clear way of getting it.

Support As Weitzer (1991) points out in his analysis, the prostitutes' rights movement failed to attract popular support and failed to build alliances with third parties. The apparent coalition between COYOTE, the NPTF, and PEN is really an illusion: they are all essentially the same organization (Jenness 1993, Weitzer 1991). Politicians have never found any advantage to supporting the movement; there is no powerful bloc of prostitute voters. The deviant image of prostitutes and the prostitutes' rights movement "contaminates" and rubs off on any outside organization that openly supports them. Further, although there have been hundreds of newspaper and television stories about COYOTE, they are almost always tongue-in-cheek pieces that do little to convey the message of the movement. In other words, COYOTE never mobilized the financial, political, or social resources necessary to create a successful movement. Prostitutes never really supported the movement. The public never supported it. Politicians never supported it. Media were willing to give some coverage to the movement, but not with enough depth or consistency to do any real good. The attitudes and behavior of the movement leaders alienated many of their early supporters. COYOTE had a tremendous amount of support among local politicians in the early 1970s (Jenness 1993), but managed to lose almost all of it by the late 1970s because of their ineffective and (to respected supporters) embarrassing public tactics (Jenness 1993, Weitzer 1991).

Conclusion

Ironically, judges appeared to be sympathetic to the prostitutes' rights movement (Weitzer 1991), but COYOTE never focused attention on trying important cases. The movement never made an attempt to gain political support from judges. Instead, it squandered the few resources available, focused attention on the wrong things, and never figured out how to actually accomplish the most important goal of the movement. No prostitution laws were changed in the state of California or at the federal level. Prostitution is no closer to being legal today than it was in 1973.

Discussion

The civil rights movement managed to totally transform American society. Thousands of state and local laws were changed or thrown out. The federal government changed the way that it treated blacks, and forced the rest of society to follow. The movement was extremely successful in changing the lives of virtually every American. The prostitutes' rights movement, on the other hand, failed to make any real changes. Prostitution is still illegal everywhere in the United States except for small portions of Nevada (where it was already legal before the movement began). Prostitutes are still viewed as deviants and criminals by the majority of Americans. The laws have not changed, social attitudes have not changed, and most Americans do not consider prostitutes members of an oppressed minority (Weitzer 1991).

This chapter is not intended to provide the reader with a complete history of the civil rights movement or the prostitutes' rights movement in the United States. It is meant to be a general guide to a successful and an unsuccessful social movement, with enough information to allow comparison and contrast between them. The same framework can be applied to any movement to help determine its odds of succeeding. The organization that can best manipulate favorable social conditions tends to be the group that wins any struggle within society. Those that fail become unsuccessful movements.

Chapter 16 will describe and analyze two social movements in the United States that are directly competing with each other for control of the same issue. Each of the four theories discussed in Chapter 14 will be applied to both movements. This may help the reader to understand why the pro-life and pro-choice movements have had relatively equal levels of success and failure over the past few decades.

Chapter 16

The Pro-Life and Pro-Choice Movements

The Pro-Life and Pro-Choice movements in the United States make interesting cases for analysis and comparison for a variety of reasons. Both have been around for several decades. Both have been partially effective in achieving some of their goals. Both have failed to convince the majority of Americans that their position is the only one that is clearly right. Both have received a great deal of media attention over the years. Finally, each draws occasional support and criticism from major political leaders.

This chapter will give a brief history and description of the abortion debate in the United States, followed by a short analysis of the development of the Pro-Choice and Pro-Life movements themselves. Each of the four major theories of social movements will be applied to the movements. This will give the reader an understanding of what each theory focuses on and how each is used.

History

Although various abortion techniques have been practiced for thousands of years, there were no laws concerning abortion in the United States before 1821 (Blanchard 1994). That year, Connecticut passed a state law making it illegal to perform abortions after "quickening," movement of the fetus in the womb that is first felt around the fifth month of pregnancy. The Catholic Church did not formally oppose abortion until the 1850s. Pope Pius IX was deeply concerned about the role of women in Catholicism, and began to shift policies about women and fertility. In 1869, the Pope declared excommunication as the punishment for any person performing an abortion. In 1917, this was extended to include the woman receiving the abortion as well. In 1931, the Catholic Church formally declared that getting an abortion under any circumstances is a mortal sin, condemning a woman to Hell (Blanchard 1994).

The first organized American campaign against abortion began in the 1860s, driven by several factors including: 1) the effort to increase medical professionalism, 2) a general call for moralism in American society, 3) increased concern for women's health, and 4) social forces created by industrialism and mass immigration to urban centers. The American Medical Association (AMA), formed in 1847, sought to ban everyone except medical professionals from performing abortions. At that time, many midwifes and amateur healers performed abortions, and over-the-counter "medications" to "restore female [menstrual] regularity" (induce spontaneous miscarriage) were widely advertised and readily available. The AMA sought greater control over medical procedures of all kinds. They also wanted to encourage chastity in women. Many doctors believed that the availability of abortion procedures allowed "bad" women to escape punishment (pregnancy) and public visibility as a "fallen" woman (Blanchard 1994). This perspective related to a general mood of moralism led by the Anthony Comstock campaigns against pornography, sexual misbehavior, and abortion.

The idea of protecting women from the dangers of abortion rose from the simple fact that abortions were risky at that time and frequently led to deadly infections, even when performed by trained doctors. Finally, urban industrial migration led to the decreased value of children. In rural life, children acted as farmhands and contributed to the well being of the entire family; in urban life, they were liabilities who needed to be fed (Blanchard 1994).

By 1890, every state in the union had laws regulating or outlawing abortion. Getting an abortion had been redefined as a moral and ethical issue by the medical establishment. However, society continued to change. After World War II, American culture seemed to divide into two fundamentally different perspectives. One side viewed husbands as companions, women's careers as important, and children as something of an obstacle to fulfillment in career and marriage. The other side viewed husbands as providers, women working outside of the home as a necessary evil, and motherhood as the highest possible vocation for a woman. The medical establishment gradually began to adopt the first perspective for reasons that are not entirely clear. Professional control remained an issue, but moralism within the AMA began to wane. By 1970, doctors had redefined abortion again. They saw it as a medical issue rather than a moral, ethical, or religious one (Blanchard 1994).

The Movements

In 1970, Hawaii, Alaska, New York, and Washington had repealed their abortion laws, and twelve other states had reformed or relaxed theirs. The AMA, ABA (American Bar Association, the national attorney's organization), American Academy of Pediatrics, and various other professional associations all passed resolutions favoring the reform or repeal of all state laws restricting access to abortion procedures (Blanchard 1994, Humphries 1977). The California Committee on Therapeutic Abortion (CCTA) was the first nonprofessional, women's group to get officially involved in the fight for legalization and was the first organized group to define the abortion debate as a women's issue (Blanchard 1994). This marked the beginning of the Pro-Choice movement in the United States.

In response to these circumstances, the modern Pro-Life movement began when the National Catholic Bishops appointed a Family Life Bureau, following the passage of abortion law reform in three states. The first organized attempt to fight the repeal of abortion laws took place in Hawaii in 1970 (Blanchard 1994).

The public battle between the Pro-Life and Pro-Choice movements really began when the United States Supreme Court handed down decisions on *Roe v. Wade* (1973) and *Doe v. Bolton* (1973). Both cases had been carefully selected and fought by lawyers working on behalf of the Planned Parenthood Federation of America (Blanchard 1994, Humphries 1977). These decisions made abortion fully legal throughout the United States for the first two trimesters (six months) of pregnancy (Blanchard 1994, Pojman and Beckwith 1994). *Doe v. Bolton* specifically prohibited states from enacting restrictive laws and legally placed the decision in the hands of the doctor. This meant that a doctor could personally choose whether or not to perform an abortion.

The *Roe* and *Doe* decisions were a major legal victory for the Pro-Choice movement, since they placed the power of the federal government against state and local authorities who might try to resist the Pro-Choice agenda. However, the battle was far from over.

In the nearly thirty years since *Roe v. Wade,* the Pro-Choice and Pro-Life movements have each been struggling to gain complete victory for their side. One of the difficulties lies in the American public: The vast majority of Americans favor the availability of abortion under at least some circumstances (see discussion in Blanchard 1994, Humphries 1977, McCarthy 1987). Only small minorities favor total, unlimited access to abortion under any circumstances, and only an equally small minority believes that abortion should be outlawed under any and all circumstances. Various studies show that around 10 percent of Americans favor the total ban of abortion under any circumstances, around 10 percent favor unlimited availability of the procedure, and the 80 percent "mushy middle" has mixed feelings (see Blanchard 1994, Pojman and Beckwith 1994). These percentages have not changed much since 1970. The moral and ethical implications of abortion itself are secondary to Pro-Choice adherents

(Humphries 1977), but not to the general public. On the other hand, the economic and pragmatic implications that are important to most Americans are secondary to most Pro-Life adherents (Blanchard 1994).

Development of the Movement Organizations

The Pro-Life Movement

The first national Pro-Life organization, the National Right to Life Committee (NRLC), was created in 1973 following the *Roe v. Wade* decision (Blanchard 1994). The mostly middle-class group relied on traditional political methods such as lobbying, political pressure, and threatened boycotts of companies that produced drugs and equipment used in abortions. More radical Pro-Life organizations began to rise in the late 1970s and early 1980s, possibly driven by frustration over the lack of change in American attitudes. These groups, which pulled most of their members from religious organizations, began to picket clinics and doctors' offices, put glue into clinic door locks, call in bomb threats to clinics, trace clinic patients to their homes, and so on (Blanchard 1994). These militant groups tended to draw their members from the working class more than moderate organizations like the NRLC. Most of them were connected through the Pro-Life Action League, which later changed its name to Pro-Life Action Network (PLAN).

Bombings and arsons of abortion clinics began in 1977. There were twelve clinic bombings and arsons in the first two years, and they peaked in 1984 to 1985. Highly visible groups like Operation Rescue, created in 1987, condoned and even encouraged such militant actions. Americans United for Life (AUL) was created to provide attorneys for Pro-Life organizations and individuals being sued or criminally prosecuted (Blanchard 1994).

The Pro-Life and Pro-Choice Movements in the United States have been evenly matched in terms of finances, public support, and political clout for the last two decades. Consequently, neither has been able to attain clear victory over the other.

Almost all of these Pro-Life organizations drew their support from religious organizations as well as conservative political groups and individuals (Blanchard 1994, Paige 1983). Leaders of militant Pro-Life organizations tend to be religious figures, politicians, or working-class, private citizens (Blanchard 1994, Humphries 1977).

The Pro-Choice Movement

Early Pro-Choice efforts in California were led by Unitarian, Jewish, and Episcopalian groups, the American Association of University Women, the American Humanist Association, and the California Junior Chamber of Commerce (the Jaycees). The Planned Parenthood Federation of America, already concerned with all matters related to contraception and population, joined the fight for total repeal of abortion laws (Blanchard 1994). In 1965, the Association for the Study of Abortion (ASA) was created in New York as the first national nonprofit, tax-exempt organization dedicated to legalizing abortion (Humphries 1977). Led by a doctor and a college professor, the ASA helped coordinate court cases challenging restrictive state abortion laws. The ASA acted as a centralizing force and information center for a variety of local and regional Pro-Choice organizations, just as PLAN later did for Pro-Life groups. In 1970, the ASA founded the Abortion Reform Association (ARA) to perform political and activist functions. That same year the National Association for the Repeal of Abortion Laws (NARAL) was formed. Both organizations were dedicated to the total repeal of laws restricting or prohibiting abortion (Humphries 1977).

These groups were primarily funded by industrial philanthropists such as the Rockefeller Foundation (Humphries 1977). Pro-Choice organizations today also get funding from liberal political groups and individuals. The majority of Pro-Choice organizations are led by middle- and upper-class professionals such as doctors and lawyers (Blanchard 1994, Humphries 1977)

Analysis

This chapter does not attempt to provide a totally complete analysis using each theory. Instead, enough information will be provided to allow the reader to compare the theories and evaluate their usefulness. This will also further understanding of the ongoing struggle between the Pro-Life and Pro-Choice movements in the United States.

Mass Society Theory

As discussed in Chapter 14, Mass Society Theory is only useful for analyzing "mass movements," movements that are anti-democratic and seek to destroy or totally transform society. As the analysis below will show, the United

States does not have enough characteristics of a mass society to support a mass movement. A mass movement cannot form in a society that is pluralistic in nature.

Readers interested in a current example of a mass movement might want to research the present state of Iranian society (see, for example, Nafisi 1999, Milani 1999). The ever-changing social policies that have been put into effect in Iran over the past few years clearly point to the sort of rule-by-mob that Kornhauser described in such detail.

Some have argued that the Pro-Life movement is guided primarily by social fundamentalists who wish to limit the freedom of women because of their own authoritarian personalities (see discussion in Blanchard 1994). Of course, many Pro-Life organizations point to Pro-Choice as an inherently "pro-death" position and argue that abortion advocates are no different than Nazis (see discussions in Blanchard 1994, Humphries 1977). Both of these arguments are exaggerations based on stereotypes and focusing on the most extreme elements of each movement.

Atomization, Access, Availability, and Intermediate Groups

Kornhauser never indicates how much *atomization* is "enough" to create a mass society. He also never tells us how to measure it. Therefore, one really can't say whether or not American society has sufficient atomization to potentially become a mass society.

The United States does not exhibit enough *access* or *availability* to be characterized as a mass society. We elect our leaders, but do not get to monitor their daily behavior. They have the power to shape society, but cannot dictate our actions. Further, the United States is loaded with thousands, perhaps hundreds of thousands, of *intermediate groups*. Rotary clubs, church associations, singles clubs, parenting groups, hobby groups, and a countless variety of other clubs, groups, associations, and organizations interconnect people to other members of their communities in the United States.

The Pro-Choice movement tends to be comprised of individuals who have a variety of other social ties, including professional associations and community activist groups (Blanchard 1994, McCarthy 1987). They do not make up a homogeneous "bloc" of like-minded people who only associate with each other.

Some Pro-Life groups, however, seem to lack these intermediate ties. Members of these specific groups tend to be from the same religious group (McCarthy 1987) and may have little or no social contact with anyone who does not share their own set of views (Blanchard 1994). However, it is generally only the smallest and most militant of Pro-Life groups that fit this profile. The larger, more moderate groups draw their members from a diverse cross section of the American population (Humphries 1977), and most of their members have social ties to people outside of the group.

According to Mass Society Theory, a mass movement is only likely to occur in a mass society. Therefore, Mass Society Theory does not explain why the Pro-Life or Pro-Choice movements exist, only that neither movement is likely to become a mass movement.

Characteristics of a Mass Movement

Mass movements have specific characteristics (see Chapter 14). All of these factors make a large mass movement dangerous to opponents and to society in general.

Pro-Life   Much has been made of the fact that the militant Pro-Life organizations fit the mass movement profile. Pro-Life adherents did bomb and set fire to 161 abortion clinics between 1977 and 1992 alone (Blanchard 1994: 55), and several abortion providers have been killed or injured by shootings and bombings. The particular organizations that carry out such terrorist acts clearly rely on what Kornhauser calls "direct methods." Such groups fit the profile of a mass movement except for one thing: their size. They are by far the smallest of the Pro-Life organizations (see Blanchard 1994, Paige 1983). They lack mass support. In fact, their methods may have kept the more mainstream Pro-Life movement from acquiring more adherents. American citizens tend to be repulsed by mass movement tactics, particularly violence.

Pro-Choice   By contrast, the Pro-Choice movement has no mass movement tendencies. There are no known examples of bombings, arsons, or shootings by Pro-Choice adherents. Protests are not terribly unusual, but they do not occur with anywhere near the frequency of Pro-Life protests (see Blanchard 1994, Humphries 1977, Paige 1983, etc.).

Culture and Personality

A mass society gives a mass movement *cultural legitimacy*. American society today simply does not support movements that attempt to wipe out diversity of behavior or opinion.

Personality, however, is a different matter. Mass people are psychologically drawn to mass movements. Although the United States cannot be characterized as a mass society, there are some Americans who would gladly outlaw anything they do not approve of. These people want a neat, orderly society where everyone agrees with them and where no one engages in any behavior that they don't like. Some research shows this general personality type to be fairly common in the most extreme Pro-Life organizations (see discussion in Blanchard 1994, Paige 1983). However, it is important to remember that the majority of Pro-Life adherents are not authoritarian or fascist personality types. It is also important to remember that there may be people with similar personality characteristics within Pro-Choice organizations. This cannot be said with certainty because no researchers seem to be doing any personality research to find them. Right-wing fascism is generally easy to recognize, while left-wing fascism can be much harder to spot (Locher 1990). Anyone who wants to force their own view of the world onto others has the personality required to become a member of a mass movement. Their political orientation does not matter. What matters is their intolerance for differing opinions and their willingness to force their own views onto others.

Conclusion

The United States is not a mass society. Freedom and individual liberty are valued more than conformity and obedience to authority. We are truly a pluralistic society, which is why the more mass-style elements of social movements do not catch on.

Is the Pro-Life movement a mass movement? Not really. There are specific Pro-Life organizations that do have some mass characteristics: rigid, authoritarian, moralistic, and unwilling to compromise. They carry out most of the disruptive protests and violence aimed at abortion providers. It is the lack of significant growth of these organizations over time that keeps them from becoming a mass movement. Even the majority of people who strongly oppose abortion do not join such groups (Blanchard 1994, McCarthy 1987). The majority of Pro-Life adherents do not engage in such direct methods and this keeps them from becoming a mass movement.

The Pro-Choice movement is not a mass movement, either. The majority of Pro-Choice adherents see the matter of individual choice for women to be more important than any other issues (Blanchard 1994, Humphries 1977, McCarthy 1987). They do not want to force anyone to do anything. They literally believe that doctors and women who are pregnant should be able to choose to have an abortion *or* choose not to. This is the exact opposite of a mass movement, which seeks to limit or restrict freedom of choice. Most groups within the Pro-Choice movement also focus on traditional, legitimate tactics such as political lobbying and courtroom maneuvering.

Relative Deprivation Theory

As discussed in Chapter 14, Relative Deprivation Theory is based on the idea that people get upset and form social movements whenever they feel relative deprivation. These feelings make a person more likely to form or join a social movement. However, research has consistently failed to support relative deprivation theory (for example, see discussion in Oberschall 1973 and Gurney and Tierney 1982). Although the theory may appeal to common sense and seem perfectly logical, many social movement participants do not seem to experience any relative deprivation prior to joining. Because of these shortcomings, this application of Relative Deprivation Theory will be brief.

Pro-Lifers didn't lose an "opportunity" when abortion was fully legalized in the early 1970s. However, researchers and interviewers have found that many Pro-Life adherents actually see their role as part of a battle to return their religious and social values to a position of prominence in American society (Blanchard 1994, McCarthy 1987; see also Nathanson 1989 for a defense of this position). It could be argued that Pro-Life adherents therefore feel decremental deprivation over the loss of primacy of their own social views.

It is easier to argue that Pro-Choicers felt a kind of aspirational relative deprivation, at least in the 1960s and 1970s. As liberal feminism grew, women increasingly decided that they should have total authority over what happens to their bodies and that no man should be able to tell them that they could not. These rising expectations led to activities intended to change existing abortion laws.

However, the early Pro-Choice movement was not led by feminists, it was led by professional medical associations and population-control organizations (Humphries 1977). It is difficult to argue that these individuals were experiencing relative deprivation. At best, one could argue that they sought more control over the practice of medicine in general and saw abortion laws as an obstacle to that goal.

The Pro-Life movement has experienced the greatest blocking of expectations over the last few decades and has demonstrated a correlated rise in discontent. Presidents Jimmy Carter (1976–1980), Ronald Reagan (1980–1988) and George Bush (1988–1992) won their offices partly because of their Pro-Life views. Many Pro-Life adherents believed that those presidents would do everything in their power to make abortion illegal (Blanchard 1994). This did not happen. It was during this time that the more extreme and militant Pro-Life organizations like Operation Rescue and the Lambs of Christ were formed. People began threatening, vandalizing, bombing, and burning abortion clinics. Doctors and nurses were threatened, shot at, and sometimes killed. This terrorism related to abortion peaked in the mid- to late-1980s. The expectations of the Pro-Life adherents are still blocked and the followers are still frustrated.

Conclusion

One could argue that there is some level of relative deprivation within each movement. However, the presence of men in both movements is difficult to explain using Relative Deprivation Theory. Several Pro-Choice organizations and the majority of Pro-Life organizations are led by men (Blanchard 1994, Paige 1983). Men cannot become pregnant. They will never be forced to decide to have an abortion, and they will never be restricted by law from getting one. Why, then, do men occupy so many of the leadership positions in the Pro-Life and Pro-Choice movements? It is impossible to explain the Pro-Life and Pro-Choice movements using only relative deprivation. Finally, there is no research that clearly demonstrates that Pro-Life or Pro-Choice adherents experience more relative deprivation than outsiders do. Relative Deprivation

Theory is not much more helpful than Mass Society Theory when looking at the Pro-Life and Pro-Choice movements.

Resource Mobilization Theory

Resource Mobilization Theory focuses almost entirely on what it takes to make a social movement organization successful. Members of a movement must organize, acquire resources, and learn to survive as a group before the movement can make a difference in society. The final success of a social movement occurs when they are institutionalized into the social order. This ends the struggle for survival and legitimacy.

Resources

The Pro-Life and Pro-Choice movements have both managed to acquire and successfully manage a wide variety of material and nonmaterial resources. However, the nature of the movements means that they have had to use slightly different methods to do so.

The Pro-Life movement has a natural membership base: religious organizations. Most Pro-Life organizations get their members from religious groups. Pro-Life organizations find it relatively easy to contact millions of potential constituents and adherents because of the close relationship between conservative social and political beliefs, abortion views, and certain religious affiliations (McCarthy 1987). They have an extensive local organizational structure, held together primarily by church associations.

Since their religious and political interests already link these people to each other, it is relatively easy to mobilize some of them for the Pro-Life cause. Early mobilization took place mostly in Catholic organizations, but since the 1970s has tended to be based on Baptist and fundamentalist Christian organizations and conservative political groups (Blanchard 1994, McCarthy 1987, Paige 1983). This ready-made "social infrastructure" made it easy and therefore less costly to communicate with millions of potential adherents.

Unlike members of the Pro-Life movement, Pro-Choice adherents tend to be religiously apathetic (Humphries 1977, McCarthy 1987). Because of this, the Pro-Choice movement does not have a ready-made network of like-minded people and organizations to call upon. Those organizations that were most active in the early years of the Pro-Choice movement tended to be professional associations or groups interested in world population issues (Humphries 1977). This organizational base was lost as the battle wore on and organizations solely dedicated to the Pro-Choice issue began to form. Direct-mail technology, which was new at the time, allowed Pro-Choice leaders to refine large and efficient mailing lists (McCarthy 1987). They began by linking together preexisting lists through magazine subscriptions, other social movement organization lists, political campaign lists, and files of private mailing firms. All of these approaches, along with demographic targeting, allowed Pro-Choice organizations to create mailing lists that rival those of the Pro-Life organizations (McCarthy 1987).

Organization and Leadership

Both movements are characterized by well-organized groups that act together whenever necessary in order to achieve their goals. These organizations are tightly knit into cooperative clusters that allow them to share resources and information whenever necessary. Many of them have newsletters, websites, and polished media spokespersons. Most of them have learned how to operate within the legal system, the political system, and the arena of media publicity. Different organizations within each movement focus on each of these three areas. This specialization makes it possible for each organization to focus on the one task (political pressure, lobbying, and campaigning; legal test cases; or public protest and media events) that it is best suited for. This plays up the strength of each particular group and makes the movement as a whole more efficient and effective.

Both the Pro-Life and the Pro-Choice movement organizations tend to be led by deeply committed people who have a minimum of other commitments. Many of them are professional movement leaders who make their living from the organization. Others are religious or political leaders who have a flexible schedule and can take part in activities without fear of losing their outside job.

Goals

According to Oberschall (1973, 1993), a social movement cannot succeed unless their goals are clearly defined and do not alienate too many outsiders. The Pro-Life agenda is fairly clear: they want state and federal laws that prohibit women from getting abortions under most circumstances. The Pro-Choice movement also has clearly defined goals: they want state and federal laws allowing women and doctors to decide whether or not they should get or give abortions with no interference from the government. Both movements have done a good job of staying focused on these goals.

However, there is a slight problem when it comes to alienating outsiders. Most Americans have conflicted views about abortion (see, for example, discussions in Blanchard 1994, McCarthy 1987). A public opinion survey given in June of 2000 by the *Los Angeles Times* found that a large majority of Americans believe that abortion is wrong at least some of the time *and* that there should be no laws against abortion under most circumstances. This situation has not changed much since opinion polls on the issue began in the early 1970s (Blanchard 1994, McCarthy 1987, Pojman and Beckwith 1994). This conflict probably exists because Americans place freedom and personal responsibility above most other values.

This causes problems for both the Pro-Life and the Pro-Choice movement. The Pro-Life movement must deal with a general population that agrees with many of the moral and ethical perspectives of the movement but does not support the legislation that Pro-Life forces hope to create. The Pro-Choice movement has more general support within the American population. However, most Americans believe that abortion is wrong and view it as a moral and ethical issue rather than a purely medical procedure. Any attempts by the Pro-Choice movement to further extend their ideology can alienate the large number of Americans who agree with their goals but not their principles. Any attempts by the Pro-Life movement to further extend their own ideology can alienate the large number of Americans who agree with many of their principles but not their ultimate goals. The same conflicts exist within the minds of politicians. Both movements are placed in a double-bind situation where neither enjoys majority support of their principles and goals.

Factors Encouraging Mobilization

Oberschall (1973, 1993) indicates specific factors that encourage mobilization of social movements within a society. The most important of these revolves around general civil liberties such as freedom of assembly, freedom of speech, and freedom of worship. The United States guarantees these rights, and each movement has benefited equally from them. Neither the Pro-Life nor the Pro-Choice movement has a clear advantage in factors encouraging mobilization.

Success

Oberschall argues that the ultimate success for a social movement organization is to be institutionalized into society. Most of the Pro-Life and Pro-Choice groups are formally institutionalized as legitimate organizations. Many are officially recognized as political organizations, lobbying groups, or political action committees.

However, institutionalization can be a drawback for an organization. A group tends to become more timid once it becomes formally integrated into daily politics. Some leaders may value their job more than they value the group's goals. Some of the smaller, more militant Pro-Life organizations, such as Operation Rescue and the Lambs of Christ, were formed specifically because their leaders and followers were unsatisfied with the moderate positions and tactics of mainstream Pro-Life organizations (Blanchard 1994, Paige 1983). Such militant groups bring negative publicity to a movement and can damage the entire movement.

The Pro-Life and Pro-Choice movements both have highly organized groups run by professionals. They are integrated into the mainstream political world and are taken seriously by elected officials. The problem is that neither has clear dominance in the world of politics. This creates a situation where each group must focus on using about the same amount of political resources in order to compete with the other. Neither side is clearly better organized. This makes it difficult to predict either side's future success.

Conclusion

Neither the Pro-Life or Pro-Choice movement has a clear advantage over the other in terms of material resources, political power, or popular support. Both sides are comprised of tiny minorities of Americans who feel strongly enough about the issue to make the commitment and give their time or money to the movement. Both sides are led by professional and semi-professional leaders with a firm grasp of modern politics and economics. The Pro-Choice adherents tend to be more upper- and middle-class and therefore have more money to give (McCarthy 1987). Pro-Life adherents tend to be more religiously devout and therefore more willing to give their time to the movement (Blanchard 1994, McCarthy 1987). These differences are relatively small.

Does Resource Mobilization Theory do a good job of explaining the rise of the Pro-Life and Pro-Choice movements? The reader must decide. Resource Mobilization seems to account for the close race that these two movements have been running for the last few decades. Each movement has successfully mobilized the resources necessary to survive, but neither has managed to acquire enough political, social, or economic resources to totally overwhelm the opposition. The only thing that Resource Mobilization Theory might be said to leave out is a careful analysis of the historical events that led up to the struggle. This is where Political Process Theory's greatest strength lies.

Political Process Theory

As discussed in Chapter 14, Political Process Theory is similar to the Resource Mobilization Theory but with an additional emphasis on the historical events and social conditions that lead to the development of a movement. It is a hybrid of Resource Mobilization Theory (which focuses on the survival and success or failure of a movement) and Relative Deprivation Theory (which attempts to explain why a movement forms in the first place).

Organizational Strength

The Pro-Choice movement grew out of large, highly organized professional associations (Blanchard 1994, Humphries 1977, McCarthy 1987). They provided Pro-Choice advocates with large constituency blocs, experienced leaders, and actively involved members.

The Pro-Life movement grew out of religious associations (Blanchard 1994, McCarthy 1987, Paige 1983). Although possibly not as politically astute as Pro-Choice leaders in the early years of the movement, Pro-Life leaders have become more sophisticated over time. Most Pro-Life organizations are still aligned with Catholic, Baptist, or fundamentalist Christian organizations (Blanchard 1994, Paige 1983). The result is an extremely well-organized and largely smooth-running network of interrelated organizations.

Cognitive Liberation

Members of both movements had to experience cognitive liberation before they could take on such a difficult task. Members of the Pro-Choice movement had to decide that they could band together and succeed in getting the old abortion laws repealed. The members of the Pro-Life movement had to decide that they could band together and succeed in getting them reinstated. From McAdam's perspective, members of both sides had to reach a point where they realized that they could influence the policies and practices of the United States government.

Political Opportunity

In order to survive, social movements have to adapt to changing political and economic conditions. McAdam (1996) identifies four key dimensions of political opportunity that relate directly to the social system: openness of the political system, stability of existing powerful groups, presence of allies among those powerful groups, and the society's tendency toward repression.

The relative *openness of the political system* determines how easily movements can form. It is virtually the same as Oberschall's concept of "factors encouraging mobilization." As discussed above, the Pro-Life and Pro-Choice movements were both aided by openness in American society. In more closed societies both groups would have had to struggle just to organize.

The *stability of existing powerful groups* negatively effect the formation of movements. The less stable and interconnected powerful groups are, the more likely a new group is to successfully change the system. There are many different liberal, moderate, and conservative political groups in the United States. None of them has total power over any aspect of American society, and they are not interconnected enough to allow them to easily band together against social movements. This was particularly true in the late 1960s and early 1970s when our culture was undergoing something like a social revolution. Clashes over civil rights, feminism, the Vietnam War, and other divisive issues created a political climate with the "good old boys' network" less in control than ever before. During that time a number of social movements formed, all with the goal of challenging the established power structure in the United States. The Pro-Life and Pro-Choice movements developed and grew during a time that was ripe for such growth.

The *presence of allies* among society's powerful is also important. In the beginning, the Pro-Choice movement had the support and cooperation of many state and federal politicians (Blanchard 1994, Humphries 1977). The AMA and ABA were powerful, firmly established associations. These allies made it possible for the Pro-Choice people to get national attention for their agenda to push their goals within the upper reaches of the political and legal systems in the United States.

The Pro-Life movement initially had the full support of large religious organizations, particularly the Catholic Church (Blanchard 1994, Paige 1983, McCarthy 1987). These allies did not carry quite the political or legal clout of the Pro-Choice movement's allies, but nonetheless made the formation and legitimization of the movement much easier. Starting in 1976, the Pro-Life movement had the most powerful ally of all: the president of the United States. Presidents Carter, Reagan, and Bush all gave their personal support to the Pro-Life movement (Blanchard 1994, Paige 1983). Reagan was the most open about this support. He officially met with Pro-Life leaders and often gave speeches indicating that he personally supported them (Blanchard 1994). However, even the president does not have enough power to force his personal beliefs into law. Both movements have held a relatively balanced level of social and political power. This is true partly because each movement has a fair number of powerful allies but neither has enough to create a clear advantage.

The society's *tendency toward repression* is the last factor that shapes political opportunity. The federal government generally tolerates any organization that does not directly threaten national security. Respected professional and political leaders led the Pro-Choice movement, and respected religious leaders led the Pro-Life movement. Neither was deemed a threat to society or social order. It was not until threats and violence at abortion clinics became common events that the government began cracking down on militant Pro-Life groups. Even then, only the most extreme groups that were monitored, and only the most extreme individuals were prosecuted (Blanchard 1994, Paige 1983). Overall, neither movement has had to deal with excessive repressive tactics from the government.

Conclusion

Does Political Process Theory do a good job of explaining the Pro-Life and Pro-Choice movements in the United States? The reader will have to determine that. Paying more attention to the social and political conditions that make movement formation possible or likely gives the Political Process Theory a more complete view than Resource Mobilization Theory. Political Process Theory retains the Resource Mobilization focus on the day-to-day factors that make it possible for the movement to grow and survive.

Each of the four theories has strengths and weaknesses. Mass Society Theory does not work well for the Pro-Life or Pro-Choice movement because it only applies to fascist, anti-democratic movements. American society is not really a mass society as Kornhauser describes one. The Pro-Choice movement, by fighting against legislation, is the opposite of a mass movement. Only the smallest and most extreme Pro-Life organizations exhibit any tendencies toward intolerance of individual freedom and personal choice. They do not characterize the majority of Pro-Life adherents.

Relative Deprivation Theory is intended to explain why particular individuals would start or join a social movement. Although it can be argued that young women might be drawn to the Pro-Choice movement for this reason, both the Pro-Choice and Pro-Life adherents tend to be older, and men are actively involved with both movements. Relative deprivation, then, is not particularly helpful and can only be used as an explanation for these two movements if we assume that the "real" issue isn't abortion itself, but the larger set of social values and relations that are represented by the symbolic meaning of abortion for adherents in both movements.

There is some evidence that this is so (see Blanchard 1994, Humphries 1977, Paige 1983). Many Pro-Life organizations talk about "returning society to traditional values." Many Pro-Choice organizations talk about the rights and freedoms of women more than they talk about abortion. However, it is also possible that both movements are simply using these related concerns in order to attract more donations and volunteers. There has been no careful research to determine if adherents of either movement experience greater relative deprivation than bystanders and outsiders. Therefore, it is unwise to assume that relative deprivation is a primary motivation for joining either movement.

Resource Mobilization Theory does a good job of explaining how each side managed to turn into a movement. Material and nonmaterial resources were readily available to both the Pro-Life and Pro-Choice movements. Skilled organizers and leaders managed to mobilize those resources effectively. As a result, both movements grew in size, power, and legitimacy until they became an accepted part of American politics. The fact that neither movement has significantly more resources than the other accounts for the near-stalemate that has existed for the last thirty years.

However, Resource Mobilization Theory does not explain why people wanted to form each movement in the first place. The theory is meant to be politically neutral but in a subtle way always takes the perspective of the dominant social structure. Social movements are viewed as intrusions into stable social order and their greatest key to success is help from "above," from established leaders and elites.

Political Process Theory is an attempt to keep the most useful aspects of Resource Mobilization Theory and combine them with elements of Relative Deprivation Theory and a broader historical and political perspective. Political Process Theory does not assume that a social movement has to receive help from powerful groups and individuals because social movements are seen as inherently powerful due to their number of followers. Social movements can force powerful elites to help them, sometimes against their will.

Political Process Theory emphasizes the political, economic, and social factors that make a social movement likely to rise and succeed. This gives a somewhat more complete and balanced picture of the Pro-Life and Pro-Choice movements than any of the other three theories. This theory's weakness may lie in its assumptions about social movements. By assuming that social movements are started and run by "average" citizens, Political Process Theory may underestimate the role of powerful outsiders as badly as Resource Mobilization Theory overestimates it.

No one theory offers a perfect explanation for a social movement. In the case of the Pro-Life and Pro-Choice movements, Resource Mobilization Theory and Political Process Theory seem to give the most useful answers to important questions.

Discussion

Neither the Pro-Life nor the Pro-Choice movement can be considered a complete success or a total failure. So far, the Pro-Choice movement has had the most success. The movement succeeded in creating a federal law to override state laws banning or regulating abortion. Abortion is currently legal throughout the United States. However, the Pro-Life movement is constantly working to change that. The Pro-Life movement has been struggling over the last two decades to achieve more power and respectability. Neither seems to have won the support of the majority of citizens or lawmakers in the United States. This is an interesting situation, because it allows sociologists to compare and contrast the two movements as they struggle for power. The final outcome of the struggle is still in doubt.

As Resource Mobilization Theory and Political Process Theory both indicate, the outcome of the abortion debate will not be decided based on who is "right" or on whose cause is the most "just." The outcome will be decided by the legal precedents, political power, and public support that each group can generate and maintain. Public support is helpful, but has only an indirect effect on lawmakers. Political power is much more central to getting (or preventing) desired changes in society. Legal precedent is most important of all. The abortion issue will not be decided in the streets of America, but in the courtrooms.

The Supreme Court of the United States has tended to take a moderate stance, making certain that new decisions do not interfere with *Roe v. Wade*. The Pro-Life movement cannot achieve their goals unless they can convince the Supreme Court to overturn *Roe*. Until then, any law limiting abortion will be severely restricted. The abortion issue, like the struggle for civil rights, will be decided in federal court and through political action. The social movement with the most effective organization, most sophisticated leaders and attorneys and the most political power on its side will prevail.

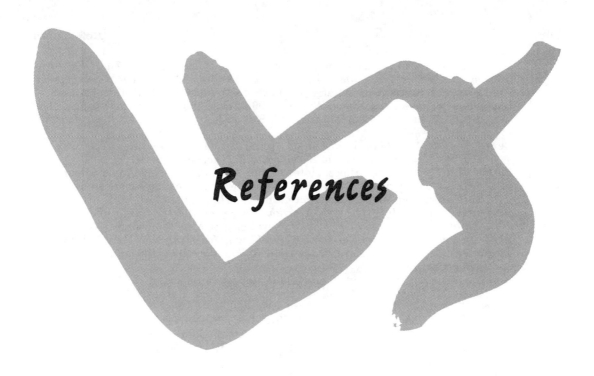

References

Abanes, Richard. 1999. "Why We Must Reject Millennium Madness." *Charisma & Christian Life.* 24(12):40–41, 44–46.

Aberle, David. 1966. *The Peyote Religion among the Navaho.* Chicago: Aldine.

Abrams, Dominic and Rupert Brown. 1989. "Self-Consciousness and Social Identity: Self-Regulation as a Group Member." *Social Psychology Quarterly.* 52(4): 311–318.

Aguirre, B. E., Dennis Wenger, and Gabriela Vigo. 1998. "A test of the Emergent Norm Theory of Collective Behavior." *Sociological Forum.* 13(2):301–320.

Allport, Floyd. 1924. *Social Psychology.* Cambridge: Houghton Mifflin, The Riverside Press.

———— 1969. *Institutional Behavior: Essays Toward a Re-interpreting of Contemporary Social Organization.* New York: Greenwood Press.

Allport, Gordon and Leo Postman. 1946. *The Psychology of Rumor.* New York: Henry Holt and Company.

Anderson, Duncan Maxwell. 1993. "Charismatic Capitalism." *Success.* 40(4):14.

Argyle, Michael. 1957. *The Scientific Study of Social Behavior.* Westport: Greenwood Press.

Asch, Solomon. 1951. "Effects of Group Pressure Upon the Modification and Distortion of Judgements." In H. Guetzkow (Ed.) *Groups, Leadership, and Men.* 177–190. Pittsburgh: Carnegie Press.

Asher, Ed. 1999. "Proctor & Gamble goes to court over rumors of Satanism." *Houston Chronicle.* 1999(May 13):A19.

Barkun, Michael. 1974. *Disaster and the Millennium.* New Haven: Yale University Press.

Bartholomew, Robert. 1997. "The Airship Hysteria of 1896–97." In *The UFO Invasion: The Roswell Incident, Alien Abductions, and Government Coverups*. Ed. Kendrick Frazier, Barry Karr, and Joe Nickell. Amherst: Prometheus Books.

Bartholomew, Robert and Simon Wessely. 1999. "Epidemic Hysteria in Virginia: The Case of the Phantom Gasser of 1933–1934." *Southern Medical Journal*, 92(8):762–770.

Bergesen, Albert and Max Herman 1998. "Immigration, Race, and Riot: The 1992 Los Angeles Uprising." *American Sociological Review*, 63(1):39–54.

Berlet, Chip. 1999. "Hate Crimes, Hate Groups, and Racial Tension in an Integrating Chicago Neighborhood 1978–1988." Paper presented at the American Sociological Association Annual Conference, Chicago, IL, August 1999.

Blanchard, Dallas. 1994. *The Anti-Abortion Movement and the Rise of the Religious Right: From Polite to Fiery Protest*. New York: Twayne Publishers.

Blasi, Anthony. 1989. *Early Christianity as a Social Movement*. New York: Peter Lang.

Bloom, Jack. 1987. *Class, Race, & the Civil Rights Movement*. Bloomington: Indiana University Press.

Blumer, Herbert. 1969 (1939). "The Field of Collective Behavior." In Alfred McClung Lee (Ed), *Principles of Sociology*. 65–122. New York: Barnes & Noble, Inc.

Bolick, Clint. 1997. "Civil Rights and the Criminal Justice System." *Harvard Journal of Law & Public Policy*, 20(2):391–397.

Bone, Warren. "So You Think Y2K Was Just a Hoax? January 1 has come and gone. Many are saying it was all a hoax. Was it? If not, then where are we?" *http://michaelhyatt.com* 1/23/00.

Boskin, Joseph. 1969. *Urban Racial Violence in the Twentieth Century*. Beverly Hills: Glencoe Press.

Boyer, Paul, Clifford Clark Jr., Joseph Kett, Neal Salisbury, Harvard Sitkoff, and Nancy Woloch. 1996. *An Enduring Vision: A History of the American People*. Lexington: D.C. Heath and Company.

Brunvand, Jan. 1981. *The Vanishing Hitchhiker: American Urban Legends and Their Meanings*. New York: W.W. Norton & Company.

——— 1989. *Curses! Broiled Again!* New York: W.W. Norton & Company.

Budge, E. A. 1978. *Amulets and Superstitions*. New York: Dover Publishing.

Bullers, Finn and David Hayes. 1999. "From blowguns to UFOs, Y2K expo at the Bartle has it all." *Kansas City Star*, 119(212):A1, A14.

Burns, Marty. 1998. "Celebration Riots: Close to Home." *Sports Illustrated*, 88(24):28.

Cannon, Lou. 1997. *Official Negligence: How Rodney King and the Riots Changed Los Angeles and the LAPD*. New York: Times Books.

Clark, Jerome and Loren Coleman. 1975. *The Unidentified: Notes Toward Solving the UFO Mystery*. New York: Warner Paperback Library.

Crum, Rex, Jennifer Merrit, Scott Van Voorhis, Ted Griffith, and Edward Mason. 1998. "The World Gets Fruit-Loopy over the new Furby Doll." *Boston Business Journal*, 18(43):2.

Davidson, Gordon and Corinne McLaughlin. 1998. "The Psychological Challenges of Y2K." p. 92–94 in *Y2K Citizen's Action Guide: Preparing yourself, your family, and your neighborhood for the year 2000 computer problem and beyond*. Ed. Eric Utne. Minneapolis: Utne Reader.

Dobratz, Betty and Stephanie Shanks–Meile. 1997. *"White Power, White Pride!: The White Separatist Movement in the United States*. New York: Twayne Publishers.

Drought, Andy. 1999. "Staff suspended in council direct selling probe." *The Glasgow Herald*, 1999(Nov.10):5.

Ferber, Abbe. 1998. *White Man Falling: Race, Gender, and White Supremacy*. Lanham: Rowman & Littlefield.

Flanagan, William. 1976. "A Monumental Thirst for Collecting Beer Cans." *Business Week*. 4/8/76:77.

Fracastor, Giralamo. 1930[1546]. *On Contagion*. New York: Putnam.

Frick, Robert. 1999. "Apocalypse, Please! Howard Ruff Peddles More Pessimism." *Kiplinger's Personal Finance Magazine*, 1999(May):28.

Galbraith, John. 1961. *The Great Crash of 1929, 2nd Edition*. Boston: Houghton Mifflin Company.

Gamson, W. 1990. *The Strategy of Social Protest*. Belmont: Wadsworth Publishing.

Giese, William. 1999. "How I'll Survive Y2K (I Think)." *Kiplinger's Personal Finance Magazine* 1999(June):120.

Girgenti, Richard. 1993. *A Report to the Governor on the Disturbances In Crown Heights, Volume 1: An Assessment of the City's Preparedness and Response to Civil Disorder*. New York: New York State Division of Criminal Justice Services.

Gleick, James. 1999. "Fast Forward-Doomsday Machines." *New York Times*. 1/24/99:6.16.

Grady, J. Lee. 1999. "Silly Rumors, Crazy Fears." *Charisma and Christian Life*, 24(12):6.

Greenberg, Jack. 1994. *Crusaders in the Courts: How a Dedicated Band of Lawyers Fought for the Civil Rights Revolution*. New York: Basic Books.

Griffin, Katherine. 1994. "Mothers Against Drunk Driving." *Health*, 8(4):62–68.

Grossman, Wendy. 1998. "Y2K: The End of the World as We Know It." *Scientific American*, Oct(1998):48.

Gurney, Joan Neff and Kathleen Tierney. 1982. "Relative Deprivation and Social Movements: A Critical Look at Twenty Years of Theory and Research." *Sociological Quarterly*, (23):33–47.

Hackworth, David. 1992. "This Was No Riot, It was a Revolt: How to stop it before it grows." *Newsweek*, 119(21):33.

Halberstam, David. 1993. *The Fifties*. New York: Villard Books.

Halpern, Charles. 1998. "The Y2K Problem Challenges All of Us." p. 9–12 in *Y2K Citizen's Action Guide: Preparing yourself, your family, and your neighborhood for the year 2000 computer problem and beyond*. Ed. Eric Utne. Minneapolis: Utne Reader.

Harvey, Donald J. 1968. *France Since the Revolution*. New York: The Free Press.

Hedges, Stephen and Betsy Streisand. 1997. "WWW.MASSUICIDE.COM: How an Obscure Cult Mixed Computers, UFOs, and New Age Theology So Its 39 Members Could Take the Ultimate Journey." *U.S. News & World Report*. 122(13):26–31.

Hensley, Thomas and Jerry M. Lewis. 1978. *Kent State and May 4th: A Social Science Perspective*. Dubuque: Kendall/Hunt Publishing.

Hofstadter, Richard and Michael Wallace (eds.) 1970. *American Violence: A Documentary History*. New York: Alfred A. Knopf.

Hogg, Michael and Dominic Abrams. 1988. *Social Identifications: A Social Psychology of Intergroup Relations and Group Processes*. London: Routledge.

Horak, Terri. 1996. "Amway Sued by Top Labels over Copyright Infringement." *Billboard*, 108(9):4, 55.

Humphries, Drew. 1977. "The Movement to Legalize Abortion: A Historical Account." In *Corrections and Punishment*. Ed. David Greenberg. Beverly Hills: Sage Publications.

Hyatt, Michael. 1998. *The Millennium Bug: How to Survive the Coming Chaos*. Washington, D.C.: Regnery Publishing, Inc.

Jenness, Valerie. 1990. "From Sex as Sin to Sex as Work: COYOTE and the Reorganization of Prostitution as a Social Problem." *Social Problems*, 37(3):403–420.

—— 1993. *Making it Work: The Prostitutes' Rights Movement in Perspective*. New York: Aldine De Gruyter.

Johnson, Donald. 1945. "The 'Phantom Anesthetist' of Mattoon: A Field Study of Mass Hysteria." *Journal of Abnormal and Social Psychology*, 40(1945):175–186.

Junod, Tom. 1999. "365 Days to the Apocalypse and We Still Don't Know Where to Hide the Jews . . . and other notes from Pat Robertson's Y2K conference." *Esquire*, 131(1):95–99.

Karlen, Arlo. 1995. *Man and Microbes: Disease and Plagues in History and Modern Times*. New York: G. P. Putnam's Sons.

Kerckhoff, Alan C. 1973. "A Theory of Hysterical Contagion." in *Human Nature and Collective Behavior: Papers in Honor of Herbert Blumer*. Ed. Tamotsu Shibutani. New Brunswick: Transaction Books.

Kerckhoff, Alan and Kurt Back. 1968. *The June Bug: A Study of Hysterical Contagion*. New York: Appleton Century Crofts.

Kindleberger, Charles. 1975. *The World in Depression: 1929–1939*. Berkeley: University of California Press.

Koenig, Fredrick. 1985. *Rumor in the Marketplace: The Social Psychology of Commercial Hearsay*. Dover: Auburn House Publishing Company.

Kornhauser, William. 1959. *The Politics of Mass Society*. New York: Free Press.

Kuehner, John. 1995. "Akron Party Turns Ugly; Students Fight Police—Again." *The Plain Dealer*, May 7, 1995:3B.

Kruh, David. 1999. "The End of the World as We Know It. . . ." *Boston Globe*, 1999 (December 13):A19.

Lacayo, Richard. 1992. "Anatomy of an Acquittal." *Time*, 139(19):30–32.

LeBon, Gustave. 1982 [1895]. *The Crowd: A Study of the Popular Mind*. Atlanta: Cherokee Publishing Company.

Levy, Steven and Katie Hafner (with Gregory Vistica, Rich Thomas, Deborah Branscum, Bronwyn Fryer, Julie Edelson Halpert, Jennifer Tanaka, and William Underhill). 1997. "The Day the World Shuts Down." *Newsweek*, 129(22):52–60.

Levy, Steven. 2000. "The Bug That Didn't Bite." *Newsweek*, 135(2):41.

Lewis, Jerry M. 1972. "A Study of the Kent State Incident Using Smelser's Theory of Collective Behavior." *Sociological Inquiry*, 42:87–92.

——— 1982a. "Fan Violence: An American Social Problem" in *Social Problems and Public Policy*. Ed. M. Lewis. Greenwich: JAI Press.

——— 1982b. "Crowd Control in English Soccer Matches" *Sociological Focus*, 15:417–423.

——— 1989. "A Value-Added Analysis of the Heysel Stadium Soccer Riot." *Current Psychology*, 8(1):15–29.

Lewis, Jerry M. and Kimberly Dugan. 1986. "Celebrating Sports Riots" Paper presented at the North Central Sociological Association Annual Conference.

Lewis, Jerry M. and Michael Kelsey. 1994. "The Crowd Crush at Hillsborough: The Collective Behavior of an Entertainment Crush." in *Disasters, Collective Behavior, and Social Organization*. Ed. Russell Dynes and Kathleen Tierney. Newark: University of Delaware Press.

Longman, Phillip. 1999. "We may be nuts, but . . .: It's official: the millennial bug is really, truly scary." *U.S. News & World Report*, 126(9):47–48.

Locher, David A. 1990. "Adding to the F-Scale." Unpublished manuscript. Kent: Kent State University.

Macionis, John. 1998. *Sociology, 6th ed*. Englewood Cliffs: Prentice Hall.

Mackay, Charles. 1980 [1841]. *Extraordinary Popular Delusions & the Madness of Crowds*. New York: Three Rivers Press.

Martin, Marty. 1986. *Modern American Religion, Volume 1: The Irony of It All: 1893–1919*. Chicago: University of Chicago Press.

Marum, Andrew and Frank Parise. 1984. *Fads and Foibles: A View of 20th Century Fads*. New York: Facts on File.

McAdam, Douglas. 1982. *Political Process and the Development of Black Insurgency 1930–1970*. Chicago: University of Chicago Press.

——— 1996. "Conceptual Origins, Current Problems, Future Directions." In *Comparative Perspectives on Social Movements*. Ed. Douglas McAdam, John McCarthy, and Mayer Zald. Cambridge: Cambridge University Press.

McCarthy, John and Mayer Zald. 1977. "Resource Mobilization and Social Movements: A Partial Theory." *American Journal of Sociology*, 82(6):1212–1241.

McCarthy, John. 1987. "Pro-Life and Pro-Choice Mobilization: Infrastructure Deficits and New Technologies." In *Social Movements in an Organizational Society: Collected Essays*. Ed. Mayer Zald and John McCarthy. New Brunswick: Transaction Books.

McCarty, James. 1994. "Off-Campus Revelers Clash with Akron Police; 7 Arrested." *The Plain Dealer*, May 8, 1994:4B.

McPhail, Clark. 1991. *The Myth of the Madding Crowd*. New York: Aldine De Gruyter.

——— 1994. "Presidential Address—The Dark Side of Purpose: Individual and Collective Violence in Riots." *The Sociological Quarterly*. 35(1):1–32.

——— 1997. "Stereotypes of Crowds and Collective Behavior: Looking Backward, Looking Forward." *Studies in Symbolic Interactionism*. 1997(3):35–58.

Melton, J. Gordon (Ed). 1986. *Biographical Dictionary of American Cult and Sect Leaders*. New York: Garland Publishing.

——— 1993. *Encyclopedia of American Religions, 4th Ed*. Detroit: Gale Research, Inc.

Milani, Farzeneh. 1999. "Lipstick Politics in Iran." *New York Times*. 148(51619):A23.

Miller, David. 1985. *Introduction to Collective Behavior*. Belmont: Wadsworth Publishing Company.

Miller, Neil and John Dollard. 1941. *Social Learning and Imitation*. New Haven: Yale University Press.

Morrison, Denton E. 1971. "Some Notes Toward Theory on Relative Deprivation, Social Movements, and Social Change." *The American Behavioral Scientist*, 1971 (May–June):675–690.

Morrison, Peter and Ira Lowry. 1994. "A Riot of Color: The Demographic Setting." In *The Los Angeles Riots: Lessons for the Urban Future*. Mark Baldassare. (Ed.) Boulder: Westview.

Nafisi, Azar. 1999. "The Veiled Threat: The Iranian Theocracy's Fear of Females." *New Republic*, 220(8):24–30.

Nathanson, Bernard. 1989. "Operation Rescue: Domestic Terrorism or Legitimate Civil Rights Protest?" *The Hastings Center Report*, 1989(Nov/Dec):28–32.

Neff, Jack. 1995. "P&G sues over rumor." *Advertising Age*, 66(36):35.

Noel, Peter. 1992a. "Kill the Jew! Kill the Nigger!: Caught Up in the Excitement of Crown Heights." *Village Voice*, 37(43):11–12.

——— 1992b. "And Justice For All?." *Village Voice*, 37(43):12.

Oberschall, Anthony. 1973. *Social Conflict and Social Movements*. Englewood Cliffs: Prentice Hall.

——— 1993. *Social Movements: Ideologies, Interests, and Identities*. New Brunswick: Transaction Publishers.

Olgeirson, Ian. 1999. "Proctor & Gamble sees stars, appeals lost lawsuit over logo." *Denver Business Journal*, 50(48):6.

O'Riley, Paloma. 1998. "Individual Preparation for Y2K." p. 70–90 in *Y2K Citizen's Action Guide: Preparing yourself, your family, and your neighborhood for the year 2000 computer problem and beyond*. Eric Utne (Ed.). Minneapolis: Utne Reader.

Paige, Connie. 1983. *The Right to Lifers: Who They Are, How They Operate, Where They Get Their Money*. New York: Summit Books.

Park, Robert E. and Ernest W. Burgess. 1921. *Introduction to the Science of Sociology*. Chicago: University of Chicago Press.

——— 1924. *Introduction to the Science of Sociology, 2nd ed*. Chicago: University of Chicago Press.

Park, Robert E. 1967. "Human Nature and Collective Behavior." In Turner, Ralph (Ed). *Robert E. Park on Social Control and Collective Behavior*. 185–193. Chicago: Phoenix Books, The University of Chicago Press.

—— 1967b. "Collective Behavior." in Turner, Ralph (Ed). *Robert E. Park on Social Control and Collective Behavior*. Chicago: Phoenix Books, The University of Chicago Press.

—— 1972. *The Crowd and the Public and Other Essays*. Ed. Henry Elsner, Jr., Trans. Charlotte Elsner. Chicago: The University of Chicago Press.

Patterson, Robert. 1965, *The Great Boom and Panic: 1921–1929*. Chicago: Henry Regnery:Company.

Pojman, Louis and Francis Beckwith. 1994. *The Abortion Controversy: A Reader*. Boston: Jones and Bartlett, Publishers.

Porter, Bruce and Marvin Dunn. 1984. *The Miami Riot of 1980: Crossing the Bounds*. Lexington: Lexington Books.

Rice, Berkely. 1981. "Gourmet Worms: Antidote to a Rumor." *Psychology Today*. 15(August):20–21.

Rist, Oliver. 2000. "Forget Y2K blame; count your blessings." *Internetweek*, (796):27.

Roberts, Ron and Robert Marsh Kloss. 1979. *Social Movements: Between the Balcony and the Barricade, Second Edition*. St. Louis: Mosby.

Salmond, John. 1997. *"My Mind Set on Freedom."* Chicago: Ivan R. Dee.

Sann, Paul. 1967. *Fads, Follies, and Delusions of the American People*. New York: Bonanza Books.

Schaefer, Richard and Robert Lamm. 1998. *Sociology, 6th Edition*. New York: McGraw-Hill.

Schmertz, John and Mike Meier. 2000. *Declaratory Judgements*. 6(2).

Schwartz, Gary. 1970. *Sect Ideologies and Social Status*. Chicago: University of Chicago Press.

Shaffer, Jeffrey. 1998. "The 'Kwazy Knot'—One Man's 'Festivus' of Christmas Fads." *Christian Science Monitor*, 91(7):11.

Sherif, Muzafer. 1936. *The Psychology of Social Norms*. New York: Harper and Row.

Smelser, Neil J. 1962. *Theory of Collective Behavior*. New York: Free Press.

Smith, Anna Deavere. 1993. *Fires in the Mirror: Crown Heights, Brooklyn, and Other Identities*. New York: Anchor Books, Doubleday.

Staff. 1990. "Selling to Beat the Devil." *Time Magazine*, 136(7):57.

Staff. 1999. "P&G is ordered to pay Amway." *Wall Street Journal-Eastern Edition*, 235(4):A14.

Stepanek, Marcia. 1999. "A Millennium Bug's Life" *Business Week*. 1/11/99:6.

Stouffer, Samuel. 1949. *The American Soldier*. New York: Wiley and Sons, Inc.

Suro, Roberto. 1998. *Strangers Among Us: How Latino Immigration is Transforming America*. New York: Knopf.

Tedford, Deborah. 1999. "Conglomerate ordered to pay attorney's fees." *The Houston Chronicle*, 1999(Dec.31):A41.

Thompson, Kenneth. 1998. *Moral Panics*. London: Routledge.

Tiene, Drew. 1995. *The Story of the Kent State Shootings* (video documentary). Kent State University, Kent, Ohio.

Tolnay, Stewart and E.M. Beck. 1998. *A Festival of Violence: An Analysis of Southern Lynchings, 1882–1930*. Urbana: University of Illinois Press.

Tumin, Melvin and Arnold Feldman. 1955. "The Miracle at Sabana Grande." *Public Opinion Quarterly*, 19(1955):124–139.

Turner, Ralph. 1996. "The Moral Issue in Collective Behavior and Collective Action." *Mobilization*, 1(1):1–15.

Turner, Ralph and Lewis Killian. 1957. *Collective Behavior*. Englewood Cliffs: Prentice Hall.

—— 1972. *Collective Behavior, 2nd ed.* Englewood Cliffs: Prentice Hall.

—— 1987. *Collective Behavior, 3rd ed.* Englewood Cliffs: Prentice Hall.

Utne, Eric. 1998. "I Am Because We Are." p. 13–14 in *Y2K Citizen's Action Guide*: *Preparing yourself, your family, and your neighborhood for the year 2000 computer problem and beyond*. Eric Utne, (Ed). Minneapolis: Utne Reader.

Vos Savant, Marilyn. 1999. "Ask Marilyn: Are You Worried About the Y2K Bug?" *Parade: The Sunday Newspaper Magazine*, 1999(May):18–19.

Weber, Eugen. 1999. *Apocalypses*: *Prophesies, Cults, and Millennial Beliefs through the Ages*. Cambridge: Harvard University Press.

Webster, William. 1992. *The City in Crisis: A Report by the Special Advisor to the Board of Police Commissioners on the Civil Disorder in Los Angeles*. Los Angeles: Special Advisor Study.

Weitzer, Ronald. 1991. "Prostitutes' Rights in the United States: The Failure of a Movement." *Sociological Quarterly*, 32(1):23–42.

Wells, Redman Lucas. 2000. *Urban Legends Research Centre. http://www.urlc.com.au*. 4/31/2000.

White, Eugene. 1990. "The Stock Market Boom and Crash of 1929 Revisited." *Journal of Economic Perspectives*, 4(2):67–84.

Young, Kimball. 1927. *Source Book for Social Psychology*. New York: F.S. Crofts & Company.

Zald, Meyer and Roberta Ash. 1966. "Social Movement Organizations." *Social Forces*, (44): 327–341.

Zald, Meyer and John McCarthy. 1988. *The Dynamics of Social Movements: Resource Mobilization, Social Control, and Tactics*. Lanham: University Press of America.

Photo Credits

Chapter 7
Page 89: Agence France Presse, CORBIS
Page 91: Joe Major, AP/Wide World Photos
Page 94: Scott Olson, Hulton/Archive
Page 96: Images, Hulton/Archive
Page 99: AP/Wide World Photos
Page 100: Jacobsen, Hulton/Archive
Page 106: Courtesy of the Library of Congress

Chapter 8
Page 113: Chris Martinez, AP/Wide World Photos

Chapter 9
Page 147: David Locher

Chapter 10
Page 164: AP/Wide World Photos

Chapter 11
Page 178: Damian Dovarganes, AP/Wide World Photos
Page 179: The Commercial Appeal

Chapter 12
Page 203: Photo by Diana Brown 1999

Chapter 13
Page 234: Lynchburg Police Department
Page 235: A. Ramey, PhotoEdit
Page 236: Mark Richards, PhotoEdit
Page 237: Library of Congress
Page 238: Rich Bachus, AP/Wide World Photos/Travers City Record-Eagle
Page 240: AP/Wide World Photos
Page 242: Joseph Sohm, CORBIS
Page 243: Bettman Archive, CORBIS
Page 244: UPI, CORBIS

Chapter 15
Page 277:   CORBIS
Page 279:   AP/Wide World Photos
Page 285:   Roger Ressmeyer, CORBIS

Chapter 16
Page 292:   Joe Marquette, AP/Wide World Photos

Name Index

Subject Index

major 12
Arundel 1